High
and
Dry

The
Texas-New Mexico
Struggle for the
Pecos River

G. Emlen Hall

University of New Mexico Press
Albuquerque

Library of Congress Cataloging-in-Publication Data

Hall, G. Emlen, 1942–
High and dry : the Texas-New Mexico struggle for the Pecos River / G. Emlen
Hall.
p.   cm.
Includes index.
ISBN 0-8263-2430-4 (paper)
1. Pecos River (N.M. and Tex.)—Water rights.
2. Texas—Trials, litigation, etc.
3. New Mexico—Trials, litigation, etc.
I. Title.
KF2576.P43 H35 2002
346.7304'32—dc21
2001006776

ACKNOWLEDGMENTS

Joseph Blecha, Eric Biggs, Beth Hadas, Delaney Hall, Chloe Hall, Gavin Hall, Renea Hicks, David Holtby, Bill Fleming, Jay Groseclose, Morgan Nelson, Ted Occhialino, Bhasker Rau, Steve Reynolds, Leo Romero, D. L. Sanders, John Shomaker, Carl Slingerland, Richard Simms, Karen M. Talley, Charlotte Uram, Sabino Samuel Vigil, Francis West, and Peter White each contributed mightily in different ways to this book. I am indebted to them and the countless others who helped me with this project.

Contents

Preface

Improbable as it sounds, *High and Dry* is a love story about a lawsuit. As things go, lawsuits are not easy to love and *Texas v. New Mexico*, Supreme Court No. 65 Original, was among the least appealing of them all. For almost twenty years at the end of the twentieth century the U.S. Supreme Court interstate water litigation between two states with a long history of enmity oozed along the Pecos River. The lawsuit was a bottom feeder, sucking up an entire river basin, the institutions built for it, the communities dependent on it and the human lives devoted to it. The lawsuit didn't so much chew up and spit out in pieces the things with which it came into contact as it swallowed them whole, leaving only the outlines of its victims, distended and struggling, in its maw.

In the process, the slow-moving, never-ending lawsuit threatened to transform many of the things that I have come to love in my thirty years as a New Mexican historian and lawyer.

I have loved the Pecos River ever since I pulled over the Glorieta Pass east of Santa Fe in late 1969 and dropped for the first time into the Upper Pecos River Basin. I came from Cambridge, Massachusetts and fell in love with Pecos, New Mexico. For more than ten years, I stayed there. I fished for trout in what is in the Pecos River's upper reaches a high mountain stream. I tried to grow gardens and corn fields, using the ancient irrigation structures of Hispanic and Pueblo Indian Pecos to get the river water to my land. I learned seventeenth-century New Mexican Spanish and its arcane, precise terms for the water I used. It took me ten more years to descend below Santa Rosa where the Pecos River Middle Basin begins and where *Texas v. New Mexico* really started and another ten years to get to

Pecos, Texas where the bitter fruits of the Pecos River management that spawned the interstate lawsuit were most directly felt.

By then I already had acquired two passionate biases about the Pecos River. First, I was a New Mexican from Pecos, New Mexico. I'd always seen the river from its top. The way the Rio Grande runs forces New Mexicans into both an upstream and a downstream perspective. The river heads in Colorado and ends in Texas; New Mexico is squeezed in-between and forced to look in both directions. By contrast, the Pecos River heads in New Mexico and runs down to Texas. New Mexicans only need to look to the state below to figure out their state's interstate rights and obligations. But from the start I had an extreme case of upstream vision, the double disability of someone who learned to see the river from the headwaters of an upstream state.

Astute observers of *Texas v. New Mexico* always attributed a lot to the river perspective of various participants and I think that they are right about me as well. For better or worse, *High and Dry* is primarily a book about New Mexico's stake in the litigation. Texas had a huge interest in it as well, but I don't see the downstream stakes as clearly, develop them as deeply, or worry over them as paternalistically as I do about New Mexico's.

I was also devoted to New Mexico State Engineer Steve Reynolds. As a journalist, I was introduced to Reynolds in the early 1970s and, as a lawyer, I made his acquaintance, starting in the mid-1970s. Shortly there-after, I joined his legal staff at the State Engineer Office and stayed until the mid 1980s. As you will learn from the story to come, I worked off and on for Reynolds on *Texas v. New Mexico* in that period, mostly in the fog of endless, ambiguous battles over laws that didn't quite work and engineering that didn't quite add up. However, the work delighted me because it was so close to New Mexico and its history, a hydroscape that endlessly fascinated me the more I learned about it. And the closer that I got to the history, the closer I got to Steve Reynolds.

Already a legend in his time when I came to know him, Reynolds was a brooding omnipresence where we all worked in the Bataan Memorial Building near the Plaza in Santa Fe. Reynolds was there when we came in to work in the morning and was still there when most of us left in the early evening. During the week, he stuck to his own beautiful corner office and ventured out from time to time, to take care of business. But on Saturday mornings, when the rest of New Mexico state government formally was shut down, Reynolds usually would show up at the office, dressed casu-ally and ready to work. Somehow he let it be known that his lawyers were supposed to show up too. I often did.

On those pared down Saturday mornings I'd work and wait for

Reynolds to come around, gathering up the small scattering of lawyers where we all worked and marching us off to the nearby Forge Restaurant for coffee and chat. A relaxed and available Reynolds would regale us with all manner of water war stories, some set in New Mexico, some in other western states, some in Washington, D.C. where he spent a lot of time and had a lot of contacts. The stories were all funny and usually directed to the follies of other western natural resource managers. We heard tales of a New Mexico Fish and Game head who was a "helluva lion hunter," in Reynolds' words, and not much more and a California state engineer who insisted on inserting language into the original 1968 Wilderness Act that was so convoluted that no one understood what the statute meant. But somehow Reynolds convinced us over many Saturday mornings like this that there was a point to all of these stories.

Over and over again, Steve Reynolds has been described as a man of singular principle. Most people took this to mean that he was a state bureaucrat who didn't curry favor and didn't take bribes. He did and he didn't, but that was beside the point. He was a man of principle because he was so sure of what the first principle of New Mexico's water policy should be: the scientific management of limited water to achieve the most economically efficient beneficial use of the state's scant supplies. *Texas v. New Mexico* swallowed Reynolds and his principle whole and disgorged them at the suit's end distended, swollen, and broken.

By then Reynolds's first principle was vying with a whole new range of competing first principles: water for Texas, water for federally protected aquatic endangered species, water for the Pecos River itself, water for all manner of other uses. Alone, first principles are elegant; together, they compete like alligators in a swamp for survival. By definition, there can only be one winner among competing first principles but it takes a long time and is certainly a mess making that determination. No winner has emerged in the aftermath of *Texas v. New Mexico*.

In the process a lot of things died. Scientific management of the river died, replaced by a much more complex political balancing of incompatible factors. The Pecos River itself threatened to die, so pushed and pulled between demands on it that it could hardly respond to any of them. Steve Reynolds died and took with him to the grave his single-minded devotion to his own first principle.

He left a lot behind, including my respect for him and his curiosity about my stumbling efforts to write. For awhile in the late 1970s I wrote a column for the *Santa Fe Reporter*. To my surprise Reynolds read them. In one of the first I wrote about the death of an old Pecos Hispanic, calling the article "a threnody." Reynolds sent me a hand-written note, praising the story and thanking me for alerting him to a word he hadn't known until then.

In July 1983 I made a big move that had a very small impact on *Texas v. New Mexico*. Giving up the full-time practice of law, I joined the faculty at the University of New Mexico School of Law. I wrote Reynolds a short note telling him of my plans. In that deeply courteous manner of his, he immediately wrote back. "You have contributed much to the effective operation of the State Engineer Office," he began,

and I have found our association both personally and professionally gratifying. I have admired and enjoyed your writing style even when you were holding me up to the opprobrium and scorn of our fellowman or giving up a million acres of New Mexico irrigation. Your contribution to the "Milagro Beanfield War" played an important part in bringing me the award of which I am most proud—A T-shirt emblazoned with "Viva Milagro Beanfield." That award was given to me by the Central Clearing House as an "earth enemy" for the part I played in killing legislation to establish a State NEPA law. I wish you every possible success in your new undertaking. The Lord knows we need some good water lawyers; it could not be in the public interest for the State Engineer to win all cases on appeal.

With that peculiarly New Mexican combination of affection, teasing and self-deprecation, Steve Reynolds let me go, back to the university world where he had begun before he became state engineer. I kept writing and *High and Dry* is the result.

I didn't write the book as a threnody to Reynolds. I did write *High and Dry* to pay homage to the institutions that made the river what it was in the twentieth century: the people, the communities, the state bureaucrats, the federal compacts and the Supreme Court lawsuits. The 21st century will remake the river in its own image even if the humans, who have struggled to force the river to behave for centuries, recede and the river itself reemerges. I have no doubt that in another hundred years the Pecos River that I describe here will be unrecognizable. But I can't see far enough into the future to know what forms that transformation will take. It will take another century to reshape it.

I pray that the Pecos River survives but, as its name implies, *High and Dry* hardly shows the way to survival. In the meantime, I leave you with *High and Dry* and the forces that made the river what it was in the twentieth century and me who I am towards the end of my working life. I grew up with Steve Reynolds and the Pecos River and now I'm looking back, seeing where we came from, how we got here and who we are.

ONE

Flying Court

————In early spring of 1976, Paul Bloom and Carl Slingerland, both high-level employees of the New Mexico State Engineer Office in Santa Fe, got together to arrange an official tour of the Pecos River. Bloom was the chief attorney for the state engineer, the legendary Steve Reynolds. Slingerland was the engineer in charge of the Pecos River basin for the Interstate Stream Commission and as close to Reynolds as anyone. Both Bloom and Slingerland had worked in the western water field for so long that they had earned former governor Edwin Mechem's sobriquet "enginawyer" (part engineer, part lawyer) to describe the combination of engineering and legal skills peculiar to the esoteric world of power in New Mexico water. Bloom was so well known for his navigation of the intricate byways of western water law that he had won an infamous place for himself as a character in John Nichols's classic New Mexico novel *The Milagro Beanfield War*. But in March 1976 the two enginawyers were acting as nothing more than Pecos River tour guides.[1]

The Pecos River began high in the Sangre de Cristo mountains, east of Santa Fe, and flowed south first through 230 river miles of eastern New Mexico and then another 300 miles of west Texas before joining the Rio Grande in southwest Texas on the Mexican border. Geologists, with their long view and their terse vocabulary, described the Pecos as a "pirate." This suggestive moniker referred to the river's theft of runoff millions of years before. The river ran south but it had cut itself north by headwall erosion, in the process establishing itself as a barrier to the slow, inevitable flow of water from the massive uplift to its west to the great plains of Oklahoma, Nebraska, Kansas, and Texas to the east. Eventually and

UNITED STATES
DEPARTMENT OF THE INTERIOR
BUREAU OF RECLAMATION

PECOS RIVER BASIN
ABOVE GIRVIN, TEXAS

SCALE OF MILES

LEGEND

⌇ EFFECTIVE DRAINAGE BOUNDARY

⬭ NON-CONTRIBUTING AREAS TO SURFACE RUNOFF

▲ ACTIVE GAGING STATION

▨ IRRIGATED LANDS

═══ MAIN HIGHWAYS

⋯⋯ RAILROADS

Chapter 1

inevitably, the geologists swore, the pirate Pecos would continue farther north, cutting off the Canadian River from its eastward run from New Mexico into Oklahoma and Kansas as surely as it had cut off the east-running rivers to the south.[2]

Now, in the meantime, the Pecos River ran south. Draining hundreds of thousands of scraggly high desert acres in Texas and New Mexico, it provided what scant surface water there was for both states, first for upstream New Mexico and then for downstream Texas. The river gave birth to the eastern New Mexico and West Texas communities on its banks and linked them together.

But in May 1976, the Pecos had just become the subject of a huge lawsuit between the states of New Mexico and Texas. The two New Mexico bureaucrats were arranging a trip that would introduce the river to the principal figures in the suit.

After wrangling over the river's water through the better part of the twentieth century, Texas had sued New Mexico in the U. S. Supreme Court in 1974. Texas claimed that upstream New Mexico had deprived downstream Texas of more than 1,000,000 acre-feet of Pecos River water. That water, Texas said, should have reached Texas according to a compact the two states had negotiated in 1948. But the water never arrived because upstream New Mexicans had used it before it ever got to the state line.[3]

By any measure, 1,000,000 acre-feet is a lot of water. It is enough to cover a million football fields, goal line to goal line, one foot deep. 1,000,000 acre-feet was five to ten times more water than the whole Pecos River usually carried in a year.[4]

Between 1974 and 1976 Bloom and Slingerland had tried to stave off the Texans, using every tactical ploy available to them. But now the Supreme Court had said that the Texas suit should proceed and the river emerged center stage, introduced by the two New Mexico enginawyers. The audience consisted primarily of an eminent Denver-based federal judge, Jean Breitenstein, accompanied by select representatives of both states. The senior judge on the United States Court of Appeals for the Tenth Circuit, Breitenstein had been appointed by the Supreme Court to

Fig. 1.1.
This Bureau of Reclamation map shows the principle features of the Pecos River Basin circa 1970 when *Texas v. New Mexico* was getting under way. In 1987 Brantley Lake and Dam replaced Lake McMillan. (Map courtesy of the Albuquerque BOR.)

hear the evidence in the water dispute between the two states and to recommend a solution.[5]

Breitenstein brought a long record of judicial experience in western water law to his job as Special Master in *Texas v. New Mexico*. As a federal judge for thirty years, first on the Colorado federal district court (1954–1957), then on the elevated Circuit Court of Appeals (1957–1970), and finally as a senior circuit judge, Breitenstein was universally recognized as a fine judge and a craftsman of elegant, straightforward expository prose. Time and again, his fellow judges and clerks remarked on two Breitenstein specialties: the simple declarative sentence and water law. The prose style he had perfected in years of writing appellate opinions. Most of his expertise in interstate water disputes predated his judicial career.[6]

For the twenty years between 1933 and 1954 Judge Breitenstein worked as a private lawyer in Denver specializing in western water matters. Those twenty years had brought him experience in all three Constitutionally authorized methods for dividing interstate waters between competing states: Congressional act, Supreme Court equitable apportionment decree, and interstate compact.[7]

In 1928 Congress had divided the waters of the Lower Colorado between Arizona and California. Breitenstein knew this decision intimately and understood its origin and its aftermath, knew how unscientific the division had been and how reluctant Congress was to exercise that power again.[8]

One alternative, Breitenstein also knew, was for the Supreme Court itself to divide interstate waters in what lawyers called "an original action equitable apportionment suit." Breitenstein had represented the State of Colorado in such an equitable apportionment suit dividing the North Platte River among Colorado, Wyoming and Nebraska. In 1945 he had written the Colorado briefs in that suit and had argued before the nation's highest court on behalf of Colorado.[9]

Like all Supreme Court observers, Breitenstein knew how the Supreme Court hated these equitable apportionment cases. Equitable apportionment involved numerous and messy facts. The legal principles of equitable apportionment were drawn from western water law and were mysterious at best to the eastern-dominated Supreme Court. They were also soft at the edges and mushy to apply. No wonder, then, that, as in the case of the Pecos River, the courts used the legal possibility of judicially imposed equitable apportionment as a threat to force states to work out shared claims to a common source by means of a preferred method: the kind of negotiated interstate compact over which Breitenstein now presided in *Texas v. New Mexico*.

4

As a young water lawyer, Breitenstein had cut his teeth on the 1927 Compact by which Colorado and New Mexico had divvied up the waters of La Plata Creek in southwestern Colorado and northwestern New Mexico. He helped write the briefs for Colorado in a 1937 United States Supreme Court case, *Hinderlider v. La Plata Ditch Company*, construing the compact. In the process, Breitenstein had helped establish the fundamental principle that interstate water compacts were superior to any rights established under the law of either compacting state. In the case of the Pecos River, therefore, what water Texas and New Mexico had to work with within their borders was only that part of the shared river apportioned to each by the compact. The compact, not state law, determined the entitlement of each state to water from the Pecos, and Breitenstein knew it because he had established the background legal principle.[10]

Time and again between 1975, when he was appointed, and 1984, when he resigned as special master, Breitenstein returned to *Hinderlider* as one of the bedrock legal principles in the growing morass of *Texas v. New Mexico*. His early reports to the Supreme Court cited *Hinderlider* as fundamental authority over and over again. Most New Mexico and Texas lawyers, knowing full well Breitenstein's early involvement with *Hinderlider,* kept referring to it. Towards the end of his part of the case, Breitenstein himself began to question new lawyers to make sure that they knew the case as well as he did. When they didn't, he got testy. He insisted that everyone recognize his important involvement in general compact law so critical to *Texas v. New Mexico.*[11]

During his tenure as special master, however, Breitenstein never once acknowledged his early involvement in the Pecos River Compact itself. In the 1930s and 1940s he was as ubiquitous in the legal aspects of western compact affairs as Royce Tipton, another principal, was in their engineering aspects. Both based in Denver, the attorney and the engineer often called on each other's expertise on different projects. Although it was hardly ever mentioned in *Texas v. New Mexico,* Tipton had called on Breitenstein in December 1948 to help translate the agreements the two states had made at the critical November, 1948 Austin meetings into what became the Pecos River Compact of 1948. In 1983, the United States Supreme Court elliptically referred to the Court's own special master as "a federal drafting expert brought in after all significant disputes had been resolved" without naming Breitenstein. The fact remained that Special Master Breitenstein understood the background to the Pecos River Compact problem he faced in his last significant case not only because of his deep general experience in western water law but also because he literally had written the compact itself. If his prior participation created a

5

conflict of interest with his current role, well, that's just the way things went in western water law, where the number of competent, knowledgeable people was so small that if the normal rules of conflict of interest applied there wouldn't be anybody eligible to adjudicate the issues. By all accounts, Breitenstein was simply delighted by his appointment as special master in the suit between the two states; no one ever objected because he had written the document he was now going to interpret.[12]

Early in 1976 Breitenstein suggested some sort of inspection of the Pecos River Basin so that he could get oriented. Bloom and Slingerland took it up with Doug Caroom, the young Austin-based assistant attorney general in charge of Texas's part in the suit. Caroom agreed to the tour. "I'm looking forward," he wrote Bloom, " to getting out of dry, dusty Texas and visiting your lush, green state."[13]

That jocular remark set the tone for the early portions of the lawsuit in general and the Pecos River field trip in particular. Every chance they got, the Texas lawyers needled the New Mexicans about how much greener eastern New Mexico was than west Texas, presumably because of the Pecos River water New Mexicans had stolen. Every chance the New Mexicans got, they needled the Texans about how much richer west Texas was than eastern New Mexico. The fate of a major western river hung in the balance of bad jokes.[14]

Slowly, through March and April of 1976, the New Mexicans and the Texans planned a serious trip that would reintroduce Special Master Breitenstein to the Pecos. The party would tour the river, inspecting "all the major dams, reservoirs, irrigation projects and natural features of the river." Slingerland, the ever-practical engineer, arranged for an air-conditioned, fifteen-person bus for most of the tour. But then, in what turned out to be the trip's *pièce de résistance*, Slingerland also arranged for a plane.[15]

The State Highway Department, Slingerland reported, had just purchased a new twin-engine, six-passenger prop plane that New Mexico could make available for the trip. In a hand-written memo to Bloom, Slingerland described the small plane. He sketched a seating arrangement that would allow up to six passengers (plus pilot) to be crammed in by putting one of the passengers in the front seat next to the pilot facing forward, two more passengers behind the pilot facing backward, and the last three passengers in the back seat facing forward. The quarters would be close, especially for opponents in a bitter, high-stakes suit, with hardly any separation between the parties and the judge. But, said Slingerland, the plane was especially "good for ground viewing."[16]

So, early in the morning of May 3, 1976, Bloom and Slingerland went to the tiny Santa Fe Municipal Airport, boarded the State Highway Department plane and flew to Albuquerque to pick up the rest of the reconnaissance party. Judge Breitenstein flew in from Denver that morning. Three Texans, two engineers, and lawyer Caroom had flown in from Austin the day before. The six passengers piled into the small plane and took off.

The itinerary, arranged by Bloom and the Texans and approved by the judge, called for the plane to fly northeast, up over the headwaters of the Pecos River high in the Sangre de Cristo Mountains. From there the plane would work its way south along the river until it reached Pecos, Texas, below which the Pecos River descended into a deep canyon where human use effectively ended. From Pecos, Texas, the plane would again ascend the river to Las Vegas, New Mexico. At Las Vegas, the party would get on the bus and repeat the trip down the river, this time on the ground. The complex four-day trip was surely a curious way to begin a lawsuit. But it couldn't be beat as a way of getting the lay of the land and the river.[17]

From the 1,000-foot elevation at which the Highway Department plane flew, the New Mexico terrain spread out nicely beneath the six passengers. The plane worked its way from above the Village of Pecos down toward Santa Rosa, some 80 river miles below. In this upper "basin" of the Pecos River, the mountains cradle what is essentially a high mountain stream. When Breitenstein, Bloom, Slingerland, Caroom, and the other passengers looked out, they saw walls, the walls of mountains, the walls of mesas, all pinching the riverine world between them.

When the passengers looked down, they could see tiny pockets of green, irrigated land tucked, here and there, into the bends of the river. These small blips were defined by the river on one side, an irrigation ditch on the other, and the long, thin lots of individual farm lands, rarely larger than four or five acres, that ran between them. They were crammed into every available nook and cranny in the sinuous upper Pecos River course, but they were small and there weren't that many of them. The terrain wouldn't allow it.[18]

These swatches of green marked the remnants of what, until the 1940s, had been very isolated, very small, fiercely independent Hispanic subsistence communities. Their names—Pecos, Ribera, Ancon, Villanueva, Anton Chico, Puerta de Luna, to name just a few of New Mexico's upper Pecos River communities—invoked the history of the late eighteenth- and early nineteenth-century settlement of the area. In late twentieth-century New Mexico, the state's cachet as a romantic, otherworldly backwater still depended on the existence of these northern New Mexican towns.[19]

From the plane the passengers could tell that this tough, resistant

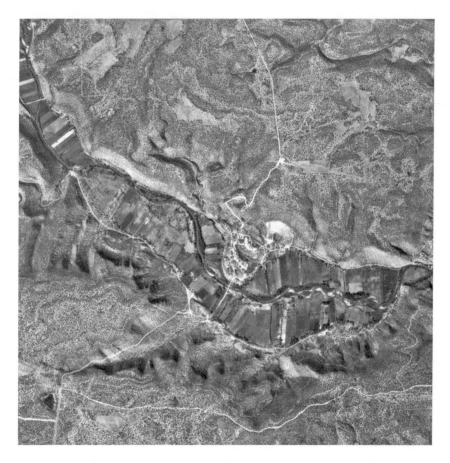

Fig. 1.2.
This aerial photograph shows the town of Villanueva, tucked into bends of the Pecos River in north central New Mexico between Pecos and Anton Chico, New Mexico. Villanueva was one of the principle settlements of the 1794 San Miguel del Bado land grant. (Courtesy of the U.S. Geological Survey.)

world had shrunk. Some of the adobe houses in these tiny communities had lost their tin roofs and stood abandoned next to neighboring buildings whose repaired roofs glittered in the bright sun. Irrigable fields that obviously hadn't been watered in years lay next to fields that were still carefully tended. Once these tiny communities had hung from the river. Now they had begun to drop off.[20]

Breitenstein and his fellow passengers would come to know this world a little better in two days when the plane flew back to Las Vegas and the bus portion of the tour began. Then the group inspected a couple of small, dilapidated irrigation systems that sometimes diverted water from the tiny, often dry Gallinas River, a tributary of the Pecos River that ran through the heart of Las Vegas, New Mexico, population 15,000.

Bloom, described by Caroom as an "amateur historian," insisted on detouring from the inspection of representative hydraulic works and leading the tour to a state historical marker. The monument identified the site in Las Vegas where in 1841, just prior to the switch in sovereignty from Mexico to the United States, Mexican officials of New Mexico had captured and penned up a rag-tag army of exhausted Texans bent on conquering New Mexico and its resources and on establishing the Republic of Texas's fantastic claim to all of New Mexico as far west as the Rio Grande. None of the irony of this stop on the tour was lost on the group of litigants. Had the Texans succeeded, Texans would have been stealing water from Texans and six-guns, not Supreme Court special masters, would have been deciding the dispute.[21]

At the start of the plane trip, the State Highway Department Cessna worked its way south, following the river out of the mountainous heartland of the upper Pecos. The view changed between Santa Rosa and Fort Sumner, about 100 river miles southeast of where the Pecos had begun. The river dropped. Canyon walls rose on both sides as if to tell the touring plane not to come any closer. In this stretch of the river, there was no room for even the small, compressed community ditch irrigation systems that the mountain stream farther north allowed.

A little farther south, the tight canyon ended abruptly in the Alamogordo (now Fort Sumner) dam, the first major man-made structure on the river. Built in the 1930s by the federal government to store water for the downstream Carlsbad (New Mexico) Irrigation District, the Alamogordo dam created behind it the first large lake on the Pecos River. The large body of sparkling water stood out in the surrounding desert.

Dams and lakes were the kind of river uses that the passengers on the Highway Department plane in May 1976 understood. To Jean Breitenstein, Slingerland, Bloom, and their ilk, river basin development always had turned on reservoirs that could store the erratic seasonal and annual flows of feast-to-famine, flood-to-drought western rivers and provide a steady source of water for the kind of economic development that water was meant to serve. They understood that the dam and lake they were seeing now from the air represented a triumph of engineering ingenuity and public will over a Pecos River that was hard to control, physically and politically. The Alamogordo Dam began the real world of the Pecos River over which Texas and New Mexico were fighting.[22]

The Alamogordo Dam also introduced a new Pecos River world to the

Flying Court

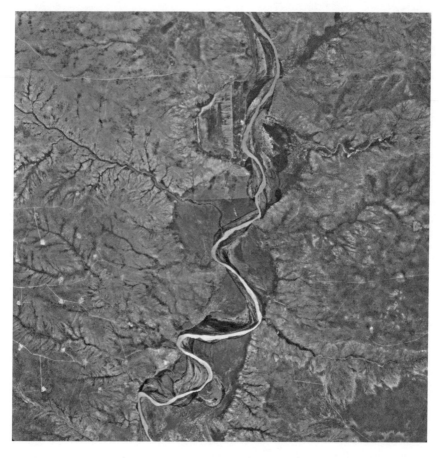

Fig. 1.3.
This aerial photograph shows the deeply incised, narrow canyon that cradles the Pecos River between the Fort Sumner Project on the north and the Acme gauge on the south. There is no room for surface water irrigation in this reach of the river and little groundwater irrigation on the surrounding mesas. (Courtesy of the U.S. Geological Survey.)

high flyers. The dam started the so-called middle reach of the Pecos, a stretch of river that ran 200 river miles to the New Mexico-Texas line. The middle reach had spawned, mostly in the twentieth century, a series of river-oriented towns that made up in rock-solid prosperity what they lacked in romance. To move below the Alamogordo Dam on the Pecos River was to enter for the first time a river world very much set in the twentieth century and built on its values. If the upper basin with its Hispanic village culture belonged to the New Mexico of ancient European sovereignty, this middle basin belonged to the New Mexico of western myth and solid American values.[23]

Flying downstream from the Alamogordo Dam also meant entering a new geological world. For the first time, the surrounding terrain spread out. To the east, the desert extended to the very edge of the horizon. To the west, the land rose and rolled a little more, but still no obvious physical barrier—no mountain, no range—was visible in that direction. Here and there dry arroyos entered the Pecos River, mostly from the west. But the land was so expansive and so flat that the passengers could hardly tell which way the arroyos ran.

This expanse of land, west of the river and east of Vaughn, was cattle country. There weren't even patches of irrigated green to relieve the monotone brown of the high-desert grasslands. That never changed east of the Pecos River. But west of the Pecos and south of Vaughn the plane soon entered another world.

About eighty river miles below the Alamogordo Dam, the land west of the Pecos River started slowly but obviously to dip south into a sink. New Mexicans generally understood that the bowl started just north of where the Atchison, Topeka and Santa Fe railroad tracks crossed the Pecos River. Bloom leaned to Breitenstein to point out the tracks. Breitenstein leaned to take a closer look out the plane window and the New Mexico State Highway Department plane turned along the river slightly to the west in order to get a clear view of the Roswell basin, a brand new part of the Pecos River and, all of the passengers on the plane suspected, the real cause of trouble between Texas and New Mexico.

From a thousand feet in the high desert air, the plane passengers could clearly see the Roswell basin's defining features. On the east it was bounded by that thin sliver of south-running river that the group had been tracking all day. On the west, about eighty miles away but still clearly visible, mountains loomed above the basin to a height of 10,000 feet, more than 6,000 feet above the river. To the south, a low range of intruding east-running mountains, the Seven River Hills, abruptly defined the basin on that side. The area enclosed by these geologic features was big, almost 5,000 square miles, but it was well defined. As with a lot of things in the desert, seeing the Roswell basin required a big perspective, which the State Highway Department plane afforded, and an enlarged imagination, which the passengers on this trip were trying to cultivate.

Small town after small town lay in a north-south line between the mountains and the river. Roswell, a city of forty-five thousand residents, stood on the north, at the head of the line. East Grand Plains, Dexter,

11

Lake Arthur, Hagerman, and Artesia came into view in turn as the plane moved south. The streets of each town were regularly laid out and the parallel and perpendicular lines looked curious and small in the desert. These towns were the heartland of the Roswell basin but they looked as if they had a precarious hold on the expanse of brown space that surrounded them.

Irrigated tracts of farmland outside the towns provided some relief. Farmers irrigated around 150,000 acres of land in the Roswell basin in 1976. That may sound like a lot but it was less by far than 1 percent of the land in the basin. The green squares that showed irrigation lay in a belt roughly six miles wide and seventy miles long, near the river but not on it. The swatches seemed as precarious and random as the small towns that they surrounded.[24]

Nevertheless, these swatches of green stood out like sore thumbs against the surrounding brown landscape. The Texans on board the flight didn't miss this unique chance to point out to Special Master Breitenstein how green the Roswell basin looked, especially in comparison with the bleak expanse of west Texas the plane was about to visit.[25]

The Roswell basin exhibited a couple of remarkable features. For one, the irrigated tracts were dispersed here and there across the even, dry desert rather than being squeezed together into bends of a mountain river like the irrigated lands farther to the north. The green swatches in the Roswell basin seemed to stay away from the thread of the river rather than being directly connected to it. The very different distribution of irrigated land between northern New Mexico and central New Mexico, the difference between Pecos and Roswell, was due to the difference between surface water irrigation, where water was drawn from the rivers and users were tied together by a shared irrigation ditch, and groundwater irrigation, where water was drawn from random individual wells, drilled helter skelter and applied to whatever land was most convenient.

Around the river itself, thickets of low green salt cedar trees dominated the riparian world. In the next eighty miles or so west of the river, intermittent patches of green irrigation dappled the terrain. Beyond, sixty miles to the west, the barren, treeless land slowly rose to the alpine terrain of the Sacramento Mountains. An occasional east-running indentation in the land's surface indicated a dry wash. Only the Rio Hondo made it almost all the way, full of water, from the Sacramentos to the Pecos. The rest of the thin water-carrying traces trying to pass for streams petered out somewhere between the mountains on the west and the river on the east.

Everywhere else in the west, extensive irrigation near big rivers meant big main-stem dams with large artificial lakes behind them, but in the

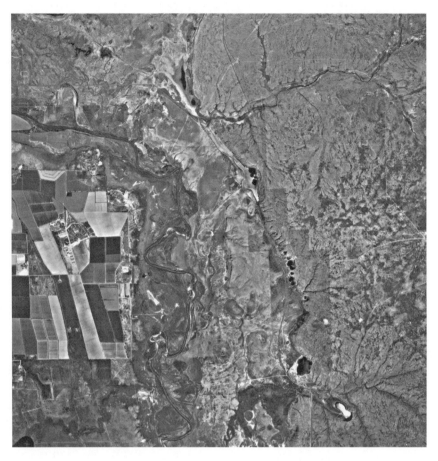

Fig. 1.4.
This aerial photograph shows the Pecos River around Roswell, New Mexico. The river frames the barren plains to the east, part of the Ogallala aquifer that underlies the south central United States. The City of Roswell sits just west of the river. West of the city, away from the river, the regular patches of farmland, irrigated from rich groundwater resources of the Roswell artesian aquifer, dominate the landscape. (Courtesy of the U.S. Geological Survey.)

Roswell basin there was neither. Instead, about ten miles west of the Pecos, the land rose up in a long, thin hump that looked from the air like the hoary back of an enormous whale swimming parallel to the Pecos just beneath the land and occasionally breaking its surface in an eighty-mile north-south line. This hump, a huge body of porous limestone tilting south and east slanted up and, here and there, broke the old surface of the land.

13

The San Andreas outcrop functioned as well as any man-made dam to collect and store the prodigious amounts of water generated by the Sacramento Mountains to the west. As things turned out, it was the water stored in this natural underground reservoir—the Roswell groundwater basin—that as much as anything else caused the trouble between Texas and New Mexico over the Pecos River. But it took a long time to figure out the geology of the outcrop and its underlying material. It took even longer to bring the natural phenomenon under legal control. By then, it was too late. Texas was without water and New Mexicans had built an extensive irrigated culture and economy on the water of the Pecos.[26]

Two days after Jean Breitenstein and the New Mexican and Texas contingents first flew over the Roswell basin, they returned on the ground in the fifteen-passenger air-conditioned bus. They drove west from Roswell on the principal road to Hondo and Ruidoso and the mountain resorts in the Sacramento foothills. They stopped where State Road 80 cut through the hump of the San Andreas outcrop. They climbed out of the bus. They looked to the walls on both the north and south sides of the road where the crews who had built the highway cut through the earth. They touched the exposed rock walls. They noticed how the obvious "beds"—separate geological strata—in the wall dipped a little to the south but mostly to the east more steeply than the surface of the land. It was as if some giant earthmover had jammed a huge slab of material right here and pounded it down under the land that ran to the river, leaving only the last edge extruded from the surface here.[27]

Later that day, the bus turned back east toward the Pecos River to inspect the other typical features of the Roswell basin. The group visited the City of Roswell well fields and the office of the Pecos Valley Artesian Conservancy District, ending up at a Roswell basin farm, aptly named "the Oasis."

Almost seventeen hundred acres of green fields, two hundred times the size of the average farm in the northern New Mexico upper basin, stretched out parallel to the Pecos River, but not on it. The Oasis had been created late in the process of developing agriculture in the Roswell area. The earliest irrigated farms had gone in a few miles west of the Oasis, up toward Roswell, in the 1890s and the first years of the twentieth century. But the Oasis used artesian water, groundwater that rose to the surface on its own.[28]

The huge chartered Greyhound lumbered down the Oasis Farm's dirt roads and finally came to a halt near a beautiful big pond surrounded by a grassy embankment and huge shade trees that already had leafed out for the year. In years past the pond had served as a public park. The current Oasis owners kept it private, but they opened it to this august group. The passengers piled out of the bus and stood awkwardly around. The New Mexico engineer Carl Slingerland finally explained to the assembled group what they were seeing in this anomalous, bucolic scene. The lake stored water that was taken out of the ground and was then delivered through irrigation ditches to the Oasis's extensive fields.

The group moved on to inspect the source of water for the ponds. Two huge wells actually pumped water into the Oasis pond but on this day the group only visited one, the larger and more powerful. When it was first sunk in the ground in 1931, the well shot the water sixty feet into the air on its own. The problem wasn't how to get water to the surface of the land but how to stop it. An early southwestern well driller, as famous for his ability to control wild water as later roustabouts would be for battling out-of-control natural gas, finally brought the original Oasis artesian gusher under control. For the next couple of decades Oasis owners had only to open the well and water rushed out of the casing and into the pond.

Now, by 1976, the pressure had dropped and the well needed a little extra help, supplied by a large diesel pump. It happened to be running on the day the Texas-New Mexico crew arrived. The motor thundered in the small copse of trees where the well and pump were located. The rusty pipes connecting the pump and the well to the pond shuddered as water poured into the pond. The needle of a gauge attached to the well bounced around, measuring the water rushing past. It showed the Oasis well pushing twenty-five hundred gallons a minute out of the ground. Somewhere amid the Oasis fields and the pump and the gauge and the well lay the real story of water in the Roswell basin. And somewhere between the San Andreas outcrop ten miles to the west and the Pecos River three miles to the east lurked the real story of the Texas-New Mexico struggle over the Pecos River.

The field trip participants in May 1976 only dimly perceived these connections. Things were not yet sufficiently clear to connect the view from the air, the view from the ground, and the unseen natural forces and human developments that brought them all together. A little farther south on the Pecos, the forces at work became much clearer from the air alone.

Immediately past the east-west running Seven Rivers Hills that bounded the Roswell basin on the south, the plane flew over two dams on the Pecos River main stem, the first dams since the Alamogordo Dam upstream from the Roswell basin. The McMillan and Avalon dams were

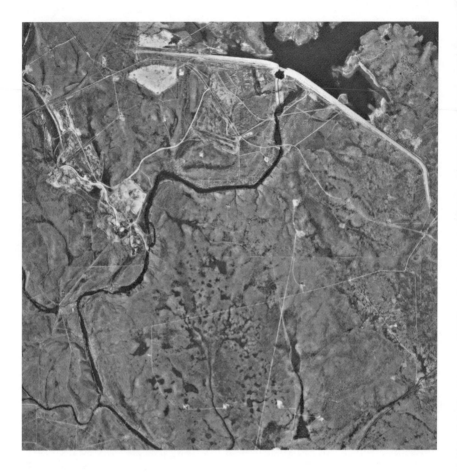

Fig. 1.5.
In this aerial photograph, the massive Brantley Dam, upstream of the Carlsbad Irrigation District, intercepts the Pecos River. Behind the dam sits Brantley Lake whose water is stored for the pleasure of southeastern New Mexico sportsmen and for the use of CID farmers below. (Courtesy of the U.S. Geological Survey.)

clearly smaller than their upstream counterpart. The pool each formed behind it seemed small from the air. In 1976 Lake McMillan in particular looked as if it were losing ground to silt from above and salt cedar trees from all sides. Nevertheless, the McMillan and Avalon dams and lakes marked the beginning of the lowest and oldest water project on the Pecos River in New Mexico, the Carlsbad Irrigation District.

The airplane passengers could see the broad canals emanating from the lowest dam on both sides of the Pecos. The canals took water to the almost twenty-five thousand acres of irrigable land that the system encompassed. Farther south an intricate web of ditches served a broad, green belt of relatively small irrigated farms.[29]

Even from the air the passengers could tell that all was not as neat as it first appeared. Many tracts of land in the Carlsbad Irrigation District looked as if they could be farmed but obviously weren't under cultivation. And a lot of wells were visible, testimony to the fact that the surface water dams and canals had not been able to deliver all the water that crops required.

In fact, the twenty-five thousand acres of irrigated land in the Carlsbad area had had trouble getting a full supply of water since irrigation had first come to the lower Pecos region in the late 1880s. The Carlsbad Irrigation District occupied a classic place in western water development. Among New Mexico lands, the district was first in time, having been developed a little before upstream Roswell, but last in location, lying as they did very near the bottom of the portion of the river in New Mexico. As Carl Slingerland often said, "those Carlsbad people always have had to scrape and fight for the Pecos water that they could get."[30]

Even from the air, the passengers could tell that the small town of Carlsbad was different. From one thousand feet up they could see the riverwalk through town, the famous Carlsbad Caverns to the southwest and the potash mines to the southeast. Obviously, farming was neither as extensive nor as central here as it was farther north in Roswell. On the ground later, talking to Jay Forbes, the home-grown, long-time lawyer for the Carlsbad Irrigation District, they would hear the town described as "precarious," just hanging onto the last of the Pecos River water in New Mexico. Of course, by the time the plane reached Texas, just sixty miles farther downstream, they would think that they had dropped off the edge of the river world.[31]

In the meantime, however, they followed the river south from Carlsbad. Staying on the thread of the river almost turned the plane around in the sinuous Malaga Bend section of the Pecos. Like some self-consuming snake the river here almost turned back on itself before returning to its original south-running course. The passengers couldn't tell it from the air but they were told that in the Malaga Bend the Pecos picked up an incredible load of natural salt. From the Malaga Bend down, drinking a cup of Pecos River water was like sipping seawater.

It wasn't fit for man or beast or, as it turned out, for lots of plants. The salt beds around Malaga Bend always had been a problem for the occupants of the Pecos River, but never more so than for the irrigation farmers at the bend and below. Twentieth-century development of the

17

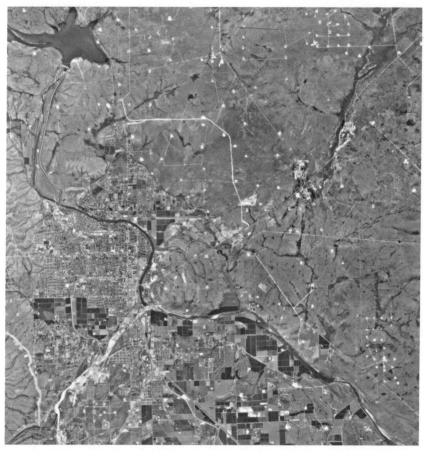

Fig. 1.6.
Lake Avalon, in the upper left hand corner of this aerial photograph, stores Pecos River water and diverts it into the irrigation system of the Carlsbad Irrigation District. The principle canals run through the City of Carlsbad and irrigate farms east of the river near the city and west of the river below it. District water serves around 25,000 acres. (Courtesy of the U.S. Geological Survey.)

Pecos River had transformed the river and natural community that it supported. Humans had changed the flow of the river. They had altered the balance of water around it. They had manipulated the plant and animal communities that depended on the river so that some plants (the salt cedars) had come and some animals (the silvery minnow and the blunt nose shiner) had gone. The one constant, the one factor that humans had not altered, seemed to be the salt that began in the Pecos at Malaga Bend and just got worse farther downstream.[32]

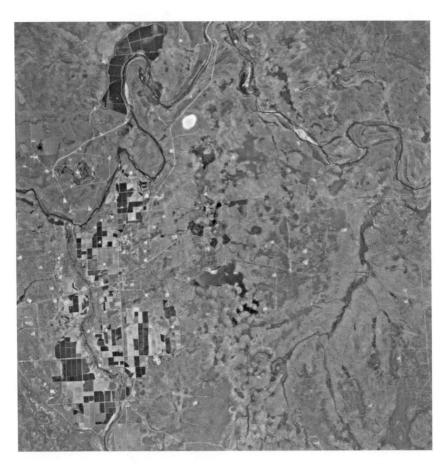

Fig. 1.7.
South of Carlsbad, still in New Mexico, the Pecos River twists in east/west contortions before heading south to the Texas border. Called "Malaga Bend," this short reach of the Pecos adds an enormous load of salt to the river water, thereby increasing its salinity and reducing its usefulness for irrigation further downstream, in New Mexico and Texas. (Courtesy of the U.S. Geological Survey.)

As the plane banked and circled and as the passengers bent and twisted to follow the river at Malaga Bend, a shimmering body of water glimmered on the earth's horizon every time the plane and its passengers turned south. This was their first sight of Texas, the Red Bluff reservoir. Constructed in the 1930s, the reservoir caught whatever Pecos River water got by the New Mexico-Texas state line and stored it for use in west Texas.

From any perspective, the Red Bluff reservoir looked huge when full. From the ground, looking north from the dam and outlet works, a

19

spectator would look at a sea of stored water. On a breezy day, the lake's surface might have the roll and chop of an ocean. From the air, the lake seemed to go on forever. But in May 1976 the works dwarfed the water. There simply wasn't much Pecos River water stored behind the Red Bluff dam that year at that time.

The looks of things only got worse as the small plane proceeded south, flying over the five Texas irrigation districts served by the Red Bluff reservoir. Paul Bloom admitted that even the irrigated parts of west Texas looked like what he called a "blasted heath," especially compared to the relative fecundity of the Roswell area. Carl Slingerland later said that Judge Breitenstein could tell at a glance at the Texas terrain that something was not right with the distribution of Pecos water between upstream New Mexico and downstream Texas.

The passengers on the plane did what they could with the parched view. The New Mexicans remarked on the multitude of oil and gas wells—"grasshoppers"—all over the barren Texas landscape as if to suggest that Texas made up in other valuable resources what it lacked in water. For their part, the Texans lamented the loss of Pecos Valley cantaloupes, famous, they said, world over for their tender sweetness.

The vision only became more stark and the lobbying of Judge Breitenstein more aggressive when the plane set down that first day of the Pecos River tour in Pecos, Texas. The town looked partly deserted. Many of the buildings were boarded up. Someone had tried to turn the abandoned, elegant downtown railroad hotel into a museum and then given up. The failed restoration was doubly depressing. Billy Sol Estes and other high-flying west Texas financiers had had as much to do with the town's decline as the lack of Pecos River water. But as the Texas and New Mexico investigators settled in for their first evening on the trip, there was a palpable sense of desiccation and decay.

The group ate together as they would for the next five days. The evening meals in particular were long and leisurely. Judge Breitenstein asked questions about what the group had seen that day. The Texas and New Mexico representatives answered as best they could.

Everyone realized that this was a unique opportunity to lobby the judge. Slingerland and Bloom didn't miss a chance to insert a jibe here, a joke there, always suggesting the justness of New Mexico's use of the river. Caroom and the Texas engineers responded in kind. The stakes were high, but so were the spirits. Everyone knew that the serious work would begin when court formally opened.[33]

In the meantime, an almost giddy sense of playfulness prevailed. Judge Breitenstein, old even then and somewhat pixie-ish, laughed and told

Fig. 1.8.
At the end of its long journey through New Mexico and just after it enters Texas, the Pecos River dumps into the Red Bluff Reservoir, the beginnings of which can be seen in this aerial photograph. Red Bluff water is stored for the benefit of several Texas irrigation districts below. (Courtesy of the U.S. Geological Survey.)

stories about old Colorado water battles. When the large bill for dinner came, he smiled and took it. "Let poppa get it," he told the Texans and New Mexicans, talking to them as he talked to his sometimes quarrelsome young grandchildren back in Denver. Of course, the two states' representatives let him pay the bill.

Everyone understood that Judge Breitenstein might be picking up the tab for dinner now but that in the end each state would pay for one half of all the expenses of the lawsuit. And everyone understood that what

21

Judge Breitenstein came to understand about the Pecos River situation would determine how the two states would share its waters.[34]

The Pecos River litigation that began with this fly-by ended the world of water as New Mexicans then knew it. *Texas v. New Mexico* transformed the world of interstate litigation that had spawned it. After the suit was done, the stakes involved in one state's suit against another over shared water resources would never be the same again. In a more fundamental and broader way, *Texas v. New Mexico* brought New Mexico face to face with the fact that its vaunted system of water law was a myth. The system had never functioned as it was supposed to, at least on the Pecos. Finally, *Texas v. New Mexico* taught water managers everywhere that it wasn't as easy as the Pecos River managers had thought to mix science and politics and law and water. A whole generation of westerners—Carl Slingerland, Royce Tipton, Jean Breitenstein, and Charles Meyers, among others—died without succeeding.

Curiously, State Engineer Steve Reynolds, the man most responsible both for New Mexico's magnificent water management system and for the debacle of *Texas v. New Mexico,* hadn't even come along on the first official run of the Pecos River. He had remained in Santa Fe, stewing over the coming challenges to his hegemony as lord of New Mexico's waters in general and the Pecos River in particular. He, too, would die before he or the courts could sort the Pecos out.

I thought I would die trying to figure out how they had died.

In May 1994 I talked a Forest Service friend, a pilot who needed flying time, into duplicating the May 1976 flight that launched *Texas v. New Mexico.* We took off in a tiny three-seated plane from the Albuquerque Airport at five o'clock in the morning when the world was still dark and cool. My friend and his fellow pilot let me sit in the copilot's front seat while the other real pilot hunkered down in the single back seat. Even in the dark, I felt vulnerable and unprotected.

There was only a tiny window between me and the black space beyond. The plane's small engine roared so loudly inside the cockpit that you couldn't be heard even if you knew what to say. As it climbed in the predawn darkness, the little plane was buffeted about, shifting in the air as if it were a three-person car changing tracks in some God-forsaken Disneyland tunnel. I felt lost in all the space and sick.

Then, headed east, the plane climbed over the Manzano Mountains. We leveled off and headed into the advancing dawn light. The fantastic, almost lunar landscape of eastern New Mexico began to spread out below us. At first the terrain looked flat and undifferentiated. Slowly, folds and dips, low hills and shallow valleys emerged. As far as I could see, there was nothing

22

else: no people, no cattle, no fences, not even many roads, just the worn-down geological shapes of the world from unobstructed horizon to horizon. By the time we reached Vaughn the sun itself was perched on the edge of the eastern horizon and, even at 6:00 A.M., it cast the flat world below us in eerie west-reaching shadows. Glancing away from the blinding sun, I looked south and east. Suddenly there it was.

Stretching like a north-south ribbon of green in front of me, the Pecos River slowly came near. At first it was just a thin green line. Then, as our plane drew nearer, I made out the shrub-like salt cedars on both of its banks. We had to fly directly over the thread of the river itself in order to see the trace of water that it carried. The Forest Service pilot took off his headphones and, over the roar of the plane's engine, yelled to me, "Do you want to turn south here and see the river course more clearly?"

"Yes," I screamed in reply. "I've never seen it in this way before, either."

TWO

The Tracys' Dream of Carlsbad

————When I first started working on the story of the Texas-New Mexico battle over the Pecos River, I didn't know much about the river below its mountainous sources in the Hispanic, northern part of New Mexico. I suspected that, like most western rivers, the upper Pecos generated the water that drove the hydraulic machinery of the lower Pecos's agricultural economy downstream. But I had only the dimmest sense of how that machinery—the dams, the diversions, the ditches, and the irrigation districts—had developed, operated and contributed to *Texas v. New Mexico*. To find out more, I got on the phone and called the Carlsbad Irrigation District (CID), the Pecos agency that controlled New Mexico surface water uses closest to the Texas state line. I had heard the name of a Carlsbad family—the Tracys—who had been involved with Carlsbad farming for years and I thought that the CID would be as good a place as any to try to find them.

"Are there any Tracys left there in Carlsbad?" I asked the polite CID secretary who took my call.

"Why, yes," she answered in that sweet, swallowed West Texas drawl so characteristic of the spoken word in that part of the world, "I'm afraid there are."

That curious blend of polite opposition and aggressive deference introduced me to the world of lower Pecos River irrigation. It was not just an attitude that ruled *Texas v. New Mexico* from its start in the 1970s, but an inclination that the Tracys had brought with them to New Mexico in the 1890s. Three generations of Tracys had struggled against nature and their neighbors to construct and control the institutions that would raise

Fig. 2.1.
An energetic New Yorker, Francis G. Tracy, pictured here as a young man, came to southern New Mexico in 1890 and never left. In the process of a long, controversial career, Tracy devoted himself to the development of the Pecos River for the benefit of his adopted community. (Photo courtesy of the Southeastern New Mexico Historical Society of Carlsbad.)

the farming community of Carlsbad out of the uninviting Chihuahuan desert. Three generations of Tracys fought to make sure that upstream users didn't interfere with the Pecos River water that nature sent down to the complicated, expensive works that they built to store and use it. The last generation of Tracys stood by, taking pot shots, while the Supreme Court threatened to tear down the century of work the family had done. The court tried to open a river the Tracys had spent a century trying to close at Carlsbad, and the court did so, God forbid, in the name of Texas irrigators even farther downstream.

Between 1890, when Francis Tracy first arrived in southeastern New Mexico from a rented farm on Long Island, New York, and the mid-1990s, when Francis Tracy's college-educated granddaughter returned to Carlsbad from a corporate career in Houston, Texas, the Tracys completely transformed southeastern New Mexico. When Francis Tracy got there, the tiny settlement had another name, Eddy. The Eddy-Bissell Company, the original Carlsbad promoters, had constructed almost the only building around, a rock structure that bore over the lintel an 1888 date and the bas-relief of a cornucopia from which poured an endless supply of sculpted vegetables. Real ones were nowhere to be seen. Carlsbad consisted then mostly of endless desert as far as the eye could see, an uninterrupted view so flat that visitors swore they could see the curvature of the earth itself. The terrain was sparsely covered with three-foot-tall mesquite and greasewood. It yielded almost no economic return. Running through the land was an unreliable desert stream, the Pecos River, by seasonal and annual turns a raging torrent and a bare trickle.[1]

Today Louise Tracy lives in her father's Santa Fe style adobe in the La Huerta ("Garden") area of Carlsbad, a town of twenty-five thousand. She sits in the kitchen of the elegant Tracy homestead, sorting through the papers of her family's remarkable 100-year love-hate relationship with the Pecos River. She talks charmingly about more Tracy plans to work around the CID, to trip up the state engineer, to enforce her version of the 1948 Pecos River Compact, and, in the 1990s, to make the 1988 decree of the Supreme Court in *Texas v. New Mexico* continue to work to support her family's Carlsbad dream.

She's a short stroll from the Riverwalk, a beautiful municipal park that straddles a Pecos River so controlled that here it looks like a pond. The nearby historic Eddy-Bissell building now houses the CID. The elegant Tracy house is itself surrounded by eighty-foot-tall elms that limit the view and shade ten acres of lush grass. Louise Tracy proudly mows the grass herself, sitting on a small garden tractor. By her own estimate the lawns require five hours of her time every two weeks to mow and an equal amount of time to irrigate.

Just across the driveway from Louise Tracy's house lie two other Tracy forty-acre tracts, one planted in sorghums, the other in alfalfa, both endlessly green thanks to irrigation and both rented to tenant farmers. The residence and adjacent farm tracts make up what Louise Tracy calls "the home place." A couple of miles down river, also on the east side of the Pecos, lie two other large Tracy irrigated tracts, the "Esperanza" and "the Orchard Farm." (In Carlsbad separate farms bear separate names, much like domestic animals.) Both additional Tracy farms are rented to tenant farmers who assemble out of pieces on both sides of the river irrigated farm units sufficiently large to come close to making money. The irrigated Tracy tracts are today among the approximately twenty thousand acres served by the Pecos River irrigation works that the Tracys helped to build and run. CID crops earn $10 million a year for local farmers.[2]

For a hundred years the Tracys have lived at the center of the battles that accompanied the transformation of Francis Tracy's Eddy to Louise

Fig. 2.2.
This December 1905 photograph shows what little was left of the Avalon Dam after the fall flood of October 1904. The roiling waters of the Pecos River wrecked the dam by carrying away the central 500 feet of the structure. (Photo courtesy of the Carlsbad Irrigation District.)

Tracy's Carlsbad. The constantly moving, constantly self-renewing water of the central Pecos River made the transformation possible. But the Tracys had to harness that fitful supply. They had to invent the means to "reclaim" the land, as they all said, from the uninviting desert and mesquite. When Francis Tracy started, little was known about the kind of aggressive human intervention required to harness wild western rivers like the Pecos. He had to work out the methods of successfully damming those rivers; of creating large storage reservoirs behind them; of diverting the stored water and delivering it for use on lands where it did not naturally occur; of making, in short, a "dependable supply" for humans of the fickle natural supply of the Pecos River's "flood flows."

By Louise Tracy's time Carlsbad has forgotten this hard-won knowledge. Its outward signs—the dams, diversions and delivery systems—exist as if they were an inevitable part of the natural landscape. A concrete

27

irrigation headgate, bearing a 1914 date and the seal of the United States Reclamation Service, delivers Pecos River water to Louise Tracy's lawn as if it has always been part of the scene. To find the inscription Louise Tracy and I have to clean off the top with a shovel.

The headgate and inscription are reminders that Louise Tracy's lawn is a product of human artifice, wrenched out of the river and the desert. The Tracys tried technique after technique to meet the various challenges to their hydraulic dreams. When their physical structures weren't big enough, they helped build bigger ones. When private money couldn't meet the increased challenges, they tapped into public sources. When existing legal institutions couldn't offer the opportunities and protections they needed, they battled the old institutions and created new ones. In the end, as *Texas v. New Mexico* would show, the Carlsbad physical structures held, but the legal ones revealed cracks and fissures that would require another round of responses and repairs.

The century of changes in Carlsbad mirrored fundamental changes in the entire Pecos River watershed. As a result of the kind of hydraulic alterations the Tracys brought, the natural landscape changed. Whole species, like the silvery minnow, disappeared from the river. New plants, especially the salt cedar, invaded. Almost as endangered as the Silvery Minnow was the ancient irrigation practiced three hundred miles upstream in the bends of the Upper Pecos. Marginal at best, subsistence-oriented, and very light in their technological touch on the land, the farmers up North struggled to hold on in the capital-intensive late twentieth-century world. The Carlsbad demands did not help. The downstream waters of the Pecos in Texas were also affected. Irrigation in Texas got a slightly later start than Carlsbad. Hampered from the beginning by saline water that entered the river below Carlsbad, Texas's prospects, though ideologically compatible with the Tracys, increasingly turned on how much Pecos River water upstream competitors at Carlsbad would allow to pass. From the start, the Tracys, located between the shrinking water world above in Hispanic New Mexico and the struggling world below in Texas, dreamed of capturing as much as they could of the transformed Pecos River and putting its water to beneficial use.[3]

In the late night hours of Saturday, October 1, 1904 Francis Tracy's dream turned into a nightmare. As manager of the Carlsbad-based Pecos Irrigation Company, Tracy had just received word of a flood disaster in the making that threatened all that he had accomplished in his fourteen years at Carlsbad. An unusually large fall cloudburst in the mountains northwest of Roswell, sixty miles upstream, had sent a torrent of water down the already rain-swollen tributaries and dry arroyos that fed the

28

Pecos River from the west. When it reached Roswell, before it hit the river, the torrent had swamped the streets of the city under as much as six feet of water. Knowing that it was just a matter of hours before the wall of water reached Carlsbad, Roswell residents frantically telephoned downstream relatives to warn them of the impending danger. Word also reached Tracy of the disaster in the making.[4]

The destructive wall of water threatened the McMillan Dam, the Avalon diversion works, and the Carlsbad flume, the three giant centerpieces in Carlsbad's plans to change nature's. Each structure in 1904 was an indispensable part of Francis Tracy's dream to make an oasis of the Carlsbad desert by capturing excess Pecos River water that would otherwise rush downstream into what was still an even more forbidding Texas desert. The McMillan dam would block the flood and store its torrent of water. The Avalon dam would divert the stored water from the river into irrigation ditches east of the river. And the Carlsbad flume would deliver the diverted water to vast acres of irrigable land west of the river and south of the city.

Together in 1904 the three Carlsbad structures embodied the essential elements of irrigation activity: storage, diversion, and delivery. By the time of the 1948 Pecos River Compact, the three elements would become central to the limitations imposed by Texas on New Mexico's use of the river's waters. Eventually, the compact limitations would become central to *Texas v. New Mexico*. There would be a direct line from the 1904 Carlsbad structures to the 1988 Supreme Court decisions, but, of course, Francis Tracy didn't know it at the time. It must have been enough that the prize he had sought for fourteen years—the flood waters of the lower Pecos—were in 1904 about to destroy the best of his work.

In October 1904, the McMillan Dam straddled the Pecos River near the Seven Rivers divide between the upstream Roswell basin and its downstream Carlsbad counterpart. The earth-and-rock dam as it existed in 1904 was more than a quarter-mile across, more than thirty feet tall, and almost one hundred yards thick at the base. It dwarfed the makeshift rock-and-log dams hundreds of miles upstream in mountainous Hispanic New Mexico, the only competitors, if you could call them that, for Pecos River water. Originally built in late 1892 and 1893, the McMillan Dam was designed by engineers to store 138,000 acre-feet. Badly damaged by an 1893 flood, McMillan had been repaired and improved in 1894–1895 by a work force that matched the original construction crews: 500 men and 165 teams of horses. By 1904 it was the biggest dam and reservoir in the world.[5]

McMillan Dam represented an investment of almost half a million dollars, about a third of the $1.5 million poured into all the Carlsbad irrigation works as of 1904. An astronomical sum of money by turn-of-the-century standards, the funds came from private, not public, sources, all outside New Mexico. Tracy's widening search for money to finance the Carlsbad structures like McMillan started in Chicago financial markets. The quest extended to New York and as far afield as Europe, where capital-rich Swiss investors were enticed by Francis Tracy and his east-coast connections to invest in making capital-poor New Mexico bloom. By 1904 the financial net had contracted again; the voracious Carlsbad capital appetite then depended on the huge resources of Colorado-based silver magnate James J. Hagerman, a robber baron of sorts.[6]

The huge structure over which Francis Tracy presided in October 1904 was a crowning success in western reclamation as it was then understood. It represented the best that capital and technology could accomplish in capturing and evening out for new economic development the erratic flood flows of desert rivers like the Pecos. Without dams like McMillan, those floods not only went to waste, but also threatened the minuscule development that the river's tiny steady ("base") flows would support. Such dams would capture the destructive floods and save them for long-term use. The river's dependable supply would even out and increase so that everyone would benefit, or so it was thought.

But on October 2, the Pecos River offered too much of what Tracy was counting on. He watched as the Pecos River flood waters reached the dam and caused the level of the lake behind it to rise at the astounding rate of fourteen inches an hour.[7] The biggest dam in the world had backed water up the river for fifty miles, way beyond its expected pool, creating a lake on both sides of the stream bed that reached all the way to Artesia.

Worse yet, the dam's spillways and outlet channels could no longer contain the backed-up water. As Francis Tracy watched in horror, the Pecos River water started to pour over the top of McMillan dam itself and work its way around the dam's eastern edge. Tracy worried that it was only a matter of time before the whole structure gave way, sending the stored water that was to be Carlsbad's salvation downstream to wipe out the young community.

Once past McMillan Dam, the flood water headed south for the Avalon dam six miles downstream. Avalon was as essential as McMillan, although in a different way, to Tracy's dreams for Carlsbad, to all pro-moters' dreams for an irrigated Eden in the West. First McMillan stored the flood inflows of the Pecos River. Then Avalon received the stored water as it was released, and forced it from the river channel on man's demand, not nature's, for use on lands that the waters never would have reached but for Avalon. Here, in the use of human technology and capital to take surface waters out of the rivers where they naturally occurred, lay the real soul of western irrigation. A half-century later, when the 1948 Pecos River Compact prohibited New Mexico from further "depleting by man's activities the flow of the Pecos River," the compact was limiting precisely the function that Avalon Dam was designed to perform. Now in October 1904 the flood rolling over McMillan and heading for Avalon threatened to provide its own limitation.

In August 1893 a previously flooded Pecos River had pounded Avalon for days until it finally gave way. The *Carlsbad Argus* had then reported that

> for days and nights the dam . . . battled with the surging sea that swept through and over the gates and mechanical contrivances for the control of the water. Down from far away gorges came the drift of a decade, to bury the barricades. From the plains came unnumbered carcasses of cattle to choke the gateways. [Once the rising water overtopped the dam] [I]t was but a few minutes after the warning came before the crest of the dam was gone. Probably in twenty minutes the water cut down twenty feet along the 900 feet of the length of the dam and in two hours more, clear to the base of the vast pile of earth and stone. . . . The opening allowed an avalanche of water to roll down upon the already choked river and whirl across bends to the slanting plains.[8]

As varied an array of national and international financiers as had built and rebuilt the much larger McMillan storage dam came to the rescue of the Avalon diversion dam. In the promoters' insatiable search for more storage, they had made Avalon serve double duty, as the principal diversion dam and as a supplemental place to store water that McMillan couldn't hold. So in 1904 Avalon dam both diverted Pecos River water and impounded a reservoir six miles long with an estimated capacity of 25,000 acre-feet.[9] Now on October 2 the fury of a new flood that had already overflowed the principal McMillan storage dam wrecked the principal Avalon diversion dam again.

For decades Francis Tracy alluded to the fact that he had personally witnessed the 1904 destruction of Avalon but no Tracy account survives. The just-formed Reclamation Service, later to become the United States Bureau of Reclamation now so infamous in the environmental history of the west, had an engineer on the scene a couple of days after the height of the 1904 Pecos River flood. "I found," reported W. M. Reed, that about 500 feet of the main Avalon dam had been carried away and the river, yet in flood, was running through Lake Avalon without interruption. Of 32 gates in the spillway, only eight, badly wrecked, were still standing.

A contemporary photograph shows a gap at the center of Avalon Dam so large that the surviving wings look unconnected by any center. Obviously the 1904 flood prevented the dam from diverting any Pecos River water from the river's main channel. Without Avalon, Francis Tracy's Carlsbad works couldn't possibly accomplish what the subsequent 1948 Compact limited, "depletions of the River by man's activities."[10]

The wall of water that destroyed Avalon on October 2, 1904, headed straight for the final structural element in Francis Tracy's Pecos River dream, a flume three miles below Avalon. The flume carried the water

Fig. 2.3.
Always central to the wildest real estate dreams of Carlsbad promoters, the flume carrying Pecos River water from east of the river to the wide-open expanses west of the river began as a flimsy wooden structure as this March 1890 photograph shows. The early structure could not withstand raging spring and fall floods, which carried it away. (Photo courtesy of the Carlsbad Irrigation District.)

Fig. 2.4.
By the beginning of the irrigation
season in the spring of 1903,
Francis G. Tracy had cobbled
together enough money to rebuild the flimsy wooden flume. He replaced it
with the massive, multi-arched concrete structure shown here. The flume still
stands today. (Photo courtesy of the Carlsbad Irrigation District.)

diverted to the east side of the Pecos River at Avalon back across the
Pecos to an labyrinth of ditches and headgates designed to deliver water
to an endless expanse of irrigable land west of the river. Rebuilt by Tracy
in 1903, using $50,000 he cobbled together from a wide variety of pri-
vate sources the new concrete-reinforced aqueduct was both massive and
graceful. Four hundred ninety-seven feet long and up to 47 feet high, the
new structure supported a trough for transporting the water across the
river that itself was 18 feet high and 20 feet wide, five times as big as any
irrigation ditch in northern New Mexico. The *National Geographic*
reported that Francis Tracy's 1903 Carlsbad flume was the largest irrigation flume in the United States.[11]

The Tracy companies' vision of limitless growth based on Pecos River
irrigation was based on the flume's ability to get water to the land west
of the river. In recalling those early years, Tracy in the 1930s mused:

The prospectuses of those days show plans for irrigating more than 1,000,000 acres of land between Roswell and Pecos. In the company's employ were the finest bunch of young enthusiasts, and inexperienced dreamers of middle age that could possibly be determined. The stage was all and properly set for limitless expansion and surely we had a great time.[12]

An early company engineer scaled that extravagant million-acre estimate back to 200,000.[13] True enough, in 1901 the irrigation system had irrigated only 10,000 acres of land, but the difference between the irrigated and the irrigable land—either 10,000 acres or 190,000 acres or 990,000 acres depending, as Louise Tracy now says, "on whose lies you believed," represented the real bonanza. The true value of the desert acres lay in getting Pecos River water, stored at McMillan, diverted at Avalon, and delivered through Carlsbad flume, to the vast irrigable acres east of the river.

In 1904 Francis Tracy's Pecos Irrigation Company owned more than thirty thousand undeveloped acres that lay within reach of existing company irrigation ditches. Tracy's company had acquired title to those acres in classic western manner, manipulating federal land laws to get around prohibitions against just the kind of large-scale land monopolies that the company had assembled. Tracy himself had first come to Carlsbad on a lark, just to help out temporarily with the land scheme. Ironically he had stayed, laid down permanent roots and by 1904 owned a part of the scheme's booty himself. The value of that dry desert land, still belonging to the Tracy companies, depended on the ability of the companies to get water to it. And that ability depended on a flume whose functions were threatened by the 1904 flood.[14]

In addition to providing the stuff of Tracy's speculative real estate dreams, the flume also promised to fulfill Tracy's legal obligation to provide water to the tracts he already had sold. By 1904 the Tracy companies had contracted to provide water to sixty-four thousand acres of Carlsbad area land, more than five times as many acres as ever had been irrigated in the area. Thus the October 2 flood threatened to wreak havoc with both Tracy's dreams and obligations, his future and his past, as the roiling water headed from the destroyed Avalon toward the flume that alone could deliver the water necessary to feed those dreams and quench those obligations.[15]

Ironically, where upstream Avalon Dam had failed so quickly, the downstream flume now functioned in its place. Its approaches acted as a barrier, slowing the pounding torrent of water. The flume's graceful concrete arches slowly released the rising water behind them to the stream below, and the wall of water partially dissipated.[16]

Chapter 2

Fig. 2.5.
While Francis G. Tracy struggled to establish the political, financial, and physical institutions that would make Carlsbad bloom, he also struggled to farm. Here, in this 1908 photograph, Tracy supervises the start of cotton planting between the young peach trees of the Tracy orchard in Las Huertas where his grand daughter Louise now lives. (Photo courtesy of the Southeastern New Mexico Historical Society of Carlsbad.)

The town of Carlsbad and the Eddy-Bissell building survived, despite extensive damage. The flume survived as well. But the equally indispensable Avalon Diversion was completely destroyed. McMillan Dam had suffered extensive damage. In other words, after the 1904 flood there was little left of the storage facilities, no diversion works, and only a damaged, incomplete delivery system dangling helplessly at the end of the useless system above it.

No private money was available to pay for the extensive repairs that the 1904 flood damage would require. It looked as if the extravagant Carlsbad project, like 90 percent of the private reclamation efforts in the West, had failed. If it had, that part of southeastern New Mexico would have returned to the scrub desert from which it had started to emerge. The Pecos River would have rolled fitfully on as it had for millions of years. Upstream New Mexico surface water uses would have posed no threat to downstream irrigation in Texas. (Eventually groundwater wells in Roswell might have presented a very different and much thornier problem.) The 1948 Pecos River Compact would not have been necessary and *Texas v. New Mexico* would not have followed.[17]

But, luckily for Francis Tracy, the federal government had just positioned itself to step in. In 1902 Congress had passed the Reclamation Act, which promised massive federal money to make the desert bloom. The newly formed Reclamation Service was casting about for high-profile projects that offered the possibility of quick, demonstrable success. After 1904, Francis Tracy worked tirelessly to convince early Reclamation officials that they had found that project in the partially wrecked Carlsbad project and that the government purchase and rehabilitation of the extensive remaining works of the private Pecos Irrigation Company, which Tracy represented, made good public sense.[18]

From the beginning, the Reclamation Service and Tracy haggled over price. Tracy insisted that the United States ought to pay at least for the $1.5 million that the Tracy companies already had invested in the dams, diversion, flumes, ditches, and headgates that, if repaired by the United States, would deliver water to the Carlsbad lands. The canals lacing the government land, argued Tracy, belonged to the private companies under existing federal law, and the government should pay to get them back. Anxious to keep the price as low as possible, Reclamation officials refused to recognize the full extent of the private companies' claims and wanted to reduce the acquisition cost accordingly. By 1905 Tracy was so desperate that his Pecos Valley Irrigation Company accepted $150,000 from the United States for its system, a fire sale price considering what the company and its predecessors had invested.[19]

The 1905 sale of the Carlsbad project to the United States brought the public interest and the financial resources of the federal government into the Carlsbad water picture. Now the Reclamation Service owned Francis Tracy's water rights, his water obligations, and his water plans. The Reclamation Service had to decide how far to go to meet Francis Tracy's obligations to provide water to previously irrigated land (13,000 acres), how much farther to go to meet Tracy's contractual obligations to supply water to previously unsupplied land (64,000 acres), and how much farther than that to go to fulfill Tracy's wildest unrealized private dreams (100,000 acres and up). And in deciding how far to extend itself, the Reclamation Service had to decide how much to disrupt the Pecos River to do it. From Francis Tracy's point of view, the bigger the Carlsbad project, the better. But from the United States' point of view, the bigger the

Carlsbad project, the more pressure on a limited, public resource and the greater the chance of impact on public interests beyond Carlsbad, to whom the federal government was responsible even if Francis Tracy wasn't.

So from the outset the Reclamation Service moved cautiously. As the Bureau rehabilitated the dams, diversions, flumes, and canals destroyed by the 1904 flood, it slowly increased the number of acres that the project would serve and charge. By 1908 only 7,000 acres of the original 20,000 acres designated by the government as "open" actually received water. For the next two decades, the irrigated acreage inched up slowly. However, by the time the Bureau turned the operation of the irrigation system over to the local Carlsbad Irrigation District in 1930, the project had been officially extended to only 25,000 acres, not all of which were actually irrigated every year. And despite more than twenty years of constant cajoling and lobbying, Francis Tracy and his band of real estate speculators could never convince the Service to include within the project the southernmost dry desert lands that they still owned west of the Pecos.[20]

Fig. 2.6.
By 1906 the United States had begun to reconstruct a massive Avalon Dam and the principle Carlsbad diversion. The scale of the undertaking made the new Avalon look like the work of ancient Incas. (Photo courtesy of the Carlsbad Irrigation District.)

The Tracys' Dream of Carlsbad

Part of the government's reluctance to embrace Francis Tracy's wildest dreams stemmed from the uncertain supply of Pecos River water. Reclamation's repair and rebuilding of the McMillan Dam had not restored its full capacity because the 1893 and 1904 floods had left a lot of sediment behind in the new delta when the water receded. But between 1905 and 1940 Francis Tracy wanted more from the Reclamation Service than just a rebuilt McMillan. He was looking for even more storage capable of capturing and making a boon of his 1904 bane, the really big floods. The government's slow response to his persistent requests revealed what the real Pecos River battle was over, how the 1948 Pecos River compact tried to resolve it, and how *Texas v. New Mexico* undid that resolution.

Even before the 1904 flood and the 1905 sale of the Carlsbad system to the United States, Francis Tracy had always hoped to build a third dam and reservoir to further even out the volatile river flows and make Carlsbad's water supply even more dependable than it was with just the small Avalon Dam and the larger McMillan Dam upstream. He never could raise the private capital to construct a third dam, but now, with the government resources available through the Reclamation Service, a third dam became more feasible. From the Bureau of Reclamation's takeover of the Carlsbad project in 1905, Tracy hounded the government to construct a new reservoir at what became known as "Dam Site No. 3," just downstream from the McMillan Dam.[21]

Even the federal government recognized that a scaled-down Carlsbad project could use additional storage. But the cost of a third Carlsbad dam and reservoir posed only part of the problem. The location of a new dam turned out to be even more significant. Simply put, the farther downstream a third dam was located, the more upstream floods it could catch and store. A new dam higher on the river, at the top of its middle reach, would catch the spring meltoff from mountains farther to the north, but would miss the summer and fall torrents in the middle basin (like the 1904 storm). A new dam at the bottom of the middle reach, just above Carlsbad, would catch the excess water yield of storms like the dangerous one in October 1904 in the middle basin of the Pecos that had proved too much for the existing structures.[22]

In a harbinger of things to come almost a century later in *Texas v. New Mexico,* the real problem with Francis Tracy's "Dam Site No. 3" turned out to be control of the flood inflows to the Pecos River. Even early in the twentieth century astute river observers like Tracy recognized that more than 80 percent of the "flashy and erratic" Pecos River flows originated not in the steady, regular flow of the river but in the fast, chaotic impulses created in the middle reach of the river by just the kind

Chapter 2

of storms that had wiped out the private Carlsbad project in October 1904. Carlsbad's bane could be converted into its boon by controlling and capturing the flood flows that had almost destroyed it and putting them to use making Francis Tracy's most fantastic dreams of a desert Eden real. The problem was that the more flood water Carlsbad caught, the less went downstream to Texas. And the lower on the river a third New Mexico dam went, the more flood water otherwise bound for Texas that dam would catch.[23]

The seeds for interstate dispute were sown in 1914. In that year, the Reclamation Service, at the insistence of the West Texas Reclamation Association, centered in the Texas towns of Pecos and Barstow, issued a comprehensive report on the state of irrigated agriculture on the Pecos River in Texas. The report found that irrigated agriculture was on the rise on the lower Pecos in Texas *and* that it was increasingly risky, both because of lack of storage in Texas and because of existing storage at Carlsbad. A third New Mexico dam would only make the Texas situation worse because the new dam would further deplete the Pecos River flows that reached Texas. Francis Tracy's constant push for a third New Mexico reservoir on the Pecos River, located as far downstream as possible, inevitably drew downstream Texas into the interstate struggle that would blossom at the end of the twentieth century into *Texas v. New Mexico.*[24]

The West Texas Reclamation Association set out in the early twentieth century not only to block Francis Tracy's plans for a third Pecos River dam but also to reign in New Mexico's upstream Pecos River uses. The association armed itself with the first of the U.S. Supreme Court's interstate equitable apportionment decisions and with an engineering advisor intimately acquainted with New Mexico water institutions. The Texans threatened to sue just as they would fifty years later, in the 1970s, for an equitable apportionment of the river. They used their Congressional muscle to block federal funding of a third dam anywhere on the Pecos River. In a parallel move the Texans also tried to negotiate an early version of what would finally become the 1948 Pecos River Compact at the heart of *Texas v. New Mexico.*[25]

The precursor 1924 Pecos River Compact set different limits on New Mexico's uses of Pecos River water from those stipulated in its 1948 successor. Unlike the later compact, the 1924 one limited New Mexico's upstream use of Pecos River water by acreage. The 1924 Compact would have restricted New Mexico to irrigating seventy-six thousand acres in the middle basin between Santa Rosa and the Texas state line using Pecos River surface waters.[26]

The proposed 1924 Compact also provided that New Mexico could build a new reservoir, presumably at an upstream site, not Tracy's preferred downstream one, to serve an additional 25,000 acres in the Carlsbad project. (Tracy claimed that the project already irrigated 24,000 acres in 1922.) Since Carlsbad irrigators had never come close to actually irrigating 50,000 total acres, the acreage limitation would simply have reigned in Francis Tracy's wildest dreams for the Carlsbad project, while allowing it to expand somewhat, using water stored behind a new upstream dam. In exchange the proposed compact would have guaranteed Texans enough Pecos River water to irrigate 40,000 acres and the right to construct a dam and reservoir at Red Bluff, Texas, just across the Texas-New Mexico stateline.[27]

Texas approved the proposed 1924 Compact. Francis Tracy and his Carlsbad-centered Pecos Water Users Association initially agreed because they knew a compact would avoid costly, uncertain interstate litigation and because they believed that any compact would have to protect the extensive senior rights of the Carlsbad project. But as the 1924 Compact got closer and closer to final approval in both states, the intricate politics of water in New Mexico bogged the process down and brought it to a halt.[28]

The 1925 New Mexico state legislature insisted on adding a provision to the proposed compact guaranteeing additional upstream storage rights in the New Mexico headwaters of the Pecos River. The proposed addition set the New Mexicans to fighting among themselves. The local fight pitted the Middle Basin—from the Texas-New Mexico state line up to Santa Rosa—against the Upper Basin—from Santa Rosa up to Pecos, New Mexico. Francis Tracy was at the center of this controversy, too. Unable to secure any statewide agreement on the compact terms, New Mexico governor A. T. Hannett vetoed the entire compact. In his March 1925 veto message Hannett explained that he was "exercising the veto power concerning this enactment in response to practically a unanimous protest against it becoming a law from the Pecos Water Users' Association, the New Mexico people most vitally concerned in the matter." In 1923 Francis Tracy's Association pushed the 1924 Pecos River Compact. In 1925 they sunk it. Without New Mexico approval, the 1924 Compact was dead, and so too were any federal plans for increased storage on the Pecos in either Texas or New Mexico.[29]

Had the 1924 Compact been approved by both New Mexico and Texas, as it almost was, the *Texas v. New Mexico* litigation that began fifty years later would have looked completely different, if it had happened at all. Groundwater wasn't in anyone's ken in the 1920s. Wells might not have been the thorny problem they turned out to be in the 1970s and 1980s litigation because the 1924 Compact restricted itself

40

to surface water. In addition, the acreage limitations that the 1924 Compact imposed on both states would have provided a much easier measure of interstate obligation than the depletion standard finally adopted by the two states in the 1948 Pecos River Compact. It would have been much simpler, as it turned out, to determine if New Mexico had exceeded its allowed acres than it was to determine if she had increased by man's activities the depletion of river flows, as the 1948 Compact required. But with Hannett's 1925 veto of the Pecos River Compact, both Texas, New Mexico, and the United States were thrown back onto less formal, less comprehensive mechanisms than compacts to work out their plans for the Pecos River. Francis Tracy and the Reclamation Service had to look to something other than increased reservoir storage to guarantee Carlsbad a full supply.[30]

Where new federal dams weren't available, new legal mechanisms might help. One was the formal adjudication of water rights claims at Carlsbad and above so that the Carlsbad water rights could be judicially defined, related to common claims to the Pecos River, and enforced against them in times of shortage. In effect, Carlsbad and the Reclamation service were using New Mexico state law to build the structures that would guarantee Carlsbad a full supply where new dams, for the moment, could not.

In 1914, the Reclamation Service turned a flood of early private suits over relative rights to the Pecos's fickle supply into the first comprehensive stream-system adjudication of all surface water claims to the Pecos River. The suit, *United States v. Hope Community Ditch et al.*, eventually involved more than five thousand water rights claimants from Carlsbad all the way to the river's headwaters in the mountains of north central New Mexico. The comprehensive litigation almost exhausted the federal government before it was finally finished twenty years later in 1933. The exhaustion tempted the federal managers of the suit to recognize what Francis Tracy always had known: nature had divided the Pecos River into two different streams, the one above the Roswell basin and the one below. The river even went underground at Santa Rosa. Working slowly upstream from Carlsbad, defining competing surface water rights as they went, the Reclamation Service asked the federal court if they couldn't stop at Santa Rosa in recognition of the fact that water claims above there didn't have much effect on water claims below. The federal court made the federal managers push on to the very beginnings of the Pecos. But the failed attempt to sever the river into two legal parts showed where Carlsbad's upstream interests really lay, in the middle watershed below Santa Rosa and above Carlsbad.[31]

Even after completion, the final *Hope* decree was cracked and leaky. It didn't include some of the ancient irrigated lands in the northern mountain valleys. More crucially, it didn't include claims to interrelated groundwater, a missing element that would always haunt Carlsbad and *Texas v. New Mexico*. But the 1933 *Hope* Decree did include a formal definition of the Pecos River water rights of Francis Tracy's beloved Carlsbad project—sort of.

The *Hope* decree recognized that the Carlsbad lands had the most senior rights to surface water in the middle reach of the Pecos River just as Tracy always had maintained. Formally at least, this seniority was supposed to guaranteed that no existing junior upstream user could withhold water from Carlsbad if Carlsbad needed it. This senior priority was the legal equivalent of a downstream dam. Carlsbad's priority subjected competing upstream uses to downstream Carlsbad's superior needs.[32]

But in defining the Carlsbad lands to which this senior priority would legally attach, the *Hope* decree confirmed only half of Francis Tracy's vision. The decree limited those senior rights to an amount of water needed to irrigate 25,055 acres, a couple of thousand more acres than had ever actually been irrigated in the Carlsbad area, but still fewer by half than the acres Tracy claimed. Nevertheless the *Hope* decree moved Carlsbad water rights one step further toward a solid foundation by cementing some, but not all, of Francis Tracy's claims, into a permanent, legal relationship of seniority to most other *existing* claims to Pecos River water.[33]

Carlsbad's protection should have been even more complete when New Mexico imposed statewide limitations and controls on *new* Pecos River surface water appropriations. Enacted for the first time in 1905, less than a year after the disastrous 1904 Carlsbad flood, the New Mexico law establishing the office of New Mexico State (then Territorial) Engineer guaranteed that the state would protect existing rights while it supervised the establishment of new ones. No new water right would be allowed unless the developer of that right could first demonstrate that the new right wouldn't harm existing rights. For Carlsbad's farmers this meant that downstream Carlsbad should be protected from new upstream depletions. For a variety of reasons, the promised comprehensive administration of Pecos River rights never came to pass and Carlsbad was left to struggle on its own for what water it could get on its own.

After New Mexico gained statehood in 1912, the New Mexico state engineer not only failed to protect the water-short Carlsbad area but also failed to protect water-short Texas from further upstream appropriations in New Mexico below Carlsbad and above the state line. For example, in a decision that would return fifty years later to haunt Carlsbad and

Texas v. New Mexico, on August 1, 1931 State Engineer George Neel granted a license to J. N. Livingston to appropriate an additional 2,000 acre-feet of Pecos River water to irrigate almost five hundred acres of desert scrub land in the Malaga area east of the river, south of Carlsbad and just north of the Texas state line. A photograph in the state engineer file, offered as proof that Pecos River was being diverted and used, shows a dapper Livingston, in a white dress shirt and a gray fedora, athwart a raised aqueduct into which a pump and raised pipe pour frothing Pecos River water. The new downstream depletion wouldn't affect upstream Carlsbad, but it would certainly reduce the flow of water that otherwise would make it to the downstream state line. At the time, the New Mexico state engineer was concerned, if at all, with the effects of new appropriations on existing New Mexican users, not Texas ones. But in the end what Pecos River water all New Mexicans had to apportion among themselves was the water left over after Texas's interstate share had been satisfied. From Carlsbad's point of view, the New Mexico state engineer's failure to protect Texas from further upstream depletions was as serious as its failed effort to protect Carlsbad, not because it deprived Carlsbad of water but because it got New Mexico in trouble with Texas.[34]

So the new legal institutions put in place by the United States and the state of New Mexico after the 1904 floods were designed to complement the repaired and rebuilt physical structures, McMillan, Avalon, and the flume. But, like the physical structures, the legal ones had flaws and cracks that would lead straight to *Texas v. New Mexico* fifty years later.

In the meantime, by the late 1920s the re-christened Bureau of Reclamation tired of actually operating the system that it had bought in 1905 and put back together thereafter. The federal government wanted to turn the day-to-day administration over to a local entity for management. Local Carlsbad interests responded by creating the Carlsbad Irrigation District, one of the water institutions authorized by the fledgling state legislature to fill the gap between individual irrigators at the bottom and the Bureau of Reclamation at the top.[35]

The statute called on new districts like Carlsbad to form by holding an election for an initial board of directors. Everyone assumed that the leaders of the Pecos Water Users Association, including its long-time president Francis G. Tracy, would simply become the directors of the new CID. But at the election held June 20, 1932 Carlsbad farmers chose a rump board of directors. Of the ten candidates on the original CID ballot, Francis G. Tracy finished last.[36]

Tracy's resounding defeat carried many lessons. For one, it showed that local farmers had tired of Tracy's cantankerous opposition to everything and everybody. His neighbors were more interested in shoring up existing irrigation works than they were in Francis Tracy's far-flung dreams of expanding the district's system to include those dry desert lands still held by the Tracy development companies.

Tracy's victorious opponents did not buy into Tracy's decades-long promotion of a third New Mexico storage dam right below the existing Macmillan Dam at what euphemistically was referred to for years as "Dam Site No. 3." The newly elected CID board wanted more storage, of course. The limited acres recognized as the measure of the Carlsbad rights by the *Hope* decree were still short of water and getting shorter. But the CID board members were also more flexible about the location of a new dam than the increasingly dogmatic Tracy had ever been.

The combination of this new CID flexibility on location and the availability of massive and cheap federal construction money in the form of various New Deal programs allowed Texas and New Mexico to begin serious negotiations that would lead to the construction of two new federal dams on the Pecos River. Until then, the two states had blocked each other's efforts in Congress to secure new Pecos River dams. Now, with Tracy on the sidelines, the New Mexicans finally agreed to support Texas's dream

Fig. 2.7.
As late as 1931 J. N. Livingston proudly watches his new diversion of Pecos River surface water flow toward his lands. (Photo courtesy of the State Engineer Office.)

Chapter 2

of a large Pecos River dam just across the New Mexico-Texas state line at Red Bluff. In turn, the Texans supported New Mexico's dream of a new New Mexican dam on the Pecos. But the Texans insisted that the New Mexican dam be located far enough upstream not to interfere further with flood inflows from torrential summer and fall rains in the middle reach of the river, between the new upstream dam site and McMillan. What had been Francis Tracy's nightmare in 1904, too much flood inflow for existing dams in New Mexico, had become Texas's dream by the mid-1930s, that portion of upstream water generated in New Mexico that couldn't be stored in the state and therefore would have to pass downstream to Texas. Francis Tracy, holding on for dear life to the downstream Dam Site Number 3 and its promise of more New Mexico access to the flood inflows, opposed the long-sought additional Carlsbad storage on the grounds of location alone. But with Tracy neutralized on the sidelines, the two states cemented the dam and related flood inflow compromise in the so-called "Alamogordo agreement" of 1935.[37]

The "Alamogordo Agreement" did not replace the never-ratified 1924 New Mexico-Texas Compact. Neither state was yet ready to agree to anything as formal as the 1948 Pecos River Compact. But by 1938 the informal agreement allowed federal construction of the Red Bluff dam in Texas and the Alamogordo Dam 260 miles north, near Santa Rosa in New Mexico. The Red Bluff dam would store the New Mexico flood inflows originating in the middle reach of the river that McMillan couldn't handle. And the Alamogordo Dam would supplement what the downstream McMillan could catch for Carlsbad, but only with water originating upstream of the middle reach of the river. The new New Mexico dam backed up a 15-mile-long lake behind it. When full, the lake held almost 200,000 acre-feet of additional water for the benefit of Carlsbad farmers 200 river miles to the south.[38]

By the time of the Alamogordo Dam construction, affairs of the New Mexican farmers were managed not by the federal government, but by the Carlsbad Irrigation District. The CID became one of the early and few Reclamation successes when it paid off its basic obligation to the U.S. government. Ownership and management of the Pecos River dams still fell to the United States, but the other physical structures—the headgates, the canals, the flumes—now belonged to the local, state-created CID as did the right and duty to distribute "available" Pecos River water among CID farmers. In the process, the CID emerged as a major player in negotiations between Texas and New Mexico over formal apportionment of the river.[39]

In 1941 nature put to the test the informal division of the river embodied in the location and construction of the new Red Bluff and Alamogordo Dams. Another fall storm in the middle reach of the river, as violent and as huge as the one that had wrecked the dams and ditches in 1904, created a second wall of water below Alamogordo Dam, headed once again for downstream McMillan and beyond. This time the rehabilitated and rebuilt dams and the Carlsbad flume held as they were supposed to, and the new Texas Red Bluff reservoir filled with the river flood flows as it was designed to do. The engineers who had designed the structures must have breathed a sigh of relief.[40]

But that 1941 flood foreshadowed new system problems that would return to haunt *Texas v. New Mexico* as much as the 1904 flood had stressed the river's physical works. The 1941 flood momentarily put so much water into the system that, while the dams could manage the surplus water, the excess could not be measured. The Red Bluff gauge had been installed by the United States Geological Survey (USGS) and the Bureau of Reclamation as one of a series of gauges that would measure water leaving New Mexico and entering Texas. But by the time the 1941 flood water reached the gauge, set in the middle of the river's normal, narrow channel, the Pecos was running in an unconfined flood a mile wide. The gauge couldn't possibly measure the flood inflows accurately.[41]

To make matters worse, existing hydrological techniques couldn't accurately describe the critical flood inflow factor that the gauges couldn't measure. Where the 1904 floods had destroyed the structures designed to control the Pecos, the 1941 floods overcame the science that was supposed to describe it accurately. At the time, however, river planners and managers were too close to the 1941 flood to see this. All they knew was that the structures, and the values those structures embodied, had held. For the moment that was enough to allow the two states to move toward a more formal apportionment of the river.[42]

Shortly after the construction of the Alamogordo and Red Bluff dams, federal officials brought New Mexico and Texas together to begin hammering out a final Pecos River Compact. They started in early 1943, in the middle of World War II, with a series of meetings in the critical irrigated areas of New Mexico and Texas. Carlsbad Irrigation District officials appeared at the April 20, 1943 meeting. The head of the CID Board told the federal officials that the CID's attorney would speak for the CID, but he never got a word in edgewise. Instead and as usual, Francis Tracy, Sr., then seventy-three years old, did all the talking for Carlsbad.[43]

What he said related principally to storage at the McMillan dam, two hundred miles downstream from the new Alamogordo Dam. McMillan, Tracy told the compact commissioners, had never stored the 130,000

Chapter 2

Fig. 2.8.
A fall 1941 flood threatened the works of the Carlsbad Irrigation District as much as the fall 1904 flood had. Here the 1941 Pecos River flood waters pour over one of the spillways of the McMillan Dam and roar downstream toward Avalon, the flume below and the Carlsbad Irrigation District works beyond. Where the Pecos had badly damaged McMillan and carried Avalon away in 1904, both structures survived relatively undamaged in 1941. (Photo courtesy of the Carlsbad Irrigation District.)

acre-feet it was supposed to hold. The floods of 1893 and 1904, he said, had greatly reduced its capacity, and even extensive repairs had not restored it. (The 1941 flood hadn't done much damage to the dam.) The new Alamogordo Dam didn't help much because it couldn't control flood inflows in the middle reach of the river. As a result, the CID irrigated acres were still water short, as usual and as always. Francis Tracy was lobbying for the same outcome he had wanted since the turn of the century: any Pecos River Compact had to protect Carlsbad's senior claims to the river, and the only physical way to do that was to provide more downstream storage at Carlsbad.[44]

The 1943 meetings ended inconclusively, and for the next five years compact negotiations sputtered along. Then, in December 1948 at a week-long session in Austin, Texas, the compact commissioners finally hammered out the details of what became the 1948 Pecos River Compact. The

The Tracys' Dream of Carlsbad

interstate compact finally established a law for the whole river, not just the part in New Mexico and the part in Texas. The Carlsbad Irrigation District sent nine representatives to the Austin negotiations, far more than any other New Mexico or Texas entity. Two, the CID's director and its long-time lawyer, had been at the earliest 1943 meeting. But Francis Tracy, Sr., did not attend the crucial 1948 meetings. His son, Francis Tracy, Jr., had replaced him.[45]

In a memoir written toward the end of his life, Francis Tracy, Jr., claimed, "I do not recall a time when the Pecos River, its watershed, or the relationship between either or both of them and the Carlsbad Project has not occupied the greater part of my waking existence." However, it wasn't until 1948 that he began to take an active interest in CID affairs and to attend the meetings of the CID's Board of Directors.

Fig. 2.9.
A relatively late formal photograph of Francis G. Tracy, probably taken in the 1940s, shows an elder statesman, removed from the early lower Pecos River controversies which had swirled around him earlier in his life. (Photo courtesy of Louise Tracy.)

Chapter 2

As a result of his new interest, Francis Tracy, Jr. was appointed one of nine CID representatives to the November 1948 compact negotiations in Austin. "As a matter of fact," he later wrote, "if the District had not been represented by such a large delegation, the compact would have been signed in [sic] behalf of the state of New Mexico by Mr. John Bliss, State Engineer, without regard to our interests and in a manner which might have been extremely damaging to our affairs." At Tracy's and the other CID representatives' insistence, however, the final compact explicitly protected Carlsbad's basic legal claim to Pecos River water.[46]

Article IX of the 1948 Pecos River Compact quietly provided that New Mexico would make up for under-deliveries of water to Texas by enforcing the doctrine of prior appropriation within New Mexico. A 1938 Supreme Court decision made the provision necessary because the court had said that compacting states did not have to follow their own law to make up for state-line shortfalls. But under the Pecos River Compact, New Mexico promised Texas that it would. The guarantee sheltered Carlsbad, with its senior priority, from compact deficits and guaranteed Texas the protection of return flows from a fully supplied Carlsbad. Article IX forever allied Carlsbad and Texas in the compact in ways that skewed the following battle between New Mexico and Texas.[47]

Immediately after final compact approval, Francis Tracy, Jr. formally joined the CID Board of Directors and then quickly, in 1953, became the district's manager, a job that he held for more than 20 years, until 1976. As the manager, the junior Tracy did everything. His letterhead showed that he functioned as the CID manager, secretary, treasurer, tax assessor, and tax collector. And none of these titles described Tracy's even more fundamental power as the CID administrative head, the power to determine what water was available to district members.[48]

But even with these extensive powers, even with intrastate New Mexico law and an interstate compact in place; even with upstream storage dams at Avalon, McMillan, and Alamogordo; even, in short, with a river legally and physically structured for the benefit of the Carlsbad Irrigation District, the Pecos River never provided enough water to reliably supply the district's lands. The volume of river water available at Avalon still varied wildly from year to year. In 1955 the Pecos provided 103,650 acre-feet of water at the CID's diversion, enough water to irrigate 25,000 acres; in 1957 only 59,981 acre-feet were available, enough water to irrigate fewer than 15,000 acres. Actual CID irrigated acreage also varied wildly from year to year, not necessarily corresponding to water availability. In the junior Tracy's almost twenty-five years as

49

Fig. 2.10. Francis Tracy, Jr., shown here at the office of the Carlsbad Irrigation District, began his memoirs saying that he could not recall a time "when the Pecos River . . . has not occupied the greater part of my waking existence." Tracy, Jr. participated in the final drafting of the 1948 Pecos River Compact and managed the Carlsbad Irrigation District from the 1950s to 1976. (Photo by Bobby Lofton, courtesy of the Carlsbad Irrigation District.)

manager of the Carlsbad Irrigation District, the records show that irrigated acreage shifted from a low of 10,000 acres to a high of 20,000.[49]

In his long tenure as CID manager Tracy did everything he could to even out and augment the water supply. He supported small-scale technological changes to increase the water supply. He was actively engaged in state and county water politics. He watched the Texans and the Pecos River Commission to make sure that nothing untoward happened. But he never took the one step that both state law and the Pecos River Compact seemed to guarantee. He never asked the state engineer to enforce priorities on the river and to shut down all upstream, junior diversions, of which there were by then a lot, in order to get downstream Carlsbad its full supply.

In the mid-1970s the knotted strands of ambiguous laws that had made up the status quo since 1948 unraveled. First, in 1974, Texas took the initial steps toward instituting the compact enforcement suit in the U.S. Supreme Court that New Mexicans had long dreaded. Then, as his last act before retiring as CID director, Francis Tracy, Jr. called the priorities on the Pecos River, asking the state engineer to curtail junior Pecos River water users until Carlsbad received its full supply. At that point, the legal structures that had held the river together collapsed as Avalon had in 1904. All the rebuilt dams, the new diversions and delivery systems that Francis G. Tracy had fought to install, and all the state-authorized districts that his son had fought to administer couldn't put the Pecos River together again.[50]

Ultimately, the job fell to the Supreme Court, sitting in far away Washington.

THREE

Royce J. Tipton Mismeasures the Pecos

————By late 1987 the Texas lawsuit against New Mexico over the Pecos River had dragged on for an incredible thirteen years. The U.S. Supreme Court already had reviewed the case four times. Jean Breitenstein, the first special master, appointed by the Supreme Court to hear the evidence in the case, had resigned in frustration and died shortly thereafter. The case's second special master, Charles J. Meyers, had just learned that he had an incurable throat cancer that probably would kill him shortly. In the course of his management of the case, Meyers had become more than a neutral arbiter between the claims of the warring states. He had become a major force in structuring the approach to the competing interstate claims to the Pecos River. Increasingly, New Mexico State Engineer Steve Reynolds, himself suffering from degenerative diabetes, fought against Meyers. The two ancient, ill titans of western water law had emerged as the principal antagonists in the battle over the Pecos. They had been acquainted since the late 1950s when Meyers clerked in a big interstate case on which Reynolds was just cutting his teeth as New Mexico state engineer. The two men had never liked each other, probably because they were so alike. Their relationship in *Texas v. New Mexico* had become more and more hostile.[1]

Imagine, then, the surprise of the small crowd of Texans and New Mexicans gathered in the vault-like chambers of the Tenth Circuit Court of Appeals courtroom in Denver on October 15, 1987 when Special Master Meyers announced that he and Reynolds shared the same opinion on one point. Reynolds had been testifying on some fundamental, technical difficulties with the 1948 Pecos River Compact. Meyers interrupted Reynolds in mid-sentence.

"You and I," he told Reynolds, "have agreed that Royce J. Tipton has a great deal to answer for. But that is behind us and we are stuck. You're stuck with Tipton and I'm stuck with him, too."[2]

Meyers was singling out for blame a long-deceased Denver water engineer. Royce Tipton had been a ubiquitous presence in Rocky Mountain water concerns during the critical years between 1920 and 1970 when western states in general and New Mexico in particular were growing rapidly and struggling to control access to increasingly stretched water resources. Tipton was foremost among the technical consultants who offered some scientific basis for the political compromises that the situation seemed to demand. So central were these consultants and so crucial were their analysis that the most influential, like Tipton, were said "to strut while sitting down."[3]

In the twenty-six years between 1941 and his death in 1967 Tipton strutted his hydrological stuff in three crucial roles in the battle over the Pecos

Fig. 3.1.
Ubiquitous Royce J. Tipton stands in the back row, sixth from the left, among various representatives of the Upper Colorado Compact states, meeting at the Bishop's Lodge, outside Santa Fe, in the 1950s. (Photo courtesy of the John Bliss Collection, NMSRCA, Santa Fe.)

53

River. First, in 1941 and 1942, Tipton brought the science of surface water hydrology, as it was then understood, to the wildly unreliable Pecos River. He gathered and analyzed the data and used them to describe how the river operated under historic, current, and hypothetical conditions.[4]

Then, between 1945 and 1948, Tipton became the driving force in hammering out the Pecos River Compact of 1948. In that role, he joined an emerging elite of pioneering western water engineers who combined a solid grounding in hydrology with an even more remarkable astuteness in negotiating interstate politics. The 1948 Pecos River Compact was largely his work; it never would have come about without him. Tipton provided what everybody then thought was an empirical formula for dividing the water of the Pecos by controlling depletions in New Mexico rather than specifying flows at the state line. He embedded that formula into the bi-state Pecos River Compact of 1948. Then between 1949 and 1967, he worked as a consultant for the Pecos River Commission. In that third role Tipton tried desperately to get the Pecos River to behave according to the scientific standards he had created for it and according to the technological improvements he designed for it. The commission and Congress cooperated for a while, but the river didn't.[5]

Without consultants like Tipton, none of the many interstate compacts, like the 1948 Pecos River Compact, that apportioned common surface waters between and among competing western states would have been consummated. Engineered by the likes of Tipton, the compacts were based on the belief that science could accurately describe western rivers, that law could apportion what science described, and that technology could improve what science saw and law regulated. In the end, the Pecos River defied Tipton on all scores. The contrast between the grand effort and the poor results showed the limits of the control that westerners could impose on regional water systems and demonstrated why, in 1987, Charles Meyers and Steve Reynolds were still blaming Royce Tipton for *Texas v. New Mexico*.

Tipton came to the Pecos River for the first time in 1941 when he became chairman of the National Planning Board's Pecos River Joint Investigation. Begun in 1939, the so-called PRJI represented a massive federal effort to bring together all available information on the Pecos River so that the warring states of Texas and New Mexico would have an accurate factual basis on which to negotiate a permanent, legal division of the river. By the time Tipton arrived in 1941, the various agencies participating in the PRJI already had spent two years gathering data and Texas and New Mexico already had spent twenty-five years sparring over the Pecos, struggling over control of flood inflows that originated in the middle reach of the river. The so-called 1935 "Alamogordo Agreement" and the subsequent construction of the Red Bluff and Alamogordo dams that the agreement had allowed had roughly apportioned access to those flood inflows. However, it remained for the two states to make that implicit apportionment explicit in a formal compact. The job would fall to Tipton.[6]

A second issue between the two states began to emerge during the pre-Compact, pre-Tipton period. The pumping of groundwater from wells in the Texas basin affected the surface flow of the river and hence affected the amount of water that reached Texas. Between 1900 and 1940 New Mexicans had discovered easily accessible groundwater between Roswell and Artesia and had developed what everyone agreed was one of the most successful well-based agricultural economies anywhere in the United States. At first almost everyone assumed, as did the laws of both New Mexico and Texas, that well water was one thing and the river water was another, so that wells in Roswell did not affect surface water arriving in Texas. Only a small band of government hydrologists, mostly working in New Mexico, suspected that the two sources were in fact one, which means that pumping groundwater in Roswell reduced the "base flow" passing downstream to Carlsbad and then to Texas. Even before Royce Tipton arrived on the Pecos River scene, the hydrologists were trying to warn both states that groundwater development in New Mexico had to be another factor in any surface water apportionment.[7]

The first inkling that Texas had of the potential base in-flow problem came from a Texan who had worked in New Mexico and knew what was going on. By the 1930s Vernon L. Sullivan was a consulting engineer in West Texas. Between 1907 and 1911, however, he had served as the very first New Mexico territorial (now state) engineer in Santa Fe at a time when artesian development in Roswell was just getting under way. When negotiations over the Pecos River began in the 1920s and 1930s, ex-New Mexican Sullivan weighed in on the side of Texas.[8]

In an August 14, 1935 letter to the Red Bluff Water Power Control District in Pecos, Texas, Sullivan reported on two factors critical to a fair apportionment of the Pecos River for Texas. First, he addressed the problem of flood inflows on which Francis G. Tracy had harped for so long. Sullivan's analysis of the Pecos River stream data showed that Texas historically had received about 40 percent of the flood flows that originated in the middle section of the river in New Mexico. Any compact apportionment of the river, he suggested to his Texas clients, should guarantee that historical percentage.

In addition, wrote Sullivan in an unexpected bombshell, the groundwater pumped from wells in the Pecos River basin "should be treated as

55

river water and its use charged against [New Mexico's entitlement to] the Pecos River water supply." In other words, when it came time formally to divide the river waters between Texas and New Mexico, any compact should recognize that diverting basin groundwater from Roswell wells was the same, as far as Texas was concerned, as storing water behind McMillan Dam and diverting it at Avalon. Getting Pecos River water to Texas, Sullivan argued, involved limiting upstream New Mexico's control over both surface and groundwater, both flood inflows and groundwater contributions to base flows.[9]

Here was a radical idea in 1935, linking flood inflows and groundwater contributions to river base flows in an interstate *surface* water agreement. But at this time, estimating flood flows was at best a guess, and no one had any idea how to measure the effect of pumping wells on the base flow of nearby rivers. By the time Royce Tipton came on the scene for the first time in 1941, he would have to deal with two recognized but unquantified and unmeasurable factors in Pecos River flows, flood inflows and groundwater interconnections.[10]

From the start, Royce Tipton warned again and again that the Pecos River Basin "probably presents a greater aggregation of problems associated with land and water than any other irrigated basin in the western United States."[11] To get a handle on those problems, Tipton coordinated the research of every state and federal agency that dealt with the Pecos. The information he and his team gathered was not restricted to the length of the 900-mile river alone. Rather, the Tipton recognized that how and when water ran in the Pecos River was a consequence of innumerable land use choices in the 44,000 square miles of the arid Pecos. In an eerie prediction of the concerns of the end of the twentieth century, Tipton even considered the deleterious effects of cattle grazing in the Pecos River uplands on the water that eventually reached the river. In 1942 the investigation was thoroughly up-too-date and even ahead of its time with its multidisciplinary resource-interrelated analysis of the watershed as a whole.[12]

The resulting 1942 publication bore a formidable title, *Regional Planning, Part X: The Pecos River Joint Investigation in the Pecos River Basin in New Mexico and Texas*. The *PRJI*, as it came to be called, provided a bewildering array of numbers in 207 different-sized pages including 2 plates, 32 illustrations, and 141 tables. For those who could understand them, the passages describing technical processes were real showstoppers. Still, for its time, the *PRJI* represented the finest effort ever made to marshal all the information "on the water problems and related problems of the Pecos basin." In some ways it is still unsurpassed.

PRJI undertook regional planning for watershed management some fifty years before most users knew enough to ask for it.[13]

Curiously, despite its extraordinary breadth, Tipton's *PRJI* never took stock of the Pecos River Basin's overall water resources. Had the *PRJI* balanced the total water coming into the basin against the total going out, the authors would have found that even in the 1940s, the river's water account was overdrawn. No matter how existing water rights were divided among existing claims, any solution would eventually fail and all solutions would be temporary so long as the basin water budget did not balance.[14]

Instead of looking at the basin water, the *PRJI* focused on the river's flow. Again and again the report emphasized how little was really known about the infinitely complex processes of the Pecos River itself. Some things, however, were clear. Here was a river whose flow depended heavily on dispersed, unpredictable flood inflows. Those flows could be evened out and the water supply for present development in both New Mexico and Texas improved if existing dams were appropriately regulated. One purpose, then, of any Pecos River compact based on the flow data assembled in *PRJI* would have to be apportionment between the two states of flood inflows originating in New Mexico but heading downstream to Texas.[15]

In addition, the report suggested, river managers would have to face the "groundwater problem" to which Sullivan had alluded earlier. The *PRJI* estimated that groundwater sources in the middle basin had contributed a whopping 235,000 acre-feet a year to the base flow of the Pecos before the development of irrigated agriculture. The geological structure that held the underground water in place leaked that much to the river every year. By 1939, estimated the report, artesian and shallow wells in the Roswell basin already had reduced that contribution to 70,000 acre-feet a year at the most.[16]

Obviously, the river had lost 165,000 acre-feet a year to New Mexico wells. That water, if it had reached the river, would have run down first to Carlsbad and then to Red Bluff. If Roswell basin groundwater should be considered part of the river, as Texans had argued as early as 1935, then New Mexico already had appropriated 70 percent of it. Tipton's *PRJI* made it clear that groundwater contributions were going to be a compact problem as well as flood inflows.[17]

The *PRJI* proposed no specific compact solution. Instead, Tipton presented a series of routing studies. They showed how far the science of surface water hydrology had come since 1889 when government officials started to gauge the flows of western rivers by installing measuring devices in the rivers themselves. Now, in 1942, Tipton could not only show how the historic river flows varied over time but could also subject those varying flows to any hypothetical set of natural conditions and man-made operations—past, existing or future—that he chose. (At that point, of course, the routing study was entirely theoretical, not even checked by the inaccurate gauges. Studies of this kind fifty years later would be done with computers and would be called "simulations.")[18]

In the short final section of the *PRJI,* imposingly entitled "Availability and Use of Water under Given Conditions," Tipton showed how much water would reach the New Mexico-Texas state line (Red Bluff) under six hypothetical conditions applied to historic river flows. Condition 1 represented actual 1940 conditions on the river with the Alamogordo, McMillan, Avalon, and Red Bluff dams in place and correctly operated; with existing irrigation demands in New Mexico and Texas; with base inflow in the Roswell area reduced (as it had been) by wells but steady (as it wasn't); and with flood inflow reaching the river as it was supposed to have. Conditions 2–6 added and subtracted dams, varied salt loads in the river, altered natural processes that consumed Pecos River water, and considered other factors that might affect the amount of water reaching the CID and Texas. All of those conditions approximated different points in time in "man's activities" on the river.[19]

The point of all six conditions was to show New Mexico and Texas how various real and possible combinations of storage (read "dams"), draft ("irrigation"), salvage ("salt cedar eradication"), and remedial measures ("channel" and "water quality improvements") might affect Texas's share of any flows originating in New Mexico and bound for Texas. For all their technical sophistication, the *PRJI* routing studies really predicted for the two states how various historic stages of river development would affect Texas's fundamental demand that New Mexico not deprive Texas of its historic share of flood and base inflows.

In Tipton's skillful hands, the six *PRJI* conditions bypassed once again the watershed balances, and focused instead on river inflows and outflows, albeit in a more sophisticated way than ever before attempted. Some earlier interstate compacts had employed gross inflow/outflow relationships to describe interstate apportionments of water. The 1938 Rio Grande Compact, for example, on which Tipton had worked, required New Mexico to deliver to a downstream gauge a certain percentage of the water that flowed past an upstream New Mexico gauge. It didn't matter what happened between the gauges. Now, on the Pecos, Tipton deepened the inflow/outflow analysis and, more ambitiously, tried to account for every inflow and outflow between the measuring points.

The deeper view was truer to the actual river operations, but, as things turned out, it strained to the breaking point the capacity of science to replicate the natural system to which it was applied. For the moment, however, Tipton's sophisticated routing studies made it possible to focus on a particular factor influencing flows, such as man-made river depletions, rather than the gross flows between two points.[20]

The publication in June 1942 of *Regional Planning Part X: The Pecos River Joint Investigation in the Pecos River Basin in New Mexico and Texas* ended the first stage of Royce J. Tipton's involvement with the Pecos River. As Tipton wrote, the *PRJI* had provided a "factual basis for the consummation of an interstate compact between New Mexico and Texas for the allocation and administration of the water of the Pecos River." For the time being, Tipton went home to Denver and left the compact negotiations to others.[21]

Begun in the spring of 1943, authorized negotiations between Texas and New Mexico started slowly. On blustery April days, first in Artesia, New Mexico, then, two days later, in Fort Stockton, Texas, officials assembled interested Pecos River farmers and let them talk about river problems between the two states. (Little did they know that almost fifty years later, in 1990, officials would organize similar meetings searching for the community will necessary not for the compact but this time for a response to the U.S. Supreme Court's forthcoming construction of the compact.) In 1943, officials listened to rancorous farmers, including Francis Tracy, argue about the Pecos River. By 1947, after four years of talk without much progress, the compact that Tipton's *PRJI* had anticipated was going nowhere.[22]

In the late spring of 1947, after a five-year absence, Royce J. Tipton reappeared on the increasingly bitter Pecos River Compact scene, this time as the federal engineering representative to the negotiating commission. With his arrival, things started to move. In a little more than a year, Tipton's presence brought about the compact that had eluded the two warring states for so long.[23]

At the first compact-negotiating commission meeting that he attended in Austin, Texas, in May of 1947, Tipton was asked whether he had anything to say. "I would prefer to listen," he said. But within moments, Tipton launched into a long, articulate analysis of Pecos River problems. For the next year and a half, until the signing of the Pecos River Compact in December 1948, Tipton barely stopped talking. "I just needed," he later told Congress, "to teach the two states a few hydrologic facts and they'd agree."[24]

Tipton first convinced both Texas and New Mexico that each would have to change its basis for dividing the river. Neither New Mexico's insistence on protection for irrigated acreage nor Texas's demand for a fixed amount of Pecos River water would work, he told them, because the river's water supply under any natural and man-made conditions varied so greatly. Either position, reported Tipton in a warning that would be forgotten in court thirty years later, could end up apportioning the whole river to one state in a dry year. How then should the two states proceed?[25]

It was easy, Tipton concluded. Texas and New Mexico should base their compact on the actual operation of the Pecos River at a particular time. By that, Tipton did not mean the supply of water in a particular year. Instead he meant the way the natural and man-made conditions of the river in a particular year and at a specific stage of development would affect the highly variable supply for any year. Tipton already had analyzed these factors through 1939. His routing studies showed, for example, how the river supply in 1927 would have been influenced had river conditions been like those in 1935. They also showed how the river flow in all years would have been influenced by conditions in one particular year. Now he proposed to bring his routing studies up to date through 1947.

Two critical factors affecting the river flow quickly reemerged as powerful influences on river water availability in any given year: the effects of New Mexico groundwater pumping in the Roswell basin and the spread of salt cedars. Tipton's *PRJI* already had analyzed both factors through 1939. Now, as he brought his routing studies forward to 1947, wells and salt cedars became the focus of the compact negotiations.

Known as the "water vampires of the west," salt cedars were scrubby, thick-growing non-native trees that had "invaded" the Pecos River riparian areas beginning in about 1914. The railroads had introduced the species to stabilize bridges; because of their plumy pink flowers they had acquired a cachet as ornamental trees. Salt cedars, it turned out, just loved the areas along the banks of the Pecos River in general and the silt-rich river areas created in places like the McMillan delta when Francis G. Tracy's nightmare 1904 flood receded. They had taken hold and spread like mad. They sent their roots straight into the water table, drinking directly from it.[26]

Tipton's *PRJI* estimated that salt cedars had encrusted 600 acres in the McMillan delta alone and consumed 5,000 acre-feet a year of Pecos River water in 1915. By 1939 the salt cedars had spread to 15,000 acres and consumption had jumped to 56,000 acre-feet a year. (It had been even higher in years of larger than usual run-off.) If nothing were done about the salt cedars, warned Tipton time and again, they would deplete more and more of the Pecos River water.[27]

60

Here, in the growing infestation of salt cedars, Texas and New Mexico at last had a common enemy. During the compact negotiations Tipton delighted in treating them as alien invaders that must be repulsed by appropriate war-like tactics. He even suggested bringing in Marine flame-throwers, decommissioned after World War II.[28]

Besides serving to unite the two feuding states, the salt cedars offered another critical element to negotiations, additional water. Here was a river where existing human development chronically outstripped the available supply. Elsewhere in the West, dams promised to capture what nature refused to reliably produce. But on the Pecos the dams were already in place, and everyone agreed that there would be no new ones. While other desperate planners looked to such exotic solutions as polar icebergs for additional water, Tipton looked no farther than the McMillan delta and saw the salt cedars. If they were removed, he predicted, the fifty-six thousand acre-feet a year that they consumed would be available for human uses in New Mexico and Texas.[29]

However, the addition of those fifty-six thousand acre-feet had to be balanced against the increasing depletion that would inevitably be caused by the wells in the Roswell reach of the river. Ever since Vernon Sullivan's 1935 assessment of groundwater, the Texas and New Mexico compact negotiators had known that those wells had some effect on the inflow to the river. It took Royce Tipton to predict the worst. As long as existing wells in the Roswell area continued to pump out of the ground more water than came in, the wells would capture more and more of the groundwater that otherwise would discharge as base inflow to the Pecos River. Sooner or later, Tipton knew, existing Roswell wells, pumped at the 1947 rate would take all of the seventy thousand acre-feet a year that was still seeping into the river from the Roswell basin.[30]

The nice fit between water being wasted by salt cedars in 1947 and water that would eventually be commandeered by the Roswell wells provided the fulcrum on which Tipton could balance the competing interests of the two states. Offering it a share of the water that would be saved by eliminating the salt cedars could accommodate Texas's demand that New Mexico take no more additional Pecos River water. Offsetting the future effects of the existing Roswell wells with the water rescued from the salt cedars could accommodate New Mexico's demand that its existing uses be protected.[31]

The diminishing base-flow contribution and the increasing salt cedar depletions that Royce Tipton's January 1948 report showed were only two elements in a forty-one-element inflow/outflow analysis. In the specific water balance scheme, the water coming into each section of the river, of which the base inflow in the Roswell area was only a small part, and the water leaving the river, of which the salt cedar consumption was only a small part, had to be equal. All forty-one elements played a necessary role in that balance, but as negotiations speeded up, the inflow element involved in base-flow and the outflow element represented in salt cedar depletion emerged as special issues.[32]

At a negotiating meeting in Santa Fe on March 10 and 11, 1948, Tipton presented to the Pecos River Commission the results of the updated January 1948 report. In addition to presenting the routing studies, Tipton summarized the report in eleven critical points and explained each in his usual articulate style. Most of the conclusions dealt with the effects of dams, salt cedars, and Roswell wells on the historic water supply of the Pecos. The dams, Tipton concluded, had not had much effect on the amount of water reaching Texas, but the salt cedars and wells had.[33]

With Tipton's analysis on the table, Texas and New Mexico exchanged their first full compact offers that hardly varied each state's original demands. When the meetings adjourned the commissioners instructed Tipton to analyze each state's offer and to estimate the ultimate effect of groundwater development in the Roswell basin on the base flow of the river.[34]

The whole group didn't reassemble until November 1948 when the New Mexico delegation, the Texas delegation, and the federal delegation (of which Tipton was the most important member) gathered for six days in Austin's elegant Driskill Hotel. With the Texas state capitol rotunda looming over it, the twenty-eight-member group met to hammer out finally the basic terms of the Pecos River compact. At least four parties were negotiating: the federal government with five representatives; Texas with eleven; New Mexico with three; and the Carlsbad Irrigation District with nine. The interests were fractured; the politics were complex. As usual, New Mexico had as many internal problems as external when it came to the Pecos River.[35]

The formal proceedings were transcribed, of course, but much of the time in Austin was devoted to separate, unrecorded caucuses by each interest group, trying to respond to issues raised in the formal, recorded proceedings. Feelings were running so high and the pressure to reach some agreement was becoming so intense that the separate Texas, New Mexico, and CID delegations had increasing difficulty even meeting in the same ballroom with one another.[36]

In the intermittent formal sessions, Tipton was obviously an increasingly dominant force in defining the terms of debate. He began melodramatically enough. "Nature is taking a terrific toll of water out of the

Pecos," he told the assembled group. "That toll is increasing and unless there is a joining of hands in order that remedial measures shall be put into effect, there will be two patients dead—one the Carlsbad Irrigation District, and the other a part of the area below Red Bluff." Typically, Tipton was trying to join political antagonists against a common enemy, nature. Typically, the prize in the battle between men and nature was the Pecos River itself.[37]

Typically, Tipton opened the sessions in Austin by using the precision of numbers to demonstrate to the warring states just how the river would kill man. If the states did nothing, he predicted to the assembled group, Roswell wells would continue to deplete the base flow of the river in greater amounts and salt cedars would consume more and more of the less and less that was left. In that event, the average safe yield from Red Bluff reservoir would plummet to less than 135,000 acre-feet a year.[38]

From these miserable prospects, Tipton moved on to the supplemental studies that negotiators had requested at the end of the March meeting in Santa Fe. If Texas's March proposal became the basis for the interstate compact—if, in other words, the salt cedars were eliminated and the base inflow remained exactly as it was under 1947 conditions—then the average safe yield at Red Bluff would skyrocket to the 198,700 average acre-feet that Texas had requested in March. If, on the other hand, New Mexico's March proposal were accepted—if the base inflow was fully depleted and the salt cedars were not necessarily eliminated but the amount of water they consumed remained the same—then the yield New Mexico guaranteed to Texas at Red Bluff dropped to 139,500 acre-feet a year.[39]

After listening to Texas's response to Tipton's analysis, New Mexico State Engineer John Bliss requested a temporary adjournment so he could confer with the nine representatives of the CID. The whole group did not formally reconvene for two days. In the meantime, the Texas group holed up in one suite of Driskill Hotel rooms, the New Mexico group caucused in another suite, and the Carlsbad group stayed in a third. Royce Tipton was the only person who still enjoyed the confidence of all three groups. For the two days of private meetings, Tipton went from caucus to caucus, explaining, trading, coaxing, and cajoling in his inimitable combination of numbers and predictions and logic.[40]

On the morning of November 13, New Mexico State Engineer and Pecos River Commissioner John Bliss reopened the formal proceedings by presenting to the commission the nine principles that ultimately would form the basis of the Pecos River Compact. The first principle went to the heart of how New Mexico proposed to apportion the water between Texas and New Mexico. "New Mexico," read Bliss, "shall agree not to deplete by man's activities the flow of the Pecos River at the New Mexico-Texas state line below an amount which would give to Texas the quantity of water equivalent of the 1947 condition as reported by the engineering advisory committee in its report of January, 1948 and supplements thereto adopted November 11, 1948."[41]

The language of this fundamental provision was so different from any previously proposed by either state that its radical implications were not immediately clear. The New Mexico proposal did not apportion flows in the river as almost all western interstate compacts previously had done. It did not affirmatively obligate New Mexico to deliver a specified quantity of water to Texas, as Texas had demanded. But neither did the proposal explicitly protect existing New Mexico uses as New Mexico had insisted. Instead, Bliss's proposal for apportioning the river prohibited New Mexico from taking more water out of the river after 1947. In its assignment of basic obligations, New Mexico's new proposal changed the focus of both original ones.[42]

But in its description of what the obligation was, New Mexico appeared to have accepted the Texas proposal. New Mexico switched from demanding that a compact protect its uses to agreeing not to further deplete the river. The switch from protected beneficial uses to prohibited further depletions moved the Roswell wells into a new category. Under New Mexico's original proposal those wells would have been fully protected as "existing uses." Under New Mexico's counteroffer those wells would have been protected absolutely only if they did not further reduce the flow of the river under the 1947 condition, as everyone knew that they would.[43]

It is tempting to say that New Mexico and John Bliss, with the blessing of Royce Tipton, thereby gave up the future of the Roswell wells. State Engineer Bliss said almost as much when he wrote an obscure paper on the "Administration of the Ground Water Law of New Mexico" for the September 28, 1950 meeting of the Rocky Mountain Section of the American Water Works Association. In it Bliss wrote

> In a state of nature, the Roswell artesian and shallow basin contributed large quantities of water to the base flow of the Pecos River. With the development of wells in the area, this base flow has been greatly reduced. The ultimate effect of ground water pumping on the River will not be felt for many years to come. Should it be such that the flow at the state line is decreased by man's activities, below the 1947 condition, the State Engineer's only recourse would be to require the junior appropriators— the ground water users in the Roswell basin—to cease their use of water.

The result of such a reduction in pumping would be reflected in the River flow only after a considerable period of time and would offer no immediate solution to this knotty problem.[44]

However, Bliss's proposals were both more complex and more ambiguous than that. Everyone expected that the savings would come from the eradication of the salt cedars. Tipton had estimated that these savings would cancel the increased draft on the river beyond the "1947 condition" caused by the Roswell wells. In addition, it was considered possible that New Mexico might bring Roswell pumping under sufficient control to prevent the further depletion of the river by existing wells. Finally, and equally as important, the definition of the "1947 condition," on which the whole New Mexico obligation would have been based, might itself be improved and the improvement might itself cancel out the anticipated future effects of the Roswell wells. So while New Mexico's willingness to change the terms of its compact obligation to Texas from an agreement not to increase use to an agreement not to increase depletions was important and fundamental, it was softened by other possibilities embedded in New Mexico's counteroffer.[45]

Royce Tipton surely had a hand in moving New Mexico from its March 1948 "protected uses" stance to its November 1948 "prohibited depletion" one. And he surely played a role in moving Texas away from a stance that would have required New Mexico to deliver a set amount of water based on 1935, not 1947, conditions. Formally, however, he only blessed the compromise. "I believe," he told the assembled group,

> that the proposal made by the State of New Mexico comprehends the major factors that are involved in the interstate problems between the two states. It is fairly obvious to me that one of the fundamental principles involved here, that of a guarantee by New Mexico not to deplete the flow of the River below essentially present conditions or, conversely, that there should be delivered at the state line that which Texas is receiving, is a fair provision.[46]

At its most basic, the compromise embodied Tipton's deep confidence in the ability of science to describe the river hypothetically and to divide it accordingly. He assumed that his formulas could accurately show how much of a varying flow in any year after 1947 would reach the Texas state line and how much should have reached it under the "1947 condition." The compromise also assumed, even more ambitiously, that the routing studies could parse any differences between those caused by man's activities in New Mexico and those caused by something else.

With that agreement, the lengthy Austin meetings adjourned, and the group agreed to reconvene in Santa Fe less than a month later to adopt a formal compact. The process involved writing the basic principles to which Texas and New Mexico had agreed in Austin into what became the Pecos River Compact of 1948. Back in Denver, Tipton called on two additional lawyers with special interstate compact expertise to help the existing legal and engineering advisors to the negotiators. One of the drafting experts was from the Bureau of Reclamation. The other was Denver-based lawyer Jean Breitenstein, the man who, thirty years later as a judge, would be called on to decipher the compact.[47]

Tipton, Breitenstein, and their helpers hammered out the actual wording of what became the 1948 Pecos River Compact in Denver between the close of the Austin meetings on November 13, 1948 and the final meeting of the negotiators three weeks later in Santa Fe. The document they produced had all the open-ended elegance of a fundamental constitution. The critical Article III provision regarding apportionment of the Pecos River between the two states incorporated almost word for word New Mexico's guarantee that it would not deplete by man's activities the flow of the Pecos River beyond the 1947 condition. The other fifteen articles showed how and under what circumstances the two compacting states would implement that guarantee.[48]

The proposed compact established a Texas-New Mexico commission with broad power. It could refine and improve definitions of the river so long as it stuck to the "inflow/outflow" method. It would determine New Mexico's compliance with the compact so long as both states agreed. And New Mexico could make up for departures from the baseline "1947 condition" so long as it used the principles of prior appropriation to make up for shortfalls. Essentially, the proposed compact generated as many questions as it answered and it did so in the context of an ongoing relationship between Texas and New Mexico.[49]

That's the way Tipton explained the compact to the Texans and New Mexicans who gathered to approve it in Santa Fe on the afternoon of December 4, 1948. Article by article, Tipton went through the proposal, explaining the provisions that he had cobbled together and then elaborately assembled in Denver. Article by article, the New Mexico and Texas representatives approved.

Tipton explained the basic apportionment provision this way:

There is apportioned to Texas the water which is equivalent to that which

66

was being received by Texas under the 1947 condition. And on the other side of the picture, by implication, there is apportioned to New Mexico that which she was using under the 1947 condition. Article III states that New Mexico shall not deplete by man's activities the flow of the Pecos River at the New Mexico-Texas state line below an amount which will give to Texas a quantity of water equivalent to that available to Texas under the 1947 condition. That again does not mean that year in, year out Texas will receive or New Mexico will consume the average amount of water that New Mexico was consuming under the 1947 condition. That means . . . that with the water supply of a given year, whether the supply is low in that given year or whether it is high, Texas will receive essentially the same quantity of water that she received under 1947 conditions with the same type of year occurring. To illustrate: For the period of study considered by the Engineering Committee, 1905 to 1946, under the 1947 condition, the least amount of water received by Texas in any one year was 98,700 acre-feet. The water supply during the year was quite low . . . The maximum that Texas received in any one year during that period of study under the 1947 condition was 1,650,400 acre-feet. What it means is that of a given inflow Texas will receive each year essentially the same proportion which she received under the 1947 condition. The only way that Texas would receive less water than she would be receiving under the 1947 condition would be by the action of nature, in other words, an increase in non-beneficial consumption by nature with no salvage. That would be outside of the ability of the State of New Mexico to take care of.[50]

Here was Royce Tipton at his best: on his feet, explaining clearly extremely complex engineering concepts, making explicit certain aspects and leaving implicit certain others, molding compact arrangements into their politically most acceptable forms. For example, here Tipton stressed on the one hand the apportionment to New Mexico of the Pecos River basin water she was using under the 1947 conditions. He didn't add that some existing New Mexico uses, particularly the Roswell wells, would sooner or later inevitably require more Pecos River water than they were using in 1947 and would thus violate the apportionment provision, all other things being equal, even though they were established in 1947. On the other hand, Tipton also emphasized for Texas the firm guarantee of a certain amount of Pecos River water every year, even though it was a guarantee of a constant share of a changing supply. Tipton's proposed Pecos River Compact represented a political compromise, but the real trade-offs were hidden in the engineering assumptions underlying the New Mexico guarantee not to deplete the river more than it did under the "1947 condition."

67

With only a few questions from participants at the December 4, 1948 meeting, the compact was approved, article-by-article, by the negotiating commissioners. Earlier that cold morning, the entire group of engineers and lawyers gathered on the steps of the U.S. District Court House in Santa Fe for a portrait. Royce Tipton stood in the third row of participants, on the highest step of the imposing Federal courthouse. His hands were clasped behind his back. His handkerchief protruded from his double-breasted suit jacket. His balding pate glinted a little in the low winter sun. His glasses framed a strong face, complete with narrow mustache. Tipton seemed to loom over the other participants. It's tempting now to see him as towering over the process that produced the terms of the Pecos River Compact of 1948. With him around, no wonder the legislatures of New Mexico and Texas confirmed the basic compact compromise and Congress blessed the states' confirmation. However, Tipton didn't stop there.[51]

Enter Royce Tipton in the third stage of his critical Pecos River role, now as the engineering advisor to the Pecos River Commission established by the 1948 Pecos River Compact. The commission was charged, as were many interstate bodies of the time, with the administration of the deal that Tipton had led Texas and New Mexico to strike. Part of that deal involved an accurate accounting of the amount of Pecos River water that should have reached the Texas state line under the "1947 condition" in any subsequent year and the amount of water that in fact had. Once that comparison had been made, then someone, somehow had to determine if man's activities, as opposed to nature's, caused any negative difference.[52]

The determinations turned out to be harder than Tipton had made them sound. Everyone knew something was wrong when in 1951, an extremely dry year, there wasn't even enough "index inflow" in the Pecos River to allow the compact's inflow/outflow formulas to indicate what the corresponding "outflow" should have been under the "1947 condition." Things got worse soon thereafter when there was sufficient "index inflow" but the corresponding outflow indicated a huge outflow deficit and there had been no changes in New Mexican uses large enough to account for the deficit.[53]

Texas initially insisted that the compact obligated New Mexico to follow the original schedules, no matter what. New Mexico and Tipton as chairman of the Engineering Advisory Committee wanted the commission to restudy the baseline "1947 condition." It took a glacial seven years to resolve the dispute, during which time the flow of the Pecos River both in New Mexico and at Texas line, continued to drop, but eventually New Mexico and Tipton prevailed. On July 30, 1957 the

Fig. 3.2.
The only surviving original photograph of the "successful negotiators of the Pecos River Commission" shows the negotiators on the steps of the Federal Court House in Santa Fe on December 4, 1948 with their hats on. Royce J. Tipton stands in the third row, in a dark suit with a mustache and a white handkerchief protruding from his jacket pocket. (Photo courtesy of the David Hale Collection, NMSRCA, Santa Fe.)

Pecos River Commission authorized Tipton and an engineering sub-committee he supervised to reexamine the "1947 condition" and recommend changes. By November 1957 Tipton was at work.[54]

Once again, he was playing on a field of his own invention: the most accurate description of the Pecos River under the "1947 condition." Obviously, the basic formula on which the compact had been based needed revision. But any revision could be highly controversial because it might affect the amount of water New Mexico owed Texas. On this front, Tipton proceeded cautiously, once again masking his recommendations for revision in the esoteric language of sophisticated surface water hydrology and stating elliptically the effect of his proposed changes on the basic obligation of upstream New Mexico to deliver as much water to downstream Texas in any year after 1947 as would have reached it under the "1947 condition."[55]

Tipton Mismeasures the Pecos

For example, between 1957 and 1961 Tipton reconsidered the relationship between precipitation under the "1947 condition," flood inflow to the Pecos River, and base inflow. This was hardly a controversial subject except to surface water hydrologists. However, it involved the three factors that were critically important to the two states: rain because it provided the water, flood inflow because that's what Texas wanted, and base inflow because that's what the New Mexico wells had to call on to keep pumping. The relationship among the three factors was not well understood. The problem was a water-accounting one: how to categorize the extraordinary rains that had fallen on the Pecos River basin in 1941 and 1942. The accounting problem had a human dimension: Tipton and the *PRJI* architects had done their longitudinal studies so close to those extraordinary years that they couldn't see how unusual they were. Now, from the longer perspective of the 1950s, they could. So, in 1961, on the advice of Tipton, the Pecos River Commission adjusted its definition of the base line "1947 condition" to eliminate the freak years 1941 and 1942.[56]

The correction only involved shifting values, not more or less water. Some of what Tipton had originally assigned in 1941–1942 to "base inflow" in the pre-compact studies he now assigned to "flood inflows" in the revised studies in order to "dampen," as he put it, the effect of the extraordinary 1941–1942 years on all other "pre-1947" years.[57]

Tipton's switch was statistically and hydrologically justified, but it had a direct effect on the calculation of New Mexico's delivery obligations to Texas because under the 1948 Compact "flood inflows" determined mandatory outflows at the state line. Under the original "1947 condition" routing studies, less "flood inflow" had produced more mandatory outflows. The old relationship had inured to the benefit of Texas. Now Tipton's revisions had changed the relationship to the benefit of New Mexico.[58]

Esoteric Tipton-inspired hydrologic adjustments like this produced the Pecos River Commission-approved Review of Basic Data (RBD) in 1961. Using the RBD, the commission found that in the 1948–1961 period, New Mexico had under-delivered water at the Texas state line by about fifty thousand acre-feet over-all and that less than five thousand acre-feet of that under-delivery was due to man's activities in New Mexico.[59]

Tipton must have breathed a sigh of relief, but Texans on the lower Pecos certainly did not. Drought continued there and local agricultural economies suffered terribly. It was easy to blame upstream New Mexico water bandits, and the Texans did. Eventually, however, in 1974, the Texans caught on to Tipton's accounting sleight-of-hand. They discovered that using the unadjusted, pre-1947 Tipton studies, New Mexico had under-delivered Pecos River water to Texas by a fantastic 1,500,000 acre-feet between 1948 and 1974. From Texas's point of view, Tipton's Review of Basic Data and new "1947 condition" study had only delayed the inevitable day when upstream New Mexico uses would have to be cut back in recognition of Texas's downstream compact rights.[60]

As Tipton struggled to delay the arrival of that day by using the sophisticated techniques of surface water hydrology, he tried to augment the supply of the Pecos River so that the inevitable day of shortages would be longer in coming. Once again he blamed the salt cedars, which now became his real bete noire. In the compact negotiations, Tipton had waxed melodramatic about the trees, saying that lower Pecos Texas irrigation and New Mexico CID farming would "die" unless something were done to eliminate the "terrific toll that nature was taking" in the form of the salt cedars. Now, he turned up the metaphors.

As early as February 1953 Tipton spoke about the Pecos River at a Santa Fe luncheon for the New Mexico governor and members of the legislature. The cover of the printed version of the speech showed in one frame a tractor working a planted field and in the other a bleached cow skull presiding over a salt-cedar-infested desert. In the speech he presented these alternatives as a dramatic choice:

> Nature has brought about conditions in certain reaches of the Pecos River which each year are depriving man of water from an already limited supply which he otherwise could beneficially use. Of greatest import is the fact that these conditions are, year by year, becoming progressively more serious and in their end result could cause abandonment of lands which are now, or in the past have been, irrigated. If no action is taken to abate the relentless course of nature and certain other conditions, a very important and prosperous economy in the Pecos River basin could ultimately be returned to its original desert state.[61]

Obviously, for Tipton, it was nature, in the form of salt cedars, making life hard for man and not vice versa. With the world arranged in that order, the solution was clear: more physical improvements by man to correct for nature. Instead of calling for reduction in human uses, Royce Tipton called for technological improvements.

Over the decade from 1955 to 1965 he set out with the help of Texas and New Mexico to secure those improvements from the only source available: the federal government. First, in the 1950s, Tipton provided the technical support necessary to justify federal financing of a channel that would

Tipton Micmanages the R

bypass water-consuming salt cedars in a critically infested area of the river. As the chairman of the Engineering Advisory Committee of the Pecos River Commission he was ubiquitous in pushing federal funding for the Kaiser Channel around the salt cedars at the head of Lake McMillan. In every venue Tipton repeated the same dark prophesy, "that unless something is done about the salt cedars, the irrigation which depends upon the water below the Lake McMillan will gradually go out of the picture. There is a segment of civilization there which depends on irrigation which will cease to exist. In my opinion that is inevitable." Evidently unable to resist this appeal, Congress funded the bypass channel.[62]

In the 1960s, Tipton went out after the salt cedars themselves. By then, with the help of Tipton, New Mexico and Texas had secured federal financing to clear large areas of the salt cedars. Before a small group of angry beekeepers stopped the Bureau of Reclamation's clearing program, fifteen thousand acres of salt cedars had been cut and their former domain plowed. Bloody but unbowed, the Bureau of Reclamation, pushed by the New Mexico state engineer, started the environmental impact analysis that the federal agency had missed the first time around and began cutting again.[63]

In spite of all this activity, the Pecos River flow apparently responded to neither the channel nor the clearing. A series of USGS studies begun in the late 1960s but not published until 1988 could never prove that Tipton's plan for offsetting the over-appropriation of groundwater in Roswell by cutting salt cedars ever produced an additional drop of water in the river.[64]

The larger problem was that man had not been able to improve much on the unimproved natural system of the Pecos River and in the end, it was this larger problem that plagued Tipton and the group of Pecos River managers who struggled to make the river behave for the benefit of man. The Tiptons of the world were smart men who believed in their souls that water existed for the benefit of man and man would most benefit if the limited supplies were stretched as far as possible. The Tiptons of the world tried to use science and technology to perfectly match supply and demand. But by the second half of the twentieth century it was clear that neither science nor technology was able to bring so closely together what nature could provide and what humans use. Tipton wanted nature to yield: it would not.

At this point the lawyers came in. After twenty-five years of accounting and augmentation failure between 1949 and 1974, attorneys for both states became interested in what it was that Texas and New Mexico had agreed to in 1948. By then almost everyone had lost the thread that connected the 1974 woes to the complex, opaque 1948 Compact negotiations. Tipton was dead and neither Texas nor New Mexico kept legislative histories. Hence there was nothing available to show what either state formally understood when its legislature approved the compact: no public debates, no official reports.[65]

On June 9, 1949, with lots of photographic opportunities and no controversy, President Harry S. Truman, surrounded by Texas and New Mexico politicians and water brokers had signed the Pecos River Compact into law by giving the federal government's prerequisite consent. Besides the compact itself, the only trace of what the federal government understood about what it was consenting to in approving the 1948 Compact was contained in Senate Document 109, 81st Congress, 1st Session.[66]

With the beginning of litigation over the compact in 1974, Senate Document 109 emerged as the Rosetta Stone of the compact. The Senate packet that accompanied the 1948 Pecos River Compact contained the

Fig. 3.3.
President Harry S. Truman signs the Pecos River Compact June 9, 1949 while various New Mexico and Texas politicians, including Texas Senator Lyndon Baines Johnson, third from the right, look on. New Mexico State Engineer John Bliss smiles and looks over Truman's shoulder. (Photo courtesy of the John Bliss Collection, NMSRCA, Santa Fe; Associated Press.)

73

minutes of the November and December 1948 meetings in Austin and Santa Fe but no minutes of the extensive negotiating minutes prior to that. In addition, Senate Document 109 contained Tipton's original January 1948 Report of the Engineering Advisory Committee and the August 1948 supplement to it. (The supplement had considered for the first time the version of the "1947 condition" that had become the basis for the compact.) Finally, Senate Document 109 also featured for the first time a "Manual of Inflow-Outflow Methods of Measuring Streamflow Depletions," which Tipton had delivered to Texas and New Mexico sometime after the December 1948 meetings in Santa Fe at which the two states had approved the compact.[67]

Tipton had designed the manual to speed the annual determinations of the amount of water New Mexico owed Texas in any year. Using the manual would enable Pecos River Commission officials to avoid routing available water downstream in order to determine how much water should have gotten to the state line. Instead, using "index inflows," engineers could shorten the process, isolate critical "flood inflows," and quickly figure New Mexico's annual obligation to Texas.[68]

Tipton couched his manual in the usual cautious language of engineers. He warned that the baseline definition of 1947 condition inflows and outflows was provisional and tentative. He warned that the post-1947 accountings would have to be provisional and tentative. And then, in the manual, Tipton included Plate 2.[69]

The vertical axis of Plate 2 estimated the annual outflow of the Pecos River at the New Mexico-Texas state line in increments of 100,000 acre-feet, beginning with 100,000 acre-feet and going up to 1,100,000 acre-feet. The horizontal axis estimated what Plate 2 dubbed the "index inflow," also defined in increments of 100,000 acre-feet. A curved line, rising exponentially as the index inflow increased and showing more outflow for more inflow, defined how much water should reach the New Mexico-Texas state line under the "1947 condition" given varying index inflows to the basin. The points defining the curve represented the year-by-year subjection of the historic flows of the Pecos River since 1910 to the "1947 condition." Flows had varied greatly. Those historic flows had never been actually subjected to the condition defining them. They scattered on both sides of Plate 2's curved inflow-outflow line, sometimes by as much as 30,000 acre-feet in any one year. However, using accepted statistical techniques, the drafters of Plate 2 had smoothed out the irregular annual points and turned the quirky approximations into a smooth inflow/outflow curve.

Here in Plate 2 you had all the problems of the 1948 Pecos River

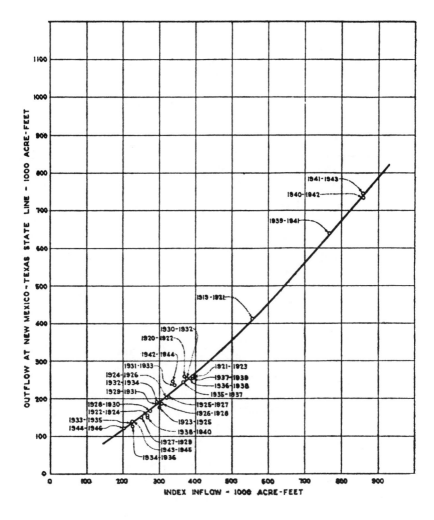

ALAMOGORDO DAM
TO
NEW MEXICO - TEXAS STATE LINE

Plate No. 2

Fig. 3.4.

The infamous "Plate No. 2," tacked on to the final compact papers, plotted index inflow measured at Alamogordo Dam, against mandatory outflow at the New Mexico-Texas state line. Plate No. 2 looked like a schedule—so much inflow, so much outflow. But Plate No. 2 turned out not to be a schedule and the 1948 Pecos River Compact itself embodied much less clear obligations. (Senate Document 109 "Pecos River Compact," 81st Cong., 1st Session, August 2, 1949, page 154.)

Compact. To begin with you had a graph that looked as if it might tell you easily and mechanically how much water New Mexico owed Texas in any year. All you had to do was locate the proper inflow, go up to the corresponding outflow, and bingo, you knew New Mexico's compact obligation to Texas. As it turned out, however, even finding the correct index inflow turned out to be much more difficult than it seemed.

In the "index inflows," all the problems inherent in the measurement of a complex natural system like the Pecos River were compounded. In figuring the "index inflow" for any year, Tipton's manual told compact administrators to start with the measured flow of the river where the water came out of the upstream Alamogordo (now Fort Sumner) dam. That much was fairly easy. A river gauge measured that physically. But to that measured inflow, Tipton's manual and plate 2 required the addition of "flood inflows" entering the river below the Alamogordo dam and above the next downstream gauge at Acme. So, manual and graph went downstream through the three reaches of the critical middle section of the river, explaining inflow possibilities.

From the point of view of Texas and New Mexico, it made sense to make flood inflows such a critical part of figuring New Mexico's obligation to deliver water to Texas. From the very beginning of compact negotiations in the 1920s Texas had been concerned lest it be cut off, by surface water irrigation, by wells, but primarily by upstream dams, from the sudden bursts of water, the "flood inflows," that dominated the water supply of an otherwise very meager river. The Tipton-designed 1948 Pecos River Compact was the only compact that so explicitly recognized that the unappropriated flood flows of desert rivers represented the real prize available for twentieth-century development in the West. But in acknowledging that fact and making "flood inflows" a primary index of New Mexico's delivery obligation to Texas, Tipton and his cohorts picked the one factor in estimating actual river flows that was most susceptible to error.[70]

In the routing studies that defined the critical "1947 condition" and that, according to Tipton's manual, would define subsequent years, "flood inflows" made up only three of the forty-one elements of inflow and outflow that described how water made its way down the Pecos River. But these three "flood inflow" factors turned out to be critical.

Of all the inflows into the river, the "flood inflows" were the hardest actually to measure. Tipton used them to create a theoretical balance between gauges that nature had to have but that the other thirty-eight elements of the routing study might not yield. In other words, the critical "flood inflows," ambiguous as they were, provided the numerical factor that was flexible enough to create the balanced mathematical inflow/

Chapter 2

81ST CONGRESS⎫
1st Session ⎰   SENATE   ⎰DOCUMENT
                                       ⎱ No. 109

PECOS RIVER COMPACT

COMPACT ENTERED INTO BY THE
STATES OF NEW MEXICO AND TEXAS
RELATING TO THE WATERS OF THE
PECOS RIVER

TOGETHER WITH

THE REPORT OF THE ENGINEERING
ADVISORY COMMITTEE TO THE
PECOS RIVER COMPACT COMMISSION

PRESENTED BY MR. O'MAHOEY

AUGUST 19 (legislative day, JUNE 2), 1949.—Ordered to be printed
with illustrations

UNITED STATES
GOVERNMENT PRINTING OFFICE
95534   WASHINGTON : 1949

Fig. 3.5.
Senate Document 109 became the frustratingly incomplete Rosetta Stone for
the frustratingly opaque Pecos River Compact. Thrown together after Texas
and New Mexico had agreed to the terms of the 1948 Compact, SD 109 contained bits and pieces of the negotiating minutes, an incomplete set of the
Compact's underlying engineering studies, and an inflow/outflow curve that
looked like a schedule of New Mexico's obligation to Texas but was not.
(Senate Document 109, "Pecos River Compact," 81st Cong., 1st session,
August 2, 1949.)

77

outflow relationships on which compact administration depended. As a result, "flood inflows" started out as the natural centerpiece of the 1948 Pecos River Compact and ended up as an indispensable part of its bookkeeping, no matter what actually occurred.[71]

Search as lawyers and historians might for some sign as to what the federal government understood the 1948 Pecos River Compact to mean, there just weren't any more clues. In the spring of 1979, the state engineer sent me to Washington to look. There were no Congressional debates and hardly any hearings. The bill approving the compact had gone to the Senate Committee on Interior and Insular Affairs, but by committee rule those records were sealed for forty years or until 1989, ten years after my trip. My boss at the time, State Engineer Steve Reynolds, convinced New Mexico Senator Pete Domenici to allow me special access to the committee records.

The cherry trees were blooming, and I could see them from the window of the small cubicle in the Library of Congress where the archivists had told me to wait while they brought the committee records. After what seemed an eternity, the archivist appeared with a 5" x 5" x 16" box, marked and sealed. I lifted off the top of the long box, feeling ever so much like Indiana Jones, and discovered nothing.

Except for a printed copy of Senate Document 109, itself long public, the Senate Committee on Interior and Insular Affairs box was empty. By then Texans and New Mexicans had lost sight of Royce Tipton's good faith efforts to master the Pecos River with the best science that anyone then knew. By then they had lost contact with Tipton's intellectual struggle with the river. They were left only with an empty box and the mechanical relationships of inflows and outflows described so imaginatively in Plate 2 of Senate Document 109.

As *Texas v. New Mexico* got under way, the Tracys were left in Carlsbad where they always had been, checking in two directions. They were looking downstream to Red Bluff and worrying about restrictions coming from that direction. They were looking upstream to Roswell and worrying about the base flow bandits pumping groundwater there from their wells. In the meantime, Roswell farmers were getting ready for the fight of their lives by considering their own water history.

FOUR

Morgan Nelson's Pecos River World

──────The century-long struggle over the Pecos River affected Roswell farmer Morgan Nelson and his family in so many ways and at so many times that the 1948 Pecos River Compact and the suit it spawned seemed to reflect the family's history. As it did the Tracys in Carlsbad, water occupied the Nelsons for three generations. But the Tracys focused on Pecos River surface water and worried about flood flows. The Nelsons focused on what turned out to be interconnected groundwater and disregarded, for the most part, river base flows. By 1948 when the Pecos River Compact was written, the Nelsons had struggled for three generations just to get established in a world that the Supreme Court was about to change.

When the Roswell area was settled around the turn of the twentieth century, Nelson's grandfather, Swann, was there to try to set down roots. When the Roswell artesian basin was over-developed in the 1910s and 1920s, Nelson's father, Fred M., was there to buy farms with existing wells and to drill some of his own. When the Pecos River Compact was presented to the New Mexico State Legislature in January 1949, Morgan Nelson, himself, a thirty-year-old freshman legislator from Chaves County, was there to approve it. And as late as 1988, when the Texas lawsuit against New Mexico had turned sour, Morgan Nelson, now aged seventy, was there to testify about New Mexico's good faith efforts to deal with the Pecos River and its endless problems. When it came to developing and regulating the Pecos River basin, Morgan Nelson's family had been around for a hundred years. Yet as a New Mexico farmer and groundwater irrigator for more than half a century, Morgan Nelson focused very much on the land

Fig. 4.1.

Roswell's Morgan Nelson tastes the salt-laden water of the Pecos River near Malaga Bend, south of Carlsbad, in 1993. (G. Emlen Hall.)

and the water in the here and the now. On a windy March afternoon in 1994 I went with Morgan Nelson, then seventy-five years old, to check on the 530-acre Nelson farm near Cottonwood Creek, fifteen miles northwest of Artesia on the Chaves/Eddy County line. The Cottonwood Creek tract is a half-hour drive from Nelson's principal residence in East Grand Plains, just southeast of Roswell.[1]

I expected a Roswell farmer bound for his land to dress for outdoors work and travel by pickup, but not Morgan Nelson. We went in his large, American-made sedan, "all the better to drive on back roads," as he told me. He wore a neat dress shirt, scuffed brogues, and a fedora. "That's what I wear," he told me, smiling.

We traveled south on paved roads and turned west at the boundary between Chaves and Eddy counties, heading toward the ten-thousand-foot-high Sacramento Mountains eighty miles away. I understood that heading west in the seventy-five-mile Roswell artesian basin usually meant quickly leaving the north-south band of easily accessible artesian water. But even the earliest maps showed an odd western bulge in the artesian zone in the Cottonwood Creek area and as we drove up out of Artesia, Nelson pointed out the natural features that confirmed the existence of groundwater under natural pressure.[2]

"There," he pointed out as we roared along the paved road. "See that rock? That's what they call 'water rock.'"[3]

Along the edge of the county road, I saw piled up dark gray boulders, some huge, some the size of bowling balls. We stopped for a second to look and feel. Holes and dents and cracks pock marked the surface of the limestone rocks, otherwise hard and cold to the touch. These were the rocks that made up the bed of limestone that underlay the whole Roswell artesian aquifer between the high mountains to the west and the low Pecos River to the east.

The thirty inches of rain that fell annually on the mountains made its way along the surface down into the holes and fissures and cracks of these water rocks. There the water lay, trapped hundreds of feet under the ground, driven by gravity from above, under increasing natural pressure, toward the lower elevations, and eventually to the Pecos River itself. "Poke a hole into these rocks," Morgan Nelson told me as we handled the boulders, "and the water just blows out. The water pressure makes it all possible."

What "it" was became clearer as we approached the Nelson Cottonwood farm. A neat, unpretentious residence sat in a copse of trees near the farm's fields. Huge farm machinery in a nearby yard marked this as a farmhouse. (It turned out that the biggest machine was a chile picker.) The house itself would have fit well in any Midwestern suburb. Nelson's daughter and son-in-law resided here. We stopped on the way to the fields to check in. Ann, his daughter, interrupted her cleaning to show her father and me around. Then Morgan disappeared into the farm's office and began to tinker with a computer.

He was working, he explained, an Auburn University computer program. The program assembled all kinds of local data collected at various stations on the Nelson Cottonwood farm—precipitation, soil moisture contents, winds, heat, daylight hours—and told Nelson and his family exactly when they should irrigate the fields and with exactly how much water. Morgan Nelson was having some trouble loading the program and making it run, but he was trying to master a technology that couldn't have even been imagined when he went into farming in the late 1940s. The Nelson family farm was clearly way beyond the marginal operations in northern New Mexico with which I was most familiar. "The narrow margins today," Morgan Nelson explained, "require the most careful management."

Soon we were tearing along back roads to inspect the farm's operations themselves. Morgan Nelson talked with irrepressible enthusiasm while the car bounced this way and that down what looked like little more than rough tracks at the edge of still dormant fields. We came to a screeching halt on a dirt track dividing a huge as-yet-unplowed field to the west and a plowed field to the east. On this second three-hundred-acre tract the Nelsons already had planted chile, and they were irrigating for the first time.

It was a windy, cool, bright southern New Mexico afternoon. The copse of trees surrounding the headwaters of Cottonwood Creek sat off to the northwest of the huge field, hunkered down in a hollow. The field sloped off to the east toward the Pecos River some ten miles away. Using laser technology, Nelson had leveled the huge field so that it dropped less than a couple of inches from its western border. You could barely see the slope.

Long east-running rows about three feet apart and about a half-mile long followed the slope to the east. The Nelsons had already planted the tops of these rows—the "beds"—with chile seeds and covered them with a cap of added dirt. The low-lying trenches between the beds—the "furrows"—awaited the water. Once the seeds had germinated and the chile plants started to grow, a Nelson tractor would remove the dirt cap, exposing the young plants to sun and air so they could really start to grow. But in March the plants were still hidden, and Morgan Nelson's farmer was getting ready to send water down the furrows to soak the beds.

The farmer, Nelson explained, was an experienced irrigator who used to farm on his own. But business was risky, and like a lot of farmers in the area, he'd discovered that he preferred to work for someone else rather than chancing the tricky weather and water that ruled Roswell farmers like Nelson. So today, he was managing Morgan Nelson's chile and water, a hired hand in a country of family farms.

The irrigation water came from one of three artesian wells on the Cottonwood farm. The well lay off to the west and still produced water at the mere opening of a valve, the natural pressure was that strong. The water ran down from its source in a fifteen-inch underground pipe into a sixty-foot-long, ten-inch, PVC pipe, capped at both ends lying perpendicular to the rows at the west end of the chile field. A line of valve gates protruded from the pipe at intervals that corresponded to the thirty-inch rows in front of them. The well water poured into the pipe and was released into the rows through the gates, ten gates at a time.

A solar-powered main valve directed the water to the open gates, first on the north side of the valve, then the south, alternating between the two sides at hour-long intervals. From whichever gates were open at the time, the water poured out and fingered its way down the furrows, which extended east as far as you could see. The first 100 yards of each furrow already had been wet; the new water raced across the moistened part and then slowed down as it hit dry ground and went slowly on for another 100 yards. At the end of that 100-yard section, the solar valve closed the set of gates on one side of the pipe and switched to another set of gates on the other side and another group of rows. Over the next couple of days, the solar valve and Nelson's hired hand repeated the process, row by row, length by length, until the water had reached the end of all the rows, a half-mile across and a half-mile away.

The irrigation method was relatively new. It had a name—"surge irrigation"—and it had a purpose—"conservation" of water. Combined with laser leveling, surge irrigation reduced leakage in clay soils like this by allowing water to seal the clay in the upper, moistened section of a row before the water was shifted to the next, lower section of the row. In this way, Nelson explained, you wasted the least amount of water possible irrigating all the rows. Saving water meant saving money, and as a prudent Roswell farmer, Morgan Nelson was interested in that.

From this perspective, a thousand feet above and ten miles away from a Pecos River that couldn't be seen, it was easy to lose sight of the fact that the water flowing naturally out of Morgan Nelson's well was water that would have run down to the river but for Nelson's interception of it. Like Nelson, I was facing the wrong direction to think about that. Carlsbad, the compact, and the lawsuit might have been part of another galaxy.

After an hour watching the water move from row to row, Nelson and I bounced back toward his farm southeast of Roswell in East Grand Plains. On the way we stopped at a new, million-dollar chile processing plant that Nelson and his son-in-law had just built and brought into operation. In the 1990s Roswell farmers like Nelson had realized that chile, theretofore principally grown farther to the west in the Deming-Hatch-Las Cruces area of New Mexico, would grow in Roswell as well. Roswell farmers began to switch to the lucrative crop. Morgan Nelson, always one step ahead of the game, realized that the new crop would require processing and built a plant complete with all the bells and whistles and pulleys necessary to deliver finished Roswell chile to various markets.

Farm production using Pecos River basin water is a complex, expensive, risky business in the Roswell area. It's not for the faint of heart, which the expansive, generous Morgan Nelson certainly is not. Neither is it for the dilettante, which Nelson also is not. In the time we spent together, he was never not working, but I never once saw him with a shovel in his hands.

Fig. 4.2.

In fall 1992, Morgan Nelson, age 73, and daughter Ann Nelson Houghtaling inspect a new solar-powered surge flow control, the latest irrigation device installed at their Cottonwood farm fields. (Photo courtesy of Morgan Nelson.)

After inspecting the Cottonwood farm surge irrigation and chile factory, Nelson drove me back to his residence in East Grand Plains. The house was steeped in the family's past. It sat beside a road shaded by huge cottonwoods that had sprung up from the green fence posts sunk into the waterlogged soil at the turn of the century by John Chisum and J. J. Hagerman, two of the earliest and most influential settlers in the area. Morgan Nelson's uncle by marriage, Oliver Pearson, hauled some of the wood for the frame house Nelson now lived in from Nebraska and had the rest shipped in on the first railroads that arrived in Roswell in the late 1890s.[4]

Just beyond the principal residence sat a small outbuilding that looked like a railroad car. Here Morgan Nelson had his office. It had two rooms. One was completely crammed with overflowing boxes themselves crammed with papers. The other room was almost as full but this one had a desk, a chair, a couple of book cases bulging with books on New Mexico history, and an ancient computer. The seat behind the desk was piled high with papers. Near the wall opposite the crammed bookshelves there was a cardboard box of unfiled papers, waiting for Morgan to organize them, a collection of papers on Pecos River water and Roswell irrigation that Morgan calls "my accumulation of history." Over the years he had collected everything that had been written on the region and its water. It was a lot of stuff. Government reports, legal testimony, court documents lay everywhere.[5]

Morgan Nelson recalled some of what he'd collected over the years. He knew where some of it was located in his office. The mess came from the material he couldn't quite remember and the locations he couldn't quite recall. As he talked about Roswell wells and Pecos River water and the connection between the two, he rummaged among the rich supply of primary documents.

When he wasn't rummaging and talking, Morgan was writing. Morgan Nelson is an engineer, and he's always had an engineer's interest in machines—farm machines, chile-processing machines, water-producing machines. When computers arrived, he didn't regard them as new-fangled intrusions. As soon as personal computers became available, Morgan Nelson got one and stuck with it. Not only did he and his daughter and son-in-law use one to help manage irrigation and business, but Morgan himself used an ancient word-processing system to re-create and record his own family's history.

Over the last ten years Morgan Nelson has struggled to write the history of Chaves County, the settlement of East Grand Plains where he lived now, and the water essential to both. "I haven't had time to do any work on my accumulation of history of East Grand Plains in over a year," he wrote to a friend in 1987, "because I have been so involved in other things. I hope to get started soon. I just want to get the information down while I can. Much is already lost. I do not intend to inflict my work on the public, but just do my thing privately."[6]

Morgan Nelson's private accumulation, as he called it, grew sporadically. By 1994 he had written more than ninety separate pieces on his life in Roswell. Some were long, running to ten thousand words. Others were a lot shorter, not even covering a page. Some were transcripts of oral histories narrated by Roswell old timers. Others Morgan Nelson had cobbled together from recollections and newspaper articles and ingrained community lore. Others still he borrowed wholesale from unpublished memoirs and out-of-print autobiographies.

Some Nelson articles dealt with families. Others dealt with farms. Some dwelled on particular political or social events. Others traced the ownership of particular tracts of land in East Grand Plains tract by tract, trade by trade, sale by sale, family by family. Together the ninety pieces made a pile almost a foot thick.

Their titles outlined the history of farming in Roswell: "The Nelsons in Eddy County From 1897," "Hub Gifford," "The Big Well—The Oasis Ranch," "South Springs—1896–1899," "Irrigation: Early History," "An Interview with Fred M. Nelson and Florence M. Nelson," "Birdie Dee Eccles: A Dedicated, Lifelong Active Democrat," "The Beginnings of Roswell Social Order of the Beuaceant No. 116," "Cotton the King," "Alice Webb Young, an Interview, 4/21/92."

Facts seasoned Morgan Nelson's writings with the same rich chaos as nuts and raisins in an applesauce cake. Details were repeated in two or three places. One article supplemented a repeated detail with a little additional information. The events described in different sketches overlapped completely or partially or not at all. To get the full picture that Morgan Nelson has sketched of Roswell water and life you have to piece together the different repeated details and patch together the different times. The cumulative effect is as confusing to the uninitiated as life itself in a community like Roswell where everybody has known everybody else and their families. Once, in a moment of introspective candor, Nelson told me that he had begun talking to me when he was seventy-five-years-old in the hope that I could bring an order to the stuff he had collected that he was not going to be able to impose in his own lifetime.

Three stages emerge from Morgan Nelson's material. The stages parallel the lives of three Nelson generations struggling to establish themselves in the desert waterscape. The efforts of Swann, Fred, and Morgan Nelson over a century are embedded in three stages in the development of Roswell water, a trajectory leading straight to *Texas v. New Mexico.* Finally, the development of Roswell water coincides with three stages in the efforts of the United States Geological Service (USGS), in cooperation with different local entities, to come to grips with the nature and extent of the remarkable resources of the Roswell artesian basin. The three overlapping screens provide a three-dimensional picture of a human struggle to master a natural miracle and of the ambiguous results that followed.

It all started with Swann Nelson, Morgan's grandfather, who emigrated from Sweden to the United States in the late 1800s and began to bounce around the new country, mostly in a westerly direction, looking for opportunity, not water. He found a wife in Galesburg, Illinois, and started a successful general mercantile store in Nebraska. When the Nebraska store burned to the ground in 1887, "he took his family in a covered wagon and headed across the plain for Roswell where he had heard of the irrigation." He navigated by compass and replaced an ox who died en route with the family milk cow.[7]

Arriving on New Year's Day, 1888, Swann Nelson and family found a world in transition. For years the Roswell area had been relatively unsettled and then, more recently, the domain of a few large cattle barons like John Chisum. Now with the arrival of the likes of Swann Nelson, the local world began to move toward irrigated farming. Chisum, unlike many of his cattle-raising brethren, apparently welcomed the change.[8]

Roswell water was what brought the farmers, but it wasn't water from the Pecos River. Near Roswell, the Pecos was treacherous. The banks were high. The riparian areas, especially west of the river, were boggy, full of mosquitoes and useless salt grass that reached to the bellies of horses moving through it. The river intercepted east-running tributaries carrying runoff from the high, water-producing mountain ranges to the west. The Pecos behaved like the pirate that it was: uncouth, unreliable, and basically unapproachable. But the uplands above that riverine hell were laced with much more inviting small tributaries and springs.

It was these that drew settlers like Swann Nelson. Roswell itself grew up in the late 1880s and early 1890s near the site of a large spring that bubbled to the surface from a then unknown source and formed a lake in the desert. East-running rivers and streams, joining the south-running Pecos, crossed the depression that began at Salt Creek on the north and ran seventy or so miles to the Seven Rivers area on the south. From these springs and rivers, early Roswell farmers took out irrigation ditches and started to farm.[9]

Swann Nelson spent his first days in Roswell on a farm on the Berrendo River. Shortly thereafter he took his family across the Pecos River at Spring Mound Valley, where he attempted to harness the water of Bottomless Lake and lead it down to flat land, east of the river. There he proposed to farm.

Swann Nelson failed, like a lot of Roswell pioneering farmers, but not for lack of water. The new irrigation ditch he and others dug ran through gypsum that dissolved on contact with water. The conveyance leaked so badly so quickly that it wouldn't carry anything.

Resourceful Swann Nelson rebounded quickly, moving downriver to Carlsbad, where he took charge of industrialist and financier J. J. Hagerman's new sugar beet fields, irrigated by water stored at McMillan Dam and diverted at Avalon. This promising new crop quickly failed too, destroyed by a particularly virulent curly-top virus. Undaunted, Swann Nelson moved back to Roswell and started a truck garden on the outskirts of the small, primitive settlement. He sold the tomatoes, which he watered by hand from a bucket, to families from town. He succeeded in establishing a small-scale business, servicing the kitchen needs of Roswell's emerging elite.

For the ten years between 1888 and 1898 Swann Nelson was still bouncing around trying to establish a firm hold, only now his range was reduced. He was moving up and down the Pecos River, from one struggling southeastern New Mexico town to another. In those moves the promise of water availability sometimes provided a direct impetus. More often, Nelson seized the indirect opportunities that the development of water created—a Hagerman job here, a truck farm there.

After 1898 New Mexico lost its hold on Swann Nelson. Using contacts established in Roswell, Swann traded his truck farm for a livery stable in Oklahoma City and for a couple of years lived there, trying to combine horse trading and farming. The new business didn't hold. By 1904 Swann left again, this time for the Yucatán Peninsula, answering what his son, Clarence, recalled as a Mexican government invitation to Americans to help settle the fertile area.

Here Clarence Nelson's voice takes over:

Here again my father Swann started a farm and planted tomatoes. He worked and watered them by hand and they did very well. He was going to send for mother, Fred and me to join him. One night, as he slept in his hammock, a robber, who thought he had a lot of money hidden there, came and stabbed him in the abdomen. He got up and carried his intestines in his hand half a mile to the nearest neighbor. He developed peritonitis and died as they had no penicillin then. He was killed there in 1906. We had sent him clippings of the San Francisco earthquake and they were returned.

When my father died, there was a $1,000 insurance policy. My mother bought a house at 204 East Bland in Roswell. It still stands there. It was her country home as there were only a few scattered houses to the south of it. My sister, Nettie, and her husband, Oliver Pearson, and the Whitemans lived across the street. Mrs. Samuelson lived in the 100 block of East Bland. Mrs. Samuelson had a very talkative parrot. My sister kept it most of the time.[10]

This is the stuff of community history: disjointed; connected, if at all, by individual memory of events long past; richly textured by the tragedies that befall the family and the ways they react. Through the dense fog, the Nelson family emerges, finally grafted by the death of Swann Nelson in Mexico onto the Roswell water world.

The Roswell in which Morgan Nelson's father and uncles grew up was shaped by water, but it wasn't the artesian irrigation water that would dominate Fred Nelson's and Morgan Nelson's lives. Instead, it was the Roswell oasis, where the boys could enjoy themselves.

Listen once again to Clarence Nelson:

Duck hunting was the passion of the time. I loved to hunt ducks and my older brothers, Ernest, Harry, and Fred did a lot of hunting, too. Mother would pick them and we would sell them in meat markets in Roswell. Mother would make feather beds and feather pillows.

The country was filled with ducks. In those days ducks were everywhere—on the Pecos and South Springs rivers, at the dams of the South Springs headwaters, on the reservoirs and in the swamps.

The Pecos River was my favorite place to hunt, but it took a while to get there. On occasions when I was in school at East Grand Plains, I would get sick and the teacher would let me go home. Since duck hunting would hasten my recovery more rapidly than anything else, I would ride to the Pecos to hunt.

My brother, Ernest, had a single barrel 10-gauge shotgun. One day it snowed and he went to the Pecos to hunt. He saw a flock of ducks on a sand bar in the river. There was a high bank on his side but to get close, he had to crawl on his belly through the snow. Unknown to him, while crawling he got snow in the end of his shotgun barrel until he shot the gun.

Fig. 4.3.
Roswell artesian well owners often filled artificial reservoirs like the one pictured here and then irrigated from water stored there. Artesian reservoirs dotted the Roswell uplands and proved fertile play grounds for boys like the Nelsons and the kids pictured here. (Photo courtesy of the Historical Society for Southeast New Mexico.)

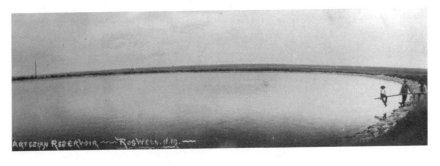

89

It kicked the whey out of him and blew the end of the gun open wider. It scattered shot over a much wider area and when he started picking up the ducks he found that he had killed ten of them. He continued using the gun because of the wide shot dispersion.

I went hunting with my cousin, Clarence Pearson, on a reservoir near the railroad tracks at South Springs. He was several years older than I as I was about 12 or 13 then. We drew straws to see who would shoot first. I won. A big canvasback duck landed and before I shot, he up and shot it. I was angry and his only excuse was that he was afraid that I couldn't hit it.

Not all was duck hunting. Although I was only 10 to 13 years of age, I used to drive horses to mow and rake irrigated alfalfa. I also drove a buck-rake we called a "go devil" to push hay to the baler. We had an old Eagle baler. It was one driven by horses going around in a circle. My brother, Ernest, would feed the alfalfa into the hopper and force it in with his feet. On several occasions he nearly lost a foot because he could not get it out before the plunger closed. We baled hay all around East Grand Plains and also in the Berrendo area.[11]

By 1916, the fatherless Clarence Nelson had left for college and medical school in Loma Linda, California, never to live in Roswell again. "No thanks," he told his nephew Morgan in 1986, " I wouldn't like to go back to the good old days. I wouldn't trade my Mercedes diesel for all the livestock we ever had." But the emerging community remained the home of Clarence Nelson's brothers, Fred and Ernest.[12]

Swann and his sons witnessed the rapid growth and transformation of the Roswell area. The growing boys focused on ducks and gardens. It fell to adults with a broader perspective to assess what was happening in a general way to the area's water resources at the time of Swann Nelson's death in 1906, water resources that were making the Roswell desert bloom and whose development was, unbeknownst to anyone, reducing the river's flow as it moved down to Carlsbad.

In 1906, the year of Swann Nelson's death, Cassius Fisher, Jr., became the first (but certainly not the last) United States Geological Survey (USGS) investigator dispatched to the Roswell basin to report on the occurrence and availability of artesian water, water from deep in the ground that would rise under its own power to the surface of the land if a well was drilled into it.[13]

Fisher found a world where wells were being drilled so fast that the Roswell area looked to some like a pincushion. As Fisher told it in 1906, "flowing wells were first obtained in the Roswell basin about ten years ago [1895]." He estimated that between 1895 and 1906 property own-

Fig. 4.4.
The cloud of ducks rising here from the Pecos River near Roswell was typical of the wildlife that gathered around the water-rich river while various Nelson generations were growing up between 1900 and today. (Photo courtesy of the Historical Society for Southeast New Mexico.)

ers had sunk more than 250 artesian wells, "about half of them in Roswell and North Spring Valley, the extreme north end of the basin." An accurate count would await the next USGS study in 1931, which stated that 476 artesian wells had been drilled by 1906.[14]

In some places water would rise so far above the surface of the land that new Roswell homes had upstairs bathrooms with water that would flow when the tap was opened. The artesian water, said Fisher, was not leaping up from an unknown source. Rather, he pointed out in his careful government prose,

(T)he water-bearing formations in the Roswell artesian area outcrop in successive zones on the higher slopes to the west. There they receive their water supply by direct absorption from rainfall and the sinking of streams. The Hondo, Felix, Penasco and Seven rivers are the most important sources. These streams rise high on the slopes of the Capitan, Sierra Blanca, and Sacramento mountains where the rainfall is relatively large. As a result they carry an abundance of water in their upper courses, all of which sink in

91

the outcrop zone of the porous limestone and the overlying formations and passes underground to the east. After the water has entered these porous formations it is confined by impervious layers of limestone or clay, and under the lower lands to the east it is under considerable pressure.

The new artesian wells mined this pressure.[15]

Clearly the Pecos River itself was going to be affected by the new turn-of-the century wells. After all, the Pecos, geological pirate that it was, had itself intercepted mountain-generated water that would otherwise have traveled to the Ogalala Aquifer underlying the Great Plains. Now, the artesian wells were robbing the pirate river's source itself!

You could see the results of the robbery in the Roswell artesian basin. Springs dried up. Streams lost flows. Surface water irrigation was everywhere failing. But at least at the moment when Cassius Fisher was writing, all the losses were replaced by the miracle of plentiful groundwater that would rise to the surface under its own pressure and go where it was directed, primarily to new irrigated farms, yielding crops and a profit where before there had only been bare desert. Hard figures weren't easy to come by, even with the USGS on the ground and counting. But reasonable estimates showed that the number of irrigated acres in the Roswell basin jumped from 10,000 in 1900 to 30,000 in 1906, most supplied by the miracle of artesian wells.[16]

The rapid growth did not worry Cassius Fisher. "It is believed," he wrote in that curious, lackadaisical engineering style, that

there is no cause for fear that the water supply throughout the northern part of the Roswell basin will give out or become inadequate for all requirements under proper economy of practice . . . There is pressing need for greater economy on the part of users of well water throughout the Roswell basin. At Roswell a city ordinance regulates the management of all flowing wells, but throughout the remainder of the district no restraint whatever is placed on the management of the wells, and, with very few exceptions, they are allowed to flow continuously. A small portion of this water is stored in artificial reservoirs, but by far the greater part runs off into pools, evaporates and seeps away on uncultivated lands or runs directly into the Pecos River. In one case noted, a ditch leads from the well directly to the River, a distance of one-half mile, and it is not an unusual thing to find water flowing from the wells to the low, marshy lands adjacent to the river, where by underflow it soon reaches the main channel.[17]

To hear Cassius Fisher tell it, the Pecos River, if anything, was gaining

Fig. 4.5.
This early promotional advertisement for the Roswell newspaper and area was designed to show the bountiful natural supply of pressurized water available from the local artesian basin. While residents sat by, reading the paper, the miraculous water shot into the desert air under its own power. (Photo courtesy of the Historical Society for Southeast New Mexico.)

from the rapid, wasteful development of the contributing artesian sources. No one, not even the USGS, was concerned with the effect that artesian pumping might be having on the river, on Carlsbad, or on Texas.

Roswell farmers like the Nelsons were too busy to worry about the future of water. Two of Swann Nelson's sons, Clarence and Harry, left the Roswell area after their father died, but two, Fred (Morgan's father) and Earnest, continued the struggle to establish the Nelson family permanently on the Roswell scene. Fred Nelson's struggle in particular seemed to embody the history of intense area land use in southeastern New Mexico.[18]

Like John Chisum and the other great cattle barons of the early Roswell days, Fred M. Nelson, born in 1892 in Roswell, started out trying to make a living in livestock combined with working rented farms. When the post-World War I agricultural depression wiped out the herd of registered Herefords that Fred had acquired over the years, he turned

93

to irrigated farming in a new place, Texas, and from an old source, the Pecos River itself.[19]

"A neighbor was going down to Texas," he later told his son, Morgan, "to farm on a new farming area they were developing in the area below Peyote, near Pecos. They had just built a new canal there on the Pecos and were talking about building a dam on the Pecos also." Of course, the dam became the Red Bluff reservoir, built in the mid-1930s just across the Texas-New Mexico border on the Pecos River. The "new farming area" which drew Fred M. Nelson turned out to be another of those early ill-begotten Texas irrigation schemes, based on Pecos River dreams and dependent on New Mexico letting an adequate supply of Pecos River water past the state line.[20]

Water availability was the least of Fred Nelson's problems when he moved to Peyote, Texas in March 1923. "We went down to break that land up and farm that," he told Morgan years later.

> It turned out to be a big mistake, but we stayed there for two years . . . I couldn't farm where I first went. It was in a large area of sand and we could hardly even get into it. We only stayed there a year. A family moved out and I rented their place. It had a much better house on it. We called it the 'Red House.' I was able to rent more land but the jackrabbits ate my cotton up the first year and the salt water killed it the second year.[21]

Peyote, Texas, is still there. Morgan Nelson, four years old at the time he moved to Peyote with his father and family, had not been back for seventy years when he and I journeyed down the Pecos River, in the fall of 1993 out of New Mexico and into Texas, inspecting the river that had spawned so much trouble in so many lives for such a long time. In nearby Barstow, Texas, we had arranged to meet Rayburn Allgood, a West Texas farmer who had testified at length in the *Texas v. New Mexico* litigation about the hardships that water shortage in Texas, presumably due to upstream New Mexico, had caused.[22]

Morgan and I found Rayburn Allgood drinking his morning coffee in the Chit Chat Cafe on the highway side of the railroad tracks in Barstow, a *Last Picture Show* town if there ever was one. The Chit Chat was a low-slung white washed building with a single door, set akimbo in the wall. It was dark inside and it took Nelson and me a moment to spot the long table in the back around which ten men, including a Texas Highway patrol officer, were gathered, talking, drinking coffee and playing liar's poker with the serial numbers of dollar bills they pulled out of their wallets.

When Morgan Nelson asked the group for Allgood, all the men

pointed at another and laughed. One thing led to another that morning, but it turned out that Allgood knew the way to what was left of the Peyote settlement where Fred M. Nelson had taken Morgan Nelson and his family to live in 1923–1924. That afternoon the three of us returned to the Big Valley to inspect another of those Pecos River settlements that had killed the dreams of would-be farmers like Fred M. Nelson.

The dirt trace that led from the state highway to what was left of Big Valley passed through desert as bleak and flat as any I'd ever seen. Suddenly, however, Allgood, Nelson, and I arrived at the edge of a sharp drop off and before us emerged a narrow valley through which the Texas part of the Pecos River ran.

I spotted a couple of abandoned houses from the top of the ridge. But there were no obvious signs of extensive cultivation. Rayburn Allgood directed us off to the west where, he said, we could see the old diversion works that used to serve the ditches that at one time provided irrigation water for the valley where Fred Nelson had tried to set up shop in the 1920s. We drove down to look.

In a bend of the slow-moving Pecos River, just before it turned to run through the Big Valley itself, we found a massive diversion structure, consisting of a rock-and-steel dam at least twenty feet tall with four gates at the bottom through which the diverted water passed. Four large wheels on top of the dam were supposed to raise the gates and let the water in. However, the flow of the river had worked its way around the dam so that no water could now reach the gates even if they were open. When the three of us clambered up on top of the dam and tried the wheels we discovered that they had rusted into place and wouldn't move.

Ruined Texas farmer Rayburn Allgood, seventy-four years old, pulled on the wheel with all the might left in his huge, mottled hands, but it wouldn't budge. Successful New Mexican farmer Morgan Nelson, seventy-five years old, yanked with all his might as well but couldn't make the abandoned works budge either. Allgood returned to Barstow that afternoon. Morgan Nelson and I turned around and headed back to New Mexico. Seventy years before, Morgan's father, Fred M., had done the same thing, unable to harness the Pecos River in Texas to his agricultural dreams.

But finally in the Roswell basin, Fred Nelson did get permanently located. He traded farms. He rented farms. He prospered and bought farms. Finally, in 1928 he settled on the East Plains farm begun by his brother-in-law, Oliver Pearson, and later on the Cottonwood Creek. All these farms depended on irrigation water drawn from the artesian aquifer, but it was a measure of the rapidity of the development of groundwater in the Roswell basin that Fred M. Nelson never had to drill a new well himself. In one instance, he took a deep dry oil well and converted it to artesian water. Generally, he acquired rights to existing wells and repaired or replaced them as needed for water on his farms.[23]

Fred Nelson's experience paralleled the development of artesian water in the basin as a whole. In 1904, when Swann Nelson left for Mexico, water seekers had drilled 485 artesian wells in the Roswell basin and irrigated less than twenty thousand acres from them. Then well-drilling activity took off. Between 1905 and 1909, 620 additional wells were drilled. The number of irrigated acres leaped accordingly. By 1928, when Fred Nelson finally landed in East Grand Plains, there were 1,424 wells irrigating more than forty-five thousand Roswell basin acres in Chaves County alone.[24]

The Oasis Ranch, lying east of the Nelsons' East Grand Plains primary residence, closer to the Pecos River, became the crown jewel in Roswell agricultural development. Visitors, like the 1976 *Texas v. New Mexico* entourage of engineers, lawyers, and Special Master Jean Breitenstein, inevitably inspected the Oasis because it was like most Roswell farms, only more so.[25]

The Oasis had more irrigated acres—almost two thousand—than most southeastern New Mexico farms. The Oasis had more water—nine good wells drilled into a relatively open artesian formation. In February 1931, when Fred M. Nelson had been back from Texas and farming up the road for four years and Morgan Nelson was a boy of seven, the Oasis Ranch fittingly became the site of the largest artesian well in the world.

Morgan Nelson again, this time on the 1931 Oasis artesian well:

The well was drilled to a depth of 840 feet and flowed 9,100 gallons per minute under a natural pressure of 32 pounds per square inch. When fully opened it would spout a pillar of water seven feet above the 13-inch casing. When reduced to 4 inches, it blasted a spray nearly 75 feet high. Ivan Gill described it when it was first opened as "a squishy kind of roar, like a hail storm."

The well was drilled by Myron Bruning who was considered one of the best water well drillers in the country. He used a steam powered rotary rig. The rig itself was wooden and had to be erected each time he drilled and torn down, board by board when he finished. The big well was his crowning achievement. He was 42 years old at the time and had years of experience in drilling for oil and sulfur in Texas before he became a water well driller. He drilled many wells in the Pecos Valley with his steam rig.

Bruning engineered the Oasis well with care. He drilled an 18-inch hole

710 feet deep to the top of the San Andres Limestone and set in 13-inch casing with every joint welded and asphalted. He sealed the entire length of the hole outside the casing with red clay.

Bruning then let down a 12-inch bit and began grinding away at the limestone, hitting water almost immediately, a flow which increased in strength with depth. So powerful was the output at the surface that the finer drill cuttings were brought up and out with the water; the coarser material drifted into holes and caverns in the underground water stratum.

Guided by geological maps of the locality and the log records from previous wells, Bruning stopped drilling at 840 feet, which he estimated was near the bottom of the San Andres limestone. The pure water reared its pressure column seven feet above the casing top and held it there in a steady rumble.

Bringing the geyser under control proved to be a job. After flanging the top of the casing, Bruning attached a steel gate valve weighing more than 800 pounds to the bottom of several joined sections of heavy drill stem for extra weight and lowered it over the well top. But, despite the weight, the five drenched men could not hold the assembly in place. The high-pressure water threw metal and men around like socks in a washing machine and half-drowned them for good measure.

Bruning then decided that if he could not lick the pressure, he would fool it. He threaded 60 feet of the 13-inch well casing into a long stem of pipe sticking up in the air over the well, lowered it neatly into place and bolted it to the flanged well top. While the drillers labored, the water climbed inside the 60 foot tower and poured over the top, drenching the men working below. Then the casing was detached from the well head and the gate valve closed, placing under control the greatest artesian well in the world, nearly four weeks after the job was started. On the following Sunday, people came from miles around to see Bruning's masterpiece with his reducer, shooting sky high.[26]

Here was an engineer's view of the Roswell water world: artesian water was a hidden, powerful, chaotic natural resource, like the Carlsbad flood inflows, that could be mastered by the ingenious intervention of great men like Bruning and Tracy. Here, too, in the farming operation that the so-called "king of wells" served, you had the perfect vision of the Roswell that might emerge if the water resource was harnessed. By the 1930s almost two thousand acres of the Oasis Ranch were being irrigated and farmed. From time to time, various owners of the ranch even made money.[27]

Developments like the Oasis's 1931 "big well" changed the Roswell waterscape even further. For the better, what had once been a bog of useless salt grass near the Pecos River became the model for what a productive New Mexico irrigated farm could be. For the worse, the development of the artesian resource had dried up most of the natural seeps and springs and rivulets that the artesian aquifer used to feed. No one except ex-State Engineer and West Texas water consultant Vernon Sullivan worried much about drying up the base flows of the Pecos River and reducing the supply at downstream Carlsbad and Texas. Artesian wells had brought so much water to the surface that a lot of the Roswell land now required not irrigation but drainage in order to remain productive. For

Fig. 4.6.
In 1931, when it was drilled, the Oasis Well shot a stream of water sixty feet into the air under its own artesian pressure. Bringing the water down under control turned out to be harder than raising it from the bottom of the 800-foot-deep well. (Photo courtesy of the Historical Society for Southeast New Mexico.)

better or for worse, the rapid development of the artesian aquifer in the Roswell basin between 1920, when Fred M. Nelson started to settle down, and 1940, when he and the Nelson family were finally in place, fundamentally altered the natural balance of the Roswell water world.[28]

Roswell farmers and bankers saw this growth and transformation and began to worry about how long it could go on. In some areas of the Roswell basin, the pressure in artesian wells had begun to decline, in a few instances to the point where existing wells would no longer produce water on demand. Local and federal banks became jittery about lending money for further artesian drilling. For a moment, Roswell development slowed.[29]

Enter the United States Geological Survey for the second significant time in Roswell's short history. In the mid-1920s the groundwater division of the USGS, at the request of the State of New Mexico, dispatched Albert Fiedler and S. Spencer Nye, an engineer and a geologist, to Roswell to update the work done by Cassius Fisher at the turn of the century. Finally published in 1933, Fiedler and Nye's Geological Survey Water Supply Paper 639, *Geology and Ground Water Resources of the Roswell Artesian Basin, New Mexico* ran to 372 pages, more than five times the length of Fisher's 1906 effort. The report included 46 plates and 36 figures, all analyzing the nature and extent of Roswell's miraculous artesian resource.[30]

From the beginning and throughout their work, Fiedler and Nye soothed Roswell concerns that the artesian supplies soon would be exhausted by existing wells. As early as September 1926, Fiedler appeared before the Chaves County Commission and announced that the artesian water supply was "permanent," as the Roswell *Daily Record* described it. However, Fiedler added, the artesian resource should be carefully regulated to prevent waste and to protect existing wells. The final 1933 publication amplified these points.[31]

Between 1926 and 1933, New Mexico moved to implement Fiedler's recommendations. In 1927, the New Mexico state legislature, lobbied by Fiedler himself, adopted for the first time anywhere, ever, in the United States basic legislation asserting public control over groundwater resources. Theretofore regarded as the private domain of the overlying land owner, Roswell artesian groundwater now became, as surface water long had been, regulated public property, available for private use on terms and conditions specified by the state. Within declared basins, of which the Roswell artesian basin was the first, the state would allow new appropriations of groundwater only if the new appropriator could demonstrate that the water could be appropriated without impairing existing rights. Within the Roswell basin, no one could do this; the real result was that appropriation of the Roswell basin by the state ended new well development in the basin.[32]

These Fiedler-inspired reforms were neither universally accepted nor universally applicable. Morgan Nelson's uncle, Oliver Pearson, for one, actively challenged the reforms in court as unconstitutionally impinging on his rights as a landowner. By 1931 he had lost.[33]

But even as finally approved by the New Mexico courts, the new Roswell artesian groundwater regulations were not complete. The new scheme controlled access to new wells, but only regulated existing ones. The fourteen hundred wells in the Roswell artesian basin that irrigated forty-five thousand acres in 1925 could continue to pump so long as their method of operation did not waste water. There was evidence that even the existing wells had over-strained the groundwater resource and clearly reduced the groundwater contribution to the Pecos River.[34]

In addition, the new scheme applied only to the deep artesian water source, not the separate shallow aquifer that lay above it. Cut off by the new laws from access to the artesian aquifer, water-hungry Roswell farmers turned to the overlying shallow aquifer. They had to lift this water, using more and more sophisticated pumps and paying higher and higher energy costs to do so, but at least the non-artesian shallow water was there. In the 1930s, Roswell area land irrigated from this new source increased threefold to around thirty-eight thousand additional acres.[35]

Besides limiting itself to the artesian source of water, the new regulatory system was limited to defined basins. Beyond the borders of those basins, anybody could still drill an artesian or shallow well anywhere he wanted without interference from the state. Roswell water prospectors, of course, went right on, developing artesian water just outside the borders of the basins declared by the state engineer. Of course, since they were unregulated, no one knew how many of these pirate wells there were, but Morgan Nelson had to deal with them all his farming life.[36]

Finally, the new public regulation of artesian water seemed to pretend the river the groundwater system fed did not exist. For all its progressive vision, the regulatory scheme did not recognize the complex but undeniable interconnection between groundwater and surface water, between the artesian wells and the Pecos River. Those two physical relatives still lived in completely separate legal worlds. It remained for the 1948 Pecos River Compact to bring them together implicitly and for the Supreme Court, more than forty years after that, to explicitly cement the two interconnected sources.[37]

For the moment, Morgan Nelson, the third-generation Roswell farmer,

Chapter 4

entered a water world significantly different than the one occupied first by his grandfather, Swann, and then his father, Fred M. Nelson. While his grandfather and father struggled to locate the family physically in Roswell, Morgan Nelson had to battle with new regulations and new claims to keep them there. Like the second generation of Tracys at Carlsbad, Morgan Nelson turned from the development of water to its regulation. When he returned in 1947 from World War II to settle and farm in Roswell, Morgan Nelson embroiled himself, willingly and delightedly, in legal battles over control of Pecos River basin water.[38]

Nelson used the new state regulatory scheme to defend the wells he had inherited from his father. He and other artesian farmers watched like hawks as the City of Roswell struggled to develop adequate municipal supplies by purchasing and transferring existing rights because developing new sources was illegal. When Nelson and his fellow members of the early Pecos Valley Artesian Conservancy District (PVACD) saw the city doing something they didn't like, they protested to the state engineer, who now had jurisdiction over the transfers.[39]

Not only did Morgan Nelson fight to defend old wells but he also fought attempts to drill additional artesian wells just beyond the declared boundaries of the artesian basin, on the grounds that those new wells were bound to shorten the life of his wells within the basin. These battles brought Morgan Nelson and other old-time Roswell artesian pumpers into direct battle with the Corn family and its efforts to establish irrigated agriculture in the Salt Creek area, fifteen miles north of Roswell, at the very northern edge of the Roswell artesian basin.

Martin Corn and his seventeen children had put down roots in the Salt Creek area at the turn of the twentieth century. Like most local farmers, the family first depended on intermittent surface waters to support their dispersed grazing operations in the area. Owing to extensive groundwater development elsewhere in the basin, those sources had dried up by the 1940s. In the spring of 1947, the Corns began an extensive well drilling operation in the Salt Creek drainage in an effort to restore the surface water resources they had lost. The proposed Pecos River Compact would make such drilling illegal, so this was an urgent campaign.[40]

Fred M. and Morgan Nelson, just home from the Air Force with an engineering degree from New Mexico State, tried to stop the Corns from further depleting an aquifer he and other well owners thought was already overstressed. But because the Salt Creek area was beyond the basin as defined by the state engineer, no one could control well drilling in those outlying areas. In one of his earliest of a lifetime's dealings with the New Mexico State Engineer Office, Morgan Nelson vividly recalls

Fig. 4.7.
In this 1958 photograph, Fred M. Nelson (right) and his son, Morgan, inspect the irrigation of a crop on their farm near Roswell. (Photo courtesy of Morgan Nelson.)

standing on a rise overlooking Salt Creek and the Corns' well-drilling rigs, pleading with State Engineer hydrogeologist Arthur Brown to extend the Roswell Artesian basin into the Salt Creek area so that the Corns' wells could be controlled. "That Arthur Brown," Morgan Nelson says, "just stood there, gnawing on an apple, telling us that the Salt Creek artesian aquifer wasn't connected to ours and that, besides, the State Engineer just didn't have the resources to control these outlying developments. I was so mad."[41]

Angry or not, Morgan Nelson stood by in the late 1940s and early 1950s and watched as his family's share of the Roswell basin shrank as the irrigated acres expanded. Exact figures were hard to come by, but the State Engineer Office knew that in 1940 farmers had irrigated 120,000 acres from artesian and shallow groundwater sources in the Roswell basin. By 1947 that number had jumped to 136,000 acres and through the mid-1950s it just kept going up, reaching a high of 158,000 acres by

1955. Despite the limitations purportedly imposed by the radical state regulation in the 1930s, to say nothing of the 1948 Pecos River Compact itself, the draft on the groundwater resource went on growing.[42]

Others besides Morgan Nelson noticed. Even the Texas compact commissioners, on their way to Santa Fe to negotiate the final Pecos River Compact in March 1948, saw well drilling activity everywhere in the Roswell basin and asked what was going on. As far as State Engineer John Bliss was concerned, nothing was going on. Again and again, he assured the Texans that irrigation from groundwater had not increased in New Mexico since the state had imposed its regulatory scheme in the 1930s. But as far as Roswell farmers and ranchers like the Corns were concerned, the frenetic well drilling activity, especially in 1947, represented a last ditch effort by New Mexicans to establish wells before an interstate compact with Texas really stopped further development of local water resources.[43]

When it came to his Roswell neighbors like the Corns, Morgan Nelson fought tooth and nail to try to limit further development of the precious aquifer to which his family long had had rights. However, when it came to Texas, Morgan Nelson fought equally hard for the right of all New Mexicans, including even the Corns, to use the New Mexico water they needed. As a local farmer, Morgan Nelson was in a position to fight the Corns. As a budding young Chaves County politician in the late 1940s and 1950s, Morgan Nelson was in a position to fight the Texans.

In 1949 Morgan Nelson won a seat in the New Mexico State Legislature. No sooner had he arrived in Santa Fe than the Pecos River Compact arrived for legislative approval in January 1949. The proposed compact must have seemed very unclear to the legislators. And ironically, it was the intent (and understanding) of the legislators that approved the compact, rather than the understanding of the negotiators, that determined what the compact really meant.[44]

As a freshman legislator who was also a Roswell farmer, Morgan Nelson was keenly interested in the proposed compact. Today, more than fifty years later, he hardly remembers why. State Engineer John Bliss, he recalls, carried the proposed compact to the legislature. Southeastern New Mexico legislators were suspicious of it and were, according to Nelson, "inclined to reject it" as they had rejected the first version in 1924–1925. But Bliss came back "almost in tears" and insisted that New Mexico had to approve this compact or face the much worse prospects of a Texas suit for apportionment of the river. According to Nelson, the legislators agreed to Bliss's desperate plea only after Bliss explicitly guaranteed that the proposed compact protected New Mexico's right to all the Roswell wells drilled up until 1949.[45]

That Bliss guarantee would have protected even the Corn wells drilled in the Salt Creek area in 1947, wells that Nelson himself had adamantly opposed. That guarantee effectively negated years of concern by the compact negotiators about the effect of Roswell pumping on the base flow of the Pecos River. At best that guarantee also ignored the ambiguity implied in the compact's Article III(A) apportionment provisions. Forty years later, the Supreme Court's flat out rejection of what became known as New Mexico's "protected use" theory—that the compact absolutely protected all New Mexico rights established prior to 1948—contradicted what Morgan Nelson understood the New Mexico state engineer to have told the New Mexico State Legislature.[46]

Still, the New Mexico State Legislature approved the Pecos River Compact of 1948 in early 1949, based on John Bliss's desperate pleas and inaccurate guarantees. What Morgan Nelson remembers most clearly now is the morning on which the legislature approved the compact that would do the Roswell wells in.

"It was," he says,

> a brilliant March morning in Santa Fe. The sun had just come up over the mountains to the east of the old State Capitol. The light flooded the cupola and bathed the chamber in light. Ellis Whitney, my Roswell mentor, had decided that we should give in to [State Engineer] Bliss because the compact protected our wells, and the rest of us went along. We really thought that in approving the compact with Texas, we had put the Pecos River problems behind us and avoided a court-imposed apportionment of the river. It must have been the light.

He laughs today after decades of litigation.[47]

Nelson served in the state legislature for 13 years. In 1962 he retired from state politics, mostly, he now says, in protest against the turn to the right that Roswell politics took between 1949 and 1965. But he never abandoned his peripatetic efforts to protect his local farming interests.[48]

Those efforts included an amazing array of activities. Morgan Nelson helped establish and then keep going a cotton association that promoted the long-staple cotton grown all over the Southwest and on his farms. He started up a savings and loan association and became deeply involved in the capital-intensive operations of many Chaves County farmers. Then, in the early 1970s, Nelson got out of the business several years before savings and loans everywhere turned sour. He joined an in-law in running a farm implement business and many years later could still drive around the back roads of Roswell, Artesia, and even

Barstow, Texas, pointing out tractors and bailers that he had sold. But, through it all, Morgan Nelson farmed.[49]

While he farmed, he watched the artesian water. Basin water levels always fell in the summer, when irrigation was heavy, and rose in the winter, when wells weren't pumped, especially after the state engineer forced artesian well owners to shut down their wells when they weren't irrigating. But beyond the inevitable seasonal variations, there was a more troublesome, apparently permanent decline in artesian water levels across the Roswell basin that gave even the most optimistic irrigator pause. Were Roswell farmers pumping themselves dry?

Everyone, including Morgan Nelson, speculated on possible reasons. Some pointed to weather conditions. The years immediately after 1949, when the 1948 Pecos River Compact became effective, were some of the driest on record. The drought stressed the artesian wells in two ways. First, the paucity of rain meant that farmers had to make up in artesian water for what their crops missed in rainfall. Second, the paucity of rain meant that the aquifer itself, an amazingly efficient natural collector of what little water fell on the upland areas, was recharged less. Anyone with common sense could see that the increased draft and decreased recharge would lead to greater stress on the aquifer itself. Maybe, said some, this was what was causing the Roswell basin water levels to drop.[50]

Others, also including Morgan Nelson, pointed to the increase in irrigated acres in the Roswell basin in the decade immediately after the signing of the Pecos River Compact despite the compact's guarantee that New Mexico would not further deplete the flow of the Pecos River. Internal state engineer figures showed a jump of 16,000 acres in the years between 1940 and 1947. Between 1947 and 1950, those acres jumped even more, from 136,000 in 1947 to 158,000 in 1950. By mid-decade, things seemed to have stabilized, and by 1960 they may even have started to drop off. But, still, the increase in acres served by artesian and shallow water might also explain the troublesome fact that the water in the basin was apparently being drained and not replaced.[51]

For the third time in the twentieth century, local officials, with Morgan Nelson still in the lead, turned to hydrology for a scientific explanation of the problems that the Roswell basin seemed to be facing. In 1954 the directors of the Pecos Valley Conservancy District funded the New Mexico Institute of Mining and Technology to study the basin and the limits of its groundwater resources. In turn, New Mexico Tech's aggressive president, E. J. Workman, selected an Iraqi hydrologist trained in Baghdad and at the University of Utah to do the work. In early 1955 Dr. Mahdi Hantush rented a house in Roswell. The world of groundwater hydrology was never again the same.[52]

Published in August 1955, Hantush's report on the groundwater resources of the Roswell area bore the imposing title "Preliminary Quantitative Study of the Roswell Groundwater Reservoir, New Mexico." Fisher in 1906 and Fiedler and Nye in 1931 had used measured well depths to estimate the hidden underground water in the area. Now Hantush took the analysis one giant step forward. Using established mathematical formulas to describe the flow of matter and energy through porous and non-porous material, he estimated the movement of water through rocks, which, if you took a broad enough view, was exactly what was going on in the Roswell basin.[53]

Pages of esoteric formulas applied to obscure Roswell well data filled the pages of Mahdi Hantush's report. But Mahdi Hantush pulled no punches when it came to what those formulas showed about the "safe yield" of the Roswell basin. In 1955 Roswell wells were removing per year a lot more water than came into the basin. For a while stored water in the ground could cover the excess. But eventually (and it was only a matter of time, noted Hantush), the level of water in all wells would drop to the point that no well could economically remove water from the ground. Hantush's implied solution was clear: reduce the human draft on the Roswell basin or suffer the inevitable consequences.[54]

Through the 1950s and 1960s Morgan Nelson and his fellow progressively minded Roswell farmers tried. They supported the state engineer's efforts to prevent waste in existing wells. They cooperated in the efforts of the courts to define and limit existing rights to water. They even arranged to purchase and retire from irrigation almost 6,000 of the 158,000 acres irrigated in 1955. Between 1955 and 1965 the number of irrigated acres in the Roswell basin dropped by almost 10,000 acres a year, hitting 147,000 acres in 1960 and 138,000 in 1965. This reduction showed remarkable restraint in a local economy that depended on agricultural growth. However, the restraint may still have been too little and too late to reach Hantush's "safe yields."[55]

Through the dry years of the 1950s and into the 1960s water levels in Roswell wells continued to drop from year to year. In some years the drop was insignificant. Like most Roswell farmers, Morgan Nelson could and did adjust on his Cottonwood Creek and East Grande Plain farms. He moved from crop to crop, from year to year, and from local battle to local battle.[56]

But the continuing declines pointed toward a time when the water resource would inevitably be exhausted by existing pumping, and

Hantush's calculations proved it. The continuing declines also guaranteed, as surely as night followed day, that groundwater contributions to the Pecos River itself would also drop until, like the groundwater itself, they disappeared. Hantush's formulas confirmed Royce Tipton's earlier warnings. In the 1950s and 1960s, this inevitable fact didn't concern Roswell farmers. Except for the few local farmers who pumped water directly from the Pecos, the river was, as always, beyond their ken. They had enough trouble with their own wells.

In the 1970s, however, that focus changed. Texas complaints about Pecos River deliveries at the state line drew attention to the Roswell wells. For the next two decades Morgan Nelson found himself embroiled with Pecos River Compact problems raised by *Texas v. New Mexico*. He watched the legal events unfold. He copied and stored court documents. ("Filed" was too polite a term for what went on in his home office.) He haunted the back rows of courtrooms in Denver and Santa Fe as one of the few interested visitors in the arcane legal proceedings.

Finally, toward the end of the endless proceedings, New Mexico called on Morgan Nelson as a witness. New Mexico's lawyers wanted Nelson to testify about farming in Roswell, about farming in Texas, about his experiences with the Pecos River in New Mexico. The case settled before he took the stand.[57]

But Morgan Nelson had a lot to say on the subject.

FIVE

Leave It to Steve

——————*Texas v. New Mexico, Number 65 Original,* started rolling in the mid-1970s. The compact-based, interstate Supreme Court suit yoked together the Tracys' and Carlsbad's surface water and the Nelsons' and Roswell's groundwater. The State of New Mexico now had to defend both worlds against the downstream claims of the State of Texas. The interstate battle ground was the setting for the emergence of State Engineer Stephen E. Reynolds as the leader of New Mexico's troops.

Just as Reynolds was readying himself for the legal struggle of his life, he emerged on the national media scene as the model of a devoted, brilliant state water bureaucrat. The process culminated in a front-page April 1980 profile in the *Wall Street Journal.* Reynolds and his already long tenure had been the subject of many articles in local publications. For awhile it seemed as if every reporter new to New Mexico, and there were a lot of them in the 1970s and 1980s, felt obliged to profile Reynolds. Publications from the *Albuquerque Journal's* weekly newsmagazine to Washington, D.C.'s *Governing* magazine featured Reynolds, too, although they tended to be more moderate in their praise and more balanced in their views. But it was the *Wall Street Journal* story that really catapulted Reynolds out of the world of the western water and into a national arena.[1]

Reynolds, like more than half of New Mexico's residents by the 1980s, was not born there. The *Wall Street Journal* retold the story of Reynolds coming to New Mexico from Decatur, Illinois, in 1935 as a Depression-driven, hungry young college student bound by what looked like chance but what turned out to be fate. It was all the more fitting, observed the *Wall*

Fig. 5.1. New Mexico State Engineer Steve Reynolds stands astride the small Santa Fe River in this 1980 photograph. At the height of his powers at the time, Reynolds strikes a characteristic pose, at once skeptical and imposing. (Photo by Danny Turner.)

Street Journal, that Reynolds looked as if he'd always been here. He was described as "a tall, rangy 63-year-old who looks more like a rancher than a bureaucrat."[2]

The articles went on to relate Reynolds's successes at the University of New Mexico as a student (he graduated first in the class of 1939, unheard of for an engineering student), as an athlete (he played end on the UNM football team), and as a politician (president of his class in 1938 and 1939). Reynolds, the articles all implied, was a huge success, just waiting to happen.

Fellow UNM graduate Governor John Simms selected Reynolds as state engineer in August, 1955, a position Reynolds would hold until his death in 1990. "He's the State Engineer of New Mexico," reported the *Journal* in 1980, "a title that doesn't describe his real job—water boss of a state with some of the strongest laws and best enforcement in the arid West, where water is the resource on which all others depend. In deciding who gets how much of a limited supply, the engineer has impartially enraged farmers, oilmen, miners and whole cities. Yet even his opponents respect him, and over the years the unflappable Mr. Reynolds has become something of a resource himself." This combination of science, power, and public control fascinated all Reynolds's fans.[3]

The fact that Reynolds had held power for a long time even by 1980 was also fascinating to the media. Working closely with New Mexico's Congressional delegation, particularly New Mexico Senator Clinton Anderson and his Senate Committee on Interior Affairs, and with the Bureau of Reclamation, Reynolds had built enduring and powerful relationships with federal officials in Washington who controlled the money for western water projects. The *Journal* noted these long-standing relationships, quoted a couple of prominent Washington officials and went on to Reynolds' even more amazing long-time survival in New Mexico state politics.[4]

To outsiders and journalists new to New Mexico, political life here seemed nasty, brutish, and very short. The state capitol, Santa Fe, in particular looked like a place where political ambitions quickly died. The very part-time, formally unpaid state legislature appeared the last place where a water bureaucrat and engineer could survive. Governors came and went, usually nowhere, and they had the power to appoint the state water boss to a short two-year term. Yet Steve Reynolds survived, session after session, year after year, governor after governor. When asked how by the journalists, state politicians always cited Reynolds's even-handed administration of the state's intricate and arcane water laws. The journalists always trotted out a story about Reynolds's cancellation of a former governor's well permit for failure to abide by its terms to show that Reynolds survived state politics by refusing to play it.[5]

Beneath the image of the state engineer as hard-boiled water saint lurked a much more complex character. There was talk in 1980 and thereafter that the *Wall Street Journal* profile had actually been arranged by a former Reynolds employee then heading the legal division of the Department of Energy in Washington as a way to shore up Reynolds's plummeting stock in New Mexico. Indeed, there was calculation in everything that State Engineer Steve Reynolds did. Reynolds got journalists to deny in profile after profile that he made any political calculations in his administration of New Mexico's water law. But his complex defense in *Texas v. New Mexico* could only have been devised by a clever politician.[6]

Astute observers took note in May 1976 when Supreme Court Special Master Jean Breitenstein and delegations from Texas and New Mexico took off in the small State Corporation airplane to inspect the Pecos River and State Engineer Reynolds did not come along. He wasn't averse to flying. For years he had flown at the front of B-17s and B-29s doing research into summer cloud formation, lightning, and rain. Instead, two other factors had indicated to Reynolds and his principal advisor, the lawyer Paul Bloom, that he shouldn't come along.[7]

First, Reynolds had decided that he himself would both direct New Mexico's legal defense against the Texas suit over the Pecos River and be the state's principal engineering witness. As state engineer since 1955, Reynolds served as *ex oficio* secretary of the New Mexico Interstate Stream Commission. That position made him *de facto* representative to the Pecos River Commission. He was as familiar as anyone was with interstate problems on the river. But when some of his advisers pleaded with him to find some less partisan representative for New Mexico's interests in the Pecos River, Reynolds rejected the idea.[8]

This decision represented both the strengths and weaknesses of Steve Reynolds's water administration as it had developed between 1956 and 1976. It was true that he did know more about the Pecos River than anyone else anywhere, except perhaps his trusted lieutenant, Carl Slingerland, just as he knew more about all New Mexico water issues. The depth and breadth of his Pecos River knowledge certainly qualified him to speak on the issues. But over the years, his voice had become the only voice that could be heard above the growing grumbling and eventual din of the Pecos River battle. Now, as the din became a lawsuit, Reynolds had decided that he alone would speak, in court and not on an airplane, about Texas's claim to the river. For twenty years, Reynolds had convinced New Mexicans that he would take care of their water problems and they had let him. Now in 1976, as a kind of last hurrah, he would take care of the Pecos, too, as legal strategist, as principal witness, but not, alas, as a passenger on the trip to acquaint newcomers with a river whose problems he already knew so well.[9]

The other reason that Steve Reynolds elected not to tour the Pecos River in spring 1976 was that he was mending political fences in Santa Fe. In November 1974 New Mexico had elected Las Cruces politician and small-time businessman Jerry Apodaca as governor. A smart, vindictive veteran of New Mexico politics, Apodaca had pledged to Hispanic constituents that he would consider appointing someone as state engineer more sympathetic than Reynolds had been to the special water problems of small New Mexico farmers and to the special claims of at least one powerful Apodaca ally.[10]

Apodaca later admitted to the *Wall Street Journal* that he had considered replacing Reynolds. "We took a long hard look at his operation,"

Leave It to Steve

Apodaca told the *Journal*. "He'd been there for so long he practically had a monopoly on water policy; it was like Hoover at the FBI. But we could find no vindictiveness, no personal involvement in any of his decisions. And he knew everything about water; that knowledge is Steve's great security." As a result, implied Apodaca, he had reappointed Reynolds to what was then Reynolds's tenth consecutive two-year term.[11]

In fact, the story of Apodaca's reappointment of Reynolds as state engineer in 1975 was more complex than either admitted and showed the balance of water politics and policy under Reynolds on the eve of the Texas suit against New Mexico over the Pecos River. As soon as Apodaca won the November 1974 general election and began trying to find a new state engineer, Reynolds started to fight back. Too much a gentleman to enter the trenches of New Mexico politics directly, he allowed his allies and subordinates to do the dirty work for him.

In December 1974 and January 1975, State Engineer general counsel Paul Bloom and former governor Jack Campbell began a quiet telephone campaign on Reynolds's behalf. The two called bankers and realtors and large mining companies across the state, telling them of Apodaca's plans to get rid of Reynolds and inviting them to urge the new governor not to do it. The Reynolds allies even went so far as to specifically target the numerous bank officers in charge of loans to an over-extended Apodaca and his businesses. These big business interests weighed in on Reynolds's side and Apodaca caved in. If anything, Reynolds's victory was more a result of Reynolds exploiting Apodaca's weaknesses than of Apodaca's recognizing Reynolds' strength as Apodaca told the *Wall Street Journal* in 1980.[12]

Reynolds was able to rally New Mexico's biggest and most conservative institutions to his side in 1975 because over the twenty years of his service as state engineer he had convinced them that his regulation of New Mexico water served the economic development interests of the state. Reynolds brought stability to the world of New Mexico water; New Mexico powers were for that. This was a far cry from where Reynolds had begun as state engineer in August 1955.[13]

Almost as soon as he was appointed state engineer, Reynolds asserted the state's jurisdiction over groundwater in most of the Rio Grande Valley from the Colorado state line to the Elephant Butte reservoir in southern New Mexico. Reynolds proposed to recognize that groundwater and surface water in the Rio Grande basin came from the same natural source, which meant that, for example, taking water from wells in the basin would diminish the water flowing in the river.[14]

In 1956, the recognition of the interrelationship of groundwater and surface water and the resulting "conjunctive management" of the two water sources shot New Mexico, once again, way in front of every other western state in terms of progressive water management. In the 1930s and in the Pecos River basin, New Mexico had taken the first step among western states by declaring groundwater subject to public regulation just like surface water. Now in the mid 1950s, with Reynolds leading the way, New Mexico took the second giant step, this time in the Rio Grande basin, by recognizing that the two public sources of water were in fact one.[15]

The 1938 Rio Grande Compact, a tri-state Texas-New Mexico-Colorado agreement, apportioned the Rio Grande by bulk flows. It required New Mexico to deliver to a downstream Texas point a percentage of flows passing an upstream New Mexico gauge. Between the upstream and downstream measuring points lay the Albuquerque-centered middle Rio Grande, rapidly feeding on groundwater for growth. Reynolds knew that the wells wouldn't affect the water passing the upper gauge but they were guaranteed to reduce the river flows below the gauge, thereby reducing the compact-required deliveries at the downstream gauge and thus violating New Mexico's measured obligation to Texas. To keep New Mexico in compact compliance he had to limit New Mexico wells.[16]

Reynolds's recognition that groundwater and surface water came from one limited source had radical implications for real estate development in the middle Rio Grande basin, particularly around Albuquerque. In the 1950s the city was perched on the edge of a growth spurt unprecedented in New Mexico. Real estate promoters and politicians touted Albuquerque as sitting on top of a bottomless ocean of underground water, free for the taking from deep city wells drilled helter-skelter into the mesas east of the city and the river. Now the brash new state engineer proposed to put the dampers on the boosters' hope for unlimited growth. According to the proposed Reynolds policy, not only would the developers have to deal with the state for public groundwater, they would also have to purchase ancient surface water rights near the river to offset the effects on the river of pumping groundwater on the mesas. Suddenly, the limitless supply that the developers and city officials had counted on evaporated. Real estate costs would go up and profit margins down.[17]

Reynolds himself loved to tell the story of his announcement of his proposed Rio Grande basin plan. Called by the Chamber of Commerce in Albuquerque to account for his water policy in early 1957, he found himself in a huge, oak-wainscoted board meeting room seated at a long, narrow conference table with every New Mexico big-shot banker and mogul. Reynolds had been invited to explain his plan for conjunctive management of the water resources in the middle Rio Grande basin. As the audience realized the implications of what State Engineer Reynolds was telling them, they became, relates Reynolds, grinning, more and more hostile. By the end of the meeting, the angry audience, led by then Albuquerque city commissioner Maurice Sanchez, pledged to fight him tooth and nail, in the courts and in the legislature.[18]

The two battlegrounds turned out to be Reynolds's favorites. Later affectionately called by a Supreme Court justice "the most litigious son-of-a-bitch in New Mexico," Reynolds often turned to the courts to vindicate policies that couldn't win immediate political approval. By 1962 he and his lawyers had beat the challenge of the City of Albuquerque to his proposed policy and had found an ally in the judiciary that he would use to advantage over the next twenty years.[19]

As for the 1957 battle in the legislature, the struggle was a little more complex. The City of Albuquerque was powerful even then. The city rallied the same conservative rural-dominated membership that would save Reynolds in 1975. City Commissioner Maurice Sanchez proposed to clip Reynolds's wings by requiring district court approval of groundwater basins of the kind that Reynolds had unilaterally imposed. The way Reynolds fought the bill in the legislature would characterize his relationship with that body for the next twenty years.[20]

He forbade his staff any contact with the legislature; he alone would articulate the state's water policy and make whatever legislative deals needed to be made. He wrote long memos to everyone on every water-related topic. He sat patiently in the back of committee hearing rooms, waiting hour after hour to offer testimony, answer questions and direct policy. Usually a cantankerous state legislature took his advice.[21]

Initially, though, Reynolds lost this early battle with the City of Albuquerque. On March 7, 1957 the state senate rejected on a 17 to 15 vote the city-sponsored bill putting groundwater power directly in the hands of the courts. Two days later, the senate reversed itself when Lieutenant Governor Joseph Montoya broke a 16-16 tie by voting in favor of the bill. Fortunately, the new governor, Edwin Mechem, a politician Reynolds described as genuinely interested in water affairs, vetoed the bill. Reynolds's power to take control over groundwater when he wanted to and for hydrological reasons was established and saved—just.[22]

What a change in attitudes and backers in twenty years in between the Albuquerque battle that started in 1955 and the Apodaca one in 1975. In the earlier one, the bankers, the real estate developers, and the big farmers fought Reynolds's seizure of control of groundwater, the last unregulated water resource available for the taking in a burgeoning New

Fig. 5.2.
New Mexico State Engineer Steve Reynolds at the center of a huge January 7, 1966 meeting of Upper and Lower Colorado River Basin interests in Salt Lake City, Utah. Just as Reynolds made his presence felt in western water affairs, he somehow stands out in this large and contentious group. (Photo courtesy of the David Hale Collection, NMSRCA.)

Mexico. In 1975, the same institutions that had tried to get rid of him now saved him. In the interim, Reynolds had won the support of the New Mexico powers-that-be by convincing them that his aggressive form of water management actually stabilized water resources and guaranteed more reliable investments of the kind that promised to make them rich.

Reynolds accomplished that switch between 1955 and 1975 in a couple of ways. First, he demonstrated time and again his almost obsessive devotion to New Mexico and her water interests. "When it comes to water," remarked Paul Bloom, for years Reynolds's chief lawyer, "he's like a Bedouin potentate. It's me against my brother and my brother and me against the clan and the clan against all the other clans in the world."[23]

As New Mexico clan leader, Reynolds's ability to exact favorable treatment in interstate water affairs was legendary. New Mexico, for example, would support a huge, controversial Arizona water project only if Arizona would support a huge New Mexico claim to the Gila

115

River that was larger than any court or legislature had recognized and a dam to go with it. Reynolds made the outrageous demand stick. When Arizona accused Reynolds of blackmailing Arizona, Reynolds replied with characteristic insouciance, "Well, if that enables you to understand our position, you can call it blackmail."[24]

By whatever name, Reynolds accomplished his success by forging powerful and enduring political alliances. He and New Mexico's long-time U.S. Senator Clinton P. Anderson teamed up as a powerful influence on federal water policy in the west in general and New Mexico in particular. Within New Mexico, Reynolds paired himself with the conservative, smart, long-standing state senator from Deming, Ike Smalley. Together they held their own in the annual legislative sessions in Santa Fe.[25]

Reynolds offered these politicians a scientific justification for the water policies they pursued. No one labored as hard as Steve Reynolds did to master the technical data about New Mexico water. He worked six or even seven days a week, at home or in his office, and did almost nothing else. For recreation, the former intercollegiate football player sailed a small boat, alone, on one of the lakes that his controversial dams produced. He read everything that had anything to do with New Mexico water, and almost nothing else. If a movie, any movie, had been filmed in New Mexico, he went to see it. When a colleague gave him a Franz Kafka parable on Poseidon because he believed that Reynolds might be interested in the story of an ancient water king, Reynolds laughed, asked who Kafka and Poseidon were, and then filed the parable without reading it.[26]

Yet what he mastered, most of it dealing with New Mexico water, he mastered so completely that he could explain it in a web of history and science and law so seamless that his analysis carried the weight of immutable truth. Governor after governor cited State Engineer Reynolds's knowledge as the principal source of his extraordinary power and longevity. Governor, then Judge, Edwin Mechem, one of Reynolds's true admirers, expressed that same respect acerbically when he remarked, "Steve's greatest source of power was that he always managed to get in the first word."[27]

These words Reynolds sometimes expressed on his feet. He was a courteous, dignified speaker who, especially late in his career, tended to read too much from texts prepared many years before and patched together for the subsequent occasion. But in public appearances his saving grace was a charming and usually self-deprecating sense of humor. After graduating from UNM in 1939, he had returned as an adjunct professor and assistant football coach in the 1940s. Three-time governor Bruce King played under him as a student and then as governor reappointed Reynolds as often to the state engineer office. "I began as the governor's coach," Reynolds loved to say, "and I ended up as his water boy."

At times, that ready wit could acquire an edge. Trapped before a hostile Hispanic audience in Española one evening, Reynolds was asked why he didn't speak Spanish. "I'm sorry I never learned," he replied. "I should have. But I never did because the Hispanic people of New Mexico were too polite to insist on it."[28]

Good as he was on his feet, Reynolds was really at his best and most comfortable in writing. His real legacy lies in the written memoranda he

Fig. 5.3.
State Engineer Reynolds makes an emphatic point at a 1976 legislative meeting. In most instances politicians and others heeded his increasingly dogmatic positions. Imagine State Engineer Reynolds approaching Special Master Charles J. Meyers (pictured in Fig. 7.1) in this way and you will see the awful clash between two titans that ended *Texas v. New Mexico*. (Photo courtesy of the *Santa Fe New Mexican*.)

Leave It to Steve

prepared and the written briefs his lawyers prepared with constant editorial help (some called it interference) from Reynolds.

Reynolds wrote like the engineer he was. His prose wasn't particularly lively. It was full of the kinds of passive constructions that engineers and scientists love and that, for most other readers, kill sentences in midflight. But a Reynolds document was careful and accurate. High-level aides and lawyers quaked at the prospect of being called into Reynolds's office to go over a document with him.

He'd be waiting at the large conference desk in his elegant corner office in the Bataan Memorial Building with what he called his "editorial tools": an unabridged Webster's International Dictionary and a pencil that had erasers mounted on both ends. The double-ended pencil had been given to him by aides whose prose had suffered at the hands of Reynolds's acute sense of diction and syntax. If the aides complained too much about Reynolds's linguistic sensitivity, Reynolds would stop erasing, lay the pencil down and, with a grin, announce, "Well, I guess we could just tear the whole thing up and start over again from scratch." The author and editor would quickly return to the text. "Let's see," Reynolds would say, "I think this sentence needs a preposition in here."

All this tinkering and editing produced innumerable briefs for courts and memoranda for the state legislature. Like good legal briefs, the legislative memoranda appeared neutral on the surface but were in fact expressed and organized in such a way as to lead inevitably to a conclusion that appeared self-evident but wasn't. Implicitly they expressed a remarkably consistent view of New Mexico water that included his views on the Pecos River.[29]

That underlying Reynolds view was fundamentally based on an instrumental view of nature in general and water in particular. Natural processes were good in his view only by virtue of what they could do for man. Water that was left in a stream helped no one and water that was left in the ground remained hidden. Steve Reynolds fought the increasingly popular notion that water in rivers—"instream flows"—deserved legal protection because he believed so fundamentally that the operative term in "beneficial use" was "use." Whatever quarrels Carlsbad and Roswell and their irrigators might have with each other, they were all users of New Mexico water and that, in Reynolds's view, deserved the highest respect.

Reynolds combined that belief in the use of water with an engineer's skepticism about theories, be they scientific or legal, that attempted to explain too much. Trained as a mechanical engineer, Reynolds understood the basic formulas that the likes of Mahdi Hantush had started to work with. But, especially when it came to the complex and poorly

Chapter 5

understood movement of groundwater, Reynolds was skeptical that the theories adequately could predict what would happen in the real world. He preferred to wait and see. All the scientists agreed that the effect of pumping groundwater in Roswell on the base flows of the Pecos River headed for Carlsbad and Texas would be slow. The delayed effect created time for Morgan Nelson to pump his artesian wells and for Reynolds to prepare his strategies.[30]

While waiting for the facts to catch up with the theories, Reynolds played what cards were available to him to protect his and New Mexico's options. Nature itself held a critical card, and Reynolds insisted on recognizing that fact. New Mexico was a desert; no massive importation of water from other regions could change that. Limited water was distributed unevenly. "You had to play Nature's water cards," he loved to say, "the way that Jesus flung 'em." If God gave the people of Roswell that amazing groundwater aquifer, the equivalent of a natural reservoir, then it was theirs alone to enjoy. No card he held could trump Roswell's ace-in-the hole, the bounty that Nature had bestowed. However, Reynolds did hold some powerful cards and one of the principal cards he held and played very well was the legal King.[31]

The courts, as well as the legislature, came to trust his judgment and did, by and large, what he asked. Reynolds had almost become a lawyer himself. He joked about practicing law without a license. He sometimes latched onto slippery legal doctrines with the unwarranted fervor of a true lay believer. He liked the company of lawyers, with all their verbal jousting. In turn, the lawyers recognized Reynolds as a skillful and fair judge in hotly contested administrative water disputes. But, insisted Reynolds's closest legal allies, he had the engineer's deep suspicion that lawyers were really just pettifoggers who wasted a lot of time and produced nothing real. He thought laws were there to be manipulated for other ends. Reynolds recognized, as he often said himself, that water in New Mexico was "extensively and intricately governed by law." That recognition didn't so much constrain him as it did create esoteric weapons in an ongoing battle to achieve various ends.[32]

Basic twentieth-century New Mexico water law was built on two bedrock principles, beneficial use and priority of appropriation. The first principle, beneficial use, insisted that public water be carefully used so that the limited public supply would stretch as far as it could. The second principle, priority of appropriation, insisted that when beneficially used water became short, as it inevitably would in a desert environment like New Mexico, the oldest established users would get their full supply before the younger users would get any. Both principles were equally embedded in the New Mexico State Constitution of 1912. But State Engineer Steve Reynolds believed in the first principle and disliked the second so much that he disregarded it.[33]

For a number of reasons, priority of appropriation struck Reynolds as a silly way of apportioning short supplies in New Mexico. First, he disliked the principle because it offered the law's most basic protection to New Mexico's oldest and least efficient uses. Reynolds could, and did, try to facilitate the market transfer of old rights to new uses so that, as he liked to say, "water would flow uphill to money." Still priority of appropriation faced backwards when New Mexico under Reynolds was trying to use its water policy to move economically forward and it was the wrong orientation.[34]

Reynolds also recognized that in the new world of interconnected groundwater and surface water, priority enforcement was physically too slow to work. Calling priorities might have worked where it was invented: on the small California streams used for mining, where turning off a junior right meant more water for senior downstream users almost immediately. But when you shut off a junior well, say in Roswell, because a senior downstream surface user, say in Carlsbad, wasn't getting enough water, that drastic act didn't do anybody any good. The junior well user couldn't use his well. In the meantime, it could take a long, long time—months, years, even decades—for the water not used by the well to reach the senior surface water irrigator's point of diversion in the stream. By then the surface water irrigator had either dried up and blown away or it had rained.[35]

Reynolds also believed that enforcement of priorities would take the power to distribute water and mold policy out of his office and put it in the hands of the courts. Far better, thought Reynolds, to use the tools of science in the hands of experts, rather than the crude club of priority in the hands of the unscientific courts to manage New Mexico's scarce resources.[36]

Reynolds used science as the tool to enforce the state constitution's real command that "beneficial use shall be the basis, the measure and the limit" of the right to use water. For most of his regime as state engineer, "conservation of water" meant one thing: dams. "Beneficial use" meant another: using as little water as possible to achieve any desirable end. By insisting that all water rights holders use no more water than they had to, Reynolds hoped to save enough water to delay and even avoid having to use priorities to apportion the limited supply.

In the meantime, while clamping down on uses within New Mexico, Reynolds hoped to hold at bay other states with interests in New

Mexico's waters. The other side of his fanatic devotion to New Mexico was his equally fanatic antipathy to the claims of other states, especially downstream Texas, to New Mexico water. At the outset of his regime in August 1955, New Mexico was already a party to seven different interstate agreements that apportioned common water sources between New Mexico and every surrounding state. Reynolds recognized that these compacts bound New Mexico but from the outset he fought hard and successfully to minimize the limitations they imposed on his own tough water rights administration.[37]

Early in his regime he had succeeded in controlling the efforts of neighboring states to limit New Mexico's power to regulate the use of water within its own boundaries. In early February 1957 the U.S. Supreme Court threw Texas out of court in its effort to sue New Mexico over the 1938 Rio Grande Compact. The Supreme Court ruled that the United States itself was an "indispensable" party to any attempt to enforce the interstate Rio Grande compact. New Mexico, partially under Reynolds's direction, had both argued that the suit couldn't proceed without the United States and convinced the United States not to join in. The result: Texas couldn't even get its Rio Grande Compact complaint into court. Less than a decade later, when Texas and New Mexico joined forces against upstream Colorado, Reynolds succeeded in getting the United States to enter a new Rio Grande Compact suit. From the Texas perspective, it looked as if Reynolds controlled access to the federal courts, the only way outside states could gain access to New Mexico water.[38]

For twenty-five years Steve Reynolds brought these developed tenets and attitudes to bear on the Pecos River Compact. His responses, always favorable to New Mexico, were as multi-faceted as his water interests. But he maintained with the certainty of a true believer that the compact negotiators understood that the compact recognized and protected New Mexico surface and groundwater uses established as of the end of 1947. He bolstered his position by getting former New Mexico State Engineers John Bliss and John Erickson, both present at the compact negotiations, to agree with him and by consigning Royce Tipton's quite different explanation to the archives.[39]

As a matter of science, Reynolds regarded the compact's central apportionment provision as hopelessly vague and technically impossible and he used his verbal skills to exploit the ambiguities. When asked whether Roswell wells weren't violating the compact by further "depleting" the Pecos River with their continued pumping as Tipton had said they would, Reynolds stopped the discussion by saying that the wells "intercepted ground water inflow," rather than actually "depleting" the river.[40]

121

Finally, as a matter of law, Reynolds was convinced that Texas could never prove, as the compact required, that "man's activities" in New Mexico had caused an alleged violation of the compact's vague guarantees. If all else failed, New Mexico could hide behind the law's assignment of the burden of proof to Texas. If no one could prove why state-line deliveries changed, then Texas lost. To every compact question, Reynolds had a New Mexico answer.[41]

Reynolds could do nothing about the Pecos River Compact, but he could try to control the Pecos River Compact Commission. From his earliest days as state engineer between 1956 and 1961, Reynolds moved on every front to shore up New Mexico's Pecos River Compact positions on the Pecos River Commission.

As secretary of the Interstate Stream Commission, Reynolds was bound to be close to the Pecos River Commission. Not only did he effectively appoint the commission's New Mexico representative, but he himself served as a member of the commission's critical Engineering Advisory Committee ("EAC"). Year after year between 1956 and 1976 Reynolds was reappointed state engineer and thus, year after year, returned to the Pecos River Commission and the EAC. To this aspect of his job, Reynolds brought the same single-minded devotion to New Mexico and the same complete mastery of technical and legal detail that he brought to all his water work. But it was nowhere so apparent as in the first five years of his involvement with the Pecos River Commission between 1956 and 1961.[42]

The brash new state engineer started shaking up the Pecos River Commission soon after he attended his first meeting of the Compact Commission's Engineering Advisory Committee in October 1955. From the outset, Reynolds's relationship with Royce Tipton, the father of the compact and now the chairman of the EAC, was "rocky." At that first meeting Reynolds challenged the validity of three of the factors used to calculate both the Tipton-inspired "1947 condition" standard and subsequent compliance with it.[43]

Reynolds's challenges came at a particularly sensitive time in the early history of the Pecos River Commission. Unable early to make any compact computations at all, the commissions' EAC had struggled to make minor adjustments in the "1947 condition" baseline and companion inflow/outflow manual. Finally, in early 1957, a subcommittee of the EAC submitted to the EAC proposed findings that would have found New Mexico 129,000 acre-feet behind in compact deliveries through 1955. The Texas member of the EAC moved the adoption of the findings and New Mexico member Reynolds refused to second the motion. There the matter lay in a position that the Supreme Court would find troubling twenty years later, the commission paralyzed by its two-vote voting structure that enabled new-comer Reynolds use of what in effect was a veto power.[44]

Over the next six years, the commission got itself back on track. In 1962 it adopted the Reynolds-inspired, Tipton-executed Review of Basic Data restudy of the "1947 condition" base-line. Using the new methods and data that Reynolds had insisted on, the commission found that through 1961 there had been 53,300 acre-feet of under-deliveries since 1950 but that New Mexico could be held responsible for no more than 5,300 acre-feet of those, only 5 percent of the amount the engineers had come up with in 1957. Texas went along with new figures in 1962, which were not only much lower but ran over a period twice as long (1948–1956 v. 1948–1961). By any measure the 1962 standards and cal-culations represented a great victory for Reynolds and New Mexico.[45]

But instead of unlocking the Pecos River Compact commission and freeing it to move forward, the 1962 resolution only stalled it again. The Texas engineers always had blamed Reynolds for the delay and then for the sharp reduction in figures. They claimed that commission cooperation had ended as soon as brash trouble-maker Reynolds had come onto the EAC in 1956. Now beginning in 1962 the Texans themselves refused to cooperate. In 1977 the Supreme Court's special master determined that starting in 1962 Texas showed "a complete lack of desire to agree to anything that New Mexico wanted."[46]

Texas's general disregard for commission affairs in the 1960s played right into Reynolds's hands. In contrast to Reynolds's steadfast attention to commission business, Texas chose to make its Pecos River commissioner a salaried minor functionary whose job, a small, patronage plumb in Texas politics, changed frequently. The job often went to someone collecting a political debt with little knowledge of or interest in the Pecos River. So New Mexicans loved to tell the story of the Houston lawyer/minister appointed as Texas representative to the Pecos River Commission who barely found his way to commission meetings and then only as part of an extended vaca-tion with his mistress. True or not, the story showed how little attention Texas paid the future of the Pecos River Commission.[47]

Under Reynolds's direction, the Pecos River Commission turned to the past. Apparently uninterested in future compact compliance, in 1961 the Pecos River Commission published a 284-page book praising the progress the commission had made between 1950 and 1960. Long and not very illuminating, *The Pecos River Commission: A Decade of Progress* seems naïve and self-serving in light of the twenty years of bitter litigation that would begin in 1974. But from Steve Reynolds's 1961 point of view, the book, which one of his staff wrote, must have looked just fine. After all, it made Pecos River interstate affairs look hunky-dory as of 1960 and for the foreseeable future.[48]

That left Reynolds free to deal with the Pecos River on his own New Mexico terms, without much considering Texas. And deal he did, primarily by insisting that Pecos River users abide by the important terms of state law as he saw it. Reynolds set out in the 1960s to make sure that well owners in the middle Pecos Valley limited their beneficial use of water to the minimum necessary, not because the compact required it but because New Mexico law did.

By then farmers, especially in the water-rich Roswell area, had gotten used to irrigating from their wells in their own way. No court had ever formally determined the extent of their rights. Their wells had never been metered so they were in the habit of pumping as they pleased. In some parts of Roswell artesian pressure was so still so good that if well owners left their wells open, water would just run out all winter, when irrigation dropped off and well levels rose. In other areas farmers had increased the acreage that they farmed over the years as they felt like it. All these signs that groundwater development was running in Roswell by its own possibly wasteful lights offended Reynolds's understanding that beneficial use of water was the limit of a water right in New Mexico and that he, as state engineer, was in charge of what that limit was.[49]

So in the late 1950s and 1960s he sent his carpet-bag Santa Fe lawyers down into Chaves County, where Morgan Nelson welcomed them and many others didn't, to adjudicate groundwater rights in the middle Pecos River basin. In a couple of massive lawsuits that still aren't finished, Reynolds set out to define groundwater rights and limit their use. One by one Roswell farmers were hauled into court and required to prove how much land they had a right to irrigate and how much water they had a right to use for irrigation.[50]

The "conservation" results were spectacular from Reynolds's point of view. The courts found that ten thousand acres of land in the crucial Acme to Artesia middle reach of the basin were being illegally irrigated under New Mexico state law. The court ordered that those diversions stop. Some other Roswell wells were so carelessly operated that the court found that they had forfeited valid underlying rights for wasting water. For the rest of Roswell wells, Reynolds insisted, and the court agreed, that well owners install meters for the first time and report exactly how much water their wells had pumped.[51]

Roswell farmers and their New Mexico Farm Bureau association groused and groaned. The pointy-headed engineers from Santa Fe, they said, didn't know anything about irrigation and knew less about farming. Reynolds didn't care. When some of the farmers went on just as they had before, Reynolds sent his lawyers into Chaves County, seeking to hold farmers in criminal contempt for failing to abide by the limits of their decrees. People, especially from Carlsbad, had always called Roswell groundwater farmers "water bandits." Now Reynolds and the courts were treating them like thieves.

The Roswell contempt proceedings produced some classic New Mexico confrontations. When big-time Albuquerque criminal lawyer Billy Marchiondo came to Roswell to defend his in-laws, the Moutreys, against criminal charges that they had taken more water than their decree allowed, he ran into Reynolds's chief lawyer, Paul Bloom. In the hearings, Marchiondo insisted on calling Bloom "Mr. Blum." In frustration, Bloom started addressing Marchiondo as "Mr. Macaroon." Designated District Judge Joe Angel, a veteran of many northern New Mexican legal battles, finally got matters under control. He upheld the state engineer's authority, and groundwater use in Roswell went down.[52]

How much was unclear, but it was a lot. Removing 10,000 acres from irrigation in the 1960s saved at least 30,000 acre-feet a year. Tightening up controls on valid wells probably saved another 20,000 acre-feet a year. Cast in its most favorable light, Reynolds's success meant that New Mexicans were taking 50,000 acre-feet a year less from the Roswell Basin than they had been in 1947. If Royce Tipton and the designers of the Pecos River Compact had been right about the connection of groundwater and surface water in the middle reach of the river, then Reynolds's reduction had to mean that more water reached the river. (Whether that additional water reached the New Mexico-Texas state line was another matter altogether.) Reynolds's enforcement of New Mexico's own law might incidentally have made it easier for New Mexico to meet its interstate Pecos River compact obligations, whatever they were.[53]

Priority enforcement, that other great factor in New Mexico water law, was also supposed to have made it easier for New Mexico to comply with the compact. Everyone suspected that the Carlsbad Irrigation District had the oldest rights on the river and that its priority should have guaranteed it a 100-percent supply. If Carlsbad got all of its supply, then Texas stood a much better chance of getting its share in the form of return flows from the CID's relatively inefficient surface water system. If, however, Carlsbad didn't get 100 percent of its supply, then no amount of curtailment of upstream uses would benefit Texas much; the CID would grab the added water first.[54]

Leave It to Steve

The Pecos River Compact in Article IX had guaranteed that if man's activities in New Mexico produced shortages in Texas, then New Mexico would use priority enforcement to make it up. In the twenty years between 1956 and 1976 State Engineer Steve Reynolds did everything in his power to make sure that that didn't happen. It wasn't easy because year after year there wasn't enough water stored at the shrinking McMillan Dam or diverted at Avalon to satisfy the demand of irrigated acres within the Carlsbad Irrigation District. But Reynolds and his chief lieutenants worked hard with the officials of the Carlsbad Irrigation District, including Francis Tracy, Jr., to convince them not to enforce the senior rights on the river that the district held.[55]

Reynolds told the district time and again that enforcing the district's senior priority wouldn't work, either physically or legally. Physically, priority enforcement wouldn't work, according to Reynolds, because shutting down the junior Roswell wells wouldn't produce any more water at Carlsbad for a very long time. And legally, according to Reynolds, priority enforcement wouldn't work because first he would have to ask the courts to readjudicate all the surface and groundwater rights in the whole Pecos River Basin and that too would take a very long time. Reynolds turned out to be wrong on the legal grounds. Correct as he was as a matter of hydrologic time, calling priorities would have worked to bring diversions and stream flow into a more realistic balance, eventually. But Reynolds had a much quicker solution than priority enforcement to the chronic problem of Carlsbad shortages.[56]

Instead of shutting down upstream wells in Roswell in order to satisfy the Carlsbad Irrigation District's senior surface water rights, suggested Reynolds, the CID and its members ought to drill wells of their own. These wells would produce additional wet water for CID lands much more quickly and much more reliably than priority enforcement could. The New Mexico Supreme Court had approved in a Roswell case the use of what it called a "supplemental well," that is, a well used to make up in groundwater for what a stream wouldn't yield to a surface water right holder. CID farmers would drill supplemental wells on their lands and make up in well water for what the Pecos River wouldn't yield.[57]

So during the first fifteen years of Reynolds's tenure as state engineer up until 1972, but especially during the early years, CID farmers filed into the state engineer's office district in Roswell and, showing nothing more than a CID certificate indicating that they owned irrigated land within the district, received permits to drill wells. Within a few years, more than half of the twenty-five thousand irrigable acres within the Carlsbad Irrigation District were being served by wells that "supplemented" the ancient but insufficient surface water rights on which the district had been founded in the 1890s.[58]

In a subsequent memorandum to the state legislature, Reynolds termed the supplemental wells "a reasonable alternative to priority enforcement on the Pecos River." Within the CID a curious network of combined surface and groundwater practices evolved. In one year one farmer would combine his surface water right with another farmer's to get enough surface water for his lands while the other farmer would combine his supplemental well with the first farmer's and take all his water from the ground. The next year the two would switch. So long as the CID water levels remained high and pumping costs low, use of the supplemental wells was an easy and efficient way to keep the CID lands at 100 percent supply without reducing the Roswell wells at all. Everyone seemed to win.[59]

Except, as Reynolds himself had demonstrated on the Rio Grande, the Pecos River itself. The supplemental wells made up for what the river didn't produce, true enough, but they did it by doubling the groundwater impact on surface flows, further reducing the water in the river. (To make matters worse, the CID wells captured water that was otherwise bound for the state line as return flows, diverted by CID but unused.) On the Rio Grande, Reynolds had slowed down groundwater development "to keep the river whole," as the lawyers and hydrologists were fond of saying. On the Pecos, Reynolds speeded up groundwater development in order to keep surface water users fully supplied for as long as possible. If the Rio Grande policy kept the Rio Grande whole, the Pecos policy had to further dismantle a river already subject to the prior claims of the Carlsbad Irrigation District under New Mexico state law and to the superior claims of Texas under interstate compact law.

The policy worked so long as the CID and Texas did not raise the fundamental issue and assert their basic rights. Through the 1950s and 1960s neither had. But in the 1970s, the loose understandings and administrative compromises and indifference that had held Carlsbad and Texas temporarily in check began to come unglued.

The appointment of West Texas lawyer R. B. Magowan as Texas commissioner to the Pecos River Commission in the 1970s started the trouble. Magowan was a colorful, outspoken advocate for lower Pecos River irrigators in Texas. He had gained fame prosecuting West Texas's own Billy Sol Estes and had made a lot of money investing in pot-boiler movies like "The Texas Chain Saw Massacre." Magowan was not inclined, to say the least, to follow the lead of Steve Reynolds on the commission as the previous Texas commissioners had. Magowan pointed out that year after year less and less water had crossed the New Mexico-Texas state

127

line. He balked at Reynolds's continued insistence that the commission come up with an accurate measure of the river performance before it tried to determine whether or not New Mexico had depleted the flow of the river below the 1947 condition. Finally, he went back to the original inflow/outflow curves as set out in Royce Tipton's initial 1949 manual for the start of Pecos River Compact administration.

When he did, Magowan discovered that in the twenty-five years of the compact New Mexico had chronically under-delivered Pecos River water to Texas. Using Plate 2 of Senate Document 109 was simple: you took the annual index inflows since 1947, used the curve to show how much outflow at the state line that inflow should have produced and then compared it to how much actually arrived. It took Texas more than fifteen years to get around to that computation. But when it did, it discovered that over the life of the compact, the original Tipton curves showed that New Mexico had under-delivered more than 1.4 million acre-feet to Texas.[60]

That was enough to start R. B. Magowan fuming at the Pecos River Commission meetings. While Steve Reynolds muttered about refining the description of the river, Magowan insisted more and more stridently that New Mexico meet its initial obligation, right or wrong. Finally, at the 1974 Annual Meeting of the Pecos River Commission Magowan rose, rejected all the work the commission had previously done and demanded that New Mexico deliver to Texas the 1.4 million acre-feet that it owed. If New Mexico did not, said Magowan, Texas would sue. "Fine," said Steve Reynolds. "Let the interstate battle begin."[61]

In the meantime, as relations between Reynolds and Magowan and New Mexico and Texas deteriorated, the Carlsbad Irrigation District fell out of line. The rising power costs started real trouble in the 1960s and '70s at Carlsbad. Increasingly expensive electricity powered the CID supplemental wells. As the groundwater became more expensive, surface water started to look better and better to CID irrigators, who began to talk more and more of their prior right to Pecos River surface water. State Engineer Reynolds and Carl Slingerland found it increasingly difficult to convince the CID board to forego its legal right to surface water in favor of water from supplemental wells.[62]

In early 1976 the matter came to a head. Retiring CID manager Francis Tracy, Jr., instructed the district's attorney, Jay Forbes, to draft a short letter to Reynolds demanding what everyone had feared for twenty-five years. The state engineer should do what the state constitution and law required: enforce Pecos River priorities and shut down junior well appropriators in Roswell so senior surface appropriators in Carlsbad would get 100 percent of their supply from the river.[63]

The separate Texas and Carlsbad moves threatened the heart of Steve Reynolds's water regime. R. B. Magowan's suit meant that Reynolds could no longer put the Texans off while New Mexico worked out its own internal Pecos River problems. Carlsbad's priority call threatened Reynolds with a loss of administrative control over the river to the courts. Even worse, judicial enforcement of senior surface water priorities at Carlsbad against junior groundwater in Roswell threatened to end Reynolds's decades-old reliance on groundwater to make up for over-appropriated surface water supplies. On both the Texas and Carlsbad scores, Reynolds was in trouble.

He responded, as always, by working harder. By the mid-1970s Steve Reynolds focused more and more of his prodigious energy on Pecos River problems. By the mid-1970s Reynolds was spending 80 percent of his time on the Texas-New Mexico struggle over the river and that was 80 percent of a lot of time.[64]

At the outset, Reynolds was playing on a field that he liked: the courts. And he was playing according to a strategy that suited him: his own. But where once he had counted on the delayed effect of groundwater on interconnected surface water to buy him time, he now could only count on his ability to delay and confuse lawsuits. In the end, the strategy turned on him, and the court turned out to be less friendly to his positions than he expected. Increasingly isolated as the litigation progressed, Reynolds watched the water world that he had so carefully constructed come crashing down around him.

I went to work for Steve Reynolds in 1977 when the edifice of his water rights structure looked most impressive but its foundation already had begun to crumble. Almost ten years around northern New Mexico as an editor, journalist, and fly-by-night lawyer concentrating on endless local squabbles over land and water had brought me to the job.[65]

In 1970 I had written a rabble-rousing attack on federal and state plans to build the Cochiti Dam and Reservoir near one of New Mexico's ancient Pueblos. The article won me first a written rebuke from State Engineer Reynolds and then an audience with him. In both, he courteously buried me in details contradicting the position that my article developed. The article and the audience began a love/hate relationship between the two of us that went on for twenty years. In 1973 I sued him on behalf of some woebegone Hispanic farmers, complaining about the shenanigans of resort developers. In 1977 I was suing developers on Reynolds's behalf. By then I had eased sideways into the world of *Texas v. New Mexico* and neither my world nor Reynolds's would ever be the same.[66]

SIX

Jean Breitenstein Tackles
the 1947 Condition

───────August 30, 1978. Denver, Colorado. Late afternoon. A cavernous, almost empty courtroom on the fourth floor of the Federal Court building, one of the homes of the Tenth Circuit Court of Appeals. The room sweltered, caught between late summer monsoons outside and weak air conditioning inside. Even the deceased judges peering down from the portraits hung around the room looked hot.

The Honorable Jean Salas Breitenstein, a seventy-eight-year-old Senior Judge on the Tenth Circuit and since November 1975, the U.S. Supreme Court's special master in what the lawyers call *"No. 65 Original–Texas v. New Mexico,"* looked up from the dais where he sat. The lawsuit had been moving forward by fits and starts since 1974 and Breitenstein was tired.

"Gentlemen," Breitenstein said to the assembled group, "it is quarter after four and it's pretty hot in here. I think that you are going to hold the Master's attention better if you go over to tomorrow morning. Is there any reason why this can't go over until tomorrow morning?" No one objected.[1]

So Judge Breitenstein postponed until the following morning a presentation that I had been scheduled to make that afternoon. It was an overnight break in a lawsuit that was constantly interrupted by weeks of waiting, months of wild-goose chases, years of jockeying for position in a legal world that kept changing.

Indeed, *Texas v. New Mexico* "went over" so many times that it lasted from 1974 to 1988 and isn't really over yet. The suit yielded a numbing ten thousand pages of recorded testimony, religiously (and expensively)

Fig. 6.1.
The Honorable Jean Salas Breitenstein, senior Circuit Judge of the United States Court of Appeals for the Tenth Circuit, intended to finish his career where he had begun, in an interstate battle over water between two states. In the 1930s, as a young water lawyer, he had represented Colorado in a bitter dispute with New Mexico over the La Plata River Compact. In the 1980s, as a semi-retired judge, he heard the dispute between Texas and New Mexico over the Pecos River. (Photo courtesy of Peter Breitenstein.)

produced each night as if the fate of the lawsuit hung daily on a single line of testimony. The suit produced hundreds of highly technical reports and exhibits requiring thousands of man-hours to assemble. New Mexico and Texas lawyers in the suit came and went, those coming missing any glimmer of understanding that their predecessors had gleaned, those leaving often taking with them the disturbing sense that they weren't quite sure what they had been working on. The suit survived three special masters, two of whom died while the suit was still pending. Judge Breitenstein's weariness on the eve of my first—and only— actual appearance in the suit was just a moment in fifteen years of exhausting, inconclusive litigation.[2]

In the end, *Texas v. New Mexico* was profoundly boring. The suit bored the human community it affected with its endless, esoteric, incomprehensible legal and engineering jargon. It bored Pecos River communities from Pecos, New Mexico to Pecos, Texas. In a different sense it bored New

Mexico's vaunted water law, leaving it so full of holes that no one was quite sure what was left when the suit was done. Just as the Carlsbad dams had failed at the very start of the century, at the end of the twentieth century the structures of the state's water law were so weakened that everything threatened to come tumbling down.

There is some irony in the setting and the medium. A complex, beautiful 450-mile-long desert river was brought inside a large, windowless room and filtered through the lenses of engineering and law. Its fate was consigned to a few lawyers, judges, and expert witnesses whose presence was barely noticeable in the large room where they worked. Genuinely public decisions affecting a river and the human communities built on it were shaped by a small group of lawyers and engineers speaking esoteric languages of their own, barely able to communicate with each other, let alone speak in one public voice.

So, waiting on the night of August 30, 1978, the prospect of *Texas v. New Mexico* struck me as profoundly boring.

State Engineer Reynolds had hired me in 1976 because he needed someone with my esoteric interest in Spanish and Mexican water law, an area becoming important in several massive water adjudication suits that were pending at the time. My enthusiasm for arcane sources from ancient pre-1848 Spanish and Mexican archives spilled over to the equally arcane engineering archives of the Pecos River Commission.[3]

On May 2, 1978, at Special Master Breitenstein's direction, Texas and New Mexico agreed to present alternative legal histories of the Pecos River Commission's efforts to administer the Pecos River Compact between 1949 and 1974. At this point Breitenstein wanted to know what glosses the two states had added to the compact and which administrative interpretations might help him now. "We have agreed," Texas lawyer Doug Caroom intoned, "to do this with a minimal amount of argument and each of us will be as objective as we can." Reynolds and his chief Pecos River assistant Slingerland assigned the New Mexico job to me.[4]

Slingerland brought the minutes of the Pecos River Commission to me in battered cardboard boxes at the end of May 1978. For the next three months I pored over the badly organized, lengthy, frustratingly elliptical and incomplete documents. I tried to organize them by date, from 1950 to 1974. I also tried to separate the minutes by working group: the commission itself, its Engineering Advisory Committee ("EAC"), and the EAC's working subcommittee. For documents that were so important to *Texas v. New Mexico*, the records of the Pecos River Commission were certainly a mess. By mid-July my tiny office, a remodeled bathroom in Santa Fe's Bataan Memorial Building, looked like a scholarly battlefield with piles of documents scattered here and there. As I piled, I read and took notes.

My reading sent me more and more frequently to see Slingerland and Reynolds. Only they could explain the gaps and fill in the holes. I had no background in surface water hydrology or engineering. Special Master Breitenstein was, as he himself admitted, "awfully poor in mathematics," and so was I. I had neither the breadth of historical knowledge nor the depth of technical understanding to make real sense of the archives.[5]

Slingerland and Reynolds were always generous with their time. They went over my text, word by word, line by line, commission meeting by commission meeting. They made changes, "for the sake of accuracy," they said. In the end what I wrote hardly mentioned Reynolds's hard-line paralysis of the Pecos River Commission in the late 1950s. Instead it emphasized the Reynolds-inspired *Review of Basic Data* of the early 1960s. Of course, I went along. Neither ever told me explicitly what to say, but they didn't have to. I was dependent on them for any order that I could impose on the bizarre documents out of which I was supposed to construct the narrative that became on the August 1, 1978 deadline, *New Mexico's 4(b) Statement: Pecos River Commission Administrative History.*[6]

My *Statement* had the look of most of the formal legal documents—the hundreds of briefs, the more than fifty orders, the more than ten special master's reports, the five Supreme Court decisions—making up what lawyers call "the record proper" in *Texas v. New Mexico.* My history was an odd size—6 × 9"—cut to the specifications of the U.S. Supreme Court. It contained ten thousand words in thirty single-spaced, printed pages. It was full of arduous sentences like, "(s)ome expressed concern that the element of base inflow—an important one in calculating resulting outflow—had inflated unnaturally predictable outflows under the 1947 condition because the high precipitation had recharged an already partially depleted aquifer." As with the document as a whole, I didn't really understand what I had said or why I had said it.[7]

When Reynolds got the final, printed text of my *Administrative History,* he wrote "Summary Judgment, New Mexico!" on it and returned it to me. It was partly his engineer's way of complimenting legal work. In the borrowed language of esoteric civil procedure, Reynolds was saying that the *History* was good enough on its own to win the case right then for New Mexico. Insecure about what I had done and about my relationship to a man whose respect I very much wanted, I was pleased by his reaction.

Reynolds's cryptic note reflected the lawyer half of his "enginawyer" identity. He had many legal defenses against the Texas claim. One of the first line of defenses was administrative and procedural. When all was said and done (and it would take a long time to say and do everything that this interminable suit would require), my *History* proved that the Pecos River Commission already had apportioned the Pecos River between Texas and New Mexico and so Breitenstein's court could not. If this Reynolds plot succeeded, as he believed it should, the special master would never hold a trial and would never reach the question of what the original compact had meant.

I suppose that I should have seen that my *History* was just a pawn in Reynolds's multi-faceted strategy when I looked at the Texas version of the commission history. It was not printed as New Mexico's was. It was fifteen hundred words long, about one twentieth as long as mine. It lacked the narrative detail and analytic structure of New Mexico's administrative account. At the time I thought that the difference between the two histories reflected the fact that we New Mexicans worked harder and knew more than our Texas counterparts. It wasn't until much later that I realized that the difference between the two histories turned on different legal strategies. Reynolds and New Mexico emphasized the history because they thought that the apportionment of the Pecos River had already been done and there was nothing that a court could do about it. Texas glossed over the history because it thought that the compact itself had apportioned the river and there was nothing that a commission, no matter what it had done, could do about it.[8]

I didn't see much of this as I waited for the long night of August 30 to pass. I would find out how much more clearly Special Master Breitenstein saw when court opened on August 31. Then he'd start asking me questions, and I'd hear what was on his mind. Breitenstein had had the case for four years by then and his frustration with lack of progress was starting to show.

The causes for delay were the usual suspects in any legal proceeding. From the start, both states struggled to position themselves advantageously before Breitenstein. While they maneuvered, they snapped and bit at each other like angry dogs.

From the beginning, Breitenstein lamented the inability of Texas and New Mexico to get along when it came to the Pecos River Compact. Litigious Steve Reynolds and suspicious, defensive, aggressive R. B. Magowan didn't help. Breitenstein's long history in interstate water disputes had taught him, as he himself said, "that in inter-state controversy the principles of the Golden Rule are entirely forgotten. And I think that they have been forgotten in this case." Early on, perceiving the animosity between Texas and New Mexico, Special Master Breitenstein stopped a New Mexico lawyer in mid-thought and asked, "How can the court make these two states cooperate? This suit is just like a divorce action in the divorce court." Of course the stakes were higher, involving as they did a whole river and the communities based on it. But, as in a marriage gone bad, the parties to the Pecos River Compact had lost, if they ever had them, the subtly interwoven considerations of a common enterprise that made a shared life possible. And the Pecos River Compact, with its broadly charged, ambiguously constrained commission, demanded that shared life. Divorce was not a possibility for two states forever bound by a common border, a shared river and a binding compact and now, alas, a lawsuit.[9]

Delay was one of the bitter fruits of all that animosity. However, delay in the lawsuit served New Mexico just fine, as it always had when it came to Texas and the Pecos River. After all, the compact guaranteed to downstream Texas its negotiated fair share of the river by limiting upstream New Mexico's uses of it. So long as compact enforcement was stalled, no limitations on New Mexico were imposed. Initially, Breitenstein tried to stay clear of the relative fault of the two states in the compact's long failure to do anything, writing that an "(e)xploration of fault for failure would be unproductive" and that "Texas does not, charge New Mexico with bad faith." Still the taint of New Mexico's upstream position never disappeared. It resurfaced ten years later in a much harsher light when a second special master momentarily held that Reynolds intentionally had strung Texas along for years and years.[10]

Texas's delay was due simply to lack of interest in Pecos River affairs. Officials in Austin could easily ignore the water problems of the marginal western hinterlands. They didn't know much about the Pecos River and weren't inclined to invest the resources to find out. When Pecos River Commissioner R. B. Magowan finally drove the Texas attorney general to file the suit in 1974, the original Texas complaint simply adopted the Senate Document 109 curves as the measure of New Mexico's failed compact obligation. Two years later, prompted by Special Master Breitenstein's request for more specific information, Texas finally started to investigate what New Mexico had been up to on the Pecos River since 1948.[11]

In the summer of 1976 the Texans dispatched a young law student to Santa Fe, where he spent a summer in the state engineer's water rights files. The New Mexicans there had treated the law student courteously enough, but they hadn't helped him any more than they had to. They politely showed him into the cavernous room of row after row of dull green metal filing cabinets in the State Engineer Water Rights Division and left him there, all alone. The seventy years of records, organized water right by water right and according to an arcane filing system, were not easy to access. The state engineer employees were not about to offer a Texan working on *Texas v. New Mexico* the Rosetta Stone that their years of experience had given them. Still the law student emerged from the isolated, mysterious summer in the heart of the enemy camp in Santa Fe with enough information at least to make Texas's complaint more concrete. Now, in a 1977 amended complaint, Texas detailed just how New Mexico had depleted the flow of the Pecos River by man's activities below the "1947 condition."[12]

The catalogue of increased depletions since 1947 included all kinds of post-1947 wells, authorized under New Mexico state law: supplemental wells allowed in the Pecos River basin when surface supplies proved short, domestic wells automatically allowed to homeowners, and extra-basin wells, unregulated by the State Engineer. These post-1947 wells, the Texas Amended Complaint now claimed, had indirectly caused what the compact explicitly prohibited: increased post-1947 depletions of the Pecos River flow in New Mexico.[13]

From the looks of that 1977 Amended Complaint, what had started as an esoteric but not unusual interstate compact suit was headed toward becoming the first major interstate case anywhere in the United States on the legal relationship between groundwater and surface water. Within its borders, New Mexico and State Engineer Reynolds had led the way in conjunctive management of the two interconnected water sources. Within its borders, Texas clung much longer legally to the geological myth that groundwater and surface water sources resided in different worlds and appropriately belonged to entirely separate legal regimes. Some claimed that New Mexico State Engineer Steve Reynolds had said that he would be damned if he would saddle New Mexican Pecos River well users with a progressive idea that Texas herself had refused to recognize: conjunctive management of interrelated ground (wells) and surface (river) sources of water. But Texas's 1977 Amended Complaint did just that when it asked Special Master Breitenstein to rule that New Mexico wells had depleted the flow of the Pecos River in violation of the compact.[14]

There the issue lay like a land mine, looking for any opportunity to explode, including my cameo appearance as a historian a year and a half later. In the meantime, everyone set out to first determine what the compact meant by the base-line "1947 condition" against which departures could be judged. In blistering decisions in May and June, 1977 Special Master Breitenstein indirectly indicated that he would reject the legal positions of both states. The central "1947 condition" was neither the original 1948 one which Texas had insisted on nor the subsequently adopted

1962 one which New Mexico clung to. Instead, suggested Breitenstein, the compact's "1947 condition" was the actual condition of the river in 1947. A full trial, he ruled, would now define what that condition had been, starting from scratch. For two weeks, in late February and early March 1978, the base-line fight over the Pecos River Compact finally began.[15]

Breitenstein and, finally, attorneys for the two cantankerous states, had agreed that this initial stage would determine what the base-line compact "1947 condition" was in fact. What that determination involved became slowly apparent as seven witnesses—four for Texas and three for New Mexico—produced exhibits on and explained their version of the "1947 condition." Texas witnesses Bell, Whittenton, Chang, and Murthy explained in detail how the original "1947 condition" had been assembled "reasonably" and how some of the changes in that definition made in 1961–1962 had not been "reasonable." New Mexico witnesses Erickson, Reynolds, and Slingerland countered by showing that the original definition was considered temporary, was in fact in many instances flatout wrong, and was, in any case, improved by the 1961–1962 revision.[16]

The two weeks of slow-moving technical testimony introduced Special Master Breitenstein to the immense problems he created in *Texas v. New Mexico* when he ruled that the critical "1947 condition" base line standard was still an open factual question. For one, he encountered the Texas witnesses, some of whom were foreign trained and whose English, let alone highly technical explanations, he found hard to understand. Breitenstein had to chide these Texas witnesses continuously, to speak up, to slow down, to enunciate more clearly. Aware that their witnesses were hard to understand, the Texas lawyers flooded the record with accompanying technical reports designed to make up for what the Texas witnesses lacked in speaking skills. In addition, these Texas witnesses had come to the Pecos River problems only with the relatively young lawsuit, and their lack of experience showed. They were often tripped up on or stumped by details that the New Mexicans knew better. One of these early Texas witnesses, Dr. V. R. Krishna Murthy, exemplified all the problems that Special Master Breitenstein faced. He would play a critical role in *Texas v. New Mexico* eight years later, long after Breitenstein was gone.[17]

Here, at his first appearance, Murthy began by laying out his impressive civil engineering training as an undergraduate in India and then as a Ph.D. candidate at the University of Pennsylvania. Under questioning from Texas lead attorney, Doug Caroom, Murthy launched into a criticism of the 1961–1962 Review of Basic Data's revision of the base-line "1947 condition." His conclusion that several aspects of that revision

Breitenstein Tackles the 1947 Condition

were "unreasonable" was easy enough to understand, but his reasons confounded everyone in the room except the other engineers.

At one point Special Master Breitenstein asked witness Murthy for a definition of the term "linear relationship" used in one of Murthy's criticisms. Murthy went on for four transcript pages in soft-spoken, idiosyncratic English until the special master interrupted again.

"By 'linear' you mean 'straight line'?" asked the special master.

"Yes, 'linear' means 'straight line,'" answered Murthy.

"Okay," retorted Breitenstein in exasperation, "I can understand 'straight line.'"[18]

Between the judge and the witness, things went from bad to worse. For example, one factor in any version of the Tipton-inspired "1947 condition" had to be estimated leakage from existing dams under the "1947 condition." In showing how to do the estimation correctly, Murthy had gone to a courtroom blackboard that not everyone could see and had drawn a graph that no one could understand. The illustration produced the following exchange between Texas lawyer Caroom, witness Murthy, and Special Master Breitenstein:

Caroom: Dr. Murthy, let me ask you another question. This equation which you put up on the board and which you have just described, is that applicable to describing a stage-leakage relationship in a reservoir?

Murthy: Your Honor, this is a very general hydraulic equation, and then for various situations we modify the equations by multiplying by some coefficient. But these coefficients have constant values, they do not alter the general shape of the curve. So, depending on the nature of the flow phenomena that is occurring we compute or estimate the coefficient.

Caroom: All right, Dr. Murthy, let me ask one final question, then. Is it possible for this equation which you have described and which you have said is more or less applicable to this situation, is it possible for that equation to produce a straight-line?

Murthy: No, Your Honor, this is a parabolic equation, we call it, a non-linear, and it cannot be a straight line because of the velocity and the head and the discharge is the velocity times the area. So the discharge and the head relationship also cannot be a straight line.

Breitenstein: Mr. Caroom, I think I am in a parabola. We will take the afternoon recess.[19]

Accustomed as all water lawyers were to the peculiar technical tilt of water hearings, where audiences didn't gasp at surprising testimony so much as reach for their calculators to check statistical testimony, this kind of exchange in *Texas v. New Mexico* stretched to the breaking point the relationship between law and engineering. As the 1978 hearings dragged on, it became more and more clear that the compact was based not so much on the river as the engineering construct of it and that the law couldn't do much to clarify the construct. And now Breitenstein had said that his court would have to reinvent that construct.[20]

In the nine-year course of the proceedings over which he presided, Breitenstein heard only engineers testify and lawyers argue, mostly past each other. No irrigators, no biologists, no ecologists appeared. After the initial inspection trip up and down the Pecos River in 1976, all the proceedings took place indoors, in a huge, empty courtroom in Denver, Colorado. There weren't even any aerial photographs. There were only lawyers and their questions, engineers and their calculations, fighting over a river that had never existed.[21]

"The engineers—God bless them, I love them, I have represented them," Special Master Breitenstein joked early on in the proceedings as the parade of engineer witnesses began. "But by means of assumptions, by the formulas that they use, they can take the same basic data and come out one to the North Pole and one to the South. That's the sort of thing I want to avoid in this case." As the parade of expert engineer witnesses grew longer, Breitenstein enumerated three problems he had with the technical evidence. It involved mathematical and statistical techniques he wasn't prepared to deal with. The evidence was so opaque that he couldn't make anything of it. And when he looked at the opaque statistical conclusions through his lawyer's lenses, he only saw contradictory "1947 condition" descriptions based on the kind of triple hearsay that lawyers regarded as completely unreliable. So the Breitenstein jests about engineers continued for a little while and then turned into snarls.[22]

He accused engineers for both New Mexico and Texas of "just playing with numbers" and of "sophistry." He assessed one of the infrequent engineering agreements between the two states as "a mass of words and figures which challenge ingenuity but destroy clarity." Finally, when a Texas hydrologist began talking about "negative discharges," an oxymoron if there ever was one, Breitenstein turned to irony. "Well," he broke in, "I think I am attaining one of my life-long desires. All my life I have wanted to live in a world of theory and had to live in one of practicality. I now find I am living in a world of pure theory."[23]

Breitenstein Tackles the 1947 Condition

Try as they might, the lawyers in *Texas v. New Mexico* could never bring the engineers back to the special master's earth. Often it was because the lawyers didn't know what questions to ask or what to make of the responses. One Texas lawyer conceded that he was "totally confused." Another admitted that the testimony of one of his own witnesses was "all above my head." New Mexico's early lead lawyer confessed that he "was not sure" he was "engineer enough to understand it [an engineer's testimony]" to which Special Master Breitenstein responded, "I know I am not."[24]

Some of this was just lawyer posturing, trying to make a sympathetic ally of a confused judge. In the hallways the engineers came and went, whispering about the Master's "senility." (At least once, the Master overheard them as he entered an elevator New Mexicans were leaving.) On a couple of occasions, Texas's chief lawyer tried gallantly and successfully to take Special Master Breitenstein through some of the complex attempts to describe how the river operated in 1947. Breitenstein graciously acknowledged the help. But ultimately, a suit that should have brought together law and engineering only sent them farther apart. In the end, there was no clear law to apply and no comprehensible engineering to adopt.[25]

The March 1978 proceedings did yield one engineer who spoke clearly: New Mexico State Engineer Steve Reynolds. Of all the engineering witnesses, Reynolds had had the most experience on both sides of the bench. As a water rights judge, he had won a great reputation as a fair, firm decision-maker in the contentious water contests over which he often presided. For years he also had testified as a witness in all kinds of proceedings and had a wonderful gift for the give and take of courtroom testimony. He was articulate and precise. He knew just how much information to give and just how to phrase his answers. Of course, on direct examination, he was responding to questions asked of him by his own lawyer. As in any high-stakes litigation, like *Texas v. New Mexico*, both the questions and the answers had been rehearsed over and over again. But when it came time for the Texans to cross examine him, the process took on a more spontaneous cast and witness Reynolds emerged as a star courtroom performer.[26]

Reynolds always responded politely to Texas questions asked of him, no matter how silly he considered them. When he could, he refreshingly began his answers with a simple "yes" or "no" and without the usual equivocation. To those questions that required a more elaborate response, to make the answer clearly consistent with his underlying position, he answered more fully. To those questions he didn't understand or didn't like, he simply rephrased the question and answered himself. The Texas

140

attorneys had been told that it was impossible to get anything out of Reynolds as a witness that he didn't want to say, and his first appearance in *Texas v. New Mexico* certainly justified that reputation.[27]

But even if there was no way to trip Reynolds up, his beautifully orchestrated performance still startled Special Master Breitenstein. As what Reynolds said about the "1947 condition" sunk in, it became clear that his version of the bargain that Texas and New Mexico had struck was so one-sided that it left no room for the kind of compromise that Breitenstein had been looking for ever since he flew the river with the parties, a compromise that would give Texas some relief without ruining New Mexico. Here, in March 1978, Reynolds said for the first, but not last, time that in New Mexico's view, the "1947 condition" included all the New Mexico uses established in 1947 or earlier. "It is certainly our view," testified Reynolds, "that New Mexico is entitled to continue uses that were—groundwater uses that were established in 1947 or earlier, even though the continuation of those uses might cause the rate of artesian inflow to the river to fall below what it was in 1947."[28]

This blunt statement made identical "use" and "depletions" so that the compact's prohibition against further New Mexico depletions only meant that New Mexico could establish no *new* post-1947 water rights. Existing rights as of 1947 could, under the compact, further deplete the river after 1947. This highly partisan view of the "1947 condition" would have given compact protection to the extensive new wells developed in the North Roswell artesian basin during 1947. It would have protected those supplemental wells drilled in both Carlsbad and Roswell in the 1950s and 1960s. (Under New Mexico law, those new wells were only a part of much older pre-1947 rights, usually ancient surface water rights for which there was no surface water left after more recent, but still pre-1947 wells, had dried the river up.) It would have protected those wells still being drilled on the margins of the state engineer's declared Pecos River basins even as Reynolds testified. In short, Reynolds would have awarded to New Mexico every benefit that groundwater development could offer even if it thereby affected the Pecos River New Mexico shared with Texas.[29]

The Texans, who had just discovered New Mexico's wells, slowly caught on to the most obvious implications of Reynolds' position. "Mr. Reynolds," cross-examined Texas lawyer Frank Booth,

under your view of the Compact and the way that it is approached in the administration of your position, does it follow that if the supply of all uses existing in 1947 require all the flow of the Pecos River in New Mexico, that still would not be a "depletion by man's activities" insofar as the Compact is concerned or Texas is concerned or Texas is concerned.

Reynolds: Under that hypothesis, yes.

Booth: Is it possible, as you have testified here today, that Texas was apportioned nothing under this Compact?

Reynolds: Under a hypothetical question, I suppose that's possible.[30]

To an engineer of Reynolds's precision, the answers were correct and beside the point. The compact didn't guarantee Texas any water. It only limited New Mexico uses. But the Reynolds response directly contradicted what Royce Tipton had told the compact negotiators in 1947: that an apportionment based on a fixed number of New Mexico acres, or, in this case, "guaranteed uses," which was the same thing, wouldn't work because in years of low supply New Mexico would get all the water. Reynolds either had lost the history or arrogantly disregarded it for the moment. And Frank Booth, like a good trial lawyer, had stumbled unwittingly on a central point. If Booth didn't catch the implications of what State Engineer Reynolds had just said, Breitenstein surely did. If the special master accepted what became known as "New Mexico's 'use' theory," it would be very difficult to find a principled basis for providing Texas with any relief.

Still witness Reynolds stuck to the view that the "1947 condition" included all New Mexico water rights lawfully established by December 31, 1947. As the special master realized the full extent of that New Mexico claim and the devastating impact it would have on downstream Texas's claim to water, he grew increasingly skeptical of everything that New Mexico said about the "1947 condition" compact term.

As a result, Breitenstein found himself losing any hold on the compact he was supposed to construe. The engineering evidence wasn't teaching him anything about the "1947 condition." The lawyers were too confused to help. That "enginawyer of enginawyers" State Engineer Steve Reynolds, who had built a career on the common ground between the two disciplines, had developed a hide-bound definition of the critical term that was useless. After four years, after more than ten briefs, after more than sixteen days of exhausting testimony, Breitenstein was actually worse off than he had been at the start. He'd have to go back to the beginning.

Breitenstein already had scheduled a final hearing for late August to conclude, he then believed, the phase of the lawsuit concerned with the first-step legal definition of the base-line "1947 condition." My *Administrative History* had been a small part of that final first step. Now he seized the opportunity afforded by the long-scheduled final hearing to add two new elements in a desperate, contradictory effort to rescue *Texas v. New Mexico* from the morass of numbers into which it was falling.

First, Special Master Breitenstein hired an independent engineering expert of his own to advise him. Picked from lists submitted by each state and paid for by them both, Raymond Hogan, Breitenstein's own engineer-advisor, became a key player in critical technical issues for the special master. In effect Breitenstein's solution consigned the centerpiece of the 1948 Compact—the mathematical description of the way nature actually operates—to technicians, meeting privately and speaking to themselves in a language that the public could not understand.[31]

In addition, at the end of this crucial trial segment, Breitenstein threw in a new concern that sent the whole proceeding on a new track. After the states had submitted lengthy briefs on the evidence offered in March and the Administrative History on which I had struggled for so long, Breitenstein himself sent out an unusual letter, saying that at the final August 30 hearing he wanted each state to address not only what the "1947 condition" was but "how the theory of his state can be used in the practical administration of the Compact. I realize that, in the present status of the case, the special master is expected to make his determination of the 1947 condition. No determination of that issue will be helpful if the position of neither state results in a workable method of administration."[32]

The "workability" issue had lurked behind the strategies of both states for some time. If the Court's compact rulings became too partisan, either state could argue that the compact was invalid because it had never worked. In that event either state could fall back on the more fundamental, although hardly more precise, underlying right of each state to an equitable portion of the Pecos River. Up to that point, Steve Reynolds preferred the compact alternative because he thought the compact offered New Mexico two distinct advantages: a 1961 favorable decision as to how much water New Mexico owed Texas for the 1950–1960 decade and, more importantly, a commission that he might not be able to control but that he could certainly stall. In a world where time was water, that meant a lot. For their part, the Texas representatives preferred the compact because the equitable apportionment alternative was even stranger terrain, if that was possible. But now the special master was bringing the issue forward on his own and adding it to the

Br[...]n T[...]les the 1947 Condition

already confusing brew of issues coming to a head at the August hearing at which I was scheduled to appear.[33]

August 31, 1978. Denver, Colorado. Cool, early morning.

After an awful night, I rose, took my place behind the podium and introduced myself to Special Master Breitenstein. "Nice to have you here," he replied warmly. I was prepared to talk about the meager law of interstate compact commissions. As far as I was concerned the cases all confirmed State Engineer Reynolds's first-line position that the Pecos River Commission had resolved the issues before the court and so there was nothing for Breitenstein to do. "This has been a case," I said , "that is really long on hydrology and short on the law."

"I completely agree with you on that," Special Master Breitenstein responded.[34]

From there I launched into what had become for lawyers in the case an obligatory analysis of Breitenstein's own *Hinderlider* case from the 1930s, this time using the case to prove the legal proposition that interstate commissions had the power to define what compacts meant. "Well, frankly," said Breitenstein, "I had *Hinderlider* in mind when I wrote this (August 18) letter." (When I again referred to the case later in the two-hour argument, Breitenstein snapped, "[y]ou don't need to argue that [case] to me. I wrote the Colorado brief.")[35]

"Yes," I thought here at the start, "now I've got him on the high, common legal ground where all lawyers like to stand."

"I am here this morning," I continued, "to try to specify to you four fairly basic issues that don't involve engineering methodology, that don't involve questions of the kind that would involve your choosing between scalping a hydrograph and using a water balance procedure. For example, the base inflow issue is one that can only be answered by the Compact which . . . suggested that the Compact Commissioners understood that New Mexico uses in 1947 were to be protected and so the increased depletions caused by 1947 uses were also protected."[36]

I hadn't been in court in March when Reynolds had said the same thing. I hadn't read the briefs that his other lawyers had submitted in August along with my *Administrative History* and I didn't know that the New Mexico briefs had repeated the same "use/depletion" refrain. I hardly knew what the words I just said meant. But now, when I inadvertently raised the "depletion versus use" compact issue again, Breitenstein pounced. "You are the first one that I have heard," he interrupted in the inimical style of legal oral argument, "that has made that distinction clearly. 'Use' isn't 'depletion,' at least in my book." Flustered, I didn't know what to say.[37]

Chapter 6

"That," I said in ambiguous reply to a central question, "is an issue that should be resolved."

Special Master Breitenstein would not accept my attempt to evade a question I didn't understand and an answer I couldn't give. "Is 'use' different from 'depletion'?" he asked again.

"I think they are," I replied, "and I think the compact can be read to protect the uses in New Mexico in 1947 specifically with respect to base inflow."[38]

My reply was precisely the kind of double talk Breitenstein had been trying to cut through for months. My answer's first part—that "use" wasn't "depletion"—contradicted the second part—that New Mexico uses were protected. Instead of straightening out the problem, I ducked again.

"I would like to say, " I now added, "that Mr. Tansey [yet another New Mexico lawyer] and I have divided up those issues that he would prefer to address, and one of them was base inflow. I am primarily concerned with the Review of Basic Data."[39]

In effect, I was telling the judge to ask another New Mexico lawyer, not me. "Go ahead," Breitenstein said, giving up, and I did. For the next forty-five minutes I rolled on uninterrupted, talking about the history of the administration of the Pecos River Compact. Breitenstein said nothing until I stopped. "Thank you, Mr. Hall," he perfunctorily said and that was that. When Tansey, the next New Mexico lawyer, came on that afternoon, the argument took yet another turn and never returned to the fundamental "depletion"/"use" question.

That night, in our suite in the elegant old Brown Palace Hotel, New Mexico's third and chief lawyer, Richard Simms, took me aside and told me I had done well. "You argued," he told me in that unconsciously egotistical way of many lawyers, "just as I would have argued." Carl Slingerland was more critical. "You did well," he remarked, "except for the 'depletion'/'use' stuff. We have to make them the same."

At the end of those late August 1978 hearings, Special Master Breitenstein tried to seize control. The Master decided that a new routing study would be needed to describe the base-line "1947 condition." In so doing he rejected both Texas's reliance on the original "1947 condition" routing study and New Mexico's reliance on the commission-adopted 1961–1962 alternative. He directed his own technical expert to determine the unmeasured values, the engineering techniques, and the judgment calls necessary to a new definition of the compact's base-line "1947 condition." The new Inflow-Outflow curve that the study produced, the third in compact history, would look very much like the 1961 curve that New Mexico lawyers preferred.[40]

But early in 1979 New Mexicans were dismayed to learn that despite their wins in specific technical battles it looked as if they might lose the all important war over the relative rights to the river described by the "1947 condition." Slowly over that spring and summer it became clear to them that Breitenstein intended to limit upstream New Mexico's rights to the river not to its 1947 uses but to its 1947 depletions.

Things began well enough for the New Mexicans in early February 1979 when Breitenstein issued a typewritten seventy-one-page draft of his decision on the "1947 condition." (In the rare world of special masters a "draft" was a proposed decision circulated so that the parties could comment on it before the Master made it final.) Broken up into sixteen subsections, each one angular, elliptical, and discrete, Breitenstein's draft was sometimes hard to follow. However, some parts were crystal clear. In it the special master proposed to adopt his engineer's rulings on the technical issues; chalk one up for New Mexico.[41]

He also rejected Texas's flat-out reliance on the original "1947 condition" studies. The "1947 condition" was not the condition described in the original compact studies on the basis of which Texas originally claimed to have been bilked by New Mexico out of 1.4 million acre-feet of water. Chalk up another for New Mexico. Instead, ruled Breitenstein,[42]

the 1947 condition is that situation in the Pecos River Basin which produced in New Mexico the man-made depletions resulting from the stage of development existing at the beginning of the year 1947 and from the augmented Fort Sumner and Carlsbad acreage.

Chalk up a third big victory for New Mexico, or so Reynolds and the New Mexicans preferred to think. After all, "the situation in the Pecos River Basin" in 1947 included all New Mexico uses existing at the time and the "stage of development" surely included the increasingly controversial Roswell wells drilled at any time in 1947. True, the special master's setting the compact date at the beginning, not the end of 1947, would cut off from compact protection the New Mexico wells drilled during 1947 to get in under the compact wire. Clearly Breitenstein had selected the earlier date simply to give water-pressed, down-stream Texas some marginal relief. But that was a discrete problem on which State Engineer Reynolds and Simms thought Breitenstein had clearly erred. On the big underlying issues, on the "1947 condition" and the New Mexican rights that it recognized, Breitenstein's definition of the "1947 condition" looked okay.

This reading, however, like a lot of other New Mexican gleanings from compact and lawsuit proceedings, conveniently overlooked equally compelling and contradictory parts of the Breitenstein draft report. In an early section entitled "Ground Water," Breitenstein weighed the arguments of the two states and concluded that New Mexico was entitled to deplete by wells the base flow of the river only to the extent that New Mexican wells were affecting the river at the beginning of 1947. In other words, New Mexico wells were protected but only to the extent that they didn't affect the river more than they affected the river in 1947. New Mexicans knew as surely as they knew anything that existing pre-1947 and post-1947 wells were bound by nature's laws to do exactly that: deplete the river after 1947 more than they had in 1947. Even Tipton had told them so.

Realizing the possibility that this might be what the special master meant, the New Mexicans used the opportunity Breitenstein offered to criticize his draft report to ask for clarification. In written objections and then in late April 1979 oral arguments, Richard Simms pushed Breitenstein to say that the "situation" he was talking about when he defined the "1947 condition" included all New Mexico wells drilled through 1947.

"Is New Mexico entitled," Simms asked in frustration, "to the depletion manifest on the river in 1947 as a result of groundwater pumping, or depletions that would result from that stage of development existing in 1947?"[43]

"As long as it [the pumping] doesn't increase the depletions below what they were at the time," replied Breitenstein, "you comply with the compact."

Simms, increasingly panicked, tried again. If the Master meant that the compact limited New Mexico to its river depletions in 1947, not its groundwater uses, then the Master's decision would "roll back history in New Mexico." "It is to say," Simms continued, that

> the New Mexico Legislature ratified a compact that wiped out the economy of . . . southeastern New Mexico . . . You are taking away from New Mexico what the Legislature never would have taken away. I find that utterly impossible to believe, if that is your decision.[44]

Simms's earlier victory was turning into a disaster. Now Simms resurrected the ghost of Royce Tipton to prove that Breitenstein's ambiguous ruling couldn't be. "Your Honor," he continued,

> Royce Tipton, who guided these negotiations, told the negotiators at the point in time when they were touching this issue, that the New Mexico

Legislature would never ratify such a Compact. In his mind, what was ultimately produced and agreed upon by the negotiators and later ratified by
the New Mexico legislature, was not what Your Honor is now saying it
is. I don't know what says it clearer in the record.[45]

Finally, Judge Breitenstein himself weighed in. "You may be right,"
he told Simms and the others assembled in the courtroom,

I have been wrong lots of times. All I can do is my best. But let me say one
thing, Mr. Simms, it is completely beyond my realm of comprehension as
to why New Mexico and Texas did not make some legislative history when
they had this Compact before the Legislatures for ratification. You didn't
do that . . . All I can do is the best that I can on the way that you've got it,
and your Compact is written that New Mexico shall not deplete.[46]

The text of the compact Breitenstein knew. After all, he had written
it thirty years before. The murky politics he was just discovering. On that
curious note, the April 1979 hearings closed.

In response to the various objections, Breitenstein did rework his initial draft report. For one, he dropped all references to the particular technical issues that would go into the "1947 condition" routing study. His
September 7, 1979 Final Report limited itself to the broad definition of
that critical condition.

In place of the deleted technical material, Breitenstein included a second section dealing with what he called "the ground water" issue. Now
his Final Report to the Supreme Court discussed it twice.

In Section V Breitenstein read the compact's treatment of groundwater
in the context of the apportionment of the base flow of the Pecos River
between the two states. "The 1947 routing study," he concluded, "did not
consider the base flow fully depleted. Instead it was based on present conditions. The question is the depletion of the base flow at the beginning of
1947." Everyone connected with the suit understood what this meant:
New Mexico wells, whenever established, could not deplete the flow of the
river more than they were depleting the flow on January 1, 1947.[47]

In Section XIII, tacked on after he had heard the written and oral
objections of both Texas and New Mexico, Breitenstein came back to
New Mexico's wells. "Although hidden in a mass of semantics and mathematics," he said,

the heart of this controversy is the pumping of ground water in New
Mexico. Texas says that pumping reduces the base flow. New Mexico says

that it may continue the pumping practices of 1947 . . . The New Mexico position is no more than a reiteration of the "use" theory which the Master has consistently rejected.[48]

Having said that so clearly and having jettisoned once again State Engineer Reynolds's fundamental version of the compact bargain, Breitenstein postponed applying his "depletion" theory either to the actual description of the "1947 condition" or to New Mexico's compliance with it in the years thereafter. That determination would await the suit's second stage, determining whether New Mexico wells caused impermissible departures from the required "1947 condition state line flows," which included groundwater contributions as of January 1, 1947. For the moment, Breitenstein was sticking to the unadorned principle that the compact protected New Mexico depletions, not uses, and that New Mexico couldn't reduce base flows more than it had under "1947 conditions."

With respect to his basic resolution of the "1947 condition," Breitenstein decided to allow a full review by the supervising U.S. Supreme Court. So in late 1979 and early 1980 the Supreme Court for the first, but certainly not the last, time got ready to hear the tortured Texas/New Mexico battle over the Pecos River. First in written briefs and then in oral arguments, New Mexico and Texas objected to different aspects of Special Master Breitenstein's definition.[49]

Simms, Reynolds, and Slingerland produced New Mexico's first written presentation to the Supreme Court. For almost a month, the three worked together day and night at the large conference table in Reynolds's elegant ground floor office, usually surrounded by stained Styrofoam cups, half full of cold coffee; by unemptied ashtrays, and by Reynolds's large supply of sharpened #2 pencils. Out of the mess, they constructed a printed eighty-five-page, thirty-thousand-word attack on Special Master Breitenstein's rulings.

The first half of New Mexico's lengthy "Brief in Support of Objections to the Report of the Special Master" told in neutral terms the complicated history of the Pecos River Compact and Commission. In any lawsuit, the initial story plays an important role in the subsequent legal argument. This was especially true of the Pecos River story, flooded as it was with thirty years of science and law and politics. The tale that Reynolds and Company told tried to simplify the complex history so that the Supreme Court would understand the issues. The three valued me as a narrator. From time to time they invited me into the room and asked for my advice. By the time New Mexico's argument began on page 42 of its "Brief in Support," they had composed a version of the Pecos River interstate history that implicitly showed the court how to resolve the two fundamental legal issues that followed.

The two New Mexico legal issues went to the heart of the threat that Breitenstein's rulings posed to Roswell groundwater rights in particular. First, New Mexico objected to Breitenstein's setting the compact cut-off date at the beginning of 1947, rather than the end. The history showed, argued New Mexico, that the compact negotiators knew and that the commissioners assumed that the correct cut-off date was December 31, 1947, not January 1. In the twelve-month balance of that argument hung the Corns' wells, the whole North Roswell extension, and the frenzied 1947 drilling by New Mexicans trying to beat a compact deadline they saw coming.

Then, in a more comprehensive second objection, New Mexico argued that the Pecos River Compact did not make New Mexico liable for increased base flow depletion to the Pecos River after 1947 caused by groundwater pumping existing at the beginning of 1947. Much of the New Mexico argument was based on the compact text itself; this part of the brief had the weight, the feel and the liveliness of hermeneutics. But in the balance of that argument hung Roswell wells dating as far back as the 1930s.

After a lot of discussion, Reynolds, Slingerland, and Simms had decided, as Reynolds said, "to lay the cards on the Supreme Court's table." They recognized that it almost always was a mistake to cry wolf. They knew what often happened in lawsuits when one side exaggerated the bad effects of a proposed ruling: the court disregarded even the more modest real effects. In this case Reynolds and company were cautious about over-predicting the disastrous effects of Breitenstein's rulings. But, in this instance, they decided that they had to do it. In their judgment, they had to alert the Supreme Court to the practical effect of affirming Breitenstein's definition of the "1947 condition."

So at the end of the brief they repeated in writing the dire prediction of disaster that lawyer Simms had first made orally to Special Master Breitenstein in April 1979. Now, in November 1979, the New Mexicans ended their first brief to the Supreme Court by bluntly concluding,

(t)he fact of the matter is that the Master's construction of the Compact would obliterate the economy of the Pecos River Basin in southeastern New Mexico . . . The Master's decision could slice in half the 125,000 acres of ground water irrigation in existence in New Mexico in 1947 . . . [50]

Texas was also dissatisfied with Breitenstein's September 1979 ruling and, like New Mexico, had appealed. However, Texas was concerned neither with the January 1, 1947 date nor with New Mexico wells. Instead, Texas argued, in a brief less than one-third the length of New Mexico's, that the compact's "1947 condition" referred to the original engineering studies that had defined the condition, right or wrong. The Texas lawyers had never budged from their square one.[51]

The Supreme Court scheduled oral arguments in Washington, D.C., for late March 1980. Steve Reynolds designated his chief lawyer, Richard Simms, one of the few Supreme Court veterans from New Mexico, to present New Mexico's case. Simms was a natural choice. In 1978 he had argued and won in the Supreme Court what Reynolds had dubbed "the whole enchilada" in a suit between New Mexico and the United States over Forest Service water rights. When it came time to switch from the Forest Service to Texas as the next external threat to New Mexico's internal water world, Reynolds went back to Simms.[52]

Simms spent weeks getting ready for the oral arguments in *Texas v. New Mexico*. "I was very confident about our position," he later recalled, "and I spent a hell of a lot of time trying to anticipate questions, writing down the answers, going through arguments, writing out alternative forms of argument, outlining them all, trying to get myself prepared for carrying on a dialogue the course of which is directed by questions that you in most instances, can't anticipate." He even went to Washington a week early and assembled some friends into a pretend panel of justices presenting New Mexico's case to them in the classic moot court format and answering questions they threw his way. When at 2:09 P.M., Monday, March 24, 1980 Chief Justice Warren Burger announced that "We will hear arguments next in *Texas v. New Mexico*," Simms felt as ready as he could be.[53]

In the meantime, of course, Doug Caroom, the Texas lead lawyer, had been getting ready too. Unlike Simms, Caroom had never appeared before the Supreme Court before and so he wasn't as familiar with the Washington courtroom where he would argue, with the layout of the tables and podium and dais, or with the system of podium lights that warned lawyers of time limitations. Caroom, however, felt that he had one huge advantage. His basic argument, which he believed was right and had even convinced Simms for awhile until Steve Reynolds started relentlessly to work on him, was simple: right or wrong as a matter of science, Texas and New Mexico had agreed in 1948 to a definition of the baseline "1947 condition" and that agreement now bound both states. From the Texas point of view, the special master had erred when he had ruled that the compact's "1947 condition" was the real situation on the Pecos River, not necessarily the one described in the studies. (Caroom's position didn't even address New Mexico's concern with "use" and "depletion" and so the positions of the two states hardly crossed.)[54]

When Chief Justice Burger called the case, Caroom rose to argue first. He'd hardly started with his fundamental point when Associate Justice Byron White, a Coloradan, a long-time friend of Special Master Breitenstein's, and one of two Supreme Court Justices familiar with western water, interrupted from the dais with a question: "And you would say that would still hold true if it turned out that there was a printing error in the engineering report . . . even if everybody conceded the report just made an outright, obvious mistake in describing what the condition on the river was?"[55]

Justice White was probing in classic lawyerly manner, taking the basic Texas position and pushing it to its logical limits far beyond what Caroom actually had written or said. "That would be the strict literal consequence of our case," Caroom had to admit, lamely adding, "We don't want to be unreasonable about it." Apparently satisfied that he understood the Texas position and that it couldn't be correct, Justice White stopped asking questions for awhile.[56]

By the end of Caroom's thirty minutes, Justice Stevens had emerged as Caroom's chief interrogator. Clearly Stevens believed that every version of the "1947 condition" was an artificial construct and that therefore the compact's "1947 condition" might as well be the one that the two states had agreed to at the time the compact was made.

When his turn came, New Mexico's Richard Simms realized that he would have to focus on Justice Stevens and did so by addressing Stevens's concerns immediately, rather than starting as he had originally planned. Despite this display of flexibility, he couldn't get much of a rise out of Stevens or any of the other justices, for that matter. Part of the problem, he later realized, was the large exhibit he dragged to the podium with him. An enlarged version of the forty-one-column routing study that made up the "1947 condition," it showed each element had a different value for every year from 1910 to 1947. Simms had been convinced that once the Supreme Court saw the columns and what they represented it would see what the original routing study depicting the "1947 condition" had intended to do. But he soon realized that the point was difficult and, worse, that most of the justices couldn't see the exhibit's one thousand nodes from the dais. As they craned their heads this way and that, just trying to catch a glimpse, they missed parts of Simms's complex explanation. Some of the lawyers in the large hearing room were actually seated behind Simms's exhibit and couldn't see it at all.[57]

As a result of the visual confusion, Simms found himself arguing to a preoccupied, uncomprehending audience much of the time. On a couple of occasions justices interrupted to ask questions. Justice Stevens challenged Simms twice on why the Court shouldn't assume that the two states had agreed to the original river operation study, right or wrong, as the base line for compact performance. Simms explained in terms of the exhibit that few could see. Otherwise, the Supreme Court simply let him go.[58]

As a result, Simms never directly described the dire impact that Special Master Breitenstein's ruling might have on irrigated agriculture in the Roswell basin. Simms referred in a few places to the special problem of "base flow depletion" in the 1947 condition studies. Among the active, long-time participants in *Texas v. New Mexico* that term had become code for the threatened groundwater wells in New Mexico, but the Supreme Court must have had trouble understanding it, buried as it was in the chart that they had trouble seeing. The last half of Simms's argument was scarcely interrupted, often as much a sign of lack of interest as of agreement. After a short rebuttal by Texas's Caroom, Chief Justice Burger closed the proceeding with the traditional, "(t)hank you gentlemen. The case is submitted."[59]

Simms and Caroom went back to Santa Fe and Austin and waited while the Supreme Court went to work. Exchanges of memos among the justices and their clerks showed great confusion about what was involved in the suit at that point and how the Court should proceed on what, after all, they knew, would not be a decision that ended the lawsuit. In the end, eight of the nine Supreme Court justices followed the lead of Chief Justice Warren Burger and agreed simply to uphold the decisions of the special master to that point and to wait and see how things developed afterwards. Only Justice Stevens, who had participated so actively in the oral arguments, strongly disagreed.[60]

In mid-May 1980, a short two months after oral arguments, the Supreme Court issued its first decision in *Texas v. New Mexico*. The opinion was issued anonymously by the court, not authored by any identified justice. It was all of one, nine-line sentence long:[61]

> Upon consideration of the report filed October 15, 1979 by Senior Judge Jean S. Breitenstein, Special Master, and the exceptions thereto, and on consideration of briefs and oral argument thereon, IT IS ADJUDGED, ORDERED AND DECREED that all exceptions are overruled, the report is an all respects confirmed and the ruling of the Special Master on the "1947 condition" as that term appears in Arts. II(g) and III(a) of the Pecos River Compact is approved.

After all the writing, after all New Mexico's dire predictions, after all the oral presentations, this is the most that the majority of the Supreme Court justices were willing to say. The ruling was brief but full of implicit messages.

The good news for New Mexico (and the bad news for Texas) was that the Supreme Court had confirmed Breitenstein's definition of the fundamental "1947 condition." In so doing, the Court had rejected, once and for all, the bottom-line Texas claim that the "1947 condition" was the one contained in the original 1948 river operation studies. With that rejection, the mechanical basis for the Texas claim that New Mexico owed more than a 1,000,000 acre-feet of water finally disappeared. But in place of the 1948 studies, the Supreme Court had accepted the actual 1947 condition of the Pecos River as the true compact "1947 condition."

Reynolds and company gleaned this message from the Supreme Court's elliptical decision and recognized it for the serious problem it posed. The actual 1947 condition of the Pecos included groundwater contributions allowed by preexisting wells whose full effect had not reached the river. The bad news for New Mexico (and the good news for Texas) was that the Supreme Court seemed to have rejected Reynolds's use theory, once and for all, and accepted the depletion alternative. New Mexico's prediction of disaster, voiced clearly in late 1979 and early 1980, could turn out to be true. The next step, turning Breitenstein's Court-approved basic definition into numbers, would tell.[62]

Before the two states and Breitenstein could take that next step, *Texas v. New Mexico* twice veered off course and took another three years to get back on the track laid down by the Supreme Court in 1980. First, Texas insisted on introducing an entirely new, supposedly judgment-free statistical technique, "double mass accounting," to determine New Mexico's compact obligation. When the special master listened in early 1982 to another week of esoteric evidence, primarily from University of Texas at Austin professor Abraham Charnes, a world-renowned statistician, he learned that Charnes's "more robust" method for relating Pecos River inflows and outflows wasn't any form of the "inflow/outflow method" that the compact required. More importantly, he was also told that Charnes's method wouldn't eliminate the judgment calls that had paralyzed the Pecos River Commission in the first place. As a result, Breitenstein rejected the Texas statistical solution to the compact impasse.[63]

Instead, he created a solution of his own: the special master would appoint a third member of the Pecos River Commission to break ties between Texas and New Mexico. Both states balked at the possibility, especially New Mexico. To State Engineer Steve Reynolds the Breitenstein proposal directly threatened New Mexico sovereignty. Worse yet, from Reynolds's perspective, a third, presumably federal voting representative on the Pecos River Commission would allow the federal government to defeat a New Mexico decision with respect to compact administration by siding with Texas on an issue.[64]

To the special master, it didn't matter. So long as New Mexico held what amounted to a veto power over compact administration, especially with State Engineer Reynolds at the helm, it would simply block any of the determinations necessary for downstream Texas to get its share of water. Finding no authority in the Pecos River Compact for appointing a tie-breaker, Breitenstein turned back to his inherent powers as a judge to craft a solution: he could appoint an additional member of the Pecos River Commission not because the compact authorized it but because the legal situation demanded it.

Up the case went to the Supreme Court for the second time in less than five years, this time, everyone thought, on the two narrow issues framed by the special master's rulings since the first 1980 decision: Could the special master consider Texas's double mass alternative and could the special master appoint a tie-breaking third member of the commission?

In the interim, Texas's chief lawyer, Doug Caroom, who had developed an impressive command of the engineering issues in the case, left for private practice. He tried to take the Pecos River case with him but Texas was unwilling to pay his hefty new fees and instead brought in a new lawyer, Lambeth Townsend, who had to start, painfully, from the beginning.[65]

New Mexico underwent a similar transition when Richard Simms left for far more lucrative private practice. Unlike Texas, New Mexico allowed Simms to continue to work on part of the case, figuring that his high fees were low given what was at stake and considering the risks of putting in a rookie substitute. However, when it came to presenting New Mexico's arguments to the Supreme Court for this second time, State Engineer Reynolds balked.

He was fiercely loyal to his own legal staff, thank you, and refused to send an outsider, even one who, like Richard Simms had been an insider for so long. Instead, to Simms's chagrin, Reynolds chose a smart, aggressive Midwesterner named Charlotte Uram to present New Mexico's 1983 arguments to the high Court. The first woman ever on Reynolds's small legal staff, Uram approached *Texas v. New Mexico* with the clear head of a novice, which some found refreshing and others found naïve.[66]

The danger, of course, was that neither Texas's Lambeth Townsend nor New Mexico's Charlotte Uram would be able to find the thread, if there was one, that held the suit together. Luckily, the issues at this point seemed discrete and legal rather than messy and scientific as they had been up to that point. For the first time, there was a lot of case law dealing with the issues: the power of a court to do either as Texas had asked in adopting a new method of apportionment or as Special Master Breitenstein finally had recommended in appointing a third member to the Pecos River Commission to break ties. The 1982 New Mexico and Texas briefs to the Supreme Court showed that the two states and their new lawyers understood that they were now fighting on the high, familiar ground of legal issues and principles.

In the increasingly monomaniacal legal view of State Engineer Reynolds, *Texas v. New Mexico* now turned on the proper relationship of courts, even the Supreme Court, to administrative agencies, like the Pecos River Compact Commission (PRCC), set up by compacting states to deal with interstate problems. New Mexico's brief drew on a mountain of federal administrative law to demonstrate that any court could only review what an established administrative agency already had done as opposed to doing what the agency hadn't done. New Mexico's lawyers argued that only the PRCC had the power to adopt a new definition of the "1947 condition." Similarly, only the bi-state PRCC had the authority to substitute the "double mass accounting" method of determining post-1948 river flows. If, as Special Master Breitenstein had said, the PRCC had not intended its revised 1961–1962 definition of the critical "1947 condition" to apply in the future, then there was in fact no commission action for a court to review. In Reynolds's highly legalistic view, the Supreme Court now could only do what Special Master Breitenstein should have done: dismiss the compact suit and leave Texas to whatever alternatives it might have. Texas's brief, of course, was as full of legal authority as New Mexico's but it pointed in a different direction.[67]

Because the issues at stake were legal ones, the oral arguments presented on March 30, 1983 in Washington were relatively easy to follow. Unlike the arguments in 1980, there were no confusing charts showing the "1947 condition" studies in all their esoteric detail. There were many fewer long silences from the nine justices hearing the case.[68]

New Mexico's Charlotte Uram used every technique of high-level oral advocacy to unfurl New Mexico's position and to demonstrate her complete mastery of the compact issues at that point. After weeks of meticulous, exhausting preparation, she appeared relaxed and confident before a Supreme Court on which, finally, a fellow female lawyer sat. Peppered by questions, she responded quickly and surely to the expressed concerns of particular judges. Indeed, Uram later said that her first argument before the Supreme Court had "all the give-and-take of a good tennis match," a game which the unathletic Uram hardly played. Uram's performance impressed Supreme Court Justice Sandra Day O'Connor enough to have O'Connor recall it a couple of years later when she ran into Uram at an American Bar Association meeting.[69] But the textbook briefs and arguments took on this less awkward cast precisely because in the end they had so little to do with the Pecos River and its interstate problems and so much to do with the proper legal relationship of courts and administrative agencies set up by compacting states to deal with the those problems. The engineering had dropped out and the river and its condition had disappeared with it. The law had replaced them.

Indeed, the engineers now disappeared as the chief culprits in the Pecos River problems and Special Master Breitenstein himself emerged. Several Supreme Court Justices expressed surprise that Breitenstein hadn't been able to get quicker, firmer control over the suit. If Breitenstein couldn't, they seemed to suggest, then the Supreme Court itself could, especially if, as now seemed true, the issues were classic legal ones. In that atmosphere, lawyers for Texas and New Mexico awaited what they thought would be a fairly quick legal decision that would not so much resolve the compact problems as stake out the legal boundaries of Special Master Breitenstein's authority.[70]

The process began just three days after the March 30 oral arguments when, on April 2, 1983, the Supreme Court assembled in private conference to discuss, among twelve other cases that also had been "argued and submitted," how to resolve this chapter of *Texas v. New Mexico*. Oddly enough, Justice William Brennan, Jr., an unlikely expert on western water rights and a justice who hadn't said a word in either the 1979 or 1983 oral arguments, now brought with him to the conference a terse memorandum on the case. "We have to decide two things," Brennan's two-page memo to the other justices began,[71]

whether we can accept the Special Master's recommendation to appoint a tiebreaker to the Pecos River Commission, and, if we do not accept the recommendation, what instructions to give the Special Master. There is really no doubt about the first question. We have no authority to appoint a tiebreaker. What to do next is considerably more difficult.[72]

The remaining page and a half detailed "the proper next steps":

(1) to decide how to measure the 1947 condition, giving effect to the compact's "inflow-outflow method" requirement, (2) to quantify the 1947

condition using the measurement system chosen, and (3) to determine whether, during the years covered by Texas's complaint, New Mexico has complied with its compact obligation not to deplete state-line flows beyond the 1947 condition.[73]

Brennan ended the brief memo in capitalized recommendations for what the Court should now do: "SUSTAIN FIRST NEW MEXICO EXCEPTION (tiebreaker appointment); RETURN TO SPECIAL MASTER TO DEFINE 1947 CONDITION AND DETERMINE TEXAS RIGHTS UNDER COMPACT." There followed an astonishing third recommendation: "APPOINT A NEW SPECIAL MASTER." Neither state had asked that Breitenstein be replaced, and he hadn't yet asked to be relieved. Brennan thought the special master couldn't do the job anymore.[74]

A quick vote at the April 1, 1983 conference, tabulated by Brennan, showed that the whole Court agreed with the first two Brennan recommendations. (The third Brennan recommendation, appointing a new master to replace Breitenstein, apparently disappeared without a trace.) Given the agreement about Justice Brennan's proposed result, it was no surprise that the Chief Justice Burger assigned Justice Brennan the job of putting together the first formal Supreme Court opinion in *Texas v. New Mexico* up to that point. After all, Brennan's three-page April 1 memorandum would form the core of the formal opinion.[75]

Justice Brennan's assignment in *Texas v. New Mexico* was only one of nine opinions for which he was primarily responsible in April 1983. Some of the opinions took longer to complete than others. Some turned out to be more controversial than others. But, despite the other demands on him, Justice Brennan and his two clerks managed to turn out the first draft of the formal opinion in *Texas v. New Mexico* in two short months. By June 10, 1983 Brennan circulated among the other eight members of the Court the first draft of the 1983 opinion in *Texas v. New Mexico* and the first Supreme Court analysis of the case ever.[76]

What had begun as a five-hundred-word memorandum to fellow court members in April had grown by early June to a 7,500-word formal opinion, complete with footnotes and graphs. Of course, Brennan's 1983 draft had to address the particular legal issues raised by the briefs and oral arguments presented to it this time around and it had to do so in the manner that Brennan had outlined in his early memorandum. Fully half his draft amplified in elegant prose and supported with rich legal reference the result that Brennan had outlined in his April 1 memorandum.

He now formally proposed to confirm Breitenstein's rejection of Texas's double mass accounting, describing that technique as just too different from the compact-specified inflow/outflow technique. Brennan also rejected Breitenstein's own proposal to add a neutral tiebreaker to the PRCC. That, too, said Brennan, was beyond the bounds of the original compact and the authority of the judiciary. However, determining what the "1947 condition" was, how it should be defined, and how it should be applied in the years after 1947 to determine whether or not New Mexico was meeting its delivery obligations to Texas, these questions were within the scope of judicial scrutiny. Reynolds was wrong in his insistence, first implicitly developed in my *Administrative History,* that the suit be dismissed until such time as the Pecos River Commission itself had determined them. In other words, the draft affirmed the power of the courts to construe the original bargain that Texas and New Mexico had struck.

As the draft opinion circulated among his fellow justices in the second week of June, 1983, only this point about judicial authority raised any questions. Justice (now Chief Judge) William Rehnquist thought that Brennan hadn't expressed clearly enough the judicial authority of the Supreme Court to resolve the interstate compact problem. In reply on June 14, Brennan wrote Rehnquist. "Dear Bill," he began,

> I certainly hadn't meant to give an impression that we were throwing up our hands in this case. Rather, I hope that this opinion signals a firm willingness to decide it. I do not think it inappropriate, however, to observe first that the total amount of water in dispute in this case—probably not more than 50,000 acre-feet/year, and most likely a good deal less than that—may not justify the expense of maintaining an original jurisdiction action in this Court for close to a decade (and counting), and, second, that we are not about to appoint a "Pecos River czar." Since the second point is made earlier in the opinion, there is no need to reiterate it at the end. Would it dispel the air of defeatism if I simply eliminated the sentence in the final paragraph that (creates that air)?
>
> Sincerely,
> Bill[77]

Brennan's prediction of the amount of water involved turned out to be way off, but his reassurance (and proposed editorial change) allayed Justice Rehnquist's relatively minor concerns. On June 15, Rehnquist became the last Supreme Court justice to join in the Brennan draft. On June 17, 1983 the Supreme Court announced its decision in *Texas v. New Mexico* as embodied in the unanimous Brennan opinion.[78]

Brennan was the first to lay out a clear map of the tortured course of the litigation to that point. His description showed the twists and turns that the suit had taken over its first nine years, imposed a badly needed order on its increasing chaos, and finally made it all seem part of a logical process. Brennan also described, clearly and succinctly, the history of compact negotiations and the engineering debates that had preceded the compact, had informed the terms of the compact itself, and, finally, had been the focus of Pecos River Commission battles. In text and in footnote, Brennan's opinion set out in plain language the first accurate account of the engineering efforts to define the compact's base line "1947 condition" and the subsequent efforts to refine that definition.[79]

Richard Simms's 41-column river routing study, which had so confused the proceedings in the Supreme Court in 1980 that the Court never mentioned it, now showed up as a central part of Brennan's background analysis even though it had not been mentioned in the 1983 oral arguments. The Roswell wells, whose demise Simms and Reynolds had predicted in 1980 and about which the Court had said nothing, also resurfaced. "Due in large part to many natural difficulties," wrote Brennan, "the Pecos barely supports a level of development reached in the first third of this century. If development in New Mexico were not restricted, especially the groundwater pumping near Roswell, no water at all might reach Texas in many years."[80]

It didn't take much reading between the lines to gather that the Supreme Court believed that groundwater development in Morgan Nelson's part of the Middle Pecos had deprived Texas of its compact-guaranteed share of the Pecos River surface waters. Clearly the Supreme Court thought that New Mexico would have to cut back on the Roswell wells to comply with the compact's obligations. For the moment it looked as if the legal and engineering institutions that had sired the Pecos River Compact finally might get back together again.

The 1983 Supreme Court finally was clearing the way to implement the 1948 Pecos River Compact. At least that's what the Justices and Special Master Breitenstein believed. Concerned that Breitenstein might take offense at the Supreme Court's rejection of his tiebreaker suggestion, Justice Byron White, who had arranged Breitenstein's appointment as special master in the first place, called Breitenstein in Denver. On July 1, 1983 White reported to his fellow justices that he had "chatted with Jean Breitenstein about *Texas v. New Mexico*." White reported that Breitenstein was

> not at all upset about the opinion. On the contrary, he anticipated the tiebreaker result and believes that the rest of the opinion clears the air a

good deal. He also appreciated the suggestion that if he preferred to get rid of this dog, we would understand and find a replacement. He thinks, however, that he should not get out immediately but try to get a pre-trial conference order together in the near future. He has a meeting with counsel set for July 21. He will have to rely a good deal on an engineer, which will be expensive. He did say that the Social Security amendment will cost him a fair amount of money beginning January 1. Thus, unless the law is changed, someone else will have to take over by that time. I shall be in Denver in an office next to his sometime after July 20 and will keep track of what is going on in this miserable case. Perhaps with the rejection of their major submissions, the two states will be more cooperative.

Cheers.

Byron[81]

At the July 21 meeting, Special Master Breitenstein repeated to the Texas and New Mexico representatives Brennan's admonition that interstate problems were best solved by the states themselves. Breitenstein then focused on Brennan's first step—the final definition of the base-line "1947 condition." In his opinion, Brennan had suggested with respect to that base-line that "there seem to be no more than three or four issues upon which the Special Master will have to resolve difficult questions of fact or of hydrological method." Now Special Master Breitenstein proposed to address those issues, quickly, so that the case finally could proceed.

He first forced New Mexico and Texas engineers to negotiate in late 1983 and early 1984 the few remaining technical issues. The negotiations primarily involved exchanging proposed coefficients for missing factors in the "1947 condition" formula. Texas and New Mexico, after almost a decade of bitter litigation, finally managed to produce a mutually acceptable technical definition of the base-line "1947 condition" at the heart of the Pecos River Compact. In his final January 9, 1984 Report to the Supreme Court Special Master Breitenstein wrote,[82]

(I)n accordance with Compact III(a) New Mexico shall not deplete by man's activities the flow of the Pecos River at the New Mexico-Texas state line below an amount which will give to Texas the quantity of water represented by (the inflow/outflow curve) represented by Texas Figure I and Table I in Exhibit 68.

The New Mexicans knew that the inflow/outflow curve to which they had just agreed showed that New Mexico was contributing less to the base flow of the Pecos River between Roswell and Artesia than under the river's "1947 condition." Reynolds and Slingerland had allowed me to admit that much in my 1979 argument to the Master. State Engineer Reynolds still clung to the often rejected notion that the compact protected "uses" established by the start of 1947. But he knew that base flow depletion was only one in many factors affecting Pecos River flows at the Texas-New Mexico state line.[83]

Above all, Reynolds relied on what he regarded as an even more fundamental card that New Mexico had not yet played: Even if Texas could demonstrate that, using the newly agreed on definition of the "1947 condition," less water was reaching the state line than should have been, Texas could still never prove that New Mexico was responsible for the diminution. It wasn't enough that the approved curve tried to account for all natural changes to the "1947 condition." Texas would have to demonstrate just which activities by man in New Mexico had caused departures from the base-line "1947 condition."

Brennan's 1983 opinion contributed to Reynolds's faith in his ploy. The Supreme Court recognized that the ultimate question of whether New Mexico owed Texas water "necessarily involves two subsidiary questions. First, under the proper definition of the '1947 condition' . . . what is the difference between the quantity of water Texas could have expected to receive in each year and the quantity it actually received . . . Second, to what extent were the shortfalls due to man's activities in New Mexico."[84]

The 1983–1984 agreement as to the inflow/outflow curve only established the definition needed to answer the first question. Using that definition someone still had to figure out what the Pecos River flow had been in the years after 1948 and to compare what it should have been under the "1947 condition." If the speed of previous progress was any measure, just completing this first step could take a long time. And time, as Reynolds knew, favored upstream New Mexico.

Brennan also had recognized that completing the first step would require a second step before the compact finally could be fulfilled: someone would have to decide whether the difference ("negative departures") between what water arrived at the New Mexico/Texas state line in post-1948 years and what water should have gotten there under the "1947 condition" had been caused by "man's activities in New Mexico." This fundamental determination, Reynolds believed, would provide a victory for New Mexico. He was convinced that no one could tell which Pecos River shortfalls were caused by man and which weren't. So long as the burden of so parsing annual shortfalls fell on Texas, Texas could never show that "man's activities in New Mexico" had caused departures from the "1947 condition."

Brennan had not got that far in his 1983 opinion, but Special Master Breitenstein had. From the very beginning of *Texas v. New Mexico* he had emphasized that it was up to Texas to show that New Mexico had caused "by man's activities," as the compact said, negative departures from the "1947 condition." Sometimes Breitenstein simply had said that that "burden" would fall on Texas. At other times the special master had assigned the job to Texas because he knew that no one could prove a negative. "So it seems to me," he ruled. "that the burden is on Texas to show that departures have been caused by the activities of man." If Texas couldn't prove them, then New Mexico wouldn't be responsible, even for negative departures.[85] So long as Breitenstein remained as special master, New Mexico was safe on that critical issue.

But in July 1984, Breitenstein tendered his resignation and the Court accepted, disingenuously noting "deep appreciation for his long and invaluable service to the court." Almost immediately the Supreme Court replaced Judge Breitenstein with a complex Texas native who had served as dean of the Stanford Law School. The world of *Texas v. New Mexico* would never quite be the same. Steve Reynolds, as it turned out, had met his match.

SEVEN

The Presumption of Charles J. Meyers

──────── "That son of a bitch," Carl Slingerland muttered for the first, but certainly not last, time as he left the eleventh floor conference room of the law offices of Gibson, Dunn and Crutcher in Denver, Colorado one afternoon in the fall of 1984.[1]

The setting was enough to make the feisty, austere New Mexico engineer nervous. The Los Angeles-based firm had spared no expense when it had expanded in the early 1980s into the Rocky Mountain West to capture a share of the legal work sure to be generated by the predicted energy boom there. Its spacious conference room had floor-to-ceiling windows with a view of downtown Denver and the peaks beyond. Slingerland's modest Santa Fe home looked onto the industrial back of St. Vincent's Hospital. The Gibson, Dunn, and Crutcher conference room's burnished hard wood floors didn't look anything like the clean, slightly worn carpeting of Slingerland's living room and office in Santa Fe. No New Mexico meeting room had a polished silver tea service like the one sitting dead center on the long hardwood table. But it wasn't so much the ostentatious physical setting that upset Slingerland. He had just met the lawyer the Supreme Court had selected to replace Jean Breitenstein as special master in *Texas v. New Mexico* and he liked neither what he saw in nor what he heard from Charles J. Meyers, Jr.[2]

Between July 1984 when he took the case over from Breitenstein and July 1986 when he issued his first formal report to the Supreme Court, Meyers assembled the engineers and lawyers from New Mexico and Texas in seven informal conferences in his opulent Denver offices. At the first meeting Slingerland, Steve Reynolds, and Richard Simms, now a

Fig. 7.1.
Charles J. Meyers peers ferociously out from his desk at the Stanford Law School where he served as dean before moving on to private practice in Denver and a final assignment as Special Master in *Texas v. New Mexico*. Charming, mercurial and very bright, he did not react well to the kind of didactic certainty embodied in the Steve Reynolds of Fig. 5.2. (Photo courtesy of Professor Dan Tarlock.)

private legal consultant, sat on one side of the conference table, opposite Texas lawyers Renea Hicks and Paul Elliot and Texas engineer V. R. Krisha Murthy. Meyers meant to force the cantankerous parties to honor Justice Brennan's 1983 admonition that "the parties try to settle their differences in a spirit of cooperation." To promote settlement and speed the suit to an end, Meyers described for the warring parties where the suit was and what he needed to conclude it.[3]

"Right there," Slingerland later reported, "at that first meeting, in that fancy goddamned room, Meyers just up and said that as far as he was concerned there was no question that New Mexico owed Texas water under the Pecos River Compact. The only question was how much. Well, we all knew that no one had yet decided any such goddamned thing."

His voice rising, Slingerland continued. "Old Breitenstein had only determined what the '1947 condition' was. He hadn't decided whether Texas had received the water it was supposed to have in the years after

Presumption of Charles J. Meyers

1947. And Breitenstein certainly hadn't determined whether a negative departure in any year after 1947 had been caused by 'man's activities in New Mexico.' So when, right there and then, old Meyers said that he was there to decide how much water New Mexico owed Texas, well, old Richard Simms, he nearly fell out of his chair."[4]

Texas lawyer Renea Hicks remembered these early meetings differently. Hicks thought of himself as cut out of Meyers's Texas cloth; both were very quick, anxious to get to the bottom line. Steve Reynolds, recalled Hicks, had opened the first informal meeting with a statement about the sequence of seemingly endless steps that would be necessary to bring *Texas v. New Mexico* to a close, an end whose contours no one could then know. Reynolds was accustomed to having his analysis accepted as the first and only word on the state of water affairs. According to Hicks, as Reynolds finished his presentation to Meyers, he lit a cigarette and inhaled deeply. Meyers himself had been listening and smoking while Reynolds talked. Now, as Reynolds lit up, Meyers set his cigarette down. Rather than simply accepting what Reynolds said, Meyers responded with his remark about the amount of New Mexico's water debt to Texas. Reynolds, astonished as much by the fact that Meyers had responded at all as by what he had said, lit a second cigarette while the first burned on in the ashtray in front of him. With these two, where there was fire, there was smoke.[5]

From the beginning of their relationship in 1984 until Meyers's death in July 1988, these two titans of western water law rubbed each other the wrong way. Meyers found Reynolds imperious, expecting everyone to accept what he said simply because he had said it. Reynolds found Meyers injudicious, actively participating instead of just refereeing, saying exactly what he thought as he thought it instead of inscrutably waiting and weighing.

Meyers had moved to Colorado as the leader of the Gibson, Dunn, and Crutcher's interstate natural resources expansion. In 1981 the Los Angeles law firm had lured him away from a prestigious academic career as professor first (1962–1976), then as dean (1976–1981) of the Stanford Law School. As a teacher, Meyers had won the affection of decades of ambitious, very bright law students, beginning at Columbia in the 1950s and ending at Stanford in the 1970s. A man of interests ranging from Mozart, whose birthday he celebrated every year, to oil reservoir engineering, which he sometimes wrote about, Meyers, was above all engaged in the world around him. Now he would end his career passionately engaged in bringing *Texas v. New Mexico* to its conclusion, an end that Steve Reynolds did not want and began to dread as soon as he met Meyers.[6]

When it came to describing Meyers, admirers resorted to a string of provocative, vaguely contradictory adjectives. An academic and personal friend tried with this catalogue: "Charlie was the most energetic, passionate, volatile, warm, tough, kind, brutally honest, compassionate, feisty, generous, and above all, expansive person I have ever known." To the much more restrained New Mexicans with whom he would deal in the second half of *Texas v. New Mexico,* this "array of qualities," as his friends called it, was bound to cause trouble. Asked to sum up those qualities in one word, the same friends always chose another adjective: above all else, Charles Meyers was a Texan. To the New Mexicans no summary could be worse.[7]

Meyers had approached being dean at Stanford with the same verve that he brought to *Texas v. New Mexico.* At Stanford, he proved a terrific money raiser, cajoling, pleading and ultimately producing large increases in annual giving and endowments. He had less success, however, in turning Stanford into the preeminent school for the economic analysis of law, as he wanted to do. Meyers's effort failed, as his successor pointed out, because Meyers as dean inherited "a diverse group of strong-willed faculty members pursuing a multitude of visions" who wouldn't all play to Meyers's tune. The lack of cooperation never stopped Dean Meyers from accepting his peers or pushing his vision.[8]

That vision—that only economic analysis could explain the law's past and guide its future—informed Meyers's scholarship in his specialty of natural resources law. His writings on oil and gas law emphasized the wisdom of fashioning rights to oil and gas so as to maximize a free market in the resource, unconstrained by bureaucratic regulation and artificial monopolies. While not the primary focus of his writings, the water rights aspects of natural resources also caught Meyers's attention as a writer and scholar.[9]

To water resources Meyers brought the same abrupt critical intelligence and the same stated ideological biases that he had forged in the oil and gas area. When he reviewed water work he considered inadequate, he minced no words criticizing it. When the first multivolume legal treatise on water law appeared, Meyers's review in the prestigious *Yale Law Journal* called it "repetitious, inconsistent and episodic" and nothing more than "a collection of individual papers, of varying quality, dealing with the assorted problems of water law." Meyers stated his own consistent, comprehensive view of western water law in two other traditional legal forums, the case book and the working papers of the first national water commission.[10]

The first edition of *Water Resources Management* was a collection of cases and commentaries designed for use in water law courses in law schools around the country. There was no mistaking its theme. Water resources were constrained on all sides by arcane and archaic rules that prevented the free flow of limited water resources to their highest and best use in a changing world through the operation of property rights and private markets. That theme, implicit in the case book, Meyers made explicit in his simultaneous work as assistant legal counsel to the National Water Commission in 1971 and 1972.[11]

The final report of the commission, *Water Policies for the Future*, proved Meyers's most enduring scholarly legacy to the water law field. In it, Meyers joined forces with then University of Chicago professor, now federal appellate judge, Richard Posner, the most famous "law and economics" star on today's legal scene, to advocate incorporating efficiency principles into water allocation. Steve Reynolds was no particular fan of low value community uses of water of the kind made by ancient New Mexico Pueblos and Hispanic villagers. He, too, believed that his job was to allow water to flow uphill to money. But Meyers and Posner went much farther in their advocacy of market efficiency than Steve Reynolds ever did. The two academics argued for dismantling the very water bureaucracy, which Reynolds so carefully had built and over which he presided. So, as early as 1972, law professor Meyers had set out to poke holes in the world that State Engineer Reynolds was building.[12]

The collision toward which the two were headed had even been hinted at in Meyers's earliest and most magisterial piece of legal writing on water resources, "The Colorado River." As a graduate student and then law professor at Columbia University in the 1950s, Meyers had secured for himself a temporary job as chief legal assistant to Supreme Court Special Master Simon Rifkind, assigned to decide the monumental legal contest between Arizona and California over the water resources of the lower Colorado River. Between 1956 and 1960, Meyers sat in on the endless struggle between the two water-thirsty southwestern boom states and lived to tell about it. Although he never mentioned his role in the thirty-thousand-word, seventy-five-page 1966 law review article or in the 292 footnote references that accompanied it, "The Colorado River" article summed up what Meyers had seen and learned in the California-Arizona battle and foreshadowed how he would react twenty-five years later in *Texas v. New Mexico*.[13]

In many ways Meyers's "The Colorado River" introduced personalities and issues that would reappear in *Texas v. New Mexico*. It referred to both Breitenstein and Tipton. The article also revealed a fascination with the financing of the special master's proceeding, a topic that would embroil Meyers in disputes with Texas and New Mexico and, in 1987, with the Supreme Court itself. Finally, the article demonstrated Meyers's facility for constructing complex compact terms and his ability to parse the texts of interstate water agreements with the eye of a hermeneutics scholar and the attitude of a Machiavellian political scientist. Time and again in "The Colorado River" Meyers demonstrated ambiguities in the 1922 Lower Colorado River Compact and other important Lower Colorado legislation and then suggested how that ambiguity probably intentionally masked a lack of fundamental agreement among the parties. When it came time to look at the Pecos River, not as an observer and an academic but as a judge himself, Meyers already had been there and done that on the Lower Colorado.[14]

Most of all, "The Colorado River" showed Meyers at his complex, contradictory best. Compared to the usual cold, analytic approach of law review articles of the time, Meyers's article was a potpourri of styles and inclinations. The article's language was often rich and esoteric. (Meyers's description of "the clangorous strife in the Lower Basin where Arizona and California have been in baleful opposition for at least forty-four years" would have driven the word-wise Steve Reynolds to the library-sized Webster's International Dictionary in the corner of his Santa Fe office.) Some of Meyers's sentences were short and direct, others ran on and on. Sometimes Meyers spoke in the editorial "we." At other times he reverted to the more usual indefinite third person, referring to himself as "the author." At still other times, he disappeared (although not for long) from the article; then the lawyers spoke for themselves.[15]

Nothing so captured the rich contradictions of Charles Meyers's style as the following passage, so unusual in law review literature, describing the 1956 opening of the hearings in *Arizona v. California*:

For thirty years the states had been unable to reach agreement, and no evidence exists of a serious effort to do so after the committee's resolution. A little more than a year later, apparently with an understanding that the United States would intervene to give the Court jurisdiction, Arizona filed another suit in the Supreme Court in an effort to get a judicial determination of her water rights. Nearly four years were devoted to the filings of pleadings and motions, the holding of pretrial conferences, and the preparation and entry of a pre-trial order. On June 14, 1956, twenty-six years after Arizona made her first attempt to obtain an adjudication of her water rights in the Colorado, the trial on the merits began before a Special Master.

The courtroom was overflowing. Dozens of lawyers were there, representing not only Arizona and California but also three other states having Lower Basin interests—New Mexico, Nevada, and Utah—each of which had joined the litigation, though not all voluntarily. Present also, of course, was the United States, a brooding omnipresence, which could have been going along for the ride but which, as it turned out, laid a claim to a large part of the vehicle and to the right to drive besides.

The personalities present were a rich assortment. For Arizona there were the contrasting figures of the local lawyers, with tanned and weathered skin, and of outside counsel—the elegant New Yorker, Theodore Kendl, and the loquacious John Frank, a writer of popular works on law, ex-law teacher at Yale, and now a resident of Arizona, though hardly a native. Both would in a year or so fade from the scene, leaving the case in the hands of long-time Arizona practitioners.

On the California side the contrast was as great, although not of the same kind. Leading counsel, with the task not only of defending against Arizona (and, as it turned out, against the United States) but also of suppressing any mutinous tendencies in his own ranks, Northcutt Ely, a Washington, D.C. lawyer who had spent a career on the Colorado River beginning as an aide to Ray Lyman Wilbur, President Hoover's Interior Secretary and author of the Boulder Dam water delivery contracts with the California agencies. In the courtroom Ely is a human computer—dry, unemotional, imperturbable, loaded with information instantly available. At his right hand sat M. J. Dowd, for years the chief engineer of the Imperial Irrigation District, a veteran of many a tangle in the hearing room, and a quick-witted, well-informed, cagey witness. To provide the drama on the California side was Harry Horton, long-time attorney for the Imperial Irrigation District, highly emotional, quick-tempered, absolutely certain of the justice of his cause, and suspicious of everybody—even (it would seem) of his erstwhile allies.

These and many, many more were present on that opening day, and an air of Armageddon pervaded the room—though of course there was sharp disagreement over the identity of the forces of Good and Evil. Men were present on both sides who had literally spent their lives on the battle over the Colorado. And for Arizona, it was the long-awaited moment; it was now or never. For California, who had long played the waiting game, the crisis was now at hand—having contracts and works for 5.362 million acre-feet, she had nothing to gain, only water to lose.

Promptly at ten o'clock, Judge Simon H. Rifkind took his place on the bench to begin the trial. He is a short, energetic man with quick, alert eyes. A highly respected federal district judge who resigned to engage in an extremely successful New York litigation practice, Rifkind very quickly captured the respect of the lawyers for his rapid perception, his intelligence and his forthright willingness to rule. . . . This was June 14, 1956.[16]

Substitute for Rifkind, a former judge, Meyers, a former academic. Substitute New Mexico, an upstream state with nothing to gain, only water to lose, for California, a downstream state in the same position. Substitute Texas, since the 1960s struggling to rescue something from the Pecos River Compact, for Arizona, for at least as long trying to save something from the Colorado River. Substitute 1984, when *Texas v. New Mexico* finally got under way, for 1956, when *Arizona v. California* started. All the elements of the start of *Texas v. New Mexico* under Special Master Charles J. Meyers's reign were foreshadowed in his article of almost thirty years earlier.

The choice of Meyers to replace Breitenstein demonstrated a switch in Supreme Court policy from using the free services of semi-retired senior federal judges as special masters in original jurisdiction cases to a policy of hiring—and paying hefty fees to—private legal specialists like Meyers. By 1987 some members of the Supreme Court itself would balk at the high price of Meyers's services, writing that the $260 an hour he billed for time spent on the case was an outrageous charge for what should have been prestigious public service. This opinion horrified Meyers's partners in the Gibson, Dunn, and Crutcher firm. Characteristically, Meyers himself didn't care. In his view he'd done the work, and the parties had to pay the freight. He'd made that clear right from the beginning of his tenure as special master. Indeed, the first order that he entered in the case directed Texas and New Mexico to cough up $25,000 each to cover his fees and other litigation expenses.[17]

The first substantive task that Meyers set in 1984 was determining for the years 1950–1983 how the arrival of water at the New Mexico-Texas state line compared with what the just-established "1947 condition" said should have arrived. This determination involved mathematically sending the water down the Pecos River for each year after 1949 to see what got to the state line and how much should have under the "1947 condition." To begin, Meyers hired for himself a new technical assistant. (The Texas lawyers did not want someone like Breitenstein's assistant, an engineer who consistently had sided with New Mexico's approach to the highly technical river routing questions.) Meyers turned to a Denver water firm, Wright Engineering, with whom the New Mexicans had had previous unhappy dealings. New Mexico protested, but to no avail.[18]

Beginning with April 1985 meetings in Dallas, followed by May meetings in Albuquerque, the technical experts for New Mexico and Texas got together without the lawyers or the special master or his expert, to hammer out the details of the computations. There was trouble from the start. The engineers could not agree, for example, on such esoterica as the computations of flood inflows for the Alamogordo to Artesia reach of the river and for the Artesia to Damsite 3 reach. Other equally esoteric statistical problems plagued the efforts of the two states to come up with their own model of how the Pecos River had performed in the 1950–1983 period under the compact-imposed "1947 condition."[19]

The New Mexicans knew that if the two states couldn't agree, Meyers's expert technical assistant would impose his own solution. Given their mistrust of Wright Engineering, this possibility was worse than anything they might agree to. So Slingerland and Reynolds set out to propose acceptable solutions to particular problems in defining the 1950–1983 river deliveries.[20]

They did so by marching across the hall of the Bataan Memorial Building from their offices to the office of their technical people and delivering a range of possible coefficients for particular factors in the river routing. They asked their hydrologists and computer wizards, using these arbitrary values, to run the model for the whole river and the entire 1950–1983 period in order to gauge how the particular choice would affect the next question: whether New Mexico had under- or over-delivered water at the state line for each year. (Only if New Mexico had under-delivered would they then need to worry about how much of that under-delivery had been caused by "man's activities" in New Mexico.) This tinkering, factor by factor, gain by gain, loss by loss, went on for months in the spring and summer of 1985 and always began the same way. Either Reynolds or Slingerland or, to the horror of the scientists, sometime both, would cross the hall bearing a new number and ask the hydrologists to try a new value.[21]

This pragmatic approach was one that Special Master Breitenstein had warned against early on in the *Texas v. New Mexico* proceedings. He had admonished engineers from the two states to proceed on the basis of good science, not acceptable results. Now here were Reynolds and Slingerland, only eight years later, going against that early advice.[22]

The profoundly unscientific approach attitude of the two New Mexico water leaders also offended some of their own technical people, from whom they asked for particular answers to particular problems without ever explaining why the specific questions were being asked. To the hydrologists and computer modelers in the state engineer's own office, New Mexico was missing a good chance to assemble a modern, holistic view of the Pecos River basin. But Reynolds and Slingerland were not interested in what Royce Tipton had called a "realistic model of the way that nature actually operates." When one of the state engineer's own people offered to determine the effect of man's activities on the flow of the Pecos River, using updated data and techniques, Reynolds and Slingerland were not interested. It was Texas's problem, not New Mexico's.[23]

The two New Mexican water leaders were practical men dealing with inexact science. They were interested not so much in an accurate portrait of the Pecos River as they were in establishing a delivery obligation that wouldn't saddle New Mexican water users with an impossible obligation in the future. Already, in a nightmare that would recur over and over again in *Texas v. New Mexico*, effect had overcome cause and result had overcome analysis.

Regardless of one's view of Slingerland and Reynolds, it wasn't too hard to come up with most of the numbers that would show how the Pecos River had performed between 1950 and 1983 compared to how it should have performed under the base-line "1947 condition." By November 1985, the two states had agreed on many of the previously disputed, highly technical choices. It looked as if Texas and New Mexico engineers would agree on the total amount of water ("departures from the 1947 condition"), which should have, but had not, reached the state line during the thirty-three-year-period. In the meantime, however, during the summer of 1985, a new, even more critical legal issue began to surface in the *Texas v. New Mexico* proceedings when Special Master Meyers resurrected an issue that the New Mexicans assumed already had been decided, in their favor, by Special Master Breitenstein.[24]

The trouble started in June 1985, when Meyers directed Texas and New Mexico to file briefs on the so-called "burden of proof" issue. He was trying to determine which state, Texas or New Mexico, would be responsible for deciding which departures had been caused "by man's activities in New Mexico," for which the compact made New Mexico responsible, and which by something else, for which New Mexico wouldn't be responsible. It was a critical question in Steve Reynolds's litigation strategy, for he assumed that Texas would have to answer it and couldn't, thus assuring an ultimate New Mexico victory. Meyers's predecessor seemed to have explicitly ruled that the burden would fall on Texas. In 1983, the Supreme Court itself seemed to have agreed. But in 1985 Meyers was treating it as an open question.[25]

By then New Mexico and Texas each had a third generation of lawyers arguing the *Texas v. New Mexico* suit. New Mexican Peter White and Texan Renea Hicks brought their own styles to the critical burden of proof issues. White had worked for the legal division of the New Mexico State Engineer Office ever since he graduated from law school in 1969. By 1985 a sixteen-year veteran of the office, he was

Presumption of Charles J. Meyers

steeped in New Mexico water law although he had not had much to do either with interstate litigation generally or with *Texas v. New Mexico* in particular. Not having lived through Special Master Breitenstein's 1977 pronouncements on the burden of proof issue he now faced before Special Master Meyers, White could regard them as new. A shy, scholarly attorney who read philosophy for fun, White was a fan of the Austrian philosopher Ludwig Wittgenstein. Like Wittgenstein, White wrote in a compressed, almost aphoristic style.[26]

The first briefs that White filed in the case, dealing with the burden of proof issue, revealed his penchant for elliptical analysis. He argued that Texas had assumed the burden "of proving the two essential elements of its cause of action, namely, that there are negative departures in stateline flows *and* that man's activities caused the departures." Almost as an afterthought, White added that there was no basis for presuming that man's activities had caused negative departures. "There is an equal likelihood, *a priori*," he wrote, "that natural forces caused the departures." Even if there were a presumption, he concluded, New Mexico could still show that, as a matter of fact, the presumption wasn't justified. In the end, Meyers seized on these second two New Mexico points and, in classic lawyer-like fashion, turned them against Peter White, Steve Reynolds, and New Mexico.[27]

In the meantime, Texas's new lawyer Renea Hicks responded in his own style. Hicks was a tested trial lawyer. He had no previous experience in water law, but he was a skillful, no nonsense attorney who was not impressed by the esoteric hydrological lingo all around him. The combination of a completely fresh perspective and a sharp, skeptical intellect gave him an advantage over those who were mired in the decade of confusing litigation to that point. When New Mexico's opening brief on what turned out to be the critical "burden of proof" issue arrived in the summer of 1985, Hicks figured out how to turn it to his advantage.

The question, he argued, was not which party—Texas or New Mexico—had the burden of proving that man's activities in New Mexico had caused post-1947 departures. That burden fell initially on Texas. But Texas already had met it because the court-adopted "1947 condition" routing studies accounted for all natural factors in the river flow including channel losses, salt cedar losses, and all other natural losses to the system. Therefore, "state line departures are presumptively due to man's activities. . . . (C)onsequently in this phase of the case," wrote Hicks, "New Mexico bears the burden of going forward with evidence to rebut the presumption and of persuading the Master that the departures derived from causes other than man's activities."[28]

Hicks justified switching the burden from Texas to New Mexico on two practical grounds. First, argued Hicks, the compact itself required New Mexico as the upstream state to meet downstream Texas's rights by limiting its own uses. It was only fair that the state where the harm originated—New Mexico—demonstrate that the causes of the harm—state line departures from the 1947 condition—were legally permissible. Second, Hicks added, New Mexico had "superior access to the evidence of the causes for under deliveries of water to Texas" because the causes all originated under New Mexico's "relatively elaborate state regulatory system for both surface and ground water." Hicks had taken the compact, which Reynolds regarded as not enforceable, and New Mexico state water law, which Reynolds regarded as advanced, and turned them both against him.[29]

Hicks' startling approach had the virtue of honoring the distinction between natural departures from the 1947 condition and departures caused by man's activities while at the same time eliminating the difference between them. It overturned Steve Reynolds's assumptions. Not only had Texas answered a question that Reynolds assumed couldn't be answered, but New Mexico was left with the difficult task of challenging that answer. In effect, Hicks had turned Steve Reynolds's ace-in-the-hole into Texas's.

There, in the summer of 1985, the evidentiary issue lay. In late July, Special Master Meyers called New Mexico lawyer White. Meyers let him know that he was "inclined" to adopt Texas's view that the annual 1950–1983 studies of how the Pecos River had performed under the "1947 condition" automatically accounted for natural changes in the river and, therefore, "by force of logic," had to mean that "man's activities" had caused departures. However, Meyers told White, he wouldn't formally rule until all the evidence was in on the river's performance in the period. In the meantime, the engineers and lawyers returned their attention to determining total shortfalls in the state line deliveries between 1950 and 1983.[30]

Early on Slingerland had done some informal calculations that estimated that New Mexico might end up 5,000 acre-feet a year short during the period. When the final tinkering was done, Texas and New Mexico agreed that New Mexico had under-delivered water at the state line by 370,000 acre-feet over the thirty-four-year 1950–1983 period. Conveniently, that amounted to around 10,000 acre-feet a year, a figure a little larger than Slingerland's early guess. Even though neither the total deficit nor the additional annual obligation accurately reflected the best scientific description either of the "1947 condition" or the Pecos River in the years thereafter, the New Mexicans were not worried.[31]

The total deficit did not worry the New Mexicans because no interstate Supreme Court decision ever had awarded to any state (here Texas) damages for the unintentional failure of one state (New Mexico) to abide by the terms of a compact with another state. Instead, the Supreme Court had restricted itself to directing the non-complying state (New Mexico) to comply with the compact in the future. In other words, in the future New Mexico might have to deliver at the most an additional 10,000 acre-feet a year at the Texas state line and that would only be true, the New Mexicans still assumed, as long as Texas could show that "man's activities" in New Mexico accounted for all 10,000 acre-feet. Otherwise, the 10,000 acre-feet would be reduced by the amount not attributable to "man's activities."

In the view of Steve Reynolds and Carl Slingerland that future was still a long, long way off. When the day finally came, if it ever did, Texas's claim to additional Pecos River water would come close to Slingerland's twenty-year-old 5,000 acre-foot guess. Figured that way, New Mexicans might have to give up 1,000 irrigated acres and they'd probably already done so. As the time approached for the first formal *Texas v. New Mexico* hearings supervised by Special Master Meyers in late November and early December, 1985, there wasn't yet much cause for the New Mexicans to worry.[32]

At those hearings, vestiges of Steve Reynolds's overall strategy surfaced in bits and pieces such as the earlier Reynolds-inspired 1962 Pecos River Commission determination that between 1950 and 1961 total state line departures had amounted to only 50,000 acre-feet, of which almost none should be charged to "man's activities in New Mexico." Reynolds now told Meyers that he had to accept that determination. The issue involved complex administrative law analyses of obscure and by then ancient PRC minutes. Eventually Special Master Meyers sided with New Mexico on the narrow issue, but the victory was almost Pyrrhic. On the broader question of the jurisdiction of the court to do anything in the absence of a prior commission decision, Special Master Meyers was clearly favoring the court.[33]

In that role, Meyers was confronted with two other Steve Reynolds ploys for reducing the Texas claim. First, for some time Reynolds had maintained that New Mexico was entitled to a credit for a decrease in the number of irrigated acres since 1947 in the upper reach of the Pecos River. Texas and New Mexico had agreed that the decrease amounted to 2,719 acres. The precise number measured the general decline of irrigation in New Mexico's Hispanic northern communities. Meyers finally agreed that the decrease since 1947 entitled New Mexico to a credit of almost 7,000 acre-feet against any increased depletions chargeable to New Mexico during the 1950–1983 period.[34]

Meyers got another glimpse of the Reynolds approach when New Mexico claimed for the first time that oil and gas operations in Texas, conducted just across the border and thirty miles from Carlsbad, had depleted the river in New Mexico by almost 100,000 acre-feet over the 1950–1983 period. Unlike the long-standing Upper Reach claim, Reynolds and Slingerland had cooked up this theory late in the game.[35]

With no notice to Texas, little notice to Meyers and not much more to their own technical division, the two instructed Deborah Hathaway, a hydrologist in the state engineer office, to testify that pumping water for secondary oil recovery in Texas took Pecos River water away in New Mexico. Their theory was simple enough: pumping in the Capitan Aquifer in Texas reduced the water level in the aquifer, causing the surface flow of the Pecos River at Carlsbad Springs to diminish, thus reducing the river's flow at the state line. They aimed to secure for New Mexico another large credit because a Pecos River depletion by Texas surely couldn't be charged to New Mexico.[36]

Hathaway did the best that she could in the short preparation time allowed to her, with no more geology to go on than a very controversial and very out of date Ph.D dissertation, and with a foregone conclusion dictated by her bosses. However, when it came time to present her Capitan Reef study to the special master in November and December 1985, Meyers lit into her in his inimitable fashion for being unprofessional, and, ultimately, unconvincing. It was as if *Texas v. New Mexico* was just another Stanford Law School class and Ms. Hathaway just another unprepared first-year law student.[37]

In the end, Special Master Meyers accepted New Mexico's claim for credits based on diminished irrigation since 1947 in the Hispanic upper Pecos River basin and rejected New Mexico's claim for an offset based on Texas groundwater pumping in the Capitan Reef.[38]

However, astute observers couldn't help but notice the irony of both claims in the context of the suit as a whole. Even if New Mexico got a small credit for irrigating less land in the upper reach since 1947, the real problem in *Texas v. New Mexico* was that New Mexico had irrigated more land and taken more water in the middle reach since 1947. And New Mexico's rejected claim that Texas had misappropriated Pecos River water by groundwater pumping was tiny compared to New Mexico's misappropriation, if that's what it was, of Pecos River water through groundwater pumping in Carlsbad and Roswell. On those two much more critical aspects of human impact on the Pecos River, the New

Mexicans said not a word. This was a lawsuit. They weren't about to help Texas prove its case against New Mexico. Slingerland and Reynolds never stopped believing those subjects fell to Texas to address.[39]

They should have given the idea up when they read Meyers's draft report issued in March 1986. Meyers began the third section by accepting the list of departures from New Mexico's "state-line 1947 obligation" for the 1950–1983 period that Texas and New Mexico had agreed to. In the next sentence, Meyers delivered to New Mexico a time bomb. "This computation," he wrote, "accounts for all non-manmade depletions and thus shows depletions that are the result of man's activities." In one fell swoop, Meyers had bought the analysis first suggested by Renea Hicks that summer. In so doing Meyers eliminated what New Mexicans believed would be years of litigation trying to separate those departures caused by man's activities in New Mexico from those not. Instead, Meyers proposed to rule that New Mexico should be charged for failing to deliver to Texas 343,100 acre-feet of water, all of which was attributable to "man's activities in New Mexico."[40]

As if that wasn't bad enough from New Mexico's point of view, Meyers's proposed ruling brought him to the unimaginable consideration of what remedy to grant to Texas for New Mexico's failure to comply with the compact over all those years. Here, once again, Steve Reynolds and the New Mexicans had been counting on the fact that if the day of reckoning ever came, which they believed it never would, the Supreme Court would only order the state to conform to the compact as ultimately construed in the future. At the worst New Mexico would have gotten away free with its forty years of past Pecos River uses. But that's not how Special Master Meyers saw it in March 1986.

Acting pretty much on his own, primarily because he was himself so far ahead of the curve of the litigation, at least as New Mexico saw it, Meyers added a last section to his Draft Report concerning remedies. New Mexico, he proposed to rule, would not only have to figure out a way to get an average 10,000 extra acre-feet a year to the Texas state line in the future. In addition, New Mexico would have to pay back the 340,000 acre-feet that it had not delivered between 1950 and 1983. For the past wrongs, said Meyers, New Mexico would have to pay in water because that's all the compact authorized. Because the flow of the Pecos River at the New Mexico-Texas state line averaged only 75,000 acre-feet a year, even Meyers acknowledged that New Mexico couldn't repay the water debt in one year. So he proposed to give the New Mexicans ten years. In those ten years New Mexico would have to deliver an average 34,000 acre-feet a year (340,000 total debt divided by ten years) for the debt and another average additional 10,000 acre-feet a year to meet its current obligation. If New Mexico failed to make that delivery of an average additional 44,000 acre-feet in any year, then the Meyers proposal would assess water interest, the debt plus current obligation would increase, and New Mexico would fall even further behind.[41]

It didn't take a computer modeler to see what a drastic position this proposal put New Mexico in. The annual assessment of 44,000 acre-feet was more than half the 75,000 acre-feet of water that usually reached the state line; to produce that amount New Mexico would have to increase by half the state line flow. The 44,000 acre-feet also amounted to enough water to irrigate 10,000 acres of land in New Mexico; to produce it New Mexico would have to dry up more than one hundred serious New Mexico farmers like Morgan Nelson. "Could madman Charles Meyers be serious?" the New Mexicans wondered.

Indeed, Meyers was. He justified this harsh remedy because, he said, he had to find a way to force New Mexico to comply with the terms of his decree. New Mexico, he believed, would avoid and postpone meeting the terms of any ruling unless it was in her interests to do so. "It can be argued," Meyers continued in his draft report of March 18, 1986,

> that the interest component of the proposed decree places an undue burden on New Mexico, for it adds a burden to the already onerous task of cutting back existing uses. *But it must be recalled that New Mexico has known since 1961—if not earlier—that it has been in default under the Compact, and so far as the record shows it has not sought to perform its obligations, but rather has sought to avoid them, or at least delay performance as long as possible.*[42]

When Reynolds and his lawyers saw this proposed language, they almost died. Once again, Meyers had contradicted a previous finding of his predecessor. Special Master Breitenstein explicitly had ruled in 1978–1979 that both Texas and New Mexico had been proceeding in good faith all along. Now here was Special Master Meyers, seven years later, saying that New Mexico had knowingly and in bad faith cheated and delayed Texas for twenty-five years. Steve Reynolds must have known that there was some truth in what Meyers wrote, but in the state engineer's mind any delay was based on the fact that no one ever told New Mexico what its compact obligations were and New Mexico never knew. Now Meyers was saying that New Mexico knew all along.[43]

Reynolds and his lawyers panicked in particular at the damages implicated by this totally unwarranted finding. Standard contract law, they knew, provided that a party to a contract who intentionally breached its

Resumption of Charles J. Meyers

terms might have to pay damages measured not by the harm to the other party, in this case the poor Texas farmers, but by the benefit to itself, in this case the relatively prosperous farmers of Carlsbad and Roswell. As long as water was the medium of damage exchange, the measure of damages didn't make that much difference, but if money ever measured the damages, then Meyers's finding posed a huge economic threat.

The New Mexicans lit into Meyers's draft report as best they could. With respect to the bad faith issue raised by Meyers himself, the New Mexicans took the high road. In oral arguments in the spring of 1986, they simply told Meyers that he was wrong. Quiet, scholarly Peter White quoted the Meyers report and then simply said,

> there is no justification in the administrative history of the Compact before 1974 or in this litigation after 1974 for this disparaging statement. The Pecos River Commission has never notified appropriate officials of New Mexico that it has not met its delivery obligation.[44]

On this point even Meyers couldn't quarrel. He'd made a mistake. To Meyers, it was nothing more than an "impression" he'd "gleaned" from the minutes of the Pecos River Compact Commission. It was easily corrected. In his final July 1986 Report he deleted all references to New Mexico's intentional default and now found, as his predecessor had, that New Mexico and Texas had proceeded all along in good faith. But to the New Mexicans, Meyers's mistaken first "impression" simply confirmed his outspoken and impolite bias against New Mexico.[45]

With respect to Meyers's attribution of all 1950–1983 departures to "man's activities in New Mexico," the New Mexicans also took the high road at the April oral arguments on the draft report. Peter White approached the special master's radical analysis from two perspectives. First, he argued, Meyers's view that departures were caused either by nature or by man's activities was fundamentally wrong. There was, argued White, a third category of causes for departures from the "1947 condition": "unknown causes." This category, suggested White, comprised all those departures that couldn't be attributed to either "natural" or "human" activities.

White's approach had the virtue of coming at Meyers on his own lawyer-like terms. If Meyers, like most lawyers, made sense of the world by carving it into discrete categories that, as Meyers himself said, "contained the universe," then White's suggestion of a third category was true to Meyers's conception of the world. It just added another category to a contained universe, carving it up in a slightly more complicated way.

Into that third category of "unknown causes" White and New Mexico could have poured all the scientific limitations of the "1947 condition" routing study and the subsequent determinations of inflows and outflows. For example, base inflow to the Pecos River around Roswell had always been a critical factor in the compact's apportionment of water between Texas and New Mexico. Its amount was deeply influenced by groundwater pumping—a classic "man's activity in New Mexico"—and rainfall—a classic "natural" activity in New Mexico. But the precise relationship between pumping and base inflow was as unsure as the precise relationship between precipitation and base inflow. As a result, it was very difficult to say whether increased pumping, for which New Mexico was responsible, or decreased precipitation, for which it was not, had caused an impermissible drop in base inflow in any post-1950 year. Out of that uncertainty White proposed to create his third category of "unknown causes."[46]

Special Master Meyers quickly saw where this third category would take him: into a lengthy, ambiguous, complex second-stage determination of the cause of departures, just the kind of proceeding that Steve Reynolds had been counting on and that Meyers was struggling to avoid. When Peter White proposed the existence of the third category, Meyers shuddered.

"I really need help on this question," he pleaded in one of his rare insecure moments, "on the basic notion of Mr. White's contention that the inflow-outflow methodology doesn't take care of everything. If he is right about that, that is serious in terms of the validity of this Draft Report."[47]

As it turned out, Peter White himself offered Special Master Meyers a way out of the third category problem when he suggested that there was an evidentiary as well as a conceptual problem with Meyers's approach. White suggested that no witness had testified that the routings of the river from 1950 to 1983 in fact accounted for all natural changes in the river so all departures had to come from "man's activities," as Special Master Meyers said. Meyers shamelessly began casting about among the remaining Texas witnesses for one who would agree with his position.

He began with Texas engineer Robert Whittenton. Whittenton had worked on the Texas version of a manual for the Pecos River Commission's compact administration of the river for over a decade. As long ago as 1978 he had testified about how the commission and the manual should handle differences between "1947 condition" flows and reductions in flow caused by "man's activities in New Mexico." In 1978 he had acknowledged New Mexico was only ultimately responsible for

Presumption of Charles I. Meyers

the latter, and that any manual had to find some way to account for the difference between "1947 condition" flow reductions and "1947 condition" flow reductions caused by "man's activities in New Mexico." In 1978 Whittenton had found a way out by artificially increasing "natural" causes of flow reduction in order to guarantee that the rest were man-made. In May 1986, he stuck to his approach.[48]

In 1978 Whittenton had confounded Special Master Breitenstein. Now, in 1987, he infuriated Special Master Meyers. Time and time again, late into the evening of May 1, Engineer Whittenton said exactly what Special Master Meyers did not want to hear: the routing studies required a two-step process in order to make the compact work. First, the commission had to determine gross departures from the 1947 condition and then it had to determine which of those New Mexico had caused by man's activities. Hearing Whittenton's testimony and recognizing that what he was saying almost contradicted what he himself was saying about the "logic" of the routing studies, Meyers lit into Whittenton. When he couldn't get Whittenton to stop saying that a two-step process would be required to isolate man-caused departures from all "1947 condition" departures, Meyers abruptly cancelled the evening session. He advised Texas not to re-call Engineer Whittenton in the morning, and told them to find another witness overnight who would testify that only one step was needed to make compact determinations because the initial gross departures were all caused by "man's activities" in New Mexico. First thing the next morning, Texas re-called V. R. Krishna Murthy as a witness.[49]

Murthy already had earned the enmity of the New Mexico engineers with whom he had worked in hammering out the technical agreements that had produced the mostly agreed upon definition of the "1947 condition." The New Mexicans had found Murthy unreliable, inconstant and unprincipled in those endless, highly technical, lawyerless meetings. Now, on the morning of May 2 Murthy willingly played straight into the hand of Special Master Meyers.[50]

On this occasion Murthy began as Texas's witness and ended as Meyers's. Shamelessly interjecting himself into the litigation process, Meyers quickly made Murthy the special master's own witness and then, stranger still, the Master became the witness himself.

"You testified a minute ago," began Texas lawyer Hicks in the traditional courtroom mode of lawyers asking witnesses questions and judges listening to the question and the answers, "(t)hat you conclude that the . . . departure is all attributable to man's activities in New Mexico?"

Chapter 7

"Yes, your honor," responded Murthy, "because we have adjusted for all the known natural losses . . . So the remaining we are ascribing to man's activities."[51]

At that point Myers himself jumped in:

Special Master: That is the way that I have felt about it for a long time. I have made no secret about that. Both parties have been informed. But you do need to go one step further and you need to say—maybe you've got it—you have to say why you ascribe it to man's activities. What is the reason for ascribing it to man's activities?

Murthy: Because, Your Honor, we adjusted the computations for all the natural causes. For instance, the channel losses Alamogordo Dam to Acme, we revised that channel loss equation to reflect the actual losses that are occurring 1950–1983. Acme to Artesia inflows—

Special Master: Let me shorten it. I think that is what I have understood all along, and I will put it probably in law terms. You have attempted by your best efforts to account for every natural loss in the system?

Murthy: Yes, your honor.

Special Master: Through various changes and correlations, and the only additional losses more likely than not are due to man's activities. Isn't it just a logical proposition that if the universe is here and you have accounted for everything in the universe except one element and that one element is man's activities, the formula is so constructed that everything is accounted for except that one ingredient, namely losses due to man's activities. Is that an accurate description of Texas's . . . [testimony]?

Murthy: Yes.[52]

Meyers went on to prod Murthy into saying that the inevitable wild variations from year to year in the difference between "1947 condition" and actual flows were produced by innocent annual differences in flood inflows, nothing more sinister than the "perturbations" or "vagaries" of the Pecos River, as the New Mexicans had become fond of calling them. With that explanation, Special Master Meyers had an "independent" expert opinion to back up the position that he had independently arrived at months before.[53]

That was all Meyers needed to revise his March draft report and issue his Final Report in July 1986. To his credit, he did drop all references to New Mexico's bad faith over the long period after 1961 when the Pecos River Commission had been badly stalled. But when it came to dealing with the fundamental problem of whether all departures from the "1947 condition" in the years after 1950 could automatically be attributed to "man's activities in New Mexico," he stuck to his guns.

Now, however, he no longer had to base that ruling on logic alone. Now he based it on Texas witness Murthy. "Dr. Murthy's testimony made it clear," Meyers wrote,

> that the procedures followed . . . accounted for all non-man-made depletions so that any residual departure was, by force of logic, the result of man's activities. . . . Nothing in the New Mexico cross-examination of Dr. Murthy or in the rebuttal testimony of Mr. Carl Slingerland convinced me to the contrary. Dr. Murthy's testimony was credible, consistent with the view of my technical consultant, and I accept it.[54]

Meyers was surely attributing more independence to Murthy's opinion than it deserved. Special Master Meyers on this occasion himself had called the witness and then had testified for him and asked him to agree as an expert with his (Meyers's) own preconceived conclusion. It was just this kind of extrajudicial behavior that infuriated the New Mexicans. Their anger didn't move Meyers at all. He had said over and over again that he didn't think the Supreme Court would be interested in the highly technical hydrological details of the Pecos River Compact. Now he had diminished the centerpiece of the compact's hydrology, dismissing it as an esoteric debate among expert witnesses, which he resolved as a matter of fact in favor of Texas.[55]

The New Mexicans had started to fall apart under Special Master Meyers's blitzkrieg attack. Meyers had been ruthless in cutting them off. In a panic the New Mexicans realized they had themselves presented no evidence on "man's activities in New Mexico" and never would get a chance to. When they had tried to reopen the subject at the May hearings, Meyers stopped them in their tracks.

"You can argue the question of man's activities to the Supreme Court," an increasingly testy Meyers had told Peter White late in the long first day of hearings in May, "but I don't think that I will open it back up." The ugly exchanged continued:

> *Meyers:* You had plenty of notice that if you wanted to get into man's activities, in fact I told you a long, long time ago that you would have the

burden of proof on man's activities. I may be wrong and the Supreme Court may reverse me. That's something else. But the motion is out of order because you had plenty of notice what my views were and that you would have to come forward, if you wanted to, with any evidence of manmade depletions.

White: There was no specification on this matter until the Draft Report was issued. There was no order on this question even though it was briefed last summer. I do acknowledge there were telephone conversations and that is the impression you gave me, but my impression was that without expert opinion to predicate a judgment that you can presume that the negative departures are a residual caused by man's activities, that there would be no foundation in the record to support the presumption, it would be clearly legal error.

Meyers: I think that it is too late . . . for you to claim now that you should be allowed to put on your evidence about man's activities. I deny the motion. Proceed.[56]

Late on the second day of the two-day May hearing, White tried again. When once again he asked for permission to show that departures in state line deliveries weren't necessarily caused by "man's activities in New Mexico," Meyers shut him off again. "If that's possible," said Meyers, "if there is a likely explanation or a plausible explanation (for the departures), you should have put on evidence as to that fact."[57]

White: I don't think that's fair. I think that until today there was no evidence in support of the inference, which you are relying on for the basis of the presumption.

Meyers: You were taking a very high risk, weren't you? You were taking a high risk that I was technically wrong and that I would be technically reversed or something. That's no way to try a lawsuit. Do you see what I am saying? If you had any substantive evidence [that departures were not caused by man's activities] you should have put it on.[58]

The beleaguered Peter White was the epitome of an honorable attorney, almost an innocent in the constantly shifting, psychologically complex hardball world of interstate water litigation. He had to shoulder the burden of the position that Reynolds and Slingerland had developed long ago: that Texas had to prove that man's activities in New Mexico had impermissibly reduced the Pecos River flow at the state line after 1947.

The engineers had stuck to their story like true believers, but Meyers had burned them on the stake as it were, and Peter White suffered the consequences. The May 1986 hearings ended with his curious confession that he had intentionally avoided offering evidence on an issue he believed fell to Texas."[59]

Special Master Meyers gracefully accepted Peter White's explanation, acknowledging to him that he had "no sense that you in any way were unprofessional." But Meyers stuck to his view that New Mexico had lost its chance to explain why the post-1947 diminishment in state-line Pecos River flows did not result from man's activities in New Mexico. New Mexico, the state that had articulated the need for scientific management of man's activities in water resources, was silenced in *Texas v. New Mexico*. Meyers rudely had cut off State Engineer Steve Reynolds, the architect of that management, early in the May hearings, and now was sure that he wouldn't have to listen to his explanations thereafter.[60]

At the close of the two-day hearings, May 1986, Meyers emphasized again and again that, as he said, "we are at the very end of this thing . . . we have come to the final, final end." He even bid adieu to the assembled contestants. "I thank you again," he began in the courtly Texas manner that sometimes shone through his short-tempered abruptness. "Despite occasional difficulties," he continued,

> not anything as serious as Judge Breitenstein led me to believe when he turned this over to me, I think that you have conducted yourselves in a highly professional manner, lawyers, engineers, all the people who have participated, and I thank you very much and I hope that we meet again under other circumstances.[61]

With that farewell, Meyers withdrew to write his final report. His intent was to wrap up *Texas v. New Mexico*. The report finally construed the Pecos River Compact's obligations: New Mexico was responsible for all negative departures from the "1947 condition." The report also assessed the damages that New Mexico owed Texas for past breaches of the compact: New Mexico had to repay Texas in water and with water interest the 340,000 acre-feet that it had illegally withheld between 1950 and 1983.[62]

Finally, the Report set out the procedures by which New Mexico's future obligations would be determined: A neutral river master would make annual computations based on an approved manual that would allow a short-cut determination of New Mexico's annual deliveries of Pecos River water to Texas. The river master would promptly let New Mexico and Texas know how much water, if any, New Mexico owed

Texas every year thereafter. New Mexico would have to deliver any shortfalls within six months.[63]

Meyers believed that in four years he had concluded *Texas v. New Mexico*. Little did he know that his July 1986 report hardly ended the twelve-year-old lawsuit. He couldn't have guessed that the suit would outlive him just as it had outlived Special Master Jean Breitenstein. As far as he knew, he had completed his task. Now, for the fourth time in the course of the lawsuit, it was up to the Supreme Court to review what Meyers believed was his final work.

Both Texas and New Mexico appealed the July 1986 decision. Texas complained about one small part of the Meyers report. Basically, Renea Hicks regarded the decision as a resounding victory for Texas and appealed simply to make the Meyers decision look less lop-sided than he really believed it was.[64]

For the New Mexicans, the appeal was a desperate matter. The costs of complying with the decision, they honestly believed, would be disastrous, especially in the initial ten-year period when they would have to both pay back to Texas the water Meyers had ruled New Mexico had wrongfully withheld in the 1950–1986 period *and* increase the state-line flow to meet the new definition of the "1947 condition" that would apply in the future. In fact, the hard-nosed Meyers decision had thrown the state engineer lawyers and engineers into such a funk that for almost the first time ever in the agency's proud history, they turned to outside legal help for representation before the Supreme Court.

After consulting with Reynolds and Slingerland, state engineer chief counsel Peter White got on the phone in the late summer of 1986 and called Charlotte Uram, who had helped write the briefs and had argued *Texas v. New Mexico* the last time the case had been in the Supreme Court in 1983. By 1986, Uram had left New Mexico, where she had lived for only a couple of years, and moved to San Francisco, where she had taken a job as a litigator with a high-rolling West Coast firm. When Peter White called, the ambitious, peripatetic Uram was about to move again. He explained to her that he felt that he wasn't quick enough on his feet to argue in the Supreme Court and asked her if she would consider repeating her 1983 performance. Uram hadn't been bruised as White had been by Charles Meyers. She had enjoyed the 1983 argument. No wonder she accepted Peter White's invitation immediately.[65]

Through the fall of 1986 and into the winter of 1987, Uram and White, Slingerland, and Reynolds struggled to assemble for the Supreme Court a comprehensible attack on Special Master Meyers's July 1986 Report. They focused primarily on the most immediate problem that Meyers had created: the requirement that New Mexico pay back to Texas in only ten years and in water the 343,000 acre-feet that Meyers said New Mexico had illegally withheld from Texas in the 1950–1983 period. There was no way, the New Mexicans believed, that they could produce an additional 34,000 acre-feet a year for ten years at the state line without shutting down completely the irrigated agriculture of southeastern New Mexico. It would be far better, they argued, to follow a suggestion that Meyers himself had toyed with at the hearings but had rejected: to allow New Mexico to pay money, not water, damages. Monetary payment would adequately compensate Texas for past wrongs.[66]

The New Mexicans also attacked Meyers's scheme for determining New Mexico's obligation in the future, which collapsed into one category negative departures at the state line from the "1947 condition" and departures caused by "man's activities in New Mexico." In their briefs to the Supreme Court, Uram, White, Slingerland, and Reynolds finally found a simple structure into which to fit the complex argument. The 1948 Pecos River Compact, they wrote, had compromised the claims of Texas and New Mexico to the Pecos River. Texas had received a guarantee stabilizing the river at the "1947 condition." New Mexico had received a guarantee that she would only be charged for those changes from the "1947 condition" that had been caused by "man's activities in New Mexico." By eliminating the difference between the "condition" and the "activities" and by making them identical, Meyers had deprived New Mexico of the benefit of the bargain she had struck in 1947. At least, the New Mexicans now wrote, the compact required that New Mexico have the opportunity to show that "man's activities in New Mexico" had not caused departures from the "1947 condition."[67]

At the April 1987 oral arguments before the Supreme Court it became apparent that Colorado's Justice Byron White had taken the lead from Justice Brennan in the Court's review of *Texas v. New Mexico.* Just as Special Master Meyers had predicted, the Court, led by Justice White, was primarily interested in the problem of past damages and not much concerned with future administration and the esoteric distinction between the "1947 condition" and "man's activities." In contrast to the 1983 arguments, Charlotte Uram found the 1987 dialogue between herself and the Court flat, a measure, she guessed, of the Court's fatigue with the case. The few questions that came her way suggested that, while the Supreme Court was skeptical about New Mexico's argument that compact law didn't allow damages for past actions in any form, the Court was inclined to allow New Mexico to pay money, not water. About "man's activities" the court asked few questions.[68]

Sure enough, when the Supreme Court issued its decision less than two months later, on June 8, Justice White's formal opinion upheld the Meyers report and rejected the objections of both Texas and New Mexico. In so doing, White curtly dismissed New Mexico's argument that Meyers's refusal to separately consider "man's activities in New Mexico" had deprived New Mexico of its half of the bargain struck by the two states in the 1948 Compact. "We find no merit," White wrote, with no further explanation, "in and reject the exceptions filed by . . . New Mexico with respect to the Master's calculation of the shortfall that is chargeable to New Mexico." In an accompanying footnote, White added that New Mexico's compact obligation "as now construed and applied by this Court" would require New Mexico to deliver "on the average" 10,000 more acre-feet per year at the state line than it had in the past. It was as if Justice White really thought that he could get rid of what he had called "this dog" of a case by arbitrarily specifying an additional number even though he must have known that it was just such a fixed schedule that the two states had rejected in 1948. He didn't even mention "man's activities."[69]

White also addressed Special Master Meyers's recommendation that New Mexico pay Texas in water for her past failure to perform. The Supreme Court White rejected Meyers's finding that water damages were the only available ones. New Mexico, he wrote, could also compensate Texas by paying money. But standard contract law, not esoteric interstate water law, would measure those damages, and Special Master Meyers would have to determine them.[70]

In the end, it was this White ruling that transformed interstate water litigation thereafter. Academics bitterly disputed the application of standard contract law to interstate water compacts, but practicing water lawyers chomped at the bit. Now for the first time in compact litigation there was a substantial possibility of recovering huge damages for past breaches. White's ruling in *Texas v. New Mexico* started a cottage industry in suits by one state against another for breaches of interstate water agreements. For the moment, Supreme Court Justice White returned the case itself to Special Master Meyers to assess the damages in terms of money and clean up the details for the future by adopting a manual to be incorporated in a new final decree.[71]

Back in Denver and Santa Fe in the summer of 1987, things took a curious and personal turn for the worse before *Texas v. New Mexico* got back on its final course. Special Master Meyers was diagnosed with a particularly virulent form of esophageal cancer. As the cancer took hold, the articulate Meyers had a harder and harder time speaking. In the meantime, the New Mexicans watched their own leader deteriorate.[72]

State Engineer Steve Reynolds had suffered for years from acute diabetes and had managed it well. Now, however, late in his life, his blood sugar sometimes dropped so low so quickly that he went into mild insulin shock, especially as he tired in the afternoon of a long workday. At these times he would lose some of his usually clear diction and precise phrasing, and sometimes it would be difficult to understand him. The October 1987 hearing at which Reynolds was the only witness and Meyers the only judge threatened to turn into a debacle of great men turned old, articulate men rendered dumb.[73]

The Denver hearings in the fall of 1987 focused primarily on the question of how New Mexico's obligation to Texas would be determined annually in the future. The Supreme Court had approved appointment of an administrative "River Master" who would determine the annual amount. He would need directions on how to do it. To that end, both Texas and New Mexico had drafted manuals. The Texas version struck New Mexicans as Draconian. Under it, New Mexico could accumulate credits, but not deficits. Once it fell behind, it would have to make up any shortfalls within six months. Meyers was now to choose between the different versions.[74]

New Mexico called only State Engineer Steve Reynolds as a witness. By the time he began to testify on the first day of the two-day hearings, it was afternoon, not the best time for his blood sugar levels. As Reynolds got under way, he made a couple of uncharacteristic factual mistakes and the New Mexicans quaked at the thought that their long-time leader might drop into the momentary incoherence that increasingly struck him late in the day. However, Reynolds righted himself almost immediately and proceeded, under the guise of discussing the manual for future Pecos River operations, to destroy Special Master Meyers's whole approach to the case.[75]

Reynolds accomplished this feat with a short exhibit that he and Carl Slingerland had prepared just before the hearings. The exhibit was just five pages long and bore the unpretentious designation "New Mexico 137." The two New Mexicans had plotted the estimated annual Pecos River flows for each year from 1919 to 1946 (the accepted version of the "1947 condition") against the inflow/outflow curve that, according to Meyers and the Supreme Court, now defined New Mexico's annual compact obligation. Of course, the annual points scattered on both sides of the curve. Some of the points fell as much as 25,000 acre-feet below the statistically smoothed out mandatory curve.[76]

These annual negative departures, Reynolds testified, would violate the compact's "1947 condition" standard according to Meyers's definition.

But how, Reynolds now asked, could these departures violate the "1947 condition" obligation when they defined the "1947 condition" itself? And how could New Mexico make them up in six months if they couldn't be tied to increased depletions?[77]

Startled for a second when he realized the implications of what Reynolds was saying, Special Master Meyers expressed for the first time in the course of the hearings some genuine doubt about his approach. He began by admitting that he "didn't understand . . . what all of this truly represents." When Reynolds explained again, Meyers caught on. "Well," he complained, "you're putting me really in an awkward position, aren't you, because you are saying that everything that the Supreme Court did and that Judge Breitenstein did, even before I came on the scene, was wrong."[78]

Reynolds responded by saying that until then the decisions had been acceptable, but that Meyers had cut the process of determining New Mexico's compact obligation artificially short. Meyers needed to allow the river master, said Reynolds, either to inquire into "man's activities" in the annual determinations or to spread the accounting period from one year to many years so that the wild annual variations, which were inevitable, could even out.[79]

The moment defined the clash between Reynolds and Meyers. Reynolds, the engineer, saw the compact's science as only a very rough approximation of New Mexico's obligation to Texas. Reynolds counted on that approximation perhaps to delay, maybe to stall, but certainly to complicate any determination. The 1938 Rio Grande Compact had used a crude but easily measured method of determining New Mexico's obligation to Texas—the measured flow of the river at one upstream and one downstream point—and had worked because the compact allowed for the accrual of credits and debits over a long accounting period. The Pecos River Compact, as construed by Meyers, had to work the same way.[80]

Meyers, the lawyer, saw the Pecos River Compact's science as creating a bright standard by which New Mexico's obligation to Texas could be quickly determined and fixed. At these October 1987 hearings, lawyer Meyers realized that engineer Reynolds was right.

Special Meyers Master responded in two ways. First, he turned solicitous. When the direct examination of aging Reynolds was done, Meyers announced, "I have a couple of things on my mind. In the first place, I want to ask how you [Reynolds] are doing, if we should take a break now and then go on to cross-examination, or would you prefer for us to try to do something else and do cross-examination tomorrow morning?"[81]

Then Meyers turned hard. He agreed to consider a couple of minor changes to the proposed river manual, but he finally shut the door to New Mexico's fundamental objection that his plan would inevitably yield wild variations in year-to-year delivery obligations that would create chaos for both New Mexico and Texas. If New Mexico had trouble in any year getting the water needed to make up deficits, suggested Meyers, it could just take it from the Carlsbad Irrigation District. According to his clerk, New Mexican Diana Pool, Meyers took this position not because he believed that Steve Reynolds was wrong, but because he knew that the compact's apportionment couldn't work if it got bogged down every year in a debate about how much of any annual

Fig. 7.2.
New Mexico State Engineer Steve Reynolds and his chief assistant Carl Slingerland also attached this chart to New Mexico Exhibit 137 late in *Texas v. New Mexico*. Both charts showed that "the 1947 condition" at the heart of the Pecos River Compact, as interpreted by Special Master Meyers, violated itself. "The 1947 condition" had been based on subjecting the flows of the river between 1920 and 1946 to "1947 conditions" on the theory that after 1947 New Mexico would have to limit its depletions to the same conditions. But New Mexico Exhibit 137 showed that the "1947 condition" was so inaccurate that even in the base line 1920–1946 period, New Mexico would have been in annual violation of the compact for almost the whole period. (New Mexico 137, October 15, 1987, *Texas v. New Mexico*.)

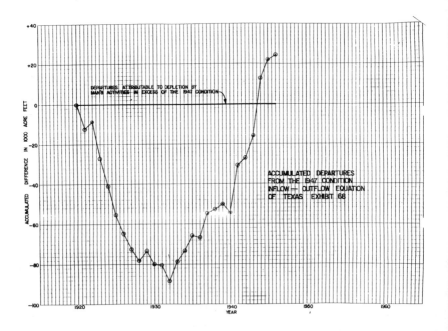

Chapter 7

departure had been caused by "man's activities" in New Mexico. Like most lawyers, Meyers was above all interested in a solution that would work, not one that would do justice to Pecos River hydrology or to the compact. Soon to be silenced himself by throat cancer, Meyers now silenced State Engineer Steve Reynolds by disregarding a fundamental point that he knew was both true and impossible.[82]

From time to time Meyers had blamed Royce Tipton, Steve Reynolds, and Peter White for burdening New Mexico with full responsibility for all the departures indicated by the application of the "1947 condition" to subsequent years and not just those departures that could be connected to "man's activities" in New Mexico. In his last Report to the Supreme Court, filed in early December 1987, Meyers added Jean Breitenstein to the list of those responsible for New Mexico's dilemma. In that Report Meyers told the Court that Breitenstein already had approved the use of the "1947 condition" curve to determine New Mexico's obligation to Texas without any calculation of man's activities. That decision was "the law of the case" and not open to further debate. In early 1988, the Supreme Court, without oral argument, agreed. In a short, anonymous decision announced March 28, the Court rejected New Mexico's objections, adopted the Meyers report, appointed a Pecos River Water Master, and issued an amended decree governing future administration of the Pecos River Compact.[83]

That solution left Special Master Meyers only the matter of following the Supreme Court's final mandate that he compute in money the damages that New Mexico might owe for its past breaches of the compact. Finally the parties were playing on a field whose boundaries Meyers himself had been struggling for decades to create and define: law and economics. What was the value of the water that New Mexico had withheld from Texas between 1950 and 1986? By the end of 1987, he had completed the task of deciding how the compact would operate in the future. Now Meyers set out to determine the dollar amount of New Mexico's past transgressions against Texas.

He never did. The aggressive esophageal cancer required major surgery. As a result, in early 1988 Special Master Meyers completely lost his ability to speak. His law clerk, Diana Poole, had to communicate for him. Through Poole, Meyers asked the New Mexicans if they objected to his continuing, practically voiceless, as special master. They didn't have the heart to object.[84]

New Mexico and Texas twice delayed hearings in order to put together their cases. Each party hired economists to make the estimates. The economists worked slowly, assembling farm costs and crop prices to calculate the direct and indirect benefits to New Mexico and harm to Texas of the Pecos River water that ought to have reached Texas but had stayed in New Mexico between 1950 and 1988. The New Mexican water rights lawyers felt that they were in over their heads when it came to assessing monetary damages in what was now a complex contracts case. They turned to an outside business lawyer, accustomed to the world of high-stakes commercial litigation, to represent them in the monetary damages phase of the suit. Hank Bohnhoff, an attorney in the Rodey firm, one of New Mexico's most respected and prestigious law firms, also needed time to get up to speed.[85]

While ailing Special Master Meyers waited, the economists went to work. Setting the value of water had been generally controversial ever since the Bureau of Reclamation had begun using cost/benefit analyses to justify its huge dam projects on western rivers. Things had gotten so bad that in the early 1980s President Jimmy Carter had restricted the use of certain economic data, including ubiquitous "secondary benefits," in project justifications. Meyers himself had announced that he didn't believe in "secondary benefits," the ripple effect through the economy of direct investment in water projects. So the economists working on both sides of *Texas v. New Mexico* proceeded cautiously, trying to stay within the bounds of the new national rules and the existing skepticism of a judge who was as devoted to economic principles in the application of legal rules as he was suspicious of inflated economic claims.[86]

The numbers that started to emerge in the late spring and early summer of 1988 were astounding. They were also astoundingly different. On May 25, 1988, Texas released two studies by economist Charles Howe, one analyzing the economic benefit to New Mexico from the breaches of the Pecos River Compact from 1950 to 1986, the other analyzing the harms to Texas from the same breaches for the same period. Howe's "conservative" estimates set the benefits to New Mexico at a whopping one billion dollars ($980,625,522) and the harm to Texas at a slightly diminished but still hefty forty million ($42,561,071). New Mexico subsequently weighed in with its own studies which pegged the benefits and damages much lower. By any measure, however, the stakes in this portion of the proceedings were very high and they only covered past damages, not future administration.[87]

In the meantime, the health of both Charles Meyers and Steve Reynolds continued to decline. Reynolds's diabetes was increasingly hard to manage and, late in his long working days, he would become uncharacteristically irascible and incoherent by turns. Meyers's throat cancer had not responded to aggressive treatment and he was losing more than his voice. Before the two titans could meet on the issue of how much money Reynolds's administration of New Mexico water had cost Texas over thirty years, Meyers died in his sleep early in the morning of July 17.[88]

The shock of Meyers's death cast another pall over the *Texas v. New Mexico* proceedings. The Supreme Court's Byron White had to search for a third special master to complete the now fourteen-year-old suit. By the fall of 1988 the Court settled on D. Monte Pascoe, a well-respected Denver water lawyer who worked for the Denver Metropolitan Water Board. According to Texas's Renea Hicks, Pascoe's position gave him an upstream state perspective on interstate river claims that Pascoe shared with the first Special Master, Jean Breitenstein, but not the second, Charles Meyers. That perspective made Pascoe suspicious of Texas's extravagant claims, a suspicion that was bolstered by New Mexico's well-prepared counterattacks on the Texas economic studies.[89]

New Mexico argued that the harm to Texas, not the benefit to New Mexico, should measure Texas's damages for the water withheld between 1950 and 1988. So, New Mexico set out to prove that the additional water would have benefited the Red Bluff Irrigation District farmers very little.

At the hearings that finally began in Denver in the summer of 1988, the New Mexican economists estimated that Texas farmers would have made a lot less from the additional water that New Mexico should have provided between 1950 and 1987 than the $51 million that the Texas economists had estimated. The New Mexicans explained the difference by pointing out the extreme inefficiencies in the Texas irrigation system. Of the additional water delivered at the state line, their studies showed, 70 percent would never reach the Red Bluff farmers because of channel (river) and conveyance (ditch) losses between the state line and the farms. The 30 percent that would have made it would have been so saline that it would have been hard to use for irrigation. They also argued that the Red Bluff dam had never functioned to even out the Pecos River flow of water in Texas. According to the New Mexico economists the small amount of unregulated bad water that would have reached the head gates of Texas farmers had New Mexico delivered the water would only have produced about $8 million more in Texas profits.[90]

As Pascoe listened to the beginnings of this testimony in late 1988, he became increasingly convinced that New Mexico should pay money, not water, for its past sins and that the amount of money should be a lot less than Texas economists had estimated but somewhat more than the New Mexican economists had. Two weeks into what promised to be at least a month-long hearing, Pascoe broke in to tell the parties where he stood. In what New Mexico's Henry Bohnhoff termed "an unusual move," Pascoe indicated that New Mexico should offer to pay Texas some money, but not too much.[91]

Representatives of the two states then met and in mid-trial settled on $14 million as the appropriate sum. Some restrictions were added in order to guarantee that the lion's share of the proceeds would in fact reach the Texas Pecos River farmers who had been harmed.[92]

Reynolds would have to go to the 1990 New Mexico State Legislature for the money. On announcing the settlement, Texas lawyer Renea Hicks had told the newspapers, "I want New Mexicans to know that they have Steve Reynolds to thank for this $14 million bill" as if the debt would get Reynolds into trouble at home. But Steve Reynolds had a way of turning adversity to advantage, especially in the legislature, and raising the money to pay for the past didn't look like an insurmountable problem. It was the future that gave him pause.[93]

Special Master Meyers had adopted and the Supreme Court had approved a new manual for figuring New Mexico's annual Pecos River water obligation to Texas beginning in 1990. Reynolds had proved, even to Special Master Meyers's satisfaction, that the manual would be highly variable from year to year, hardly a reflection of increased depletions by man's activities in New Mexico. Nevertheless, the manual required a river master to account for New Mexico water delivered every year at the state line. If in that accounting New Mexico came up short, it would have to pay the water back by the beginning of the next water year. It had looked to the Supreme Court as if New Mexico might have to produce an additional 10,000 acre-feet a year, but that figure might vary widely in any year and no one, not the engineers, not the lawyers, not the judges, knew why or by how much.[94]

When Steve Reynolds returned to Santa Fe, he knew he would have to figure out how to make the Pecos River produce the extra water that New Mexico would owe every year in the future. Reynolds had molded New Mexico water institutions to squeeze for beneficial use in the state every drop of Pecos River water that he could find. There was none to spare.

At the end of his illustrious career, what was he to do with this, his last and most serious challenge?

EIGHT

New Mexico Stumbles

By the fall of 1989 Steve Reynolds realized that the U.S. Supreme Court, in confirming the decisions of the recently deceased Special Master Charles Meyers, had added a large, new stress to the Pecos River system. Reynolds had spent a lifetime tightening up public controls on private water development in the river basin with one hand and, with the other, fighting off Texas's efforts to gain access to New Mexico water. He'd used the tools available to him and the ideology that informed his soul. But he also knew that any Pecos River Basin water budget would show that the New Mexico system couldn't sustain itself forever. Eventually it would have to adjust. Now the Supreme Court had told Reynolds that New Mexico would have to comply with its definition of the Article III(a) apportionment provisions of the 1948 Pecos River Compact. The Court-approved manual for compact administration was supposed to embody that construction. Together Article III and the manual meant that New Mexico had to get ready to produce immediately and annually an additional 10,000 acre-feet of water on the average at the New Mexico/Texas state line for the benefit of Texas. In any particular year that amount might reach 30,000 acre-feet. Like any good general, State Engineer Steve Reynolds had a plan to meet the worst case. And, like any really good politician, he knew how to mount a campaign. This was the time.

On October 19, 1989, he went to Roswell and had lunch with the Chaves County Rotary Club. (Morgan Nelson attended.) As dessert was served, Reynolds addressed the assembled group of politicians and farmers. He began in the wonderfully ironic, self-deprecating style that he had developed over more than thirty years as the New Mexico water boss.

"You can thank Jack Russell," he said, "for arranging for me to talk to you about *Texas v. New Mexico*, Original No. 65, and administration of the Pecos River system including its groundwater tributaries. Please understand that I did not conspire to impair your digestion or spoil your day." The audience laughed nervously.[1]

In praising Jack Russell with faint damnation, Reynolds acknowledged the local leader in past Chaves County efforts to get the Roswell basin under control. Russell was an astute Roswell lawyer who for years headed the Pecos Valley Artesian Conservancy District (PVACD), an organization of groundwater users devoted to reining in its own excessive pumping. Russell had supported Reynolds's controversial efforts to bring basic water law controls to the basin. Reynolds had supported Russell's success in getting the PVACD to purchase and retire almost seven thousand acres of existing Chaves County irrigated acreage in the 1970s and 1980s, part of a valiant local effort to bring water supply and demand into a better balance.[2]

Now the demand for 10,000 more acre-feet a year, slapped on by the Supreme Court, threatened those already limited local Chaves County resources. To make matters worse, the Supreme Court had blamed junior Roswell wells for the new debt. The formal New Mexico water law of prior appropriation and the compact itself made those wells most vulnerable in the times of shortage that the new Texas demand would bring. These were bad signs in Roswell, but New Mexico State Engineer Steve Reynolds had a bold plan that he was about to announce.[3]

Before he did, Reynolds got in some self-serving jabs at the Supreme Court that had made his new plan necessary. He remarked how Texas had argued that New Mexico had benefited by $1.1 billion from the Pecos River water supposedly stolen from Texas. The State of New Mexico would have to pay only $14 million for it. "I think the people of New Mexico," he joked, "would thank the State Engineer any time that he can buy $1.1 billion worth of water for $14 million."

"While I remain convinced," Reynolds continued, drawing on one of his old saws, "that New Mexico never failed to meet her Compact obligation, we all must understand that we cannot expect the Supreme Court to always be right; but it is always Supreme." Reynolds then announced his plan for producing the required additional water at the state line.

He proposed to create a giant, new state well field capable of pumping 30,000 acre-feet a year and delivering the additional groundwater to the river at Roswell. The augmented river supply would somehow pass the Carlsbad Irrigation District's downstream dams and arrive at the Texas state line. The Reynolds plan called for seventy new state wells, located five miles north of the City of Roswell, twenty-six miles of collector pipe and between three and nine miles of larger transmission pipes. The well field would cost between $20 million and $30 million to build and another $2 million a year to operate.[4]

The Reynolds "super well field" plan was the resurrection of an earlier one that Reynolds had first floated in 1976 when the Carlsbad Irrigation District's Francis Tracy, Jr., had formally invoked ("called") its seniority ("priority") on the Pecos River. Later, Reynolds allowed as how the original well field plan "had not been well received." Now, however, he told his Roswell audience, the well field looked like the only way to achieve the quick response required by the Supreme Court.[5]

The Roswell well field solution was in some sense vintage Reynolds. For one thing, it bought time. With the new wells pumping additional groundwater into the Pecos, everyone, including Texas, would stay at full supply for as long as possible. Reynolds had used groundwater within New Mexico for thirty years to avoid surface water shortages and priority calls. Why not extend this approach to a grander scale?[6]

There was another precedent for the plan. Reynolds knew something similar had worked elsewhere in the west. He knew that Colorado had worked its way out of Rio Grande Compact problems with New Mexico and Texas by pumping unused groundwater near the San Luis Valley straight into the Rio Grande before it crossed the New Mexico state line and so alleviated compact shortfalls. He suspected that New Mexico had worked its way out of its own Rio Grande Compact problems with Texas by taking credit for groundwater pumped by the City of Albuquerque from distant wells and dumped as clean waste water into the river.[7]

Reynolds's plan offered what looked like a viable physical solution to the problem of delivering 10,000 additional acre-feet per year at the state line. Reynolds always had been suspicious of the grandiose physical solutions to legal and political water problems that appealed to western hydraulic engineers. But this one cut through the difficult hydrology of the river, the arcane mechanics of the Supreme Court's River Manual, and, indeed, the still obscure Pecos River Compact itself. If the Supreme Court said New Mexico had to produce 10,000 acre-feet at the state line, then New Mexico should focus on the extra water and not worry about exactly why.[8]

Still, there was something so plainly ironic about the Reynolds plan as to make it a caricature of the hundreds of more subtle solutions that he had crafted for New Mexico over his long career. The most obvious irony was the fundamental premise of the Pecos River Compact itself. The compact was based on controlling river basin depletions in upstream New

Mexico. The compact assumed that if New Mexico depletions became too great, then New Mexico would reduce those depletions and thereby increase the state line flows. The Supreme Court had just said that New Mexico's depletions had gotten too big. In response, the New Mexico state engineer now proposed to make the too big depletions even bigger, not reduce them. Had he gone mad?

As if that weren't enough, Reynolds's proposal avoided basic New Mexico water law on how to reduce those depletions. Both Article IX of the compact and New Mexico's own state constitution prescribed priority enforcement—entirely cutting off the most recent rights in order to guarantee a full supply for the older ones—as the way to balance limited, changing water supplies and permanent water rights. Because Reynolds's super well field proposal would increase the flow of the river for a while, he never had to face the priority principle that increased depletions seemed to require. He'd spent a career pretending priorities did not exist. Why should he start now?

As usual, the downstream Carlsbad Irrigation District (CID) loomed as the biggest physical obstacle to Reynolds's physical well-field solution. Even if the state wells at Roswell could add enough water to the river to meet the Supreme Court mandate, how could the state get that water past CID's McMillan (now Brantley) and Avalon dams to Texas? Historically, the Pecos River had not fully supplied Carlsbad irrigators. Surely they would grab a new slug of water put into the river at Roswell, as state law entitled them to do. The water would never reach the state line where it would count for compact purposes.[9]

But before anyone caught on to these complications, Reynolds left the Roswell Rotary Club lunch and returned to Santa Fe to get ready for the 39th State Legislature.

Appearing in November, 1979 before an interim legislative committee, the Committee on Energy, Natural Resources and Extractive Industries, which already had begun to consider the Pecos River problem, Reynolds repeated, almost verbatim, the speech that he had tried out a month before at the Roswell Rotary Club. He didn't mention Jack Russell and the ruined appetites this time out. But otherwise he told the same jokes, complained about the Supreme Court in the same plaintive way and held out the same hope that eventually the Supreme Court might see the error of its ways.

Until then, Reynolds began, the legislature would have to appropriate the $14 million necessary to satisfy the stipulated price to which he had already agreed as compensation for the 344,000 acre-feet owed to Texas through 1988. For the future, Reynolds repeated, the legislature should "carefully consider the option of creating a well field in the

Fig. 8.1.
Beleaguered, ebullient Tom Davis, the current "treasurer, assessor, collector, secretary and manager" of the Carlsbad Irrigation District, finds that the Pecos River and its problems occupy all of his waking hours, just as they have his predecessors. Here he stands, smiling, in front of the same Carlsbad building that housed Francis G. Tracy's Pecos Valley Water Users Association at the turn of the twentieth century and that house the CID at the turn of the twenty-first. The bas-relief inverted cornucopias above Davis's head have been there since the 1890s. (G. Emlen Hall.)

Roswell basin to be used to pump water into the river when needed to satisfy a delivery shortfall or a priority call by downstream senior surface water rights."[10]

As it turned out, the 39th Legislature bit the bullet and approved the $14 million for past damages. But in dealing with the future, this legislature, unlike most in the past, would not swallow the Reynolds program whole. By midsession it became apparent that the legislature was not willing to commit itself to Reynolds's state well-field solution. Instead, it wanted to consider other solutions to the future problems created by the Supreme Court decree.

Besides considering the well field, legislative leaders expressed interest in the possibility of actually enforcing priorities on the Pecos River as the state constitution and the compact itself seemed to require. They wanted to consider importing additional water from other basins to increase the Pecos supply. Finally, they wanted to consider acquiring and retiring existing rights in order to reduce demand and hence presumably to produce more water at the state line. Committee leaders from Carlsbad and Roswell drafted a memorial requesting the state engineer office to investigate the alternatives and to report the results to the two-month 1991 legislature.[11]

As usual, Reynolds himself responded to this legislative proposal. In what turned out to be the last of more than thirty years of responses to proposed legislation, on February 5, 1990, Reynolds sent a memorandum to key legislators on the proposed study. Backing off from his original, exclusive focus on the Roswell well field, Reynolds's memo indicated that he would consider the local response to the other possibilities that the legislature had mentioned. "House Memorial 47," he wrote,

> appropriately cites the options available to meet and satisfy future delivery shortfalls. Careful study and discussion of those options in a public forum seems the best way to arrive at a selection of options that are economically justified, financially possible, equitable and politically feasible.[12]

Although he did not intend it to be his last statement on New Mexico water policy, the concluding list of criteria summed up Reynolds's whole approach over three decades. Because it committed the state to nothing more than study, the memorial, with Reynolds's still indispensable backing, unanimously cleared the House and Senate. In the early spring of 1990, at the end of the legislative session, Reynolds was ready to consider the range of options the legislature had specified.[13]

He never even got started. In late March, while he was driving back to Santa Fe from a heated water meeting in the northwest corner of the state, his left leg began to throb. When it didn't improve, he consulted the doctor who took care of his diabetes. The doctor ordered him into Santa Fe's St. Vincent Hospital. Concerned and devoted employees were led to believe that they should not visit him there but should instead rely on reports from Phil Mutz and Carl Slingerland, two trusted thirty-year lieutenants who would monitor the chief's progress. Alone, the diabetic seventy-year-old Reynolds did not improve.[14]

His weak blood distribution deteriorated. In a desperate effort to reverse the collapse, doctors amputated first his left foot and then his left leg below the knee. As he lay dying, Reynolds still tried to joke that he would leave with his boots on, meaning that they would have to carry him out of the State Engineer Office. But towards the end an oxygen mask constantly covered his mouth and he couldn't even speak. By the end his system had shut down so far that there was hardly a body left to wear boots. On April 25, 1990, Reynolds, still the state engineer, died.[15]

His death left the whole New Mexico water world in confusion, but no situation was so tenuous as the Pecos River one. First, the lame duck Republican governor appointed Reynolds's senior lieutenant, Phil Mutz, a veteran of many an interstate water battle, as state engineer. Mutz lasted less than two months; a heart attack forced him to retire. Next, the same governor replaced Mutz with Carl Slingerland, another thirty-year veteran of the Pecos River battle. The son of an Anglo rancher in the frigid San Luis Valley, an ex-Marine and an ex-Bureau of Reclamation employee, Slingerland seemed tough enough to take on Reynolds's job. He said he'd only do it for six months, maximum, when a new governor would have to find a new state engineer. True to his word, he retired from the agency altogether in 1991. In the meantime, the agency, rudderless without Reynolds at the helm, struggled to meet the 1990 legislature's command that the state engineer office consult local southeastern New Mexico communities to see which of the Pecos River options outlined in House Memorial 47 seemed best.[16]

To accomplish that, what was left of the State Engineer Office took to the road in the fall of 1990. Between September 17 and 20 the office held public meetings in Las Vegas, Fort Sumner, Roswell, and Carlsbad. The road trip duplicated the Pecos River public meetings held in 1943, when the Pecos River Compact Commission finally got serious about formulating the 1948 Pecos River Compact, and the 1976 tour on the eve of the serious start of *Texas v. New Mexico*. Now in 1990 state officials were dealing with the fallout from both the compact and the lawsuit that had spurred the two earlier trips. The SEO lawyer Peter White and the ISC engineer John Whipple prepared an informational packet to describe the legal situation to those who attended. The packet laid out four basic "possible alternative options other than priority administration for delivering water to Texas under the amended decree." It invited southeastern New Mexicans to respond at the public meetings.[17]

Respond they did. The September 18, 1990, meeting at Roswell was typical. More than a hundred farmers and local politicians showed up, including Morgan Nelson, now more than ever passionately involved in Chaves County water affairs. Instead of weighing the state engineer's options, the audience complained about the compact, complained about the Supreme Court, even complained bitterly that the state had lost *Texas v. New Mexico* through incompetence. Why should local interests have to pay for legal obligations they had not created, courts of law to which they had not submitted, lawsuits in which they had not participated? Far better, the Roswell farmers thought, that the state pay for its incompetence by purchasing from willing sellers enough existing water rights from lower Pecos River farmers to produce the extra water that the Supreme Court required.

All the possibilities were bad, but the least bad of a poor bunch, from Roswell's point of view, was the one involving state purchase or lease of water rights. The state would peremptorily curtail no Roswell water rights by priority enforcement; it would force no sale of Roswell water rights by condemnation. Instead, the state would pay top dollar to those Roswell irrigators who preferred to sell and whose forbearance presumably would produce more compact water at the state line.[18]

At Carlsbad the next day state officials heard equally strong complaints. But the Carlsbad Irrigation District spokesmen wouldn't even grudgingly back the lease/purchase alternative chosen by their upstream Roswell neighbors. Instead, they returned to a familiar theme: priority enforcement should make up for any shortfall at the state line as required by the state constitution, state statute, and the federally approved Pecos River Compact itself. In 1948 CID representatives had said the same thing at the Driskill Hotel in Austin, Texas when they insisted that the compact include the same priority guarantee already in the 1912 New Mexico Constitution. They had repeated themselves in 1976 when, as a last gesture, Francis Tracy, Jr., had written State Engineer Reynolds and demanded that Reynolds enforce priorities on the Pecos River. Now in 1990 in Carlsbad they presented a written statement to state officials, asking once again that New Mexico use the fundamental priority principle of New Mexico water law to get the additional water to Texas.

The state, the CID statement said, should start by permanently eliminating all water rights established after 1946, including those of municipalities. (This shot was clearly aimed at the compact's 1947 cut-off date.) If there still were water shortages, the state could shut off pre-1946 rights in reverse order until the CID received 100 percent of its entitlement. (This second shot was aimed at post-1947 depletions caused by pre-1947 Roswell wells.) If the CID finally got a full surface water supply after a century of waiting, the statement concluded, Texas would get its compact rights in return flow from Carlsbad irrigation.[19]

Sponsoring state officials later complained that neither consensus nor leadership emerged from these southeastern New Mexico meetings in the fall of 1990. That was putting it mildly. The Pecos River emergency just ignited the smoldering flames of the century-old battle between Roswell and Carlsbad.[20]

A parallel battle emerged in the State Engineer Office in late September 1990. The office sorely missed the steady hand of Steve Reynolds, one of the few men who could balance the concerns of engineers and lawyers because he was both. He had kept the small, ideologically focused group of engineers and lawyers under autocratic control. Now the unruly bunch threatened to burst the bounds that Reynolds had imposed; the possible explosion would make managing the Pecos River far more difficult.

Nowhere was this possibility more obvious than in the state engineer's legal division. When *Texas v. New Mexico* got started in 1974, there were only three state engineer lawyers, all highly attuned to Reynolds's version of prior appropriation water law. By 1990, the number of SEO lawyers had grown to eight, only one of whom had been employed at the start of *Texas v. New Mexico.*[21]

The chief lawyer for the Pecos River emergency became Laura Harper, a tough, no-nonsense Colorado-trained attorney. Harper had moved to Santa Fe to reinvent herself. She became a massage therapist but drifted back into legal work to keep food on the table. As a Colorado water lawyer, Harper came from a state that really did enforce priorities in times of short supply. When she looked at the Pecos River Compact and basic New Mexico water law from that perspective, she knew what to do to solve the Pecos River problem: enforce Pecos River priorities. Shut down junior users in New Mexico, presumably Roswell well owners, until the required water got to Texas.[22]

From the outset, the engineers in the State Engineer Office, more deeply steeped in the Reynolds tradition and wary of abstract legal principles, resisted the lawyers' preference for priority enforcement. At the tail end of 1990, Interstate Stream Commission (ISC) engineer John Whipple, by everyone's measure a skilled geohydrologist but a somewhat enigmatic character, a man of very few words who constantly wore a long-billed baseball cap yanked low over his eyes, presented to the legislature the agency's response to the alternatives explored in southeastern New Mexico on that fall's trip. "Administration of priorities in the Pecos River Basin by the State Engineer," Whipple began on December 17, 1990, "is the only option currently available for meeting the delivery obligation under the Amended Decree. That option should be avoided at all costs." Lawyer Laura Harper must have shuddered.

Whipple went on to dismiss option after option as either physically impossible or economically impractical. Only a "water rights acquisition and retirement program," he concluded, "would reduce, but not eliminate, the risk of shortfalls in state-line flows under the Amended Decree." For $60 million, he said, the state could purchase enough water from willing sellers in southeastern New Mexico and retire enough Pecos River water rights to get the required average 10,000 additional acre-feet to the state line.[23]

Like Reynolds's rejected "super well field" plan, Whipple's proposal went against the fundamental principle of prior appropriation. Shortages were a risk that the system explicitly acknowledged. If there wasn't enough water to go around to all rights holders always (and there never would be), the newest rights suffered first. You curtailed their water and sent the rest to the holders of older rights. You didn't compensate those high-and-dry junior water rights owners. If they wanted water, they could buy out the holders of more senior rights. In a true prior appropriation system, public water ran uphill to private money. Whipple's proposal reversed that. Now public money ran downhill to private rights, even risky junior ones.

Tensions like this between fundamentally different readings of New Mexico water law exacerbated other tensions the 1991 New Mexico legislative session, the first, but certainly not the last, to consider the water shortage problem on the lower Pecos created by the 1988 Supreme Court Amended Decree. Carlsbad legislators groused at their Roswell counterparts despite warnings that they needed to present a unified front. Northern New Mexico Hispanic representatives disliked both the State Engineer Office and their cowboy southern New Mexico counterparts. Nambe State Representative Ben Lujan, a sworn enemy of both Steve Reynolds and the rednecks from the south, even threatened to take the legislature to court for using state money on such a local problem. (Eventually he did.) In angry response, southeastern New Mexico representatives reminded their northern colleagues that their region of the state, rich as it was in oil and gas, for years had financed through severance taxes and strong local economies a large percentage of the capital outlays for the much poorer rest of the state. Perhaps, they suggested, it was time for the rest of the state to pay southeastern New Mexico back in its time of need.[24]

Amid these acrimonious cross currents, the 1991 legislature still managed to appropriate $6.8 million to the Interstate Stream Commission to start to acquire water rights in the Pecos River basin. The total didn't come close to the $60 million that Engineer Whipple had told the legislature that the water rights acquisition solution would require. But the legislature had directed that the money be spent on acquiring those water rights that would "most quickly aid" the state in complying with the

Pecos River Compact. The $6.8 million would get the State Engineer Office and the Interstate Stream Commission started.[25]

A new state engineer was appointed in 1990, the third in twelve months in an agency whose head hadn't changed for the previous thirty years. Eluid Martínez was a twenty-year veteran of the office with experience in almost every aspect of the water agency and was an ambitious Santa Fe County politician in his own right. Veteran governor Bruce King, recently elected to a third term, selected Martínez to steady the agency at this rocky time. Martínez was head of the state engineer's technical division, a prestigious branch of the office in charge of the serious science in the agency's operation. Colleagues recall that King, as governor elect, called Martínez away from a November 1990 Pecos River strategy meeting. When Martínez returned to the meeting, he was state engineer.[26]

The group assembled at that meeting became, under Martínez's regime, the "State Engineer's Pecos River Task Force," and was soon large and formal enough to create an organization chart. "Reporting Assignments for the Management of the Pecos River" looked as if the State Engineer Office was an army getting ready for the Normandy invasion. Lieutenant Laura Harper was "legal planning coordinator," sitting over a bevy of interconnected lawyers, all working on one aspect or another of the Pecos. Lieutenant Peter Kraai, as "technical planning coordinator," headed an even larger group of engineers. At the apex sat State Engineer Martínez. But just below him, at the heart of the organization and at a place where all other lines of authority led, sat an agency outsider brought in to coordinate everybody else's work.[27]

Dr. John W. Hernández, Jr., a peripatetic, very bright, charming New Mexico State University professor of civil engineering and a specialist in waste water design, was no stranger to water politics or to the State Engineer Office. A member of an old, aristocratic Hispanic family with deep roots in the state, Hernández seemed never to be at his university post, always hovering on the edge of national or New Mexico scandals.

In the early 1980s Hernández, a Republican activist, was appointed deputy administrator of the federal Environmental Protection Agency (EPA). At the time conservative Republican president Ronald Reagan was accused of using his EPA appointments to gut the agency. Thereafter allegations of perjury, conflict of interest, "sweetheart deals" with industry, and political manipulation of toxic waste clean-up engulfed the EPA. Hernández's immediate boss, EPA administrator Anne McGill Burford, was forced to resign. Hernández hung on for a little while as her temporary replacement and then fled the EPA too.

In the mid-1980s State Engineer Steve Reynolds lured Professor

Hernández back to New Mexico. This time he served as Reynolds's proxy in a high profile controversy involving the City of El Paso's effort to export southern New Mexico groundwater to Texas. At the time Reynolds had come under sharp criticism for his lack of understanding of southern New Mexico and for his conflicting roles as judge, witness, and advocate in the case. Hernández offered Reynolds a way out of both criticisms. Hernández had deep connections in southern New Mexico. He also would do exactly what Reynolds wanted him to, thus allowing the legendary water boss actual, if not formal, control over a dispute that he (Reynolds) was hearing as judge.

Finally early in the 1990s new State Engineer Martínez brought his close friend, Professor Hernández, back from New Mexico State to help him and the office out in the messy Pecos River affairs. The situation

Fig. 8.2.
In late 1990 Governor-elect Bruce King appointed veteran Eluid Martínez, shown here, as new state engineer to steady the house that Steve Reynolds had built. State Engineer Martínez had trouble finding a way out of the morass created by the Supreme Court's Pecos River decrees, local politics in southeastern New Mexico, and state engineer politics at home. (Photo courtesy of the *Santa Fe New Mexican*.)

must have looked a little like the EPA ten years before. The State Engineer Office and the Interstate Stream Commission had $7 million in public money to spend on buying and retiring private New Mexico water and few restraints on how to do it.[28]

Hernandez and the Interstate Stream Commission started by going back to the 1992 legislature for more money. The two agencies were aided by some even more alarming economic predictions of what it would mean for New Mexico to depend solely on priority enforcement to make up for inevitable shortfalls. Hydrologist Whipple and Norm Whittlesey, the economist whose testimony had won the last phases of *Texas v. New Mexico,* told the 1992 legislature that if New Mexico suffered a five-thousand-acre-foot shortfall in any year and had to depend on priority enforcement to make it up, the state would be forced to retire water rights dating back to January 1, 1944. As a result 48,922 irrigated acres would go dry and farmers would lose $12 million for the year.

From that disastrous starting place, the predictions got worse. A 10,000-acre-foot shortfall would force the cut-off date back to 1929, take 86,252 acres out of production and cost $21 million. A 15,000-acre-feet shortfall corresponded to a 1920 cut-off, a loss of 100,692 irrigated acres and a $24-million annual direct economic loss. Similar calculations, always with different numbers, had been surfacing in *Texas v. New Mexico* for decades, but that didn't make these estimated effects any less startling.[29]

To make matters worse, in 1990 and 1991 the Pecos River Master found that New Mexico under-delivered by more than 14,000 acre-feet each year. While surpluses from previous years still left a positive New Mexico balance, the 1990 and 1991 annual figures must have scared the 1992 legislature to death. A 30,000-acre-foot shortfall, well within the limits of the "1947 condition" historic variations, was a catastrophic possibility.[30]

Not surprisingly the legislature coughed up an additional $6 million in early 1992 to solve this disaster in the making. Half of that money, the legislators decided, would come from the sale of severance tax bonds, a particularly appropriate source of money for bailing out southeastern New Mexico. The other half would come from the sale of general obligation bonds. Sale of those bonds would require statewide approval in the fall 1992 general elections, a difficult proposition, given opposition and the very local benefits. But to the amazement of some and thanks to Hernández's political skills, the bond issue passed. At the start of 1993 Hernandez and the Interstate Stream Commission had close to $20 million to spend on buying compliance with the Supreme Court's 1988 Amended Decree.[31]

By then, the Interstate Stream Commission had developed a short working plan for spending the money to lease or purchase and thus take out of use lower Pecos River water rights. By then the agency Pecos River Team also had both a short-term and long-term "Action Plan."[32]

The Pecos River Team plan tried to make it clear that the acquisition program was only the first step in bringing Pecos River uses into line with the Supreme Court's decree. In addition to leasing, buying, and retiring existing rights, the state would also encourage conservation and, last of all and only if absolutely necessary, enforce priorities. The lawyers on the team insisted on that last step as a nod to basic New Mexico water law. The engineers had gone along in the hopes that the state would never have to stoop so low. The lawyers were not so confident, but the engineers firmly believed that the lease-purchase program would take care of the problem.[33]

Not until early 1993 did the Interstate Stream Commission complete the lease/purchase program outlines by setting price guidelines. On March 5, the commission formally decided that the state would pay $1,750 per acre-foot for surface water. Until then the state as buyer had freely negotiated with willing sellers the price of water rights.[34]

In 1991 the lease-purchase program had gotten under way with the state's lease of water rights owned by the City of Carlsbad downstream from the Carlsbad Irrigation District. For around $450,000 a year the City agreed to make available 9,000 acre-feet a year that it didn't then need. But the ISC-City lease would expire in 1997. It was neither large enough nor permanent enough to cover all state-line compact contingencies forever.

So, while exploring other interim options, what was dubbed the "WRAP" ("water rights acquisition program") portion of the Pecos River Project set out to purchase and permanently retire other water rights in the basin. In the effort to locate willing sellers, state buyers, led by Hernández, were helped by the general decline in southeastern New Mexico irrigated agriculture. As Morgan Nelson's career attested, farming in southeastern New Mexico was financially risky and physically hard. More and more farms were going out of business. Those that remained were actually worked by tenant farmers, and these farms were particularly precarious. Fewer and fewer children were willing to follow in the footsteps of their farmer parents. The state offer to buy came at a time when some were more than glad to cash in and sell out.[35]

The Interstate Stream Commission in the early 1990s started looking for water rights to buy in the Roswell reach of the Pecos River on the assumption of state officials that retiring such rights would, as the authorizing statute said, help "most quickly" in increasing river flows and thereby in complying with the 1988 Amended Decree in *Texas v. New Mexico*. With lots of public money to spend and be spent, it didn't take long for the WRAP program, led by Hernandez, and the Pecos River Pumpers, led by a Chaves County Association of the same name, to find each other.[36]

The Pecos River Pumpers were a small group of Roswell area surface-water-irrigation farmers. They primarily diverted water directly from the river rather than taking it indirectly (and more slowly and less visibly) from interconnected groundwater wells. The Pumpers seemed to offer the state the next best thing to Steve Reynolds's twice-aborted well field plan. Reynolds's wells would have piped groundwater directly into the Pecos. Buying out the Pumpers would leave what was already in the river there. Either way Pecos River flow would increase. Isn't that what the Supreme Court said the 1948 Pecos River Compact now required?[37]

However, as with most facets of a Pecos River already fundamentally transformed by the activities of man, paying money to retire the direct diversions wasn't a simple matter. For one thing, it wasn't clear technically that leaving in the river water previously diverted by the Pumpers would in fact help New Mexico comply with the compact obligations as set forth in the river manual.

For another, it wasn't clear physically or legally how the water left in the river, after the pumpers took the money and quit irrigating, would get past the under-supplied senior CID diversions and thence to the state line where the water might count for compact purposes. For a moment, it looked as if buying out the Roswell Pumpers would only bolster the CID's water supply and do nothing for *Texas v. New Mexico*.

To compound the irony, the Interstate Stream Commission agreed to lease annually CID water rights in order to supplement the water rights permanently purchased from the Pumpers. Trouble was that the state already had purchased part of the water it then leased since the water freed from the Pumpers first was stored at the downstream CID dams and supplied CID farmers before heading downstream to the state line. In effect, the state paid southeastern New Mexico farmers twice for the same water that probably didn't need to be bought and, in any case, may or may not have helped with Pecos River Compact compliance.[38]

To enter the world of New Mexico waters in the 1990s was to pass down a dark hall and enter a brilliantly illuminated room of mirrors. The blinding refractions only showed astute observers how little the Pecos River governed by the Supreme Court's 1988 Amended Decree resembled any flowing stream. The legal world of the Pecos River, with its confused and contradictory measures and claims, had overcome what-ever was left of the river itself.

Nevertheless, by the end of 1994 the Interstate Stream Commission had arranged to purchase and retire 10,327 acre-feet of River Pumper rights in the Roswell reach of the Pecos River. The total bill came to almost $7 million spread over four purchases and four years. With those 10,327 acre-feet purchased and retired, the ISC figured to add 2,415 acre-feet a year at the compact-crucial state line. For the retired acre-feet the state paid an average $671 an acre-foot. For the extra acre-feet delivered at the state line, the state paid $2,871 an acre-foot, $1,000 an acre-foot more than the ISC formally authorized and almost double the appraised value of Chaves County water rights. It looked as if WRAP director John Hernandez had just walked into the middle of another financial scandal.[39]

Downstream purchases didn't look much better. Casting about for New Mexico water rights below CID, state officials stumbled on the water rights that the state improvidently had licensed in 1931 to J. N. Livingston in the Malaga stretch of the river. Since then, the successive land owners had made intermittent use of the extremely salty water. Now in 1994 the state had to buy back a shaky water right that it shouldn't have allowed in the first place for almost $700,000.[40]

State purchases like these hardly ended the ugly struggles that surfaced in the wake of the 1988 Amended Decree and the Pecos River Manual. In the midst of this maelstrom of activities around the Pecos River, the New Mexico institutions that governed water started to fall farther apart in the last five years of the decade. It all began with the election of a Republican governor and in April 1995 the appointment of yet another state engineer, the fifth since 1990. This time around the new governor selected an engineer who had had no connection to the State Engineer Office and precious little experience in New Mexico's arcane system of water administration.[41]

Quite quickly, the legal division's chief lawyer, a twenty-five-year vet-eran, stepped down and then retired. The Interstate Stream engineer, groomed for years to take a place in the wider world of western water, quit. Hernández, the only true Republican in the bunch, went back to New Mexico State. Some said the new state engineer had nothing to do with the resignations; others said that he "came in and took out all the tall trees."

To make matters worse, trouble plagued the WRAP program. By 1994 engineering liaison Peter Kraai and hydrologist Whipple had come to dislike each other so intensely that they couldn't meet in the same room. Scandal licked at the edges of the program over which they fought. In the mid-1990s the State Engineer Office was awash in largely unsubstantiated rumors of incompetence and corruption in the location and valuation of acquired water rights. New State Engineer Tom Turney inherited a bad situation and it almost got worse in public.[42]

In 1995, shortly after Turney took over, the independent New Mexico State Auditor launched an investigation into allegations of mismanagement and corruption in the WRAP program. (Professor John Hernández, back at NMSU, must have felt as if he'd been dragged back to the EPA in the early 1980s.) The auditors focused on the financial aspects of the program and possible sweetheart purchases of Pecos River water rights at inflated prices, among other allegations of financial corruption at the Interstate Stream Commission. A year-long, well-publicized investigation yielded no hard findings. The state auditor issued his report on March 21, 1996. The report criticized the basis of various appraisal reports and the

Fig. 8.3.
The election of Republican Gary Johnson brought newcomer Tom Turney as new state engineer in 1995. Here, at a January 2001 meeting with City of Santa Fe officials, Turney was all smiles. The situation on the Pecos River was not so bright at the turn of the twenty-first century. (Photo courtesy of the *Santa Fe New Mexican*.)

213

state engineer's acceptance of them in paying for purchased Pecos River water rights. However, the inflated prices were evidence of incompetence, not crime, said the auditor. The state engineer, the auditor recommended, should tighten up its Pecos River operation.[43]

State Engineer Turney used the opportunity to evaluate the entire New Mexican response to *Texas v. New Mexico*. Between June 1997 and June 1998 he assembled a team of independent experts to assess all aspects of the Pecos River program and to report confidentially to him and to his new Interstate Stream Engineer. The resulting sixty-six-page report criticized almost every aspect of the Pecos River management program begun in 1990 with the rejection of Steve Reynolds's Roswell well-field plan and the selection of the lease-purchase alternative.

The WRAP plan, the report said, had not been well thought out logically, legally, or hydrologically. The report confirmed what the state auditor's report had found about the program's shaky financial controls. More importantly, suggested the report, the shaky guidelines did not account for the effect of the purchases under the river accounting procedure contained in the Supreme-Court-approved River Master's Manual. After all, the 1998 report argued, that arcane procedure, not state line flows, not purchased and retired upstream rights, ultimately determined New Mexico's compact obligation and compliance. New Mexico should acknowledge the scientific reductionism of the manual, recognize that the manual's index inflows and 1947 condition outflows had nothing to do with the actual operation of the river, and proceed according to the manual's entirely arbitrary system.[44]

The confidential report didn't move the State Engineer Office at all. Beleaguered on all sides, particularly on the Rio Grande, by other more immediate problems, the state engineer and the Interstate Stream Commission stayed the course. By the end of the century New Mexico had appropriated from one source or another $40,727,000 for the WRAP program. That sum amounted to about two-thirds of the $60 million that Engineer Whipple had said, in 1990, would be needed to meet the Supreme Court's 1988 Amended Decree. By the end of the century, New Mexico had purchased and retired the 25,472 acre-feet of water appurtenant to 8,743.84 acres in the lower Pecos River Basin. The state was trying to buy more, but as usual, there were all kinds of local opposition.[45]

Despite the financial effort, insecurity showed through everywhere. The renamed Office of the State Engineer (OSE) contracted with one of the state's premier computer modelers for a badly needed up-to-date, sophisticated model of the Roswell Basin aquifers. The relationship of those aquifers to the Pecos River had prompted the 1948 Pecos River Compact, had lain at the heart of *Texas v. New Mexico*, and bore critically on New Mexico's plans to comply with the Supreme Court's decree in that lawsuit. Yet, after almost $250,000 and a couple of years, the OSE rejected the new model and adjusted it on its own.[46]

Concerned that the WRAP program might still not have enough money, the 1998 New Mexico legislature appropriated $18.5 million from the Irrigation Works Construction Fund—$2 million per year for three years to purchase and lease water and $12 million for water rights acquisitions. However, the Legislature also appropriated $500,000

> for the purpose of preparing a long-term strategy for the state's permanent compliance with the Pecos River Compact and the United States supreme court amended decree in the case of *Texas v. New Mexico,* no. 65 original and a short-term plan for responding to a net shortfall in New Mexico's deliveries to Texas as required by the court decree.

It was as if the 1992 Pecos River Action Plan had never happened. In 1998 nothing new did. The office never prepared a new action plan, instead choosing to fold its planning efforts into a joint federal/state environmental impact statement on a new operating plan for the upstream CID Dam.[47]

In the meantime all the old players outside the Office of the State Engineer still had different ideas about what to do about the problems created by the Supreme Court and the Texans. At the turn of the century, all the old Pecos River activists weighed in in different forums.

Morgan Nelson tirelessly wrote anybody who'd listen. He even wanted the state to get rid of the compact that had saddled the lower Pecos with an impossible water burden. He went so far as to draft a memorial for the New Mexico legislature repealing the compact, and he entered into private negotiations with the Texas representative to the Pecos River Compact Commission.[48]

While Nelson fought the compact and the Texans, New Mexico State University tilted, once again, against nature. The NMSU-run Agricultural Station in Roswell proposed to use the poison arsenal to get rid of the salt cedar infestations along the river, thereby creating more water for the compact. An old and controversial project, central to Royce Tipton's conception of the 1948 Compact, salt cedar clearing had never worked to produce additional river water as far as any scientist could find. When the Agricultural Research Station resurrected the clearance plan in the late 1990s, George Welder, the principal author of the critical, earlier USGS report, quietly wrote the *Albuquerque Journal* to remind everyone that the war on salt cedars had never gained the river anything as far as he could tell.[49]

While NMSU fought with the USGS over water salvage, local Roswell interests returned to old Roswell wars, jostling for position in the awkward new world that *Texas v. New Mexico* had created. For example, the Corns saw the problems as creating an opportunity to sell water rights in the North Roswell extension that local banks had written off as useless. They used the still ongoing *Lewis* adjudication to shore up, unsuccessfully as it turned out, weak water rights there.[50]

While the Corns and North Roswell fought the Nelsons and South Roswell over what was left of the Pecos River after Texas got its new share, Roswell continued to battle with Carlsbad. Everybody always had assumed that Carlsbad had the oldest rights on the lower Pecos River and that, if worst came to worst, Carlsbad would use that superiority to get Roswell's water. Now in the late 1990s Roswell and the PVACD hired a professional historian to prove that in fact Roswell's water rights had seniority. The same Roswell organizations also hired an independent hydrologist to review the underlying Pecos River Compact data; he came to no certain conclusions.[51]

Water relationships between Roswell and Carlsbad never did improve. As recently as the 2001 legislative session an obscure bill designed to improve the position of the Carlsbad Irrigation District vis-à-vis its own members and Roswell farmers almost provoked a physical battle in Santa Fe. The bill failed late in the session but not before legislative leaders had to call out the police to keep the peace. At the final, late night committee meeting which sunk the bill a lanky, cowboy-like state policeman, who looked a little like Steve Reynolds, kept the warring sides apart. Unlike Reynolds, the state policeman said nothing and made no effort to bring the two sides together.[52]

In response to this attack from upstream, Carlsbad continued fighting against itself. Carlsbad Irrigation District irrigators battled against their own district as they had for most of the twentieth century. Louise Tracy, granddaughter of the original Francis Tracy, and George Brantley, a relative of the man for whom the CID's Brantley Dam had been named, fought their own district tooth and nail, in court and out, to force the district to recognize that they, not the district, owned the rights to Pecos River water. When a state district court judge ruled that individual CID irrigators should control releases from the upstream CID dams, the contrarian CID Board of Directors turned over control of the dams to the U.S. Bureau of Reclamation, thus hoping to escape the clutches of the state court. In so doing, the CID acknowledged an even more dangerous alien competitor for control of the river at the end of the twentieth century: the federal government.[53]

In the 1990s federal control of western rivers emerged as the new, fundamental joker in water management. Until then a marginal and marginalized player in intrastate water and a passive participant in interstate compact affairs, the United States now stepped forward to take a much more central position. The Bureau of Reclamation had always had a hand in Pecos River affairs, primarily as the upstream savior of the downstream Carlsbad Irrigation District. The Bureau began by reconstructing the Carlsbad works and then constructing the badly needed upstream storage. When the CID needed protection from the likes of Louise Tracy and the Brantleys, Reclamation stepped in again, took over operation of the dams, and afforded the CID the protective mantle of federal law. Now in the late 1990s the United States began to advocate on the Pecos, as elsewhere, for species endangered by the century-long human transformation of the Pecos River water world.

In the 1990s the federal Fish and Wildlife Service determined that the endangered Pecos River bluntnose shiner required a minimum instream flow. Water would have to be released from the upstream Carlsbad dams to maintain it. The water world had come full circle from Francis Tracy one hundred years before. Where Tracy wanted water stored for the benefit of man, United States biologists now insisted that the storage benefit fish. For a moment, it looked as if the Pecos, already stressed beyond capacity by the new *Texas v. New Mexico* definition of the compact limitations of New Mexico depletions, would come completely apart with this additional, new federal demand.[54]

However, state and federal water managers this time worked their way out of what seemed an intractable problem. The federal government got the minimum flows the bluntnose shiner required, and the state got a recognition that the federal rights would have to recognize New Mexico state water law and also recognize the potential effect the federal flows might have on New Mexico's compact obligations. Compared to the preemptive assertion of federal water rights on the Rio Grande, the Pecos River is a model, temporarily at least, of intergovernmental civility.[55]

Otherwise, the history of New Mexico water life since the 1988 Amended Decree in *Texas v. New Mexico* just jumbles the twenty years of litigation that preceded the decree, the half-century since the 1948 Pecos River Compact, and the full century of southwestern efforts to harness (and unleash) the Pecos River for the benefit of a changing physical and political landscape. The competing claims to the river have grown as the scientific understanding of it has become murkier and the legal institutions that govern it have atrophied. No wonder that in the last years of the twentieth century the images of the Pecos River lie in fragments everywhere.

In March 1995 I went to my second "water rights" funeral in less than a decade. Steve Reynolds's 1990 death had been commemorated by a sparsely attended service held, at his request, well after he died. On a blustery 1995 spring day a much larger crowd gathered at a Santa Fe church to honor Carl Slingerland, the other New Mexican who had lived and breathed the Pecos River.

Formally retired from the State Engineer Office after his short 1990–1991 stint as state engineer, Slingerland continued to consult in water matters on his own, strong terms. From time to time he worked on Pecos River matters but he preferred smaller, more concrete jobs. He was particularly proud of the help he gave to a small Santa Fe County community having trouble with its municipal well. Harkening back to his earliest days at the Bureau of Reclamation in the 1950s, Slingerland figured out that recasing the well would improve its capacity. When his recommendation tripled the well's water production, everybody was happy.

In the meantime, in semi-retirement, Slingerland returned to his real loves. He was a superb eight-handicap golfer and, despite a little arthritis in his hands, now had time to work on his game. At home he had more time to build furniture in the woodworking shop behind his house. He had invented and patented a work bench that would stay even on uneven surfaces and he made a little money manufacturing these. However, he most loved the small, hard wood, in-laid jewelry boxes that he made for his devoted wife and for his own extensive collection of arrowheads. The beautiful boxes fit together much better than the equally intricate pieces of *Texas v. New Mexico*.

I worked with Carl Slingerland on that lawsuit off and on for five years between 1978 and 1983. After I'd retired to the academy in 1983 and he'd retired from the State Engineer Office in 1992, I went to find him, looking for explanations about a lawsuit that I had worked on that I needed to learn a lot more about. Between November 1992 and March 1994 we met from time to time at his house.

I won't call those sessions "interviews." They were tutorials. Slingerland took me through the science, politics, and law of the southeastern New Mexico Pecos River. After Steve Reynolds died in 1990, Slingerland alone carried the institutional history of the Pecos River and all its problems. People said that if you wanted to talk to Steve after 1990, you had to speak to Carl. From time to time, I'd ask questions or try to repeat what I'd just heard him say. "Well, Em," he'd respond, "that's not quite right. Think of it this way." The Texans always had found Slingerland abrupt, arrogant, and unyielding. To me he was gentle, compassionate, and sympathetic.[56]

Slingerland had known all the personalities involved in *Texas v. New Mexico* from "Tip," as he called Royce J. Tipton, to "Mr. Reynolds," as he insisted on calling Steve. Toward them all he'd come to take the skeptical, affectionate stance of a healthy person now slightly disengaged from an intense series of important events.

In March 1995 Carl Slingerland went to his beloved wood-working shop. He climbed up on one of his patented workbenches. He strung one end of a rope around a roof beam and the other end around his neck. He kicked the well-balanced work bench out from under him and hung himself. His family and friends were taken by complete surprise. There was talk thereafter about a history of family depression, but the suicide still didn't add up.

Slingerland took with him to the grave the last detailed, insider's understanding of the Pecos River and New Mexico's struggle to deal with it over a century. He left behind only a chart.

Twenty years before, in May 1975, at the beginning of *Texas v. New Mexico,* Slingerland had sent then chief lawyer Paul Bloom a handwritten note and chart estimating the irrigated acreage in the New Mexico section of the Pecos River in roughly five-year increments between 1940 and 1970.[57]

ACREAGE IN 1,000

	Above Alamogordo	Ft. Sumner	Roswell Basin	River Pumpers	CID	TOTAL
1940	14.8	6.0	119.8	7.5	20.2	160.8
1947	14.5	5.0	136.4	7.4	21.5	177.4
1950	14.5	4.5	157.7	8.9	19.0	195.7
1955	11.8	5.7	158.0	7.0	20.0	195.5
1960	11.6	5.6	146.8	6.4	20.0	184.0
1965	11.4	5.8	138.1	6.0	19.6	174.9
1970	11.2	6.0	133.0	5.8	22.2	172.4

In the end, after twenty years of bitter litigation, Slingerland's chart may have said it all. If we acknowledge that groundwater and surface water are interconnected, as they surely are, then the Roswell basin estimates clearly show that New Mexicans went right on developing the Pecos River Basin before, during, and well after the 1947 cut-off date set by the 1948 Compact. For other natural resources, like timber on the national forests, the decades of the 1950s and 1960s had seen the same

New Mexico Stumbles

huge leap to absolutely unsustainable levels. From a peak in the ten years *after* the compact's signing, New Mexico's use had steadily declined. Slingerland's chart suggested that, after all was said and done (and a lot had been said and done, God knows, in *Texas v. New Mexico*), New Mexico's uses had grown too fast and hadn't shrunk quickly enough.[58]

To find out whether this might be true, I went to the horse's mouth. In late 1998 I contacted the Pecos River Master, Colorado State Professor and Chairman of the Civil Engineering Department Neil Grigg, to see if I could watch him make his annual compact computations. Deceased Special Master Charles Meyers had chosen Grigg because he was a seasoned and prestigious western water engineer who had had nothing yet to do with *Texas v. New Mexico* in its long and tortured course to that point. Texas and New Mexico had to share his sometimes hefty annual fee. Professor Grigg sat down at the beginning of every calendar year and for the previous water year made the calculations according to the Supreme Court–approved manual that determined whether New Mexico had met its compact obligation for the water year.[59]

In his decade on the job, River Master Grigg had had to settle plenty of highly technical engineering debates between Texas and New Mexico. Some of the battles involved measurement techniques under the manual. Others involved engineering judgment concerning, for example, the critical question of separating base flows and flood flows. By the time I wrote him in late 1998, Grigg had straightened out most of the technical problems and was ready to proceed more or less directly to the 1998 computations. I'd asked him if I could watch.[60]

"Please plan to visit me in March here at the university," he graciously replied, "and you can watch the computations and we can talk about the case. . . .

> Basically, I use the River Master's Manual, the Weather Bureau and the states numbers, and crank through calculations on spread sheets. I check everything several times, and then send the Preliminary Report to the states by May 15. They check everything again and issue their objections. I consider them, and then issue the Final Report by June 30. While that sounds simple, there are a number of subtle aspects that involve judgment and background on the case. Give me a call when you would like to come. I usually begin this process about March 25 or so.[61]

I reserved a plane seat to Fort Collins, but before I ever got there, the Texans put a stop to the trip. Grigg had told me that he felt obligated to inform New Mexico and Texas of my plans to come and watch. The New

Mexicans did not object, but Tom Bohl, an assistant attorney general in Austin, did. Preparing the annual accounting, he wrote, was "essentially a judicial process carried out under the continuing jurisdiction of the Supreme Court." Texas wanted to keep the proceedings "formal and judicial in nature." Under those circumstances, the Texans wouldn't consent to my sitting in. However, they didn't object to Grigg's plans to address a public conference in March 1999 at the annual meeting of the New Mexico Society of Professional Engineers. So I went to that instead.[62]

The annual meeting convened March 12 in a banquet room of the Albuquerque Hilton Hotel, the same room where boxer Johnny Tapia, tattooed and surrounded by bodyguards, had held his most recent weigh-in for his welterweight title bout against Humberto Cruz. The engineering scene couldn't have been more different: one hundred or so technicians from around New Mexico with short hair, ties, and Power Point presentations about things like the City of Alamogordo water supply. I saw River Master Grigg for the first time: balding, tall, well-dressed, obviously composed. As the New Mexico engineers finished dessert, Grigg came to the front of the room and addressed the throng about his job as Pecos River Master.

Grigg began in a quiet, scholarly way by disclaiming any intent to speak specifically about how he figured New Mexico's obligation to Texas every year. Too specific a discussion, he said, would go beyond the bounds of his job as river master. He could describe in general how he determined annual Pecos River flood inflows under the manual and how he proceeded from that determination to fixing New Mexico's state-line delivery obligation.

Using slides and a hand-held microphone, Grigg moved easily through a series of graphs that showed essentially how the manual calculated index inflows and mandatory state-line outflows. Loosening up a little as he went along, Grigg alluded to the fact that there were still plenty of debates between the two states about how the routing should be done. "You all know," he told the assembled engineers, "that hydrology is 25 percent science and 75 percent politics." Everyone laughed.

At the end of his half-hour talk, River Master Grigg graciously opened the floor to questions. There were a couple of technical ones from the audience. Then I couldn't resist asking Grigg the question I had wanted to pose to him as he worked through the 1998 water year accounting.

"Professor Grigg," I asked, "Royce Tipton, the father of this compact, said that these formulas with which you work on the Pecos River came as close as possible to duplicating and describing the way nature actually works in the river basin. What do you as Pecos River Master think of Tipton's statement?"

Grigg paused for a second and then, smiling, answered.

"Well," he said enigmatically, "I think that that's exactly what Tipton would have said."

At the turn of the century Pecos River Master Grigg has left us the clear results of twelve years of his annual and accumulated Pecos River Compact calculations.[63]

PECOS RIVER COMPACT ACCUMULATED SHORTFALL OR OVERAGE
MAY 1, 2000

Water Year	Annual Overage or Shortfall, AF	Accumulated Overage or Shortfall, AF
1987	15,400	15,400
1988	23,600	39,000
1989	2,700	41,700
1990	-14,100	27,600
1991	-16,500	11,100
1992	10,900	22,000
1993	6,600	28,600
1994	5,900	34,500
1995	-14,100	20,400
1996	-6,700	13,700
1997	6,100	19,800
1998	1,700	21,500
1999	1,300	22,800

No one really believes that the annual deficits or surpluses reflect the "1947 condition" in any accounting year. No one really believes that the variations between years, sometimes as much as 30,000 acre-feet from one year to the next, reflect changes in depletions by man's activities in New Mexico in the period. In short, no one believes that the river master's calculations embody the compact's apportionment provision. If the figures show anything, they show that New Mexico is doing okay with a compact obligation that's arbitrary and unpredictable.

It's the unpredictability that most concerns Interstate Stream Commission Engineer Dr. Bhasker Rau these days. He's in charge of Pecos River Compact compliance. He moves with energetic delight from one computer file to another, from data on the water supply for the Carlsbad Irrigation District to a long list of state appropriations over the last decade for the acquisition of Pecos River water rights. The computer screen dances with columns and numbers, all of which Rau handles well and which he can move through a variety of intricate steps.

By Rau's own admission, the one thing that he worries he can't do so well is guess how the compact figures will come out next year. From accounting year to accounting year it's anybody's guess. "Right now," he says, "New Mexico's comfortably ahead, but who knows what the future will bring?"

The other thing Rau can't do is describe how New Mexico got to the place where it now finds itself. "When they assigned me this job," he says, laughing, "I went over to the Legal Division to look at the files on *Texas v. New Mexico.* My God, they filled a whole room. No one could read through all of those papers, least of all me. Don't ask me how we got here. When people ask me, I tell them to talk to you."

NINE

The Value of Water,
Inch by Inch, Row by Row

———— *High and Dry* tells the sad tale of a high stakes, little understood, seemingly interminable lawsuit over an interstate water compact. Compacts like the 1948 Pecos River Compact are important everywhere in the West because they provide the basic legal framework within which individual states, like Texas and New Mexico, deal with water they share with each other. Most of those compacts, like the Pecos River Compact, date from mid-twentieth century and represent compromises by which the rapid unfettered development of the first half of the twentieth century could be protected, regulated, and continued in the second half. Lawsuits between states over those compacts, like *Texas v. New Mexico*, No. 65 Original, reveal late twentieth-century structural flaws which indicate the lawsuits and the compacts no longer are capable of mediating between the water past and the water future.

The 1948 Pecos River Compact was based on science that promised more than it could deliver and on a legal system that exacerbated, rather than corrected, those scientific limitations. More important, the compact aimed at a target that had become obsolete by century's end. The compact focused exclusively on depletions—the consumption of water for human purposes—by limiting the depletions in an upstream state so that some water would be available for depletion in a downstream state. While Texas and New Mexico fought over the right way to measure their relative rights to deplete the river, depletion itself lost its place as the exclusive centerpiece of water policy. At the turn of the twenty-first century, many other values—environmental and cultural, among others—competed for consideration in a world previously fixated on beneficial *use* of water. Neither compacts like the Pecos River Compact nor the lawsuits that they spawned proved capable of including those new values. As a result, the outcomes, as the outcome of *Texas v. New Mexico* shows, seem arbitrary and unpredictable even though they were meant to be principled and certain.

In the course of *Texas v. New Mexico*, Steve Reynolds's two-sided vision of the New Mexico water world collapsed. Within New Mexico, he'd created a vision based on the highest and best economic use of a common resource, a use limited by science and protected by law. He'd defended that intra-New Mexico vision against all outsiders by standing at the state borders and denying all foreigners, especially neighboring Texans, access. He'd kept those two sides of his vision solid for the last half of the twentieth century by the force of his personality and quickness of his tongue.

The Reynolds vision came under attack in *Texas v. New Mexico*. Obviously the suit threatened to breach New Mexico's water borders. More subtly, it indirectly threatened the scientific and legal foundations of water law within New Mexico. More subtly still, the suit represented an alien attack on Reynolds's water regime, an attack based on values that he didn't share and whose legitimacy he didn't recognize. In the late twentieth century, environmentalists, Native Americans, and Texans asserted themselves and new claims. In the last decade of his life, between 1980 and 1990, Reynolds was not sufficiently flexible to accommodate the new values that were emerging in a changing New Mexico. In the previous twenty-five years, between 1955 and 1980, Steve Reynolds had demonstrated the constant, focused vision and the clever leadership necessary to move New Mexico into what he saw as its future. That future became New Mexico's past before it ever arrived, and he never realized it.

Reynolds fought back against the new values, including Texas's claims to the Pecos River under the 1948 Compact, with the wide range of tools at his disposal. In the case of Texas and the Pecos, delay was Steve Reynolds's game and time was his weapon. He thought he could keep New Mexicans at full supply, at least for a long while, by supplementing the irregular but self-sustaining river flows with constant but finite groundwater in storage. He thought that he could keep Texas at bay, perhaps forever, by using the tricks of the law, the ambiguities of science, and the mysteries of groundwater. But Charles Meyers caught Reynolds at those games. Finally called to account for the Pecos River in the lawsuit, Reynolds couldn't respond. The Supreme Court's final decree mechanically solved the river's interstate problems by giving an annual answer to the question of how much Pecos River water New

Mexico owed Texas. But the mechanical answer was a parody of the subtle, nature-based system on which the compact was based.

Without Reynolds in the last decade of the century, New Mexico might have escaped from the deep imprint of his ideology. Instead, in buying and retiring private water rights, the state resorted to the most primitive solution to its Pecos River problems. The solution addressed none of the river's real problems. The solution didn't even promise to meet the Supreme Court's mechanical definition of the state's obligation. At century's end, the law of the Pecos is in a shambles. It's unclear who will pick up the pieces and what form they will take when they are put back together.

For thirty years I have worked as a New Mexico water lawyer and professor. I'm a graduate of big-shot Princeton University and the Harvard Law School. As an academic, I've talked about New Mexico water to all kinds of audiences. I've written a lot about water in professional journals, in popular magazines, and in books, including this one. As a lawyer, I've sued the New Mexico state engineer. I've worked for the state engineer. I've argued for hours at a time in all kinds of courts about those esoteric issues that so frustrated the courts in their effort to bring some order to the claims of two states to the waters of the same river. I've even appeared before the U.S. Supreme Court on water matters, including a cameo appearance in *Texas v. New Mexico*. I'm a professor and a lawyer and I deal with the big legal issues that involve the large-scale management of a critical desert resource. In short, I've floated a professional career on scarce New Mexico water.

I've stayed upright and on the surface by talking the language of water law, the same language spoken by the principals in *Texas v. New Mexico*. Water talk mixes the idioms of physical science, mathematical statistics, and law. Steve Reynolds spoke the language so fluently that everything seemed to make sense as long as he talked and as long as someone as smart and aggressive as Charles J. Meyers wasn't listening and asking questions. As soon as Reynolds stopped talking, things fell apart. "What did he just say?" people would ask, shaking their heads, as if trying to grasp the fleeting moment of coherence that Reynolds offered. When he died, of course, the illusion of coherence disappeared and didn't come back.

To the uninitiated a lot of water talk sounds like parapsychology. When the water lawyers and engineers talk about one of Morgan Nelson's wells, for example, they speak of drawdown and sustained yield, of depression and recovery. It's sometimes hard to tell whether they're talking about someone's psychic state or the performance of a well. Perhaps at the end of his life Carl Slingerland couldn't distinguish the two.

After thirty years and nearing the age of sixty, I speak water talk with some fluency and that fluency has kept me afloat in the dry world of *Texas v. New Mexico* and New Mexico water. I can bat around CIR, CU, ER, and the Duty of Water with the best of them. But the formal language of prior appropriation is as magnificently accurate and as dead as Latin. The newer vernacular of conservation biology, with its "niches" and "edges" and "loose grains" and "fine grains," doesn't fit. The two are not mutually intelligible. Where are we to look for new models, new grammars, a new idiom?

I have a confession to make. I like to do something even more than talk and write about New Mexico's hydraulic systems. What I really love to do with New Mexico water is irrigate. Over the thirty years that it has taken me to master the water law language, I've also been learning to beneficially use the surface waters of the Pecos River, the Coyote Creek and, most recently, the Rio Frijoles and the Rio Grande. When I stand at the headgates of my gardens, ready to take the public water of New Mexico, behind me stand Louise Tracy, Royce Tipton, Morgan Nelson, Steve Reynolds, Jean Breitenstein, and Charles Meyers.

In taking that stance at my farm headgate as a New Mexico gardener, I have a different perspective from Steve Reynolds and work on an opposite scale. Reynolds was trying to develop water-short New Mexico and, in *Texas v. New Mexico*, trying to use the tools of science and law to defend the whole state against an alien Texas invasion. I am trying just as hard to make a small garden grow in a desert patch. Reynolds dealt with the large, incredibly complex, poorly understood Pecos River system running for hundreds of miles and draining millions of acres. As a gardener I deal with less than an acre. As *Texas v. New Mexico* shows, Reynolds's perspective was too narrow at the end of the twentieth century and the scale on which he operated was too large for the tools he had at hand. Like many books on western water, this one begins with a plane flight, pulling away from the details of the concrete world. I end it in the small world of a New Mexico garden, seeking its perspective on the Pecos River trouble.[1]

I especially love to open the headgates of my local irrigation ditch into my gardens for the first time in early May. By then I will have ploughed the plot once, added aged compost to the turned soil, and roto-tilled the soil and compost into a fine mixture. By then I will have laid out the rows for the water and the plants, raising tall furrows as borders for the water and beds for the seeds. By then I will have raked smooth the south sides of the fresh furrows. With a small wheeled planter I will have planted seeds that I harvested the year before about four inches up the sides of the foot-tall furrows. Then I will open the headgate to my garden a little, careful not to let a flood of water in on this inaugural because too much water too fast will wash out the newly planted seeds.

The water eases through the headgate like some wild animal just loosed in civilization. It bends warily this way and that, looking for the path of least resistance in the rows before it. The water dips into the low places. It searches out the secret underground passages inevitably left by all of my garden preparations. It disappears for a second and then reappears, down the furrow a little farther. It idly turns the corner to the next furrow and starts to finger its way along.[2]

Fig. 9.1.
Irrigator and author Em Hall directs the waters of the Rio Frijoles through the canals of his tiny chile patch in Cundiyo, New Mexico. (Photo courtesy of Delaney Hall.)

228

I'm perched on a high spot next to the outside furrows, leaning on a shovel, wearing tall black rubber irrigation boots, like a prison guard waiting and watching for some breakout. If it comes, if the water either escapes from the outer furrows or breaks down the division between the interior furrows, I'll dive in with my boots and shovel and plug the gap. I hate to do it because it messes up the furrows and disturbs the seeds, but there's no choice. Once free, the water that I've let loose will quickly ruin the system I've imposed on it. So if I have to, I do. If I'm lucky, I don't have to. My system works. I stand there, propped on my shovel, while the rows slowly, gracefully fill up with the same water that drives New Mexicans and Texans mad, the same water whose appearance in the world is so vastly complex that even Royce Tipton and Steve Reynolds couldn't make law master it.

I close the gates a few minutes before the gardens are full. The last water tops the rows off perfectly. If everything has gone right, I survey the domain of a New Mexico flood-irrigated garden. The late afternoon shadows lengthen. The last light of the day refracts from the surface of the water, seeping down into the bottom of the furrows, wicking up toward the tops where the seeds wait and the water hasn't yet reached. For a moment, this garden looks like a pond whose surface is interrupted by long, dry lines, the islands of the tops of the furrows between which the water settles.

At this moment, water does what it does best; it reflects. For New Mexico writers and farmers like Stanley Crawford, the standing water reflects the essential combination of light, soil, and seeds, a natural union that eludes the efforts of laws to apportion it, of courts to adjudicate access to it, even of science to measure it. But surely at the same time the water soaking into my garden is also entirely artificial. Its presence here for the moment also reflects the technology, the science, and the political choices that brought it here to a place it would never have occurred but for the intervention of man. The water standing in my garden is both spiritual and technological, both natural and artificial, involving both the life of a seed and the life of Steve Reynolds.[3]

I'll return in the morning. The water will be gone. The remaining earth will be dark with saturated moisture right to the top of the furrows. The seeds will start to germinate. And the real back-breaking, attention-demanding work of New Mexico gardening will begin. It's work that is allowed by water, even caused by water, but it's not work that water will do.

There will be endless weeds, born downstream by the irrigation water. There will be hordes of plant-devouring insects. There will be spring

229

frosts, summer hail storms, fall snow. There are many disastrous things that can happen to a New Mexico garden, some of which can be controlled, many of which cannot. Like New Mexico water, New Mexico gardening is not for the cautious, for the inflexible, for those who need to guarantee the contours of the future. But there is no one so full of precarious hope as a New Mexico gardener like me; there is nothing so full of fragile promise as a New Mexico garden replete with water on the day of first irrigation in the spring.

And at this moment there is no one so indifferent as the gardener to the broader realities that water reflects, to the wider world to which it is inevitably connected. Standing there at the farm headgate, I have enough trouble spreading the water out on the garden to make it difficult to worry about where the water came from.

But mark it: a farm headgate like mine is just the smallest in the complex set of contraptions that move scant New Mexico water around. The smallest wheel moves only because the larger ones that move it push the whole system along. All farm headgates are connected, more or less directly, to the bigger wheel at the point where water is taken, the critical point of diversion. The farm headgates are moved by the biggest wheel, the combined human and natural conditions that control the "natural" water that reaches that point of diversion. *Texas v. New Mexico* ended a century of efforts by a lot of bright, inventive people to keep all the wheels in synch and moving. In the end the wheels didn't mesh and the machine was mired down in numbers that didn't add up, words that didn't communicate, a cacophony of contradictory values expressed loudly and simultaneously.

I'm so crazy about New Mexico gardening that I have two gardens every year. My wife thinks I've gone completely mad. I have one garden in Albuquerque's North Valley where we are lucky enough to have an irrigated half acre. I have another garden in Cundiyo, just east of Nambe, in northern New Mexico, where we are lucky enough to have another irrigated acre in the middle of an old, conservative Hispanic farming community. Both gardens draw on very old irrigation systems. My North Valley garden taps the Los Griegos lateral which dates from 1745. My Cundiyo garden is the second plot down on the Acequia del Molino, a classic New Mexico community ditch which, according to the state engineer, started the same year, 250 years ago. For two and a half centuries, these ditches have made lands that they serve verdant oases. That artificial condition has pertained for so long that it must have a claim to being natural. Nevertheless the Cundiyo ditch and the Albuquerque one embody very different water values.

Cundiyo's Acequia del Molino diverts water from the Rio Frijoles, ten miles east of Cundiyo, near the Sierra Mosca, the 12,000-foot spine that divides the Pecos River drainage to the east from this Rio Grande drainage. The Rio Frijoles passes gently through a 10,000-foot-elevation meadow, the Panchuela West, and then starts tumbling through a steep, narrow canyon, gathering water and velocity as it descends. In this canyon, the Frijoles carries with it a lot of fractured granite and basalt; the creek actually roars along, combining the sound of rushing water and bouncing rock.

About a mile above my Cundiyo field, the Rio Frijoles shoots through a defile of boulders and drops into a small pool. Below the pool, it starts bouncing downstream once again. But at the downstream edge of that pool, the Frijoles has built up a thick deposit of sand and gravel. Year after year, ever since 1745 or so, at this sand bar the twenty-seven families who reside in Cundiyo, more than 90 percent of them related Vigils, have added a low rock wall, no more than a foot and a half high, across the creek. Compared to the Avalon, Brantley, and Sumner (Alamogordo) dams that serve the CID on the Pecos River, the Cundiyo dam does not intrude much on the free flow of the Frijoles and stores very little water.

But this sand and gravel bar and the rock parapet are enough to send some of the Frijoles water into a man-made ditch about two feet deep and a foot and a half across. In classic northern New Mexico fashion, the Acequia del Molino hugs the eastern side of the creek as it drops into yet another canyon defile. But the ditch works endlessly to divorce itself from the creek, to create as much distance from it and elevation above it as it possibly can and continue to run downhill. A half mile away, the Rio Frijoles passes into a tiny open valley, through which it runs placidly. By then the acequia, which started out right next to the river, is more than a hundred yards from it. For perhaps half a mile, the acequia maintains its distance and then gets pinched back into the river by yet another tight, narrow, rock canyon. But before it is cut off, the acequia has created perhaps fifteen acres of the richest, greenest, best watered land in bone-dry desert New Mexico. (There are another fifteen acres west of the north-running Rio.)

Those fifteen acres east of the Rio Frijoles and below the Acequia del Molino are divided into ten small, oddly shaped tracts. None of those tracts comes anywhere near the size of one of Morgan Nelson's five-hundred-acre fields, by many orders of magnitude.

The state engineer's hydrographic survey maps show my Cundiyo field as the second one down on the Acequia del Molino, consisting of, get this, 1.1 acres. Even that's a lie. My 1.1 acres are crossed east-west by a sandy arroyo and I've ended up with three little fields, each perhaps

Fig. 9.2.
The upper irrigated fields of the Santo Domingo de Cundiyo grant are enclosed on all sides by mountains and mesas. The Rio Frijoles runs through the 15-acre bowl at the center. (Photo courtesy of Charles Briggs.)

a third of an acre. Since 1990 I've raised chile on one of the three fields and let Sabino Samuel Vigil cut hay on the other two. My beloved Cundiyo chile patch is a small-scale, low-impact, community-based operation. I live a hundred miles from it. I'm an Anglo lawyer from Albuquerque, participating part-time in the compressed, compacted word of Cundiyo irrigation.[4]

My half-acre in the heart of Albuquerque's North Valley is no larger than the Cundiyo field but otherwise farming there contrasts sharply with it. The field lies less than ten yards south of my house, so I can get to it in seconds and on foot. I go there frequently, sometimes many times a day, to check things out, to pull a few weeds, to do a little work as a break. Unlike Cundiyo, the North Valley field is a constant part of my life.

In the North Valley I am ringed by residential housing developments that have devoured irrigated land until half the acres around here that were

Chapter 9

irrigated in 1950 no longer are. The transformation from irrigated fields to residential housing continues. My neighbor to the south, Herman Pedroncelli, is the last serious farmer in these parts as near as I can tell. His eight beautifully irrigated acres are probably worth a half a million dollars to developers. Pedroncelli drives a mail truck between Albuquerque and Las Cruces four times a week and breaks even, maybe, using his eight acres to richly feed twenty beef cattle. Compared to Morgan Nelson, Pedroncelli with his part-time, break-even operation is a hobbyist. Compared to me, Pedroncelli, with his big John Deere tractor and its amazing implements, his computer-driven laser leveler and what even his mother calls his other "lluguetes" ("toys') is an agri-businessman.[5]

Still Herman Pedroncelli and I share the same source of water: the Los Griegos lateral. An ancient North Valley irrigation ditch dating from the mid-eighteenth century, the Los Griegos ditch used to be one of eighty ditches in the middle Rio Grande that diverted water directly from the Rio Grande. These log-and-branch affairs were huge compared to the Acequia del Molino diversion on the Rio Frijoles, but still represented relatively small-scale, low-technology, noninvasive communal efforts to deliver some river water to desert lands.[6]

In the late 1920s and early 1930s, the Middle Rio Grande Conservancy District (MRGCD), which the State of New Mexico and Congress organized, consolidated all these diversions. Unlike the Carlsbad Irrigation District, whose works were built more or less from scratch, the MRGCD constructed itself out of the eighty existing community ditch systems. Now in the 120-mile stretch between Cochiti Lake to the north and Elephant Butte to the south there are only four points on the Rio Grande from which main-stem water is diverted. These four massive concrete dams have the capacity to completely control its flow most of the year. This means that the Conservancy managers can, if they choose, send the whole flow of the river, especially when it is low, into the MRGCD's intricate ditch system. This process has transformed irrigation in the Middle Rio Grande from a small-scale, community-based, largely ineffective system to a much larger-scale, government-sponsored, capital-intensive operation. Costs rose in tandem with productivity, for a while.[7]

At the turn of the twenty-first century, the 1920s industrial model infrastructure of the Middle Rio Grande Conservancy District is increasingly inefficient and increasingly irrelevant to an essentially urban population. I have no idea where the central MRGCD works are. I have no idea where the Angostura Diversion, which delivers Rio Grande water to my North Valley garden via the Griegos Lateral, actually is. I've never even seen it except in newspaper photographs.

Over the last ten years I've thought about walking from my garden headgate up the Los Griegos lateral, up the connecting feeder ditches, up past Los Ranchos, Alameda, Corrales, Bernalillo, Algodones, up the MRGCD ditches parallel to the river until I came to the Angostura Dam, straddling the Rio Grande itself. I know that I would follow increasingly large artificial water flows. I would begin with my tiny feeder ditch. I would go from the larger Los Griegos lateral to the even larger mother ditch that feeds it and so on past wider and deeper interconnected ditches. Finally I would arrive at the (dare I say it?) mother ditch, the Rio Grande. But I've never gotten around to taking a thirty-five-mile hike to the source of my water, let alone traveling hundreds of miles farther north, to the MRGCD storage dams on the Chama River. Instead, I just wait for the water at my garden headgate.

It's always there, more or less. In the irrigation season, from March to October, the Los Griegos lateral always runs as if it really were natural. Pedroncelli has enough acres and enough swack with the Conservancy pooh-bahs that he can get them to raise the level of the water in the lateral on the days that he irrigates. When he does and they do, I can get a little of Pedroncelli's extra head before it gets to him. He bitches and moans and watches, armed with a shovel, but he does so with a grin. There's really enough water for both of us. On days that the lateral is running full for Pedroncelli's benefit, I can irrigate my garden in ten minutes, as long as he doesn't catch me. (He always does.) Otherwise, it takes me perhaps an hour. Never, I often think, has such a huge, expensive, invasive construction supported so little.

Over the years I've taken great personal satisfaction in my North Valley garden, but I have felt increasingly compelled to do something more with the water that this artifact of hydraulic civilization sends my way. Given the arcane tax structure of the MRGCD, I hardly pay for it. Over the last few years, I've tried Steve Reynolds's answer. I've tried to turn my depletion of the heavily subsidized water into money.

Over the years I have increased the garden's size until it is now more than a quarter acre. Over the years, I have changed what the state engineer people call "the cropping pattern" until it's no longer a kitchen garden, supporting a wide variety of vegetables. Now my North Valley garden is about half zinnias and half basil. The zinnias I still distribute in profusion to vases in my house and to dear friends. The basil I've tried to turn into an economic commodity.

I started doing so in the winter of 1996 by keeping track of the basil-related expenses I incurred. Initially, I charged nothing to water because the water was included in the property taxes I paid for the land. I charged nothing to land because I owned it and nothing to labor because it was my own and I owned it, too. I paid nothing for seeds because I had carefully harvested them the year before.

For $7.95 I bought an Asian rice-winnowing basket at an Albuquerque junk store. It took me a long time to figure out that that basket was what I needed to go into commercial basil production. It took me even longer to see how my own choice of that $7.95 basket involved me in a battle of economic scale as real as Steve Reynolds's struggles with natural scale in *Texas v. New Mexico.*

It happened this way: Basil seeds are hard, tiny, slippery, and come encased in husks. To separate the seeds from the chaff, I started with a small, clear, 8-inch baking dish. Across the bottom of the dish I spread the husks and seeds. Using my fingers, I broke up the husks. Buried in the chaff, I could see the tiny black basil seeds spread across the baking dish's clear bottom. I tipped that dish out and blew gently across the surface. The chaff disappeared. About one hundred black seeds lay in the bottom of the dish after an hour's huffing and puffing. I smiled and scouted around for a better way to produce the seeds I refused to buy and felt compelled to harvest from my own operations. But I didn't stumble on my winnowing basket straight away.

Like a good twenty-first-century hydraulic citizen, I first went to the Internet. Various web sites and links brought me fairly quickly to Seed Tech Plus out of Salem, Oregon. For $11,995, excluding crating and shipping costs, Seed Tech offered a "lab size Precision Air Density Separator" capable of separating up to 110 pounds per hour of basil seeds in their husks. In half an hour, this separator would yield more basil seeds than I could plant in a year, even if I devoted my entire half acre to basil all year. Seed Tech Plus offered a couple of less expensive lab models, the least expensive model priced at $4,000, but they all seemed way beyond the economically responsible farming that I was after. Every choice in gardening involves an implicit decision about the value of water. The $7.95 I ended up spending for a used rice-winnowing basket from Asia fit much more the scale of the operation I had in mind.[8]

Now windy winter days find me in my dormant field, tossing up into the gale from my basket thousands of crushed basil husks. I allow the chaff to blow away in the wind, leaving in the bottom of my $7.95 basket enough precious, tiny black seeds to get my quarter acre of basil going. Were I to buy the same amount of seeds from the upscale Shepherd's Seed Catalogue, the seeds would cost almost $1,000 a year. Were I to find a seed wholesaler, I might be able to cut that in half.

Later in May, with sun and dirt and water on my side, I'll sow the winnowed seed into the ground so that the precious Rio Grande water can grow something. When I was still working with the baking dish to separate seeds, I would sow them from a regular 8¹/₂ x 11 envelope bearing a printed, return address: G. Emlen Hall, Attorney at Law, etc. The envelope should have reminded me where my real economic self-interest lay. A day's legal work would yield me a lot more money than all the basil than I could ever grow and sell in a summer. But I was using the envelope to sow basil seeds in my North Valley garden.

I would hunch over each of the two rows I originally planted to basil in my much smaller garden and back along, tapping the open envelope as I crept, releasing a steady stream of tiny basil seeds into the shallow row I previously had scratched into the south side of the furrows. In my mid-fifties, I could barely straighten up at the end of the fifty-foot rows. When I decided to go from two to fifteen rows and increase my production tenfold, I realized that I had to develop a better sowing system.

I was a little wary after my seed separator foray into the modern world of agricultural technology, but I tried again with my sowing dilemma and this time hit reasonable gold. For $99 I found an Earth Way Products "Precision Garden Seeder," a weird-looking two-wheeled contraption that released seeds at a regular rate as the farmer (me) pushed it down the prepared rows. The tiny, slippery basil seeds eluded the smallest of the Precision Garden Seeder's ten seed plates for awhile, but using tape and endless experiments, I finally got it working. Now for $106.95 I had enough seeds and could sow relatively quickly into fifteen fifty-foot rows of the finest Genoa basil, and I'd barely gotten started with my basil farming operation.[9]

Don't worry. I'm not going to run down for you every direct and indirect cost associated with my basil plan. Believe me there were lots: the amortized costs of my beloved Italian walking tractor, perfectly sized for my layout; the annual costs of fertilizer; the indirect costs of highly subsidized MRGCD water, and the denied costs of the untold hours of unaccounted labor that I poured, with love, into the project. I'll spare you those except to note that they are real, that they demand your attention and that, while you are paying attention to the fine-grained details, you don't see the loose-grained big-picture water world of which the details are a small part.

By July 15 most years, the fifteen fifty-foot rows I have planted are full of basil plants, perhaps two feet tall, big leaves shiny on the top side, a flatter patina on the bottom. I harvest my first leaves by cutting each plant back. I thereby stop the plant from prematurely going to seed and force it to develop out into bushes rather than up into lanky basil trees.

Starting with this first cut and continuing through October, I have to find a market for the leaves.

It's not easy. There are good Italian restaurants in Albuquerque needing lots of basil every day all year. Like me, most local growers can't meet any of those criteria. We can't produce the hundreds of pounds of basil leaves they use. We can't do it as regularly as they need it. And, at best, we can produce it for only six months out of the year. Berkeley's very upscale Chez Panisse may support a couple of organic vegetable growers from the California Central Valley, but can you imagine Scalo's Northern Italian Grill in Albuquerque with a sign on its door, "Closed: No Pesto. Try Later"?[10]

For a while some of the local restaurants tried to support a farmer they affectionately called "Basil Mary" who grew fifteen acres of basil in Albuquerque's South Valley. Even she was too unreliable. For basil, the local restaurants turned to a professional operation: B. Riley's Fresh Herbs.

As it turns out, B. Riley is a middle-school teacher in Albuquerque. She works on basil and other herbs in the summer. Her partner (and husband) works on the business full time. He grows the herbs when he can, in the summer months, on a small irrigated plot in Albuquerque's South Valley. In the six months of the New Mexico year when he can't produce basil himself, he buys it and makes up as a wholesaler for what nature denies him as a farmer. Scouting the world produce markets by phone, B. Riley's husband looks for the least expensive good basil he can find.

For a long time in the late 1980s and early 1990s Riley found basil in Hawaii. Maui in particular was ideal. It had a year-round climate capable of a sustained basil yield. Its volcanic soil was perfectly suited to the demands of basil. There were a lot of growers willing to farm it. So many were available, it turned out, because, after years of studied indifference, the federal drug authorities finally had cracked down on the island's significant marijuana production, and a lot of growers had to switch crops fast. Because the basil leaves were so light, Maui basil could be air-freighted to Albuquerque more quickly, more reliably and less expensively than anyone could grow it here. Maui basil, with B. Riley moving it around, took over the gourmet Albuquerque niche. For a little while.

By the mid-1990s the North American Free Trade Agreement ("NAFTA") went into effect and the Albuquerque basil market went south. Cheap and reliable as the Hawaii basil was, Mexican basil turned out to be even cheaper and just as reliable. The volcanic conditions at the southern tip of Baja California turned out to be as ideal for basil as Maui. Mexican farmers, with their cheap water and labor and adequate tourist airport, could ship their basil even more cheaply to Albuquerque than the Maui growers could and more reliably than I could deliver it from the North Valley. The basil wholesalers quit calling Hawaii and started calling herb factors in Cabo San Lucas.

I'm left standing at my farm headgate in the North Valley, watching as the water trickles in. Ponder how far afield I have to look—Hawaii and Mexico—in order to determine the commodity value of the meager basil that I can produce with this precious water. Notice that Morgan Nelson ships parts of his chile harvest to Hungary every year to be turned into paprika and shipped back in those beautiful red containers. Consider that as I stand in the evening light, watching as the water trickles in, I must pay fierce attention to the water and its never-ending tendency to get away and go somewhere else. Recognize all that and you will understand why it's so hard for a gardener like me to see much beyond the end of my headgate when it comes to water that seems like the only thing that's always there when I need it.

All of these concerns have never stopped me from continuing the struggle to make some commodity use of my North Valley basil. Cut out of the big Albuquerque markets, I've turned, literally, to the small ones, those little local farmers' markets that have popped up in recent years all over the city. I've tried a lot of them over the last few years, but I've come to focus on the Los Ranchos Farmers' Market in my own North Valley. Open Saturdays from seven in the morning until around ten, the market provides an outlet for local gardeners like me in a medieval fair atmosphere.

On market days, I will get up at 4:30 A.M. and head for the basil patch, with a miner's headlamp fastened to my forehead. It's cool and dark then and in the hour and a half before dawn I can pick two bushels of fresh basil, easy. My daughters and I take off for the market by 6:15.

At the market, we measure the basil by loosely packed cup and charge fifty cents for two cups. If we are lucky, a bushel produces seventy cups of the pungent leaves. Beginning about 7:00 A.M. the parking lot at the market starts to fill with bargain seekers and health food seekers and just plain curiosity seekers. They are full of questions about farming techniques ("No, ma'am, we don't use pesticides"), about freshness ("Yes, ma'am, we just picked these this morning"), and about the location of our basil patch ("Yes, ma'am, right here in the North Valley, just south of Columbus Park"). No one has ever asked about our source of water. Over the years my daughters have developed into effective salespersons and change-makers. On a good day we'll sell all the basil leaves we've bought. We'll end up with $35, more or less, crammed in ones and loose change into our cigar box that doubles as a cash register.

When we began at the North Valley Farmers' Market, we'd take the basil leaves we couldn't sell home with us and make pesto with it. Using a heavy duty Cuisinart my mother-in-law had given us, cheese, olive oil and pine nuts provided by a wholesaler friend, and a recipe from the toney *Silver Palate Cook Book,* the girls and I threw together enough of the strong Italian dressing to cover many times over the pasta we ate at home. After a while we started to take the excess pasta from the excess basil leaves to the Farmers' Market in eight-ounce plastic containers we begged, borrowed, and stole. To our amazement the $4 containers caught on like wildfire. Who could resist a fourteen-year-old girl and a seven-year-old, offering an experimental taste of our secret recipe pesto on a slice of fresh French bread? Pretty soon, the girls and I had reversed our production processes. Now we started out making pesto and sold the leaves we didn't use for our weekly production as garden variety basil.

In that switch we followed in our small way a model for sustained economic development that planners had been pushing for water-rich, impoverished northern New Mexico for more than thirty years. Add value locally, the planners said, to basic production factors—water, timber, grass. Capture the value added in the local community and everyone will prosper. In its small way, the switch from basil to pesto promised more prosperity to our family.[11]

The sales figures I kept for 1997 and 1998 in a small black book marked "Bayita Farm" showed it. In 1997 we made $234 in pesto and basil sales at the North Valley Farmers' Market and in 1998 we made $314. Clearly the sky was the limit. True, as my wife pointed out, we never even factored in the cost of the other materials—the cheese, the oil, the nuts, the eight-ounce containers, to say nothing of the indirect costs of the basil itself, the land and the water—to decide whether we really made money and how much. True, also, $548 wasn't enough to pay for any aspect of our middle-class life at the turn of the century.

So my daughters and I took our hard-earned money and bought a good cello for the older girl and a three-quarter-sized-violin for the younger one. The basil and pesto were music to our ears. It was an entirely appropriate use of hard-earned money and, for the moment, an accurate reflection of the fundamental, incidental, and aesthetic value of real water in my life.

I spend a lot of time these days trying to make something more of basil and pesto. I read *The Small Commercial Garden: How to Make $10,000 a Year in Your Back Yard.* Books like this are full of very concrete suggestions I can never quite bring myself to follow. Every year I expand my operations a little: planting more basil, producing more pesto, increasing expenses by amounts I do not know and profits by amounts I do not measure.[12]

Steve Reynolds would have made charming fun of my efforts in the basil area. Morgan Nelson laughed when I told him about it. Breitenstein and Meyers never personally dealt with anything so puny and mundane during their careers in western water, although the quirky, enigmatic Meyers loved to grow flowers almost as much as he loved to listen to Mozart. On the small scale at which I work as a farmer, there's not much connection with the large-scale issues to which they devoted their lives. But if beneficial use is the basis, the measure and the limit of a water right in New Mexico, then with the basil and pesto, I'm trying.[13]

What's the alternative?

I could walk away from the intense use of water on my Albuquerque half acre. I could forget it as so many property owners here have.

Or I could turn the water rights on my North Valley half acre to their highest and best use and sell the water rights to the City of Albuquerque for $4,000 (.47 acres × 2.1 af/a × $4,000 an acre = $3,948, as the water engineers show it). I'd then sell the underlying land rights to a residential developer for $33,000 (.47 × $70,000 an acre = $32,900). If I did nothing more than put the $40,000 yield into a certificate of deposit, the annual interest would amount to $2,000 a year. That's more than I'm ever likely to make growing basil and manufacturing pesto.

Or I could try to convince Bernalillo County that my basil operation really did qualify as a farm and that, as a result, I was entitled to the much lower property taxes assessed to productive agricultural land. Right now I pay $1,800 a year in real property taxes on the half acre where I garden; with a green belt exemption I'd pay less than a quarter of that. Surely, I remind my wife, that $1,400 saved is real. In this water world, I tell her, government benefits represent the real wealth and avoided taxes are real income.[14]

But those realities are as irrelevant to me as they are fundamental to the men who oversaw New Mexico water. Their measure of value is not my measure of value. Try as I may, my water won't flow uphill to money. Their limit on the use of water is not my limit. And, as *Texas v. New Mexico* suggests, their big-scale basis for the management of New Mexico water is as opaque as my small-scale basis for trying to make my use of it pay. They have their policies and I have my property rights to water. After one hundred years of active management of public water in New Mexico, no one completely understands where the public interest in water starts and the private property right to it stops. So, standing at my North Valley headgate after the first irrigation of the spring, looking

Chapter 9

at the Rio Grande water soaking into my garden, the surface of the water reflects almost nothing clear, except strong differences of opinion about the value of water.

My other garden at Cundiyo is more of the same with this difference: In Cundiyo there is not the same awful imbalance between the technological hydraulic system that supports my northern New Mexico garden and the garden itself. Here, at least, I know exactly where the water I use comes from. I help to rebuild the low diversion dam every year to take the water from the Rio Frijoles. I clean the ditches every year that bring the water to my head gate. Every time that I want to open that gate and irrigate my plantings, I have to get the permission of Sabino Samuel Vigil, the mayordomo. All of these rituals constantly remind me of the connection among nature's supply, the community works that get the water to me, and ultimately my private garden.

In the fifteen years I've farmed at Cundiyo I've grown only giant pumpkins and chile. Unlike the North Valley basil, I make no economic justification for either pumpkins or chile. I haul the pumpkins down to Albuquerque late every fall and carve elaborate Halloween ghouls with and for my kids. The chile involves me even more directly in the century-old cycles of an ancient Hispanic community.

In 1986 Cundiyo mayordomo Vigil gave me a ristra of strung red chile in return for some legal help I'd given him. The chile came from a small tract down the ditch from mine where, year and decade in and out, Sam and Andreita Vigil carefully cultivated an acre of chile from seeds they saved from the previous year's production. They and their ancestors had been doing this for so long that no one could say for sure how long Cundiyosos had been planting with chile seeds that came from the little valley. But that first gift of Cundiyo chile got me started on a system of water use and agricultural production that was almost entirely self-contained.

With my Cundiyo seeds and my North Valley planter, I slowly learned to grow and harvest a quarter acre of chile. Residents showed me how to lay out the south-facing rows so as to generate the earliest germination. They showed me how to irrigate and fertilize the emerging plants, how to thin and weed the growing chile, when to harvest the green chile and how to string up and dry the later red. Now by year's end, I have ten bushels of green chile that I roast and freeze and ten bushels of red chile that I tie into long ristras and dry.

It is magnificent stuff to my taste. The fresh green chile is small, fleshy, and hot. I claim that it tastes different from any other chile but I can't really say why. The Cundiyo red chile, however, is equally distinct and

I do know how. It is as hot as the green chile but it is also both musty and sweet. The first bite simultaneously sets my taste buds on fire and tells them that I'm eating candy. I'd know my Cundiyo red chile anywhere. But the fact of the matter is that it's the product of a small, isolated, self-contained world. In terms of water and chile, that's its real attraction and its real limitation.

Critics of Steve Reynolds's heavy-impact, large-scale water vision always make exceptions for ancient hydraulic institutions like the ones that produce my Cundiyo chile. Places like Cundiyo are so old in the history of western irrigation, so small in the over all scheme of western agriculture, so light in their technological touch on the natural landscape and utilized by people so isolated, so oft-conquered, whose culture is so old and so marginal that critics can't bring themselves to include them in the blanket condemnation of irrigation. But what Cundiyo irrigation lacks in impact, it also lacks in real economic productivity.[15]

Eloy Vigil, another Cundiyoso, calls mine the most expensive chile in the world, given the time I spend on it and the gas I waste getting to it. Among my generation of Cundiyo farmers there isn't one who makes any kind of living off the land. As a matter of fact, the Cundiyo insularity works both ways. For their chile Cundiyosos depend on nothing outside their tiny community, including water and seeds. They never sell to outsiders the delicious yield of their fields.

Like the Cundiyosos, I'm not about to give up my day job as a lawyer and university professor to farm full time. But as the pressure on New Mexico water increases, as the state grows, I've felt more and more uncomfortable with the relationship between the public water that I use and the private yield I produce. In the North Valley the public irrigation structures dwarf my basil production, and in Cundiyo my chile production disdains public markets. Water in New Mexico is supposed to balance public good and private rights. Like a lot of New Mexican farmers I'm left these days asserting my private right to water against a changing definition of what the public good in terms of water might be. In *Texas v. New Mexico* the big balance between public and private use of the Pecos River fell apart just as the much smaller balance has fallen apart in my gardens.

At fifty-seven, I'm too old to rebalance those uses as either a lawyer or a gardener. I'm not enough of a joiner to spend the huge amount of time attending endless meetings necessary to agree on a sound scientific, legal, and policy basis for reconfiguring access to New Mexico's limited water supplies. And I'm too much of a gardener to wait for a resolution before I plant my next crop. I'll bumble along in the distended, out-of-shape water world in which I've always lived. There's going to be a lot of shifting for survival in the last twenty years of my life. However, permanent new science and new shapes are going to have to come from a younger generation.

From one direction there's Interstate Stream Commission member Sonny Houghtaling, fifty years old. It's the ISC that manages the 1948 Pecos River Compact and the changes mandated by the Supreme Court's reading of it. In 1998, Houghtaling replaced long-time Roswell-area representative Phelps White III on the ISC. Houghtaling had two strong points in his favor: He was a Republican during the regime of Republican Governor Gary Johnson and a large-scale, groundwater farmer east of Artesia. A third point—he was staunch Democrat Morgan Nelson's son-in-law—wasn't so strong.

"Morgan and I still farm 1,100 acres in four or five tracts around the Roswell-Artesia area," Houghtaling reports in a deeply courteous, quietly intelligent, southeastern New Mexico voice.

We're pumping the same artesian wells, helping the natural lift with about $20,000 of electricity, as usual. The artesian water levels have been pretty stable around here. We're growing a lot of corn for silage and alfalfa. The California dairies that have moved here in the last decade created a real market for that. But the Roswell dairies won't pay our price. This summer we're sending our corn and hay to Houston. Our dairies are buying hay in Colorado. It's a funny world, the world of free markets. We still grow some cotton, but the chile is way down. We can't compete with Mexico so long as the chile has to be picked by hand. I've only planted fifty acres this year. Chile never really took in Roswell as we thought it would. A mechanical picker is the only thing that will save the business here.

I haven't been a farmer all of my life. Right out of the Artesia High School, I started a hay hauling business and had two trucks running when I married Morgan's daughter, Ann. I'd help Morgan out from time to time and I guess I showed some aptitude for the work. We kept sharing more and more of it until now Morgan's pretty much retired and Ann and I run the show. It's a tough business and we're still looking for ways to save water. We spend a lot of money searching. Laser leveling the fields, going to solar and surge irrigation, all have cost a lot of money and have helped. Last year we spent $300,000 to put in a leeper system. That's a low pressure irrigation method that'll save us energy and water if it works. We'll see.

I didn't have any previous experience in water politics when Governor Johnson appointed me to the Interstate Stream Commission. I don't really

Fig. 9.3.

In 2001, Interstate Stream Commission member Sonny Houghtaling (left) stands next to his wife, Ann Nelson Houghtaling, and his father-in-law, Morgan Nelson, in front of a massive irrigation rig at the family's Cottonwood farm. (Photo courtesy of Morgan Nelson.)

know how I got picked. I certainly didn't lobby anyone for the job. I had been on the board of the Production Credit Association, a state wide group that oversees credit for farmers. It must have been that. A friend from Las Cruces called one day and asked if I'd be interested in a place on the ISC. I hardly knew what the ISC was but I told my friend that if chosen, I'd serve. The next thing I knew I was chosen.

It turns out that I'm the only Pecos River rep on the Commission. That means, I suppose, that I have to watch out for the whole river up there in Santa Fe. Carlsbad doesn't have a representative of its own so I guess I'm supposed to look out for them, too. It's not easy, but we have a cordial relationship.

The ISC tries to meet once a month in Santa Fe. I drive the four hours from Artesia and spend the night up in the Capitol. It's taken me a year and a half to get some sense of what's going on. My father-in-law had talked to me about the Pecos River Compact before I ever got to the ISC. Like him, I thought that New Mexico had got a raw deal with Texas if the Compact meant that Roswell and Artesia wells like ours that existed at the start of 1947 weren't protected. But the Supreme Court's ruling is pretty much a fact of life and we've got to live with it.

On the ISC I've learned how little I knew after all the years in this business. Morgan always had told me that New Mexico got a raw deal with the Pecos River Compact, but I'm just beginning to understand how. Running a farm you've got to control what you can control and make educated guesses about the rest. But with this Compact, there's so little to control and so much to guess about so quickly that it's hard to plan anything. Still I think that putting more water in the river south of Carlsbad by buying water rights down there is the right way to go. We've pretty much come to the end of that and I guess that it's working, but who knows?

It's the new competition on the river that's really got me worried. The blunt nose shiner, which incidentally I have never seen, has brought a new active player to the river—the federal government—and a whole new concern—leaving water in the river for the fish, not getting it out for us farmers. I worry about the federal choice and I worry about the federal muscle, but what can you do?

I'm learning a lot in the job on the ISC. There's a lot to learn, but there's a lot that no one knows. In 25 years, the shape of the human claims to the Pecos will probably look much clearer and very different than they do today. Like any good farmer, you do what you can do with what you've got. Then you watch to see what happens.

From farther upstream on the Pecos than Sonny Houghtaling's Artesia domain there's twenty-eight-year-old Eric Biderman and his fifteen-acre Fat Duck Farm. Biderman grew up in Santa Fe, graduated from the local high school and then hit the road for his formal education on both coasts. He was trained as an architect at Yale University and as an organic farmer at the University of California at Santa Cruz. Two years ago, using $80,000 he borrowed from his maternal grandparents, he bought fifteen acres of irrigated land on the Pecos River near Ribera, forty miles southeast of Santa Fe. The tract lay east of the river in the 1794 San Miguel del Bado Grant. It had belonged to a veterinarian who had assembled a much larger tract of alfalfa from Hispanic farmers ready to sell out and move on to the cities. The vet decided to move on to Montana. Eric Biderman moved in.

Located in the village of Corruco, one of a series of ancient Hispanic villages spread like beads on a string along the upper Pecos River,

Biderman's fifteen acres have the look of any other northern New Mexico river settlement. For starters, it's a staggeringly beautiful place. The river runs through it. Cottonwood trees on both banks set against towering mesas and an impossibly blue sky beyond. In the summertime, the fields in the foreground lie deep in blue green alfalfa.

Biderman's fields seem to bear the deep imprint of northern New Mexico. Everywhere you look you see signs of a tentative, ephemeral hold on the place. At the upper edge of his fields there's a house trailer, freshly painted, true enough, but a mobile home nonetheless. The fields beyond are in various states of disarray. Some have been ploughed; others haven't. Some of those that have been ploughed don't appear to have been well tended; others are immaculately kept. Farm equipment in various states of disrepair dots the terrain. One tractor sits in the middle of the fields; a second tractor, minus its right front wheel, sits near the trailer. There's slotted irrigation pipe everywhere. In short, Biderman's "farm" has the disheveled look of many other half-abandoned northern New Mexico fields on their way to nowhere.

But Biderman hopes that what he calls the "Fat Duck Farm" is headed in the opposite direction. It's the culmination of a dream that he hopes to turn into an economic reality, a self-supporting northern New Mexico farm built on Pecos River water.

"I know how I got into this," he relates:

Just before going off to college, I went to Israel to work on a kibbutz. Talk about desert agriculture. The Israelis really know how to make the desert bloom. It's a really hi-tech hydraulic society. It's funny but I got into organic farming in New Mexico driving an avocado picker in Israel. I'd never even gardened much before that, but when I got home and got ready to go to New Haven, I knew that I really wanted to farm.

In the summers, between academic years studying architecture, some friends of mine and I grew vegetables. We'd borrow irrigated land in places like Nambe where everybody was so busy paying the exorbitant mortgages it took to buy property there that they didn't have time to grow anything and didn't know how to anyway. One Nambe resident even let us use a tractor he had on the place.

Nambe Creek wasn't very reliable. The ditch systems there aren't well maintained. Pueblo claims to the water have cast a pall over the place. But we grew different kinds of lettuce before gourmet lettuce mixes hit the big markets. We could sell all we could grow at the Santa Fe Farmers Market for $12 a pound. We had no costs to speak of. We were college kids. And we made a lot more money than any of us could have with regular summer

246

Fig. 9.4. Twenty-eight-year-old farmer Eric Biderman drives his cultivating tractor down a row of crops on his organic farm in northern New Mexico. Biderman draws his irrigation water from the upper reaches of the Pecos River, near the tiny community of Corruco in the ancient San Miguel del Bado grant. (G. Emlen Hall.)

jobs. I didn't like the social part of the farmer's market, but I found that I just loved to grow things. I knew that it's what I wanted to do when I finished my education.

It seemed natural enough to go from Yale to the master's program in Organic Gardening at the University of California at Santa Cruz. The place has a deserved reputation as a hippie bastion and the Organic Farming program fit right in. The model farm that they had there had been so well tended for so long that it looked like a fairy tale. The organic soil was so rich you could stick your arm into up to the elbow and feel no resistance at all. Try that in New Mexico and you'd be lucky not to break your wrist.

I especially liked the weekly field trips we would take to different California farms. Organic farming is much more evolved there than it is here in New Mexico. But the Santa Cruz program also took us to those huge Central Valley corporate farms and I actually really appreciated the scale and efficiency of those operations. My God, they've got the whole University of California at Davis working endlessly on corporate farm technology and they do amazing things including producing a lot of the food for the world from the waters of the west face of the Sierra Nevada. It's nothing to laugh at, like the Israeli farms.

When I finished at Santa Cruz, I knew I'd come back to New Mexico. I became one of three inspectors of organic farms for the State certification program so I got around some and saw what people were doing. I also scouted around for good, irrigable land of my own. That's how I found these fifteen acres in Corruco. I was lucky enough to have grandparents who would stake me to the place. I could have paid for it myself, but not by working a farm here. The gift from my grandparents put me thirty years ahead of schedule, the time I would have had to work another job to pay for this land. Now I can get much more quickly to the job of making this farm pay.

As you can see, I've started fairly slowly. That very clean half acre patch over there where the pumpkins are growing is part of my master's thesis in biology at Highlands University in Las Vegas. I'm testing various methods of controlling for squash bugs, the scourge of organic farmers. Those ploughed two acres over there, I've turned over a couple of times this year to control for weeds next year. That's when I figure to really get rolling.

In the meantime, I'm gathering the equipment you see lying around here. The slotted pipe I picked up at a sale in Colorado and will allow for controlled surge irrigation, a better alternative than just flooding the fields from the ditch. That red tractor over there, the one without the front wheel, which I'm repairing, is an old cultivating tractor. The driving seat and steering assembly are off-set so that you can look straight down at the ground as you drive along. Seeing like that makes it possible to weed with great accuracy. They haven't made tractors like that in fifty years. They're hard to find and, when you do find them, you have to bid against antique collectors for them. I was lucky to find this one in Rocky Ford, Colorado. There's no hope without equipment like this. It's the only way to hold down labor costs and allow enough acres to get out a reasonable crop.

As I said, I plan to really start next spring. I'm not sure exactly what I'll plant or where I'll sell what I grow. There's a growing community supported agriculture (CSA) movement in New Mexico. In a CSA a group of families agree at the beginning of a year to buy fresh produce from a farmer. The system already works well on the West Coast. It's getting started here. I could furnish up-scale restaurants and work the farmer's markets but they're both a little too undependable for me. I've thought about other high value crops that don't travel so well, like raspberries; they're ideal for local growers. There are lots of possibilities and I'm just getting started. I'm convinced I can make a living at this and it's what I want to do.

When I bought these acres, I didn't worry much about the water rights other than to check them out with the State Engineer. They're full recognized and have a very old priority. I work on the ditch with the other irrigators around here and everything works fine. I've heard about the Pecos River trouble with Texas but it doesn't seem much of a threat up here at the top of the river where there are no dams and storage anyway. Irrigated agriculture has been a way of life up here for more than two centuries. It dropped off a lot after the Second World War when the local subsistence economies collapsed. But things are coming back. Hope springs eternal and there's a new generation of idealists every ten years or so.

Abbreviations

EAC-ISC: Minutes and Reports of the Engineering Advisory Committee of the Pecos River Commission, Interstate Stream Commission, Santa Fe, New Mexico.

ISC: Files of the Interstate Stream Commission, Bataan Memorial Building, Santa Fe, New Mexico.

MNPP: Private papers of Morgan Nelson, East Grand Plains, Roswell, New Mexico.

NMHR: New Mexico Historical Review, University of New Mexico, Albuquerque, New Mexico.

NMOHP: New Mexico Oral History Project, School of Law, University of New Mexico, Albuquerque, New Mexico.

NMPRC: Minutes of Meetings of the Pecos River Compact Commission Prior to and Including the Signing of the Compact, Interstate Stream Commission, Santa Fe, New Mexico.

NRJ: Natural Resources Journal, School of Law, Albuquerque, New Mexico.

PRC: Minutes of the Meetings of the Pecos River Commission, Interstate Stream Commission, Santa Fe, New Mexico.

SER-ISC: Papers of Stephen E. Reynolds, Interstate Stream Commission, Santa Fe, New Mexico.

TvNM-Ex: Exhibits admitted in *Texas v. New Mexico*, No. 65 Original, copies in legal division of Office of the State Engineer, Santa Fe, New Mexico.

TvNM-Files: Correspondence related to *Texas v. New Mexico*, copies in legal division of Office of the State Engineer, Santa Fe, New Mexico.

TvNM-RP: Record Proper (written motions, pleadings and other formal submissions) in *Texas v. New Mexico*, copies in legal division of Office of the State Engineer, Santa Fe, New Mexico.

TvNM-TR: Transcript of testimony in *Texas v. New Mexico*, copies in legal division of Office of the State Engineer, Santa Fe, New Mexico.

WRD-SEO: Records of the Water Rights Division, Office of the State Engineer, Santa Fe, New Mexico.

WJB: Papers of Justice William J. Brennan, Library of Congress, Washington, D.C.

Notes

CHAPTER I

1. Biennial Report of the State Engineer of New Mexico for the 64th and 65th Fiscal Years, Office, July 1, 1975 to June 31, 1976, "Personnel of the State Engineer Office Legal Division and Personnel of the Interstate Stream Commission" OSE. Letter, Hon. Edwin L. Mechem, United States District Judge for the District of New Mexico to Hall, December 12, 1998, personal correspondence in Hall's files. John Nichols, *The Milagro Beanfield War* (New York: Holt, Rhinehart, 1974). In Nichols's novel about the politics of water in New Mexico, the antagonist lawyer is given the name "Bloom" in honor of the real lawyer of real State Engineer Steve Reynolds.

2. E. G. Fiedler and Nye, *Geology and Ground Water Resources of the Roswell Artesian Basin, New Mexico,* Geological Survey Water Supply Paper 639 (Washington, D.C.: U.S. Government Printing Office, 1933). John Shomaker, consulting geohydrologist, interview, Albuquerque, New Mexico, December 16, 1993. Unless otherwise noted, all interviews cited were conducted by the author.

3. See chapters 3, 4 and 5 below. See background description in Annual Report of the State Engineer 67th Fiscal year, July 1, 1978, to June 30, 1979 (Santa Fe) 47–48 and in *Texas v. New Mexico* 462 U.S. 554 (1983).

4. Journalists and water writers always struggle for some appropriate standard by which to convey the amount of water in the standard acre-foot measurement. A 208-foot square acre sometimes suffices but few people know how large an acre is. In desperation one New Mexico lawyer measured the cavernous, public courtroom of the Supreme Court in Washington, D.C. and announced to the Court that an acre-foot of water would fill the huge room almost to its lofty ceiling. The justices nodded, indicating that now they understood the basic quantity of western water law. John Draper, attorney, interview, Santa Fe, New Mexico, December 18, 1993. *Texas v. New Mexico,* 462 U.S. at 555–557 (1983) and chart of Inflow-Outflow Calculations at 576.

5. Supreme Court Clerk Rodak to Hon. Jean S. Breitenstein, Nov. 11. 1975, Notice of Appointment and Reference, Files, *Texas v. New Mexico,* Legal Division, State Engineer Office, Santa Fe, New Mexico, hereafter TvNM-RP.

6. James K. Logan, et al., eds., *The Federal Courts of the Tenth Circuit: A History*

(Denver, Colo.: U.S. Court of Appeals of the Tenth Circuit, 1992) 394–402. In 1975 Breitenstein had authored the Tenth Circuit's first opinion dealing with the nature and extent of New Mexico Pueblo Indian water rights. See *State of New Mexico ex rel. Reynolds v. Aamodt et al.* 537 F.2d 1102 (1975).

7. See *Texas v. New Mexico* 344 U.S. 906 (1952), an aborted suit by Texas to enforce the 1938 Rio Grande Compact. Breitenstein appeared on behalf of the State of New Mexico and the Middle Rio Grande Irrigation District.

8. See chapter 7 below and see Charles J. Meyers, "The Colorado River," 19 *Stanford Law Review* 1 (November, 1966).

9. *State of Nebraska v. States of Wyoming and Colorado* Nos. 5 and 6, Original, 325 U.S. 665 (1945) and 345 U.S. 981 (1953).

10. La Plata River Compact, N.M. Stat. Ann. sec. 72-15-16 (1978). *Hinderlider, State Engineer, et al. v. La Plata River and Cherry Creek Ditch Co.* 304 U.S. 92 (1937).

11. Breitenstein, "Report of the Special Master on Obligation of New Mexico to Texas under the Pecos River Compact," September 7, 1979, *TvNM-RP* refers to *Hinderlider* five times. See transcript of testimony, November 30, 1981, *TvNM-TR* 2249 and 3467.

12. Letter, Judge E. L. Mechem to author, October, 1996. Minutes of the Pecos River Compact Negotiations, morning session, November 13, 1948, *NMPRC* 60–61; *Texas v. New Mexico* 462 US at 568, fn. 14 (1983).

13. Letter, Breitenstein to Caroom and Bloom, February 10, 1976. Letter, Caroom to Bloom, February 17, 1976, *TvNM-Files.*

14. Doug Caroom, attorney, interview, June 3, 1992 in Austin, Texas and Paul Bloom, December 9, 1992 in Santa Fe, New Mexico.

15. Letter, Bloom to Breitenstein, March 15, 1976 and Letter, Slingerland to Bloom, undated, hand-written note, *TvNM-Files.*

16. Undated, hand-written note Slingerland to Bloom, (probably spring, 1976) in *TvNM-Files.*

17. Letter, Bloom to Breitenstein, April 23, 1976, *TvNM-Files.*

18. Undated note, Slingerland to Bloom, endnote 16, estimates that in 1970 there were 11,200 irrigated acres in New Mexico above Alamogordo Dam compared to 133,000 in the Roswell area and 22,000 in the Carlsbad area.

19. G. Emlen Hall, *Four Leagues of Pecos: A Legal History of the Pecos Pueblo Grant, 1800–1934* (Albuquerque: University of New Mexico Press, 1984).

20. Undated note, Slingerland to Bloom, endnote 18, shows that in 1940 there were 14,800 irrigated acres in the upper reach of the river compared to 11,200 in 1970, a drop of more than 3,000 irrigated acres.

21. Marc Simmons, *New Mexico* (New York: W. W. Norton, 1977) 114–15; Charles R. McClure "The Texas-Santa Fe Expedition of 1841," *New Mexico Historical Review* 48 (January 1973): 47–48.

22. For a recent government account of this attitude see "Dams and Rivers: Primer on the Downstream Effects of Dams," USGS Circular 1126 (Denver: United States Geological Survey: 1997).

23. Carole Larson, *Forgotten Frontier: The Story of Southeastern New Mexico* (Albuquerque: University of New Mexico Press, 1993).

24. Undated note, Slingerland to Bloom, "a quick look at bulk acreage on Pecos," spring 1976, *TvNM-Files.*

25. Paul Bloom, interview, December 9, 1992.

26. I am indebted to Albuquerque geohydrologist John Shomaker for the geological description of the Roswell basin.

27. Pinky Galloway, former state engineer geologist, interview, Roswell, New Mexico, December 16, 1992.

28. Undated, unpublished reminiscence, Morgan Nelson, "The Oasis Ranch," 18–20, Private papers of Morgan Nelson, Roswell, New Mexico, hereafter *MNPP*. See chapter 4.

29. "Carlsbad Irrigation District (CID) Crop Census and Water Delivery for the Years 1929–1998, Bureau of Reclamation, Albuquerque, New Mexico and Denver, Colorado." Bureau of Reclamation, Albuquerque. The Census shows a low of 14,000 irrigated acres and a high of 22,000 acres with variations every year in between. *United States v. Hope Community Ditch et al.* no. 739 USDC, New Mexico in 1934 adjudicated to the CID water rights to serve 25,055 acres, a number of acres that the CID has never reached. See chapter 2.

30. Doug Littlefield Ph.D., *A History of the Carlsbad Irrigation District and Its Water Rights,* unpublished study for the Office of the State Engineer, February 2, 1990, Legal Division, SEO, Santa Fe. Marc Hufstetler and Lon Johnson, *Watering the Land: The Turbulent History of the Carlsbad Irrigation District,* edited by Gregory Kendrick (Denver, Colo.: National Park Service, 1993). Interstate Stream Engineer Carl Slingerland, interview, Santa Fe, New Mexico, March 22, 1994.

31. Jay Forbes, attorney and district judge, interview, Carlsbad, New Mexico, February 19, 1993.

32. Charles Goodnight, the first big cattle operator in the area, called the Pecos "the bitter river, the graveyard of cattlemen's hopes" because of the river's steep banks and salty water. See Larson, *Forgotten Frontier,* 61–62.

33. Bloom, Slingerland, Caroom, interview.

34. State of Texas Purchase Voucher, June 7, 1976, attaching a check for $1,104.10 to cover "one half cost of inspection and orientation of Pecos River area in states of Texas and New Mexico," *TvNM-Files.*

CHAPTER 2

1. Hufstetler and Johnson, *Watering the Land,* 32, 57. Hufstetler et al. call Tracy a New York banker. He was born and raised not in Manhattan, but in the small Hudson River community of Poughkeepsie. Louise Tracy, interview, Carlsbad, New Mexico, July 3, 1998. Francis G. Tracy, Sr., "Pecos Valley Pioneers," 33 *NMHR* 3 (July, 1958): 187–205.

2. Louise Tracy, interview by author, July 3, 1998; "Carlsbad Irrigation District Crop Census and Water Delivery for years 1990–1998," Albuquerque Area Office, Bureau of Reclamation, U.S. Department of the Interior.

3. Hall, *Four Leagues of Pecos,* preface and chapter 1; *Texas v. New Mexico,* 462 U.S. 552, 557 (1983).

4. Doug Littlefield, *A History of the Carlsbad Irrigation District* (SEO1990), 43–111. Littlefield, *A History of the Carlsbad Irrigation District and Its Water Rights,* 111–12; "A Mighty Flood Sweeps the Pecos River," and "Commercial Club Acts," *Carlsbad Argus,* October 1904.

5. Hufstetler and Johnson, *Watering the Land,* 40, 41. An 1895 survey estimated the actual McMillan storage capacity at 89,000 acre-feet; Hufstetler and Johnson, *Watering the Land,* 43.

6. Hufstetler and Johnson, *Watering the Land,* 40, 43; Littlefield, *A History of the Carlsbad Irrigation District,* 139, footnote 36 citing Tracy to Meyers, August 10, 1905; Littlefield at 43–111 traces the evolution of the corporate sponsors of the project from the Eddy-Bissel company (1889) through the Pecos Irrigation and

Investment company (1901) to the Pecos Irrigation Company (after 1904). Compare Ira G. Clark, *Water Use in New Mexico: A History of its Management and Use* (Albuquerque: University of New Mexico Press, 1987), 91–93 and Ira G. Clark, "The Elephant Butte Controversy: A Chapter in the Emergence of Federal Water Law," LXI *Journal of American History* (1975): 1006–33. Lance Edwin Davis, "Capital Immobility and Southwestern Land Prices, 1865–1875," Plaintiff's Exhibit 4043, Indian Claims Commission, *Navajo Nation v. United States*, 3, Table 1, and Hall, *Four Leagues of Pecos*, 175–77; Littlefield, *A History of the Carlsbad Irrigation District*, 43–111; Hufstetler and Johnson, *Watering the Land*, 48.

7. Littlefield, *A History of the Carlsbad Irrigation District*, 111.

8. *Eddy Argus*, August 11, 1893; Hufstetler and Johnson, *Watering the Land*, 42.

9. Hufstetler and Johnson, *Watering the Land*, 26–27.

10. Testimony of Francis Tracy, April 20, 1943 in "Minutes of the Meeting of the Pecos River Compact Commission at Artesia, New Mexico," in NMPRC. Marc Riesner, *Cadillac Desert: The American West and Its Disappearing Water* (New York: Penguin Books, revised and updated, 1993); Hufstetler and Johnson, *Watering the Land*, 58, citing Reed to Chief Engineer, U.S. Reclamation Service October 10, 1904 RG 115, Entry 3, Box 443, File 651 National Archives, Washington, D.C.

11. Hufstetler and Johnson, *Watering the Land*, 54–56; Jose A. Rivera, *Acequia Culture: Water, Land and Community in the Southwest* (Albuquerque: University of New Mexico Press, 1998); Bill Blanchard, "Millions for Moisture: An Account of the Work of the U.S. Reclamation Service," *National Geographic Magazine* 18 (April, 1907): 223.

12. Francis G. Tracy, "Eddy County, New Mexico," documents of the *Federal Writers' Project* (SRC, 1937).

13. Hufstetler and Johnson, *Watering the Land*, 24; Tracy, "Pecos Valley Pioneers," 203; Littlefield, *A History of the Carlsbad Irrigation District*, 124; Louise Tracy, interview.

14. Tracy, "Pecos Valley Pioneers," 190–95. Littlefield, *A History of the Carlsbad Irrigation District*, 105, footnote 24. Hufstetler and Johnson, *Watering the Land*, 53; Paul W. Gates, *History of Public Land Law Development*, (New York: Arno Press, 1979), 463–93. Hufstetler and Johnson, *Watering the Land*, 30–31; Tracy, "Pecos Valley Pioneers," 190.

15. Littlefield, *A History of the Carlsbad Irrigation District* , 27–28, sets out one of the Pecos Irrigation and Investment Company water contracts verbatim. Louise Tracy, interview, and *Brantley et al. v. CID* 124 N.N. 698, 706; 954 P2d 763 (1998); "Table One: Water Rights (in Acres) Issued by the Pecos Irrigation and Improvement Company, 1891–1900," "Table Two: Water Rights (in acres) Issued by the Pecos Irrigation Company, 1901–1906" in Littlefield, *A History of the Carlsbad Irrigation District*, 82, 124; Hufstetler and Johnson, *Watering the Land*, 31.

16. Littlefield, *A History of the Carlsbad Irrigation District*, 112.

17. Hufstetler and Johnson, *Watering the Land*, 61; Wallace Stegner, *Angle of Repose* (Garden City, N.Y.: Doubleday, 1971).

18. Clark, *Water in New Mexico*, 67–82, 88–89; Hufstetler and Johnson, *Watering the Land*, 69–70; Littlefield, *A History of the Carlsbad Irrigation District*, 111–35.

19. Littlefield, *A History of the Carlsbad Irrigation District*, 139, footnote 36 citing Tracy to Meyers, August 10, 1905; A series of federal acts passed in 1866, 1870, and 1877 Acts allowed for self-initiated acquisition of rights-of-way across unappropriated federal public lands to convey water to private tracts. Clark, *Water in*

New Mexico, 44–45, 76. See *United States v. New Mexico* 438 U.S. 696 (1978); Littlefield, *A History of the Carlsbad Irrigation District,* 111–48.

20. Littlefield, *A History of the Carlsbad Irrigation District,* 196.

21. Letter, W. M. Reed to Bureau of Reclamation Director, February 12, 1912, Bureau of Reclamation District Office, Albuquerque, N.Mex.; Littlefield, *A History of the Carlsbad Irrigation District,* 233, referring to Tracy as "the storm centre of all personalities."

22. Philip Mutz and S. E. Reynolds, "The Rio Grande Compact of 1938," 26 *NRJ* 2 (summer 1968).

23. P. M. Fogg, "Report on an Investigation of the Pecos River Valley in Texas— 1914," SEO, 48.

24. Fogg, "Report on an Investigation," 53.

25. *Kansas v. Colorado* 206 U.S. 46 (1907). Vernon L. Sullivan was the first Territorial Engineer of New Mexico from 1905–1907. Prior to that he had worked on the controversial Rio Grande Project. Doug Littlefield, *Dividing the Waters of the Rio Grande, 1880–1936* (Santa Fe, N.Mex.: State Engineer Office, 1986). After his term, he worked for the West Texas Reclamation group. Littlefield, *A History of the Carlsbad Irrigation District,* 277–304.

26. See chapter 3 for a description and analysis for the meaning of a switch from acreage to depletion as the measure of upstream New Mexico's obligation to downstream Texas; Littlefield, *A History of the Carlsbad Irrigation District,* 296–97. Despite the fact that Sullivan knew about the problems of groundwater development in the Roswell area, there was no mention of groundwater in the proposed 1924 Compact.

27. See Robert T. Lingle and Dee Linford, *The Pecos River Commission of New Mexico and Texas: A Report of a Decade of Progress, 1950–1960* (Carlsbad, N.Mex.: Pecos River Commission, 1961), "Appendix A" 239–42; Littlefield, *A History of the Carlsbad Irrigation District,* 290.

28. Letter, Tracy to Governor Hinkle, February 1, 1923 in Hinkle Papers, SRC; Littlefield, *A History of the Carlsbad Irrigation District,* 285.

29. Littlefield, *A History of the Carlsbad Irrigation District,* 277–304; Hannett's veto message is reproduced in U.S. Congress, House Committee on Irrigation and Reclamation, *Hearings before the Committee on Irrigation and Reclamation . . . On H.R. 3862 by Mr. Hudspeth* 69 Cong., 1st Sess. 1926, 88.

30. But see *Kansas v. Colorado,* Original No. 105, 514 U.S. 673 (1995). The Arkansas River Compact was similarly limited to surface water but the Supreme Court recently has held that upstream Colorado was nonetheless responsible for Colorado wells that affected the flow of the compacted stream; Art III(a), Pecos River Compact, N.Mex. Stat. Ann. 72-15-19 (1978).

31. *United States of America v. Hope Community Ditch, et al.* No. 712 Equity, (DCNM, 1933); *City of Las Vegas v. Oman,* 110 N.M. 425, 428–429 (Ct. of App., 1994) citing G. Emlen Hall, "Bringing Water Law to the Gallinas," Legal Division, State Engineer Office, Santa Fe, N.Mex., February, 1986.

32. *Honey Boy Haven Inc. v. Roybal,* 92 N.M. 603, 592 P.2d 959 (1978); *Cartwright v. PNM,* 68 N.M. 418, 362 P.2d 796 (1961); See *State ex rel. Reynolds v. Lewis et al.* 99 N.M. 699, 663 P.2d 358 (1983); 88 N.M. 636, 545 P.2d 1014; 84 N.M. 768, 508 P.2d 577 (1973); 74 N.M. 442. 394 P.2d 593 (1964). All the *Lewis* decisions arose out of a comprehensive readjudication of surface water *and* groundwater claims within the Pecos River drainage basin "necessitated by the fact" that the *Hope Community Ditch* litigation had not included groundwater.

256

33. The 1933 Hope Decree adjudicated to the United States an amount of water, expressed in cubic feet per second. It specified neither the amount nor the location of the acres within the Carlsbad Irrigation District to be irrigated by that adjudicated flow. See Final Decree, August 16, 1933 in *United States v. Hope Community Ditch et al.* No. 712 Equity, (ISC). See also Exhibit A to "Factual Data of CID and CID Water Rights," presented by the CID to the Interim Legislative Energy, Natural Resources and Extractive Industries Committee June 22, 1987, Santa Fe, New Mexico (SEO). See also "Stipulated Offer of Judgment between State of New Mexico and the Carlsbad Irrigation District," June 22, 1994, in *State v. Lewis* Nos. 20294 and 22600, Chaves County, New Mexico.

34. Hall, "A Brief History of New Mexico Water Rights Administration Since 1907," *CLE International*, (Denver, Colo.: 1997). It turned out that the first New Mexico Territorial Engineer, Vernon Sullivan, became the leading technical spokesman for downstream Texas irrigators, thus jumping the state limitations on the territorial engineer's jurisdiction. And Francis Tracy was so busy fighting the federal Bureau of Reclamation that he apparently had no time to take on Sullivan. Nevertheless, the emergence of a powerful administrator charged with overall responsibility for the apportionment of New Mexico waters changed the waterscape in which Francis Tracy and Carlsbad operated in the early twentieth century; License No. 1712, August 1, 1931, Book J, Office of State Engineer, (SEO). See *J. N. Livingston v. James T. Neeson et. al.* No. 5144, District Court, 5th Judicial District (1927). Littlefield, *A History of the Carlsbad Irrigation District*, 243.

35. Hufstetler and Johnson, *Watering the Land*, 134–35; Sec. 73-9-1 et seq. NMSA (1978) adopted Laws 1919, ch. 41 sec. 33; "Contract between the United States and the Carlsbad Irrigation District Providing for the Transfer of the Project to the District and Payment of the Project Costs by the District," August 10, 1932 (Albuquerque: Bureau of Reclamation); *In the Matter of the Organization of the Carlsbad Irrigation District and the Authorization of Contract with the United States* No. 5493, 5th Judicial District, Eddy County, Final Decree March 9, 1933.

36. Sec. 73-9-5 et seq. N.Mex. Stat. Ann. 1978; Hufstetler and Johnson, *Watering the Land*, 136; Letter, L. E. Foster to the Commissioner June 21, 1932, RG 115, Box 277, (Denver: National Archives); Hufstetler and Johnson, *Watering the Land*, 136.

37. Littlefield, *A History of the Carlsbad Irrigation District*, 304–27; Lingle and Linford, *Decade of Progress*, 125–30; Littlefield, *A History of the Carlsbad Irrigation District*, 328; Hufstetler and Johnson, *Watering the Land*, 140.

38. Hufstetler and Johnson, *Watering the Land*, 142–43; Lingle and Linford, *Decade of Progress*, 95; Hufstetler and Johnson, *Watering the Land*, 140.

39. *Brantley v. CID* 124 N.M. 698 (1998); Memoir, Francis Tracy, Jr., 1988, typescript, partial copy in the possession of Louise Tracy, Carlsbad, New Mexico, 5–6.

40. "Downstream Flood Control," in *Regional Planning, Part X-The Pecos River Joint Investigation in the Pecos River Basin, National Resources Planning Board* (Washington, D.C.: United State Government Printing Office, 1942) 147–54.

41. John Shomaker, "Studies related to administration of the Pecos Compact for the Pecos Valley Artesian Conservancy District," prepared for the Pecos Valley Artesian Conservancy District, February, 1995 (Roswell, N.Mex.: PVACD).

42. See chapter 5. Carl Slingerland, interview by author, tape recording and transcript, March 22, 1994. Hall, "Statement 4(b) Pecos River Commission Administrative History," August 1, 1978, 18–22 in *Texas v. New Mexico*, TvNM-SEO.

43. Minutes of Meeting of the Pecos River Compact Commission at Artesia, New Mexico, April 20, 1943 and Fort Stockton, Texas, April 22, 1943 and statement of CID Chairman Beeman, Minutes, April 20, 1943 in *NMPRC*.

44. Statement of Francis Tracy, Sr., April 20, 1943 in "Minutes," *NMPRC*, 16.

45. "Appearances," November 8–13, 1948 in "Minutes," *NMPRC*, 1; "Memoirs of Francis Tracy, Jr.," 5–6.

46. "Memoirs of Francis Tracy, Jr.," 1, 5–6.

47. Article IX, sec. 72-15-19, N.Mex. Stat. Ann. 1978. *Hinderlider v. La Plata River et al.* 304 U.S. 92 (1937).

48. "Memoirs of Francis Tracy, Jr.," 9 ff; Sec. 73-10 et seq. and 73-11 et seq., N.Mex. Stat. Ann (1978); letter, Tom Davis, Manager CID to author, September 14, 2000; *Brantley v. CID* 124 N.M. 698 (1998).

49. Chart, "Carlsbad Main Canal at Head, Near Carlsbad, N.M. gauge, Annual Volumes in Acre-feet, 1939–1999" (Albuquerque: Bureau of Reclamation); Chart, "Carlsbad Irrigation District Crop Census and Water Delivery for years 1950–1998, Total Irrigable area of 25,055 acres," (Albuquerque: Bureau of Reclamation).

50. Hon. Jay Forbes, interview by author, tape recording, January 18, 1993; S. E. Reynolds, "Memorandum on Pecos River Administration," July 12, 1976, *SER-ISC*.

Chapter 3

1. The various decisions in the case are referred to in *Texas v. New Mexico*, No. 65 Original, 421 U.S. 927 (1975) and 482 U.S. 124 (1986); See chapter 8 below.

2. Remark of Special Master Meyers, October 15, 1987, *TvNM-TR*, 94–95.

3. Gerald D. Nash, "New Mexico Since 1940: An Overview," in *Contemporary New Mexico, 1940–1990*, Richard W. Etulain, ed. (Albuquerque: University of New Mexico Press, 1994); Interstate Stream Engineer Carl Slingerland, interview, March 22, 1994, Santa Fe, New Mexico. Herbert Hoover, who negotiated the 1922 Colorado River Compact, and Raymond Hill, who negotiated the 1938 Rio Grande Compact, preceded Tipton and were also described as "strutting while they sat." For Hoover, see John Upton Terrel, *War for the Colorado River: The California-Arizona Controversy* (Glendale, Calif.: Arthur H. Clark Co., 1965), 1:19. For Hill, see Raymond A. Hill, "Development of the Rio Grande Compact of 1938," *Natural Resources Journal* 14 (April, 1974): 163–98.

4. Natural Resources Planning Board, *Regional Planning, Part X-The Pecos River Joint Investigation in the Pecos River Basin in New Mexico and Texas: Summary, Analyses and Findings* (Washington, D.C.: U.S. Government Printing Office, 1942) (*PRJI*). Note that the hypothetical conditions also applied to the past. The critical "1947 condition" was assembled by subjecting historic river flows to conditions that did not exist at the time.

5. Compare the flow-based schedules of the Rio Grande Compact, Article IV, N.Mex. Stat. Ann. 72-15-23 (Michie, 1978.); N.Mex. Stat. Ann. Sec. 72-15-19 (Michie, 1978).

6. Lindford and Lingle, *A Decade of Progress*, 9–11, 15; See chapter 2.

7. See chapter 4; Wells A. Hutchins, *The Texas Law of Water Rights* (Austin, Tex.: USDA and Texas Board of Water Engineers, 1961), 557–601; In *Yeo v. Tweedy* 34 N.M. 611 (1930) the New Mexico Supreme Court early recognized that groundwater was subject to the same legal regime as surface water. It took many years longer to recognize legally that groundwater and surface waters in effect came

from the same source; Charles V. Theis, "The Relationship between the Lowering of the Piezometric Surface and the Rate and Duration of a Well Using Ground-Water Storage," pt. 2, Reports and Papers, Section of Hydrology (Washington, D.C.: USGS, 1935), 519–24.

8. See chapter 6 for a description of the difficulties a Texas law student had dealing with the New Mexico records and chapter 7 for the crucial Texas argument that New Mexico should have to explain what had happened on the river because New Mexico alone had access to the arcane river records; Clark, *Water in New Mexico*, 122–24.

9. Letter, Vernon S. Sullivan to Board of Directors, Red Bluff Water Power Control District, August 14, 1935 in Negotiating Minutes concerning the Pecos River Compact, October 2, 1945, in *NMPRC*, 19–26.

10. In 1941 as part of the PRJI, C. V. Theis developed the first mathematical formulae for making such estimates. See Theis, "The Effect of a Well on the Flow of a Nearby Stream," *American Geophysical Union Transactions 734*, presented in *U.S.G.S. Ground Water Notes* No. 14, (Washington, D.C.: USGS, 1953).

11. Letter, Tipton to Subcommittee on Irrigation and Reclamation, United States Senate, May 10, 1956, *PRJI*, 8; See, e.g. Tipton to Woods, April 2, 1942 in *PRJI*, vi–vii.

12. Linford and Lingle, *A Decade of Progress*, 3; *PRJI*, 138–40. See Deborah L. Donahue, *The Western Range Revisited: Removing Livestock from Public Lands to Conserve Native Biodiversity* (Norman: University of Oklahoma Press, 1999).

13. For example, consider the following passage: "A check on the amount of 1940 return flow as above derived is afforded by a computation of the difference between the amount of diversions and the total depletion under those diversions independently estimated." *PRJI*, 66; Barbara J. B. Green and Jon B. Alby, "Watershed Planning," 1 *University of Denver Water Law Review* (fall, 1997): 75–95. The article traces the current drive to watershed management to the Federal Clean Water Act. Watershed planning has much deeper roots in the nineteenth-century pioneering work of John Wesley Powell. See Marc Riesman, *Cadillac Desert: The American West and Its Disappearing Water* (New York: Viking Penguin, 1986).

14. John Shomaker, interview, March 3, 1997.

15. *PRJI*, 27–82.

16. Ibid., 82.

17. Ibid., 82–86.

18. The measurement of western streams had begun at the Embudo Station on the Rio Grande in New Mexico in a USGS-sponsored project in the 1880s. Powell had directed the work and Francis Newell, the father of the Reclamation Act, served as the first project engineer. See Clark, *Water in New Mexico*, 57, 67, 70.

19. *PRJI*, 171–83.

20. E.g. Rio Grande Compact of March 13, 1938, Sec. 72-15-23 NMSA 1978 (Michie); Art. IV, sec. 72-15-23 N.M.S.A 1978; Mutz and Reynolds, "The Rio Grande Compact of 1938."

21. Letter, Tipton to Woods, April 2, 1942, *PRJI*, vii.

22. "Report of Meeting of Pecos River Compact Commission with Citizens of the Pecos Valley on April 20, 1943 at Artesia, New Mexico," and "Notes on the Public Meeting Conducted by the Pecos River Compact Commission at Fort Stockton, Texas, April 22, 1943," in *NMPRC.*; Roswell meeting, September 18, 1990, footnote 37, chapter 8.

23. See "Minutes of Meetings of the Pecos River Compact Commission Prior to and Including Signing of the Compact" (hereafter "Minutes"), February 9, 1943 to December 4, 1948, *NMPRC*.

24. "Minutes," May 28 and 29, 1947, Austin, Texas, p. 12 *NMPRC*; See also "Minutes of Pecos River Compact Commission, May 28 and 29, 1947, Austin 12–14, *Senate Document 109*, (81st Cong., 1st Sess. ,1949), 131.

25. See testimony of State Engineer S. E. Reynolds, March 16, 1978, *TvNM-TR*.

26. See statement of New Mexico Senator Clinton Anderson in Senate Subcommittee on Interior and Insular Affairs, "Hearing on S.J. Res. 9 Before the 88th Congress, 1st Session" (Washington, D.C.: Government Printing Office, 1963).

27. See, e.g., statement of R. J. Tipton, May 8,1956 in the Subcommittee on Irrigation and Reclamation of the Senate Committee on Interior and Insular Affairs, "Hearing on S.J. Res. 155 Before 84 Cong. 2nd Sess. 9," (1956) and R. J. Tipton "One or the Other: A Resume of Pecos River Problems from a Talk Given at a Luncheon in Santa Fe, N.M. on February 9, 1953, for the Governor and Members of the Legislature of the State of New Mexico," unpublished in the files of *PVACD*, Roswell, New Mexico.

28. Tipton: "My facetious proposal is to get a squad of Marine flame throwers to see whether the salt cedars perform properly and, if they do, interest the Army in having a bombing training program out there, get rid of some incendiary bombs and at the same time get rid of the salt cedars. Maybe that should be off the record." Mr. Miller: "I would like for it to be on the record." Mr. Tipton: "Well, you newspapermen, just don't put it in the newspapers. This is completely off the record so far as the newspapers are concerned." Statement of Royce J. Tipton, May 28, 1947, *NMPRC*.

29. Donald Worster, *Rivers of Empire: Water, Aridity and the Growth of the American West* (New York: Random House, 1986), 314–17; S. Doc. 109, 81st Cong. 1st Sess.(1949), xxv-xvi.

30. Bruce Frederick, "Salvaged Water: The Failed Critical Assumption Underlying the Pecos River Compact," 33 *NRJ* 1 (winter, 1993): 217. Texans and New Mexicans had recognized at least since 1935 that Roswell wells directly affected surface water flows in the interconnected river. See letter, Sullivan to Board of Directors October 2, 1945, *NMPRC*, 20–26;.

31. Frederick, "Salvaged Water," 217–18.

32. See Shomaker, "Studies Related to the Administration of the Pecos River Compact," 21. The inflow/outflow method used in the routing studies depends on stream-gauging records and on calculations of flows by difference, rather than direct measurement. Both the records and the calculations are subject to error.

33. "Minutes," March 10–11, *NMPRC*, 1948, n.p.

34. "Minutes," March 11, *NMPRC*, 1948, n.p.

35. "Minutes," November 8–13, *NMPRC*, 1948.

36. Slingerland, interview, March 22, 1994.

37. "Minutes," November 8, 1948, *NMPRC*, 10. Texas Governor Jester had begun the life-or-death hyperbole when he opened the November conference by relating a long tale about a Midwestern community that had lost one of its member's children and was only able to find the child by joining hands and combing the fields together.

38. "Minutes," November 8, 1948, *NMPRC*, 16.

39. "Minutes," November 8, 1948, *NMPRC*, 17–21.

40. Slingerland, interview, March 22, 1994.

41. "Minutes," November 13, 1948, *NMPRC*, 51.

42. For example, compare the 1922 Colorado River Compact, N.Mex. Stat. Ann. 72-15-5 et. seq. (Michie, 1979), and the 1938 Rio Grande Compact, N.Mex. Stat. Ann. 72-15-23 et seq. (Michie, 1979) to the Article III apportionment provision of the Pecos River Compact; Most interstate water compacts to which New Mexico was a party were flow-based, not depletion based. That is, compacts like the 1938 Rio Grande Compact guaranteed to Texas a certain percentage of the flow of the river measured at an upstream gauge in New Mexico. A depletion-based compact like the one Bliss proposed was both more sophisticated and more difficult. See Shomaker, "Administration of the Pecos River Compact."

43. "Minutes," November 11, 1948, *NMPRC* show that New Mexico State Engineer Bliss had to contend not only with Texas but also with his own CID. The CID representatives, even as early as 1948, were extremely sensitive to the increasing impact that existing Roswell wells would have. It is possible that the CID sensitivity drove Bliss to the switch from "uses" to "depletions."

44. John Bliss, "Administration of the Ground Water Law of New Mexico," *Journal of the American Water Works Association* (June, 1951): 438.

45. The proposed compact directed New Mexico to enforce its own laws—including the laws of priority—within its own boundaries. N.Mex. Stat. Ann. sec. 72-15-19 Art. IX (Michie, 1978). This guarantee may have been redundant, but it also served the interests of New Mexico's CID, which thought it had the oldest New Mexico rights on the river. As for changes in the definition of the critical "1947 condition," Tipton always insisted that his formulas were designed, as he said, "to reflect in realistic terms the manner in which nature operates." See *Texas v. New Mexico* 462 U.S. 554 (1983).

46. Tipton statement, "Minutes," morning session, November 13, 1948, Austin, Texas, *NMPRC*, 54.

47. "Minutes," November 13, 1948, *NMPRC*, 61–62. Tipton, Miller, and Bliss approved hiring the Bureau of Reclamation's Jeff Will to help with the drafting. "Minutes," December 4, 1948, *NMPRC*, 8–9. Tipton reported that Will "assisted from time to time" in the actual drafting of the compact. "The Committee was also assisted by Mr. Jean Breitenstein, who has had considerable experience in connection with Compacts." See chapter 6 below.

48. N.Mex. Stat. Ann. sec. 72-15-19 (1978).

49. N.Mex. Stat. Ann. Sec. 72-15-19 (1978).

50. Tipton statement, "Minutes," December 4, 1948, *NMPRC*, 18–20.

51. Lindford and Lingle, *Decade of Progress,* photo of "successful negotiators of the Pecos River Compact" following page 172. Compact enacted in New Mexico by Laws 1949, chapter 6, section 1. Compact enacted in Texas by General Laws 1949, 51 and in Congress by 63 U.S. Statutes 151 (1949).

52. See Felix Frankfurter and James Landis, "The Compact Clause of the Constitution: A Study in Interstate Adjustments," 34 *Yale Law Journal* 7 (1925): 685–758.

53. Carl Slingerland, interviews, May 18, 1992 and March 22, 1994.

54. See G. Emlen Hall, "Pecos River Commission Administrative History," August 1, 1978 in *Texas v. New Mexico,* Supreme Court No. 65 Original, *TvNM-RP.*

55. Hall, "Administrative History."

56. Hall, "Administrative History," 7–18; Slingerland, interview, Santa Fe, New Mexico, March 22, 1994. Of course, the less than fifty years of stream records for the Pecos River itself was also a very short period in the centuries-old natural history of the Pecos River itself.

57. "Minutes," September, 1961, *PRC,* 19.

261

58. Slingerland, interviews, May 18, 1992 and March 22, 1994; Hall, "Administrative History," 18–22.

59. Findings, Pecos River Commission, January 30–31, 1961, *PRC.* Hall, "Administrative History," 25–26.

60. Raymond Allgood, Texas farmer and witness in the damage phase of *Texas v. New Mexico,* interview, Barstow, Texas, March 16, 1992. Deposition of Allgood, March 9, 1988, TvNM; Hall, "Administrative History," 29–30. See State of Texas Motion for Leave to File a Complaint against the State of New Mexico, June 26, 1974 in *Texas v. New Mexico, TvNM-RP.*

61. Tipton, "One or the Other," 1.

62. Testimony and statement of R. J. Tipton, May 10, 1956, "Hearing before the Subcommittee on Irrigation and Reclamation of the Committee on Interior and Insular Affairs, 84th Congress, 2nd. Sess.," (Washington, D.C.: Government Printing Office), 8–20.

63. "Hearing on S.J. Res. 49 Before the Subcommittee on Irrigation and Reclamation, 88th Congress, 1st Session," (Washington, D.C.: Government Printing Office, 1963); George Welder, "Hydrologic Effects of Phreatophyte Control, Acme-Artesia Reach of the Pecos River, New Mexico, 1967–1982," *USGS Water Resources Investigation Report 87–4148* (Washington, D.C.: Government Printing Office, 1988). See *Central New Mexico Audubon Society et al. v. Morton et. al.* USDC NM No. 10118 (1973); "New Mexico State Engineer, 33rd Biennial Report (1976–1978)," *SEO,* 58.

64. Welder, "Hydrologic Effects."

65. Remarks of Special Master Breitenstein, August 29, 1978, *TvNM-TR,* 3000. Special Master Breitenstein lamented the fact that neither Texas nor New Mexico created and maintained legislative histories of what each state thought it was ratifying when it ratified the Pecos River Compact.

66. Linford and Lingle, *Decade of Progress,* plate 4 following page 172; S. Doc 109 (1949), 73–132.

67. S. Doc. 109, xvii–xxxiv, and 133–44, 149–72; *Texas v. New Mexico,* 462 U.S. 554, 557 (1983); Slingerland, interview, March 22, 1994.

68. Letter, Tipton to Pecos River Compact Commission, December 3, 1948, S. Doc 109, 147.

69. "Plate No. 2, Inflow-Outflow relationships, Alamogordo Dam to New Mexico-Texas State Line," S. Doc. 109, 154 and accompanying tables at 155; Compare Littlefield, *Dividing the Waters of the Rio Grande,* 44–84.

70. *Texas v. New Mexico,* 462 U.S. 554, 559, footnote 5 (1983).

71. Slingerland, interview, March 22, 1994; remarks of special master Jean S. Breitenstein, March 9, 1977 in *TvNM-TR,* 299.

CHAPTER 4

1. For the details of Swann Nelson's life, see Morgan Nelson's "Notes in Dr. Clarence E. Nelson in 1986 at Loma Linda, California" (three pages), and "Dr. Clarence E. Nelson Recollections" (13 pages), in *MNPP;* Fred M. Nelson, "Acquiring Land" (six pages), *MNPP;* interviews with Morgan Nelson, December 12, 1992 and June 1, 1993 in Chaves County, New Mexico; Alicia Romero, Secretary of State, *New Mexico Blue Book, 1949–1950* (Santa Fe, N.Mex.: Rydal Press, 1950), 108, 110; New Mexico State Engineer Steve Reynolds, address to Roswell Rotary Club, October 19, 1989, *SER-ISC,* 3.

2. See map accompanying Cassius A. Fisher, "Preliminary Report on the Geology

and Underground Waters of the Roswell Artesian Area of New Mexico," Department of the Interior, USGS Water Supply and Irrigation Paper No. 158 (1906).

3. See Fiedler and Nye, *Geology and Ground Water Resources of the Roswell Basin,* plate 13, following page 68.

4. Larson, *Forgotten Frontier,* 119–22, 258–70; Nelson, "A History of East Grand Plains near Roswell, New Mexico" (17 pages), *MNPP* (no date).

5. Letter, Morgan Nelson to "Ann and Harwood" editors of *Arizona and the West,* August 24, 1987, *MNPP.*

6. Nelson to "Ann and Harwood."

7. For more details of Swann Nelson's life, see "An Interview with Fred M. Nelson and Florace M. Nelson, February 20, 1976" in *MNPP* and "Dr. Clarence E. Nelson Recollections," 3. *MNPP.*

8. Larson, *Forgotten Frontier,* 119–22; Nelson, "The Settlers Before Chisum," and "Jacob Harris and the Mormons," *MNPP.*

9. *Vanderwork v. Hughes* 15 N.M. 439, 110 P. 567 (1910); See "Composite of irrigation investigation in 1900 showing irrigation ditches in Townships 10 and 11 South, Ranges 24 and 25 East," *MNPP.* The 6,000 acres covered by the survey show the Berrendo, the North Spring and the South Spring rivers fed by springs arising in the area. Only the Hondo River had a source outside of the region itself. Roswell itself sits in parts of 4 sections approximately five miles west of the Pecos River itself.

10. "Dr. Clarence E. Nelson Recollections," *MNPP.*

11. Ibid.

12. Ibid.

13. Fisher, "Preliminary Report," *supra* note 5.

14. Fisher, "Preliminary Report," 10; Fiedler and Nye, *Geology and Ground Water Resources of the Roswell Basin, supra* note 6.

15. Fisher, "Preliminary Report," 14; This was *Vanderwork v. Hughes* 1914 description of artesian water. See footnote 15 above.

16. Fisher, "Preliminary Report," 23; "Preliminary List of Ditches by Stream System with Priority Dates and Acreage," HNMS Associates, Santa Fe, May 2, 1995; *Woodlawn Community Ditch,* 5th Judicial District (1924). "Hagerman and the Woodlawn Ditch," *MNPP.*

17. Fisher, "Preliminary Report," 21.

18. Ibid., 25; Shomaker, "Studies Related to the Administration of the Pecos River Compact."

19. Nelson, "An Interview with Fred M. and Florace Morgan Nelson," "I Was Born March 22, 1892," and "A History of East Grand Plains," all in *MNPP;* Debra L. Donahue, *The Western Range Revisited* (Norman: University of Oklahoma Press, 1999).

20. Nelson, "Peyote, Texas," in "An Interview . . . ," *MNPP;* "To Texas," in "I was Born March 22, 1892," *MNPP.* See 1914 Fogg Report, chapter 2, footnote 42.

21. "An Interview with Fred M. Nelson."

22. Deposition of Rayburn Allgood, March 9, 1988 in *TvNM-Ex.*

23. Nelson, "Acquiring Land;" Fiedler and Nye, *Geology and Ground Water Resources of the Roswell Basin,* 193.

24. Fiedler and Nye, *Geology and Ground Water Resources of the Roswell Basin,* 228.

25. See chapter 1.

26. Nelson, "The Oasis Ranch," 18–19 quoting Bob Koonce, "The Big Well," *Farmer Quarterly Magazine* (summer, 1965).

27. Nelson, "The Oasis Ranch," 19.

28. N.Mex. Stat. Ann. 73-6-1 ff, "Drainage Districts;" *In re Dexter-Greenfield Drainage Dist.* 21 N.M. 286, 154 P. 382 (1915).

29. Robert G. Dunbar, *Forging New Rights in Western Waters* (Lincoln: University of Nebraska Press, 1983) 162–72.

30. Fiedler and Nye, *Geology and Ground Water Resources of the Roswell Basin.* The pioneering study represented the first time that the USGS had paired an engineer and a geologist on the same project. Zane Spiegel, consulting geologist, interview, Norwalk, Connecticut, July 31, 1994.

31. "Fiedler Says Chaves County Water Supply is Permanent," Roswell Daily Record, September 14, 1926.

32. N.Mex. Stat. Ann. Sec. 72-12-1, 3 (1978). N.Mex. Laws 1931, ch. 131, sec. 1.

33. *Yeo v. Tweedy,* 34 N.M. 611, 286 P. 970 (1929); Dunbar, *Forging New Rights.*

34. Clark, *Water in New Mexico,* 235–38; N.Mex. Stat. Ann. 72-12-1, 2, 4 (1978).

35. A. M. Morgan, "Geology and shallow water resources of the Roswell artesian basin, New Mexico" *New Mexico State Engineer Bulletin 5* (State Engineer Office, 1938); Clark, *Water in New Mexico,* 240. Fiedler himself had recommended developing the shallow water as an alternative to further development of the artesian aquifer.

36. Sherman "Pinky Galloway," retired State Engineer geologist, interview, Roswell, New Mexico, December 12, 1997.

37. N.Mex. Stat. Ann. Article 13, sec. 72-13-1 et seq. (1978). See chapters 3 and 6.

38. Deposition of Morgan Nelson, March 24, 1988 in *TvNM-Ex.*

39. Deposition of Morgan Nelson, 11–12. See *State of New Mexico ex rel. State Engineer v. Crider,* 78 N.M. 312, 431 P.2d 45 (1967).

40. Larson, *Forgotten Frontier,* 212–18; James D. Shinkle, *Martin V. Corn: Early Roswell Pioneer* (Roswell, N.Mex.: Hall-Poorbaugh Press, 1972); See *State ex rel. State Engineer v. Lewis,* 118 N.M. 46, 882 P.2d 37 (1994).

41. Nelson, interview, December 18, 1992.

42. Slingerland, handwritten note to Bloom, undated (probably spring, 1976), giving "Acreage in 1000 for Pecos River irrigated acreage in 1940, 1947, 1950, 1955, 1960, 1965 and 1970 for Above Alamogordo, Ft. Sumner, Roswell Basin, River Pumpers, CID and Total," *TvNM-Files.*

43. Remarks of Texas Compact Commissioner Charles Miller, Minutes of "Meeting of the Pecos River Compact Commission at Santa Fe, New Mexico, March 10 and 11, 1948," *PRC.* Response of New Mexico Compact Commissioner John H. Bliss, March 11, 1948, *PRC,* 36.

44. 108, 110. See remarks of Special Master Jean Breitenstein, August 29, 1978 in *TvNM-TR,* 3000.

45. Letter, Nelson to State Engineer special projects engineer Peter Kraii, June 14, 1994, *TvNM-Files.* Nelson, interview, December 18, 1992, and June 1, 1993.

46. Report of the Special Master, September 7, 1979, *TvNM-RP,* 44–45, and *Texas v. New Mexico ,* 446 U.S. 540 (1980).

47. Nelson, interview, June 1, 1993.

48. Nelson, interview, June 1, 1983; Terry Isaacs, "Politics, Religion, and the Blue Book, The John Birch Society in eastern New Mexico and West Texas, 1960–1965," 71 NMHR 1 (January, 1996): 51–74.

49. Morgan Nelson, "Cotton the King," *MNPP*; Leah Beth Ward, "Caught in an S&L nightmare: A Collapse in New Mexico Traps a Doctor on the Board," *New York Times,* October 18, 1992, sec. 3, page 6. Nelson, interviews December 18, 1992; June 1 1993.

50. Deposition of Morgan Nelson, March 24, 1988, *TvNM-RP*, 4–8; Al Regensberg, "General Dynamics of Drought, Ranching and Politics in New Mexico, 1953–1961," 71 *NMHR* 1 (January, 1996): 25–50. The *exact* relationship between precipitation and the artesian aquifer was never well understood although the relationship was. Slingerland, interview, May 18, 1992.

51. See, for example, the remarks of Special Master Charles Meyers, May 20, 1986 in *TvNM-TR* 248 (ISC, Santa Fe). Slingerland, undated (probably 1976), handwritten note to Bloom giving "Acreage in 1000 for Pecos River irrigated acreage."

52. The first were Fisher (1906), Fiedler and Nye (1933), and Morgan (1938). See generally R. L. Borton, "Bibliographies of ground water studies in New Mexico 1873–1979," *New Mexico State Engineer Special Publications 1978*, 1980 (SEO); Spiegel, interview, July 31, 1994; Joe Chew, *Storms above the Desert: Atmospheric Research in New Mexico, 1935–1985* (Albuquerque: University of New Mexico Press, 1987); Letter, Workman to PVACD August 10, 1955 in preface, Mahdi S. Hantush, *Preliminary Quantitative Study of the Roswell Ground Water reservoir, New Mexico* (Socorro, New Mex.: New Mexico Institute of Mining and Technology, 1956).

53. Hantush, *Preliminary Quantitative Study*, following C. V. Thies, "The Effect of a Well on the Flow of a Nearby Stream," (1941) reprinted in *USGS Ground Water Notes No. 14* (Washington, D.C.: U.S. Government Printing Office, 1953), at 734.

54. Hantush, *Preliminary Quantitative Study*, 71–75.

55. Hand-written note, Slingerland to Bloom, 1976.

56. See, for example, Chart, "Water Recorder Average for Past 25 Years (1995)" in files of Pecos Valley Artesian Conservancy District (Roswell, New Mexico.) The levels show a steady decline through 1976 and then a steady rise thereafter, probably the result of increased precipitation as much as anything. Deposition of Nelson, March 24, 1988 in *TvNM-RP*, 12–32.

57. State Engineer Steve Reynolds, address to the Roswell Rotary Club, October 19, 1989 *SER-ISC*.

CHAPTER 5

1. William E. Blundell, "Hot Spot: In New Mexico, Water is a Valuable Resource— and so is Water Boss," *Wall Street Journal*, May 1, 1980 at 1. See Tom Arrandale, "New Mexico's Water Czar," *Governing* (June, 1989): 49. See also Kate McGraw, "Steve Reynolds is Nobody's Sweetheart," *Santa Fe New Mexican* Nov. 10, 1980 at B-1; Nolan Hester, "The Water Boss," *Albuquerque Journal*, Impact, May 5, 1987, p. 4.

2. Blundell, "Hot Spot," 1, note 1.

3. Ibid., 1.

4. See Helen Ingram, "Water Politics: Continuity and Change," 31 *NRJ* 4 (fall, 1991): 703. See also, Riesman, *Cadillac Desert*, for a description of this "iron triangle of western water," and Worster, *Rivers of Empire*.

5. For an academic discussion of the nature of New Mexican politics see F. Chris Garcia, "New Mexico Politics and Government," in *Contemporary New Mexico, 1940–1990*, Richard W. Etulain, ed. (Albuquerque: University of New Mexico Press, 1994), 25. Blundell, "Hot Spot," 2, note 1.

6. Paul Bloom, former N.M. Special Assistant Attorney General and General counsel, ISC, interview, Santa Fe, New Mexico, December 9, 1992. (Tapes and transcripts on file with author.) McGraw, "Steve Reynolds is Nobody's Sweetheart," Note 1.

7. See Michael Rodak, "Notice of Appointment and Reference," November 11,

1975 in *TvNM-RP*. Chew, *Storms Above the Desert,* 42–48; Byron Spice, "N.M. Tech Physicist Involved in Shuttle's Lightning Search," *Albuquerque Journal,* April 3, 1985 at B-1; Interview with Albuquerque attorney Robert Nordhaus, May 12, 1998, *NMOHP,* discussing a flight Reynolds and Nordhaus took in the drought of the 1950s, trying to cause snow by casting dried ice into clouds above the Sandia Peak ski area.

8. Bloom, interview, note 6.

9. Ira Clark, "What Authority Should Reside in the State Engineer? New Mexico as a Case Study," 32 *NRJ* 3 (summer, 1992): 467.

10. Bloom, interview, note 6. State Representative Ben Lujan from Nambe had complained bitterly about Reynolds's role in forfeiting for non-use ancient irrigation rights in northern New Mexico. The powerful Albuquerque lawyer, William Marchiondo, represented his Roswell-area in-laws in a losing battle to increase Moutray's water rights there.

11. Blundell, "Hot Spot," 37 note 1.

12. Bloom, interview, note 6.

13. See *136 Cong. Rec. S5357-02,* April 30, 1990, statement of New Mexico Senator Pete Domenici, "The Passing of Steve Reynolds" and material printed with it, particularly editorial, *Albuquerque Journal,* April 26, 1990 and editorial, *Santa Fe New Mexican,* April 27, 1990.

14. "Order Declaring Rio Grande Underground Water," November 29, 1956, *WRD-SEO;* "Memorandum on Declaration of the Rio Grande Underground Water Basin" November 29, 1956, *WRD-SEO.* "Findings and Order," and "Memorandum Decision," "In the Matter of the Applications to Appropriate Underground Waters of the Rio Grande Basin, City of Albuquerque, Applicant, Bernalillo-Sandoval County Farm and Livestock Bureau et. al. Protestants," Application Nos. RG-960, RG-961, RG-962, RG-963, Before the State Engineer of the State of New Mexico, November 4, 1957 *WRD-SEO.*

15. F. Harlan Flint, "Ground Water Administration: A New Mexico Viewpoint," 14 *Rocky Mountain Mineral Law Institute* (1968): 545–71. Flint was long-time chief counsel to State Engineer Reynolds. *Yeo v. Tweedy,* 34 N.M. 611, 286 P. 970 (1931); 1931 N.M. Laws, Ch. 131; generally see Dunbar, *Forging New Rights,* 162–72.

16. S. E. Reynolds and Philip B. Mutz, "Water Deliveries under the Rio Grande Compact," 14 *NRJ* 2 (spring, 1974): 201.

17. "Memorandum Decision," November 4, 1957, note 14.

18. Reynolds related the story in private frequently, especially at Saturday morning coffees in Santa Fe with his legal staff. He told the story publicly in more muted terms. E.g. Reynolds presentation at UNM Law School to Water Resources Management Program, May, 1988. Wayne S. Scott, "Underground Water District Draws Fire," *Albuquerque Journal,* January 4, 1957, 1.

19. Blundell, "Hot Spot," note 1. *City of Albuquerque v. Reynolds,* 71 N.M. 428, 379 P2 73 (1962).

20. H.B. 198, 23rd. Leg. (N.M. 1957) ("An Act Relating to Underground Water").

21. Reynolds to State Senator T. E. Lusk, "Memorandum on HB 198," March 4, 1957 and Reynolds to State Senator Tibo J. Chavez, "Memorandum on HB 198," March 5, 1957 *SER-ISC* and Martha Dabney, "Preliminary Inventory of the Papers of S. E. Reynolds," 1996, *SER-ISC.*

22. Official Roll Call, New Mexico State Senate, House Bill 198 ,23rd Legislature (March 7 and 9, 1957), *SER-ISC.* Hon. Edwin L. Mechem, interview, March 9, 1997, *NMOHP.*

23. Bloom, interview, note 6. See F. Lee Brown, "Water Markets and Traditional Values: Merging Commodity and Community Perspectives," 22 *Water International* (1997): 4.

24. Hester, "The Water Boss," 8 note 1; Clark, *Water in New Mexico*, 520–21; Ingram, "Water Politics: Continuity and Change," 703.

25. Riesner, *Cadillac Desert*, 143, 282. Mechem Interview, note 22; see biographical note, "I. M. Smalley," *New Mexico Blue Book, 1949–1950*.

26. Richard Simms, former General Counsel of the Interstate Stream Commission, interview, December 4, 1992. Bloom, interview, note 6.

27. Comment of Gov. Apodaca in Blundell, "Hot Spot," note 1; Gov. Carrothers in Arrandale, "Time is Running Out," 46 note 1, 50. Mechem, interview, note 22.

28. See "Public Speeches of S. E. Reynolds," *SER-ISC*. Bruce King, *Cowboy in the Roundhouse: A Political Life* (Santa Fe: Sunstone Press, 1998), 286–87. See Reynolds speech, UNM law school, May 1988. Hester, "The Water Boss," 6 note 1.

29. Simms, interview, note 26. The Reynolds papers are housed in various rooms and different file cabinets in the State Engineer Office and the Interstate Stream Commission, Santa Fe. In the early 1990s, the lawyer Martha Dabney made a preliminary and incomplete assessment of the Reynolds Papers.

30. New Mexican C. V. Theis, working out of a USGS office housed at the University of New Mexico at the time Reynolds was a student there, pioneered the application of mathematical formulas to predicting, first, well drawdowns, starting in 1935 and then well drawdown effects on interrelated surface water, starting in 1941. See C. V. Theis, "The Effect of a Well on the Flow of a Nearby Stream, American Geophysical Union Transactions," reprinted in *USGS Ground Water Notes No. 14*, (1953): 734.

31. Reisner, *Desert Cadillac*, 443–56.

32. Arrandale, "Time is Running Out," 46 note 1, 48. Reynolds's wife, Jane Iden, was the daughter of one of New Mexico's premier lawyers. He had offered to send Reynolds to law school soon after the two were married. Bloom, interview, note 6. See Reynolds, written statements, "Statement before the Water Usage and Water Resources Committee of the New Mexico Legislature by S. E. Reynolds, June 3, 1983," and "Statement Before the Committee on Energy, Environment, Natural Resources and Extractive Industries of the New Mexico Legislature by S. E. Reynolds, September 9, 1988," in *SER-ISC*. The two statements, separated by five years, begin in exactly the same way: "The use of water in New Mexico is extensively and intricately governed by law."

33. N.M. Const. Art. XVI sec. 2 (water public and subject to appropriation for beneficial use; priority gives the better right), sec. 3 (beneficial use the basis, the measure and the limit).

34. Bloom, interview, note 6; Simms, interview, note 26.

35. Donald J. Pisani, *To Reclaim a Divided West: Water, Law, and Public Policy, 1848–1912* (Albuquerque: University of New Mexico Press, 1992), 11–12; 32–35. See Reynolds, "Pecos River System Administration," July 12, 1976 in *SER-ISC; Templeton v. P.V.A.C.D.* 65 NM 59, 332 P.2d 465 (1958); Reynolds, testimony, May 20, 1986, *TvNM-TR* at 57–58.

36. Bloom, interview, note 6. Later governors felt that Reynolds had not "managed" New Mexico waters actively enough. By that they meant that he hadn't made explicit value choices among the various uses of water. Instead he preferred to facilitate the movement of water between competing uses, using market mechanisms. See Arrandale, "Time is Running Out," 48–50 note 1.

37. Clark, *Water in New Mexico,* 500–550 See Reynolds, "Summary—The Effects of Interstate Stream Compacts on New Mexico Water Supply," March 22, 1956 and "New Mexico's Interstate Compacts," August 1959, both in *SER-ISC.*

38. *Texas v. New Mexico* 352 U.S. 991, (No. 9 Original) 1957. *Texas and New Mexico v. Colorado* 391 U.S. 901, (No. 29 Original) 1968, granting motion of the United States to intervene in the new Rio Grande Compact suit. Acting alone, Texas had been unable to force New Mexico into court. Acting with New Mexico, Texas had been able to force Colorado into Court. Texans attributed the opposite results on the legal acuity of Steve Reynolds. His success contributed to the Texas belief that Texas would never get anywhere in court with New Mexico over the Pecos River. Bloom, interview, note 6.

39. Depositions of former State Engineers John Bliss and John Erickson, November 22, 1976 in *TvNM-Ex.*

40. Art. III(a). N.Mex. Stat. Ann., sec 72-15-19. Interstate Stream Engineer Carl Slingerland, interview, May 18, 1992, Santa Fe, New Mexico.

41. See endnotes 83, 84, chapter 6 and accompanying text.

42. N.Mex. Stat. Ann 72-14-1 (1978).

43. "Minutes," October 24–25, 1955 meeting, Albuquerque, New Mexico in *EAC-ISC.* Slingerland, interview, May 18, 1992, note 40. See Steve Reynolds, hand-written meeting notes, Pecos River Commission meeting at Bureau of Reclamation, Albuquerque, N.Mex., Oct. 24–25, 1955 in "Correspondence and Data of the Engineering Advisory Committees to the Pecos River Commission, 1956–1959," *EAC-ISC.*

   Reynolds wanted to restudy base-inflows, salt-cedar infestation, and water salvage.

44. Remarks of Texas assistant attorney general Caroom, March 24, 1980, in Transcript Oral Argument, *TvNM-TR,* 38–39. EAC Minutes, April 2–3, 1957, *EAC-ISC.*

45. Em Hall, "Statement 4(b)—Pecos River Commission Administrative History," August 1, 1978, *TvNM-Ex.,* 18–26.

46. Plaintiff's Brief in Opposition to New Mexico's Affirmative Defenses, attached Memorandum of Texas Consulting Engineer Lowry, *TvNM-Ex.,* referred to in Bloom, oral argument, March 9, 1977, 14 Record at 205, *TvNM-TR.* Remarks of Special Master Jean Breitenstein, March 9, 1977 at IV Record 220, *TvNM-TR.*

47. Interviews, former Texas assistant attorney general Doug Caroom, Austin, Texas, June 3, 1993, former Pecos River Compact Commissioner J. Lee Cathey, Carlsbad, New Mexico February 19, 1993.

48. Lingle and Linford, *The Pecos River Commission of New Mexico and Texas.*

49. See *United States v. Hope Community Ditch, No. 712* (D.C.N.M. Equity 1933). E.g. State ex rel. *Reynolds v McClean* 62 N.M. 264, 308 P.2d 983 (1957).

50. *State of New Mexico ex rel. State Engineer vs. L. T. Lewis et al.* Nos. 20294 and 22600 Consolidated, 5th Judicial District, State of New Mexico. A whole body of New Mexico water law emerged from these adjudications. See e.g. *State ex rel. Reynolds v. Sharp* 66 N.M. 192, 344 P.2d 943 (1959); *State ex re. Reynolds v. Massey,* 66 N.M. 199, 344 P.2d 947 (1959); *State ex rel. Reynolds v. Fanning* 68 N.M. 313, 361 P.2d 721 (1961); *State ex rel. Reynolds v. Mendenhall* 68 N.M. 467, 362 P.2d 721 (1961).

51. *McClean,* 62 N.M. 264, note 49; *Durand v. CID,* 71 N.M. 464, 379 P.2d 773 (1963). See also Reynolds, testimony, May 20, 1986, *TvNM-TR.,* 36–42 containing Reynolds's description of "conservation" efforts in the Roswell area.

52. Bloom, interview, note 6.

53. See chapter 8 below. See Reynolds, testimony, May 20–21, 1986, *TvNM-TR.*, 25–46.

54. Drafters of the 1948 Pecos River Compact assumed that the Carlsbad Irrigation District surface rights, which dated from 1893, were older than all of the Roswell groundwater rights, which did not start until some years later. No one was concerned with the obviously older, antiquated rights of northern New Mexicans who had begun their small farms around 1803. In later proceedings to set formal priorities in the *Lewis* adjudication, Roswell groundwater users tried to establish related surface water rights prior even to CID. At this writing (May, 2001) the issue is still pending.

55. Pecos River Compact, art. IX (1948); N.Mex. Stat. Ann. 72-15-19 (1933): "In maintaining the flows at the New Mexico-Texas state line required by this compact, New Mexico shall in all instances apply the principle of prior appropriation within New Mexico." See chapter 3 for a discussion of the origin of this term. Although the Hope Decree adjudicated to what became the Carlsbad Irrigation District a quantity of water, it was recognized that there were 25,055 irrigable acres within the district. Year after year, there was not enough surface water to irrigate these acres.

56. Hon. Jay Forbes, interview, February 18, 1993, Carlsbad, New Mexico. At the time of the interview Judge Forbes had just quit as the CID lawyer. He is now district judge, 5th Judicial District. See *State of New Mexico ex rel. Reynolds vs. PVACD*, 99 N.M. 699, 663 P2 358 (1983). This case allowed for expedited priority enforcement in advance of a comprehensive final decree. Despite the advice that he was giving CID in the two earlier decades, Reynolds himself argued for expedited priority enforcement and in this case finally won. In mid-1988 Lea County water users began litigation seeking to force New Mexico to abide by the priority requirements of the Compact's article IX rather than using alternative methods for making up state-line shortfalls. See *Field v. Interstate Stream Comm'n*, No. CV 98–193 (N.M. Dist. Ct, Nov. 19, 1998, 5th Judicial Dist., Lea County) appealed dismissed.

57. *Templeton v. PVACD*, 65 N.M. 59. Note that Reynolds as state engineer opposed the recognition of supplemental groundwater rights in the Roswell basin in *Templeton* even as he was encouraging them in the CID.

58. Reynolds himself quietly put a stop in 1972 to further CID supplemental wells. When it came time to set the priority of those wells in the *Lewis* adjudication, Reynolds's lawyers argued that the priority of the wells should not relate back to the surface water right that the groundwater supplemented but, instead, should date from the well drilling. Reynolds won. Interview, consulting geologist and ex-State Engineer water rights engineer Sherman "Pinky" Galloway, Roswell, New Mexico December 17, 1992. Zane Spiegel, "Ground Water Trends in New Mexico," X *N.M. Prof. Engineer* (April, 1958).

59. Reynolds, "Memorandum on Pecos River System Administration," July 12, 1976, *SER-ISC*. Galloway and Forbes, interviews, notes 55 and 58.

60. See "Plaintiff's Motion for Leave to File Complaint and Proposed Complaint," June 26, 1974, *TvNM-RP*.

61. Hall, "Statement 4(b)—Pecos River Commission Administrative History," 28–30 note 45.

62. Galloway, Forbes, interviews, notes 55 and 58.

63. Forbes, interview, note 55; Reynolds, "Memorandum on Pecos River Administration."

64. Simms, interview, December 24, 1992, note 26.

65. Em Hall, "Water: New Mexico's Delicate Balance," 61 *New Mexico Magazine* 5 (May, 1983): 15–20.
66. Em Hall, "An Exposé of Great Western Cities," and "Cochiti Lake—The Making of the Seven Day Weekend," *The New Mexico Review* (October and November, 1970). Reynolds to Editor and Review reply in The New Mexico Review, January, 1971. *Honey Boy Haven v. Roybal* 92 N.M. 603, 592 P.2d 959 (1978). *In the Matter of the Application of Angel Fire* 96 N.M. 651, 634 P.2d 202 (1981).

Chapter 6

1. Remark of Special Master Breitenstein, August 30, 1978, *TvNM-TR*, 2290–91.
2. The official transcript is housed at the Supreme Court, Washington, D.C. References here are to New Mexico's copies of the case files *(TvNM-Files)*, the record of documents filed in the litigation *(TvNM-RP)*, the exhibits *(TvNM-Ex)*, and the testimony *(TvNM-TR)*.
3. *State ex rel. Reynolds v. Aamodt et al.*, 537 F.2d 1102 (1976).
4. Remarks of Texas special assistant attorney Doug Caroom, May 2, 1978, *TvNM-TR*, 2145–46.
5. Remarks of Special Master Breitenstein, June 28, 1977, *TvNM-TR*, 305.
6. See Hall, "Statement 4(b)—Pecos River Commission Administrative History."
7. The record proper is on file with the U.S. Supreme Court in Washington, D.C. A complete copy is available in the archives of the State Engineer Office, Santa Fe; Hall, "Statement 4(b)—Pecos River Commission Administrative History," 19.
8. State of Texas Statement 4(b), July 31, 1978, *TvNM-RP*.
9. Remarks of Breitenstein, March 9, 1978, *TvNM-TR*, 1579; March 9, 1977, *TvNM-TR*, 267.
10. "Decision of the Special Master on Affirmative Defenses," May 6, 1977, *TvNM-RP*, 27, 30; Meyer's Draft Report, March 18, 1986, *TvNM-RP*, 31.
11. Doug Caroom, Texas attorney and special assistant attorney general, interview, June 3, 1993, Austin, Texas; "Plaintiff's Motion for Leave to File Complaint and Proposed Complaint," June 16, 1974, *TvNM-RP*. Remarks of Special Master Breitenstein, May 1, 1978, *TvNM-TR*, 1925. Remarks of Texas special assistant attorney general Doug Caroom, May 2, 1978, *TvNM-TR*, 2144.
12. Caroom, interview, June 3, 1993; "Plaintiff's Motion for Leave to File Amended Complaint and Amended Complaint," April 17, 1977, *TvNM-RP*. There is no record that the amendment was ever allowed even though no party ever referred to the fact.
13. *Templeton v. PVACD* 65 N.M. 59, 332 P.2d 465 (1958); N.Mex. Stat. Ann. Sec. 72-12-1 (1978); *State v. Mendenhall* 68 N.M. 467, 362 P.2d 998 (1961).
14. *Kansas v. Colorado* (No. 105 Original) 514 U.S. 673 (1995); See chapter 5, footnotes 16, 17, and accompanying text; Slingerland, interview, May 18, 1992.
15. Breitenstein, "Draft Report No. 1," May 12 and June 16, 1977, *TvNM-RP*.
16. Testimony of various witnesses, February 27-March 14, 1978, *TvNM-TR*, volumes VI-XVI.
17. Remarks of Breitenstein, March 12, 1978, *TvNM-TR*, 1822; Caroom, interview, June 3, 1993.
18. Exchange between special master Breitenstein and witness Murthy, March 13, 1978, *TvNM-TR*, 1841–44. The quote is from 1844.
19. Exchange among lawyer, witness, and special master, March 13, 1978, *TvNM-TR*, 1846–47.

20. Exchange between Texas lawyer Caroom and special master, March 9, 1978, *TvNM-TR*, 1572.
21. See chapter 1.
22. Remark of special master Breitenstein, March 9, 1977, *TvNM-TR*, 299.
23. Remark of special master Breitenstein, March 1, 1978, *TvNM-TR*, 72; Remark of special master Breitenstein, March 9, 1978, *TvNM-TR*, 1521; "Report of Special Master on Obligation of New Mexico to Texas under the Pecos River Compact," September 7, 1979, *TvNM-RP*, 20; Remark of special master Breitenstein, March 9, 1978, *TvNM-TR*, 1683.
24. Remark of Texas attorney Caroom, March 1, 1978, *TvNM-TR*, 663; Remark by New Mexico attorney Tansey, March 13, 1978, *TvNM-TR*, 1840; Exchange between Tansey and Breitenstein, March 13, 1978, *TvNM-TR*, 2012.
25. Slingerland, interview, May 18, 1992. See remarks of New Mexico special assistant attorney general Richard Simms, August 29, 1978, *TvNM-TR*, 2998–99; See remarks of Texas special assistant attorney general Caroom, August 30, 1978, *TvNM-TR*, 2223 and following for an excellent description of river routing.
26. See chapter 5.
27. Caroom, interview, June 3, 1993. Interview with Texas attorneys Renea Hicks and Paul Eliot, June 4, 1993, Austin, Texas.
28. Testimony of State Engineer Steve Reynolds, March 6, 1978, *TvNM-TR*, 1101, 1121.
29. *Templeton v. PVACD* 65 N.M. 59, 332 P.2d 465 (1958). Texas attorney Caroom, reading background New Mexico water law, stumbled on the *Templeton* case and was convinced that the doctrine explained all of Texas's Pecos River problems. Caroom, interview, June 3, 1993.
30. Exchange between attorney Booth and witness Reynolds March 6, 1978, *TvNM-TR*, 1114–15.
31. Letter, Breitenstein to Caroom and Simms, August 1, 1978, *TvNM-Files*.
32. Breitenstein to all Counsel, August 18, 1978, *TvNM-Files*.
33. Supreme Court cases had held that a bi-state compact would be enforced "absent a vitiating infirmity." Even Special Master Breitenstein's favorite *Hinderlider* case discussed the issue. *Hinderlider v. La Plata River & Cherry Creek Ditch Co.* 304 U.S. 92, 109 (1938).
34. Exchange between Hall and Breitenstein, August 31, 1978, *TvNM-TR*, 2308.
35. Remark of Special Master Breitenstein, August 31, 1978, *TvNM-TR*, 2302.
36. Remarks of Hall, August 31, 1978, *TvNM-TR*, 2303–4.
37. "New Mexico's Trial Brief Pursuant to Paragraph 5(a)(4) of the Special Master's Pre-Trial Order of October 31, 1977," August 1, 1978, *TvNM-RP*, 61–73. Remark of Special Master Breitenstein, August 31, 1978, *TvNM-TR*, 2304.
38. Exchange between Hall and Special Master Breitenstein, August 31, 1978, *TvNM-TR*, 2304.
39. Ibid., 2304–5.
40. Slingerland, interview, May 18, 1992.
41. See Rule 41, Federal Rule Civil Procedure; "Preliminary Report of Special Master," February 2, 1979, *TvNM-RP*, 58–68.
42. "Preliminary Report," February 2, 1979, 3.
43. Question of New Mexico special assistant attorney general Simms, April 24, 1979, *TvNM-TR*, 2998.
44. Remark of Simms, April 24, 1979, *TvNM-TR*, 2998.
45. Ibid., 2999.

46. Remark of Special Master Breitenstein, April 24, 1979, *TvNM-TR*, 3000.
47. "Report of Special Master on Obligation of New Mexico to Texas under the Pecos River Compact," September 7, 1979, *TvNM-RP*, 22–26.
48. Ibid., 44–45.
49. Ibid., 3.
50. "New Mexico's Brief in Support of Objections to the Report of the Special Master," November 29, 1979, *TvNM-RP*.
51. "Texas Brief in Chief In Support of Objections," November 29, 1979, *TvNM-RP*.
52. *United States v. New Mexico* 438 U.S. 696 (1978); Simms, interview, December 4, 1992.
53. Simms, interview, December 4, 1992.
54. Caroom, interview. 3, 1993. See "Instructions to Lawyers," from Rodak, Clerk of the United States Supreme Court in Container 511, *WJB*.
55. "Transcript of Oral arguments, Washington D.C. *State of Texas v. State of New Mexico* No. 65 Original, March 24, 1980," Alderson Reporting, Washington, D.C., 5
56. "Transcript of Oral arguments," 6.
57. Simms, interview, December 4, 1992.
58. "Transcript of Oral arguments," 22–23, 24–26.
59. Ibid., 42.
60. "October Term, 1979, April 17, 1980 Rehnquist, Blackmun, White, Marshall, Powell and Stewart to 'Dear Chief,'" exchanges between various justices collected in Container 521, *WJB*.
61. *Texas v. New Mexico* 446 US 540 (1980).
62. The one dissenting judge, Justice Stevens, who agreed with the Texas position and lost, indicated that he understood that affirming Special Master Breitenstein's alternative meant adopting New Mexico's "protected use" definition of the "1947 condition." See 446 US 543 (1980). Special Master Breitenstein himself hadn't thought so.
63. The tortured course of procedural events between early 1980 and March 1982 is best summarized in "New Mexico's Exceptions to the Report of the Special Master and Brief in Support of Exceptions," December 1, 1982, *TvNM-RP*, 12–13 Interview with Texas attorneys Renea Hicks and Paul Eliot, Austin, Texas, June 4, 1993. Caroom, interview, June 3, 1993. Caroom recollects a more active searching out of Charnes by the lawyers in the case. Statement of New Mexico attorney Charlotte Uram, transcript of March 30, 1983 oral argument, 34, referring to an earlier statement before special master Breitenstein; Testimony of Dr. Abraham Charnes, March 8, 1982, *TvNM-TR*, 3632. Testimony of Dr. James Heaney, March 8, 1982, *TvNM-TR*, 3492–3631; Testimony of Bureau of Reclamation engineer James Flook, March 9, 1982, *TvNM-TR*, 4361.
64. Clark, "What Authority Should Reside in the State Engineer?" Over his years as state engineer Reynolds had developed a skepticism towards the technical capacities of federal water representatives. Some, including himself, thought the skepticism was healthy. Others, like Clark, thought it bordered on paranoia.
65. Caroom, interview, June 3, 1993.
66. Simms, interview, December 4, 1992.
67. "New Mexico's Exceptions to the Report." "Texas's Exceptions to the Report of the Special Master and Brief in Support of Exceptions," December 1, 1982, *TvNM-RP*.
68. Transcript of oral argument before the Supreme Court of the United States in *Texas v. New Mexico*, March 30, 1983, (Washington, D.C.: Alderson Reporting), 1–48.

69. Ibid., 22–45. Letter, Charlotte Uram to author, July 7, 1997 (Author's file).
70. See Docket Book, *Idaho ex. rel. Evans v. Oregon* in Container No. 604, October Term 1982, *WJB*. Brennan's handwritten conference notes indicated that justices White, Blackmun, and Stevens had particular problems with Breitenstein's handling of the *two* simultaneous original jurisdiction suits in which Breitenstein served as special master, *Idaho v. Oregon* and *Texas v. New Mexico*. Justice Blackmun worried that neither was "the best Breitenstein product." According to Brennan, Justice White thought that Breitenstein "did as much as could be done."
71. Brennan memo, "For Conference Friday, April 1, 1983," in Conference Lists, 2-18-1983 to 6/83 Container 604, Folder 2, *WJB*.
72. "Texas v. New Mexico, Argued March 30, 1983 Memo for conference April 1, 1983," Container 610, *WJB*.
73. Brennan, March 30, 1983, memo for Conference, 2, *WJB*.
74. Brennan, March 30, 1983 memo for Conference, 3, *WJB*.
75. Vote tabulation, List 4 Sheet 1, Conference April 1, 1983, Container 4, Folder 2, *WJB*.
76. "Assignment Lists, October Term 1982," Container 602, *WJB*.; "Circulation Record, October Term, 1982," Container 602, *WJB*.
77. Brennan to Rehnquist, June 14, 1983, Container 602, *WJB*.
78. The Circulation Record, Container 610, File No. 65 Original, *WJB* shows that between June 10 and June 15, the proposed Opinion underwent three circulated drafts to each of which each justice responded. There were editorial changes throughout the process, but few substantive changes.
79. *Texas v. New Mexico,* 462 U.S. 562–564 (1983); 462 U.S. 557–562.
80. *Texas v. New* Mexico 462 U.S. at 558 and footnotes 4 and 5.
81. White to Conference, July 1, 1983, Container 610, *WJB*.
82. *Texas v. New Mexico* 462 U.S. 574 at footnote 21. The Brennan opinion curiously assumed that the October 31, 1977 pre-trial order still controlled the case proceedings even though Breitenstein himself had rejected the order and Texas, at least, had replaced it with another.
83. "The 1947 condition," Texas Exhibit 68, November, 1983, *TvNM-Ex*. Coincidentally the final 1983–1984 definition of the "1947 condition" and its inflow/outflow curve strongly resembled the 1961–1962 Review of Basic Data version of that condition. The new definition vindicated New Mexico's steady reliance, albeit for other reasons, on the Review.
84. *Texas v. New Mexico* 462 U.S. at 575.
85. Remark of Special Master Breitenstein, April 24, 1979, *TvNM-TR*, vol. xxix, 2945.

CHAPTER 7

1. Slingerland, interview, March 22, 1994, Santa Fe, New Mexico.
2. See Gibson, Dunn, and Crutcher, American Bar Association Directory (1998–1999); Interview, Texas special attorneys general Renea Hicks and Paul Elliot, June 6, 1994, Austin, Texas.
3. Report of Charles J. Meyers, Special Master, July 29, 1986, *TvNM-RP*, 1, 2.
4. Slingerland, interview, March 22, 1994.
5. Mechem, interview, November 7, 1997; Hicks, interview, June 6, 1994.
6. Stanford University attorney and former Meyers student Michael Hudnall, interview, April 14, 1996, Santa Cruz, California; Diana Poole, telephone interviews, June 13, 1994 and June 27, 1996, Denver, Colorado. Ms. Poole was employed as a

Gibson-Dunn associate from 1984 to 1988 and worked as Meyers's assistant in *Texas v. New Mexico* as, almost thirty years before, Meyers had worked as assistant to Special Master Simon Rifkind in *Arizona v. California,* 373 U.S. 346 (1963).

7. Remarks of Stanford Law Professor Paul Brest, "Meyers Tribute," September 23, 1988 (Palo Alto, California). Remarks of Stanford Law Professor Gerald Gunther, "Meyers Tribute," September 23, 1988 (Palo Alto, California).

8. "In Memoriam: Charles Jarvis Meyers, 1925–1988," *Stanford Lawyer* (fall, 1988): 82; Brest, "Tribute."

9. A. Dan Tarlock, "Tribute," 29 *NRJ* 2 (spring, 1989): 328–29.

10. Book Review, Charles Meyers, "Water and Water Rights: A Treatise of the Law of Waters and Allied Problems," Robert Emmet Clark, ed., 77 *Yale Law Journal* (1968): 1036–51.

11. Charles Meyers and Dan Tarlock, *Water Resources Management* (Minneola, N.Y.: Foundation Press, New York, 1971).

12. National Water Commission, *Water Policies for the Future* (1973); Tarlock, "Tribute," 327; Charkes Meyers and Richard Posner, "Market Transfers of Water Rights: Towards and Improved Market in Water Resources," Legal Study No. 4, July 1, 1971, *National Water Commission* (1973); Compare Helen Ingram and F. Lee Brown, *Water and Poverty in the Southwest* (Tucson: University of Arizona Press, 1987).

13. Meyers, "The Colorado River;" *Arizona v. California* 373 U.S. 346 (1963) (opinion), 376 U.S. 340 (1964) (decree). Retired law professor Robert Emmet Clark, interview, January 10, 1992, Albuquerque, New Mexico.

14. Meyers, "The Colorado River," 29 footnote 110 (Breitenstein); 30 footnote 115 (Tipton); Meyers, "The Colorado River," 48 footnote 297. Special Master Arthur Littleworth, in charge of the 1990s trial of *Kansas v. Colorado* called Meyers just before he died and asked for advice on how to conduct interstate water litigation. Littleworth said that Meyers told him, "First off, charge each state a hell of a lot of money." Remarks of Littleworth at "Dividing the Waters" Conference, March 17, 1997, Albuquerque, New Mexico. For the fee disputes between Meyers and the Supreme Court see *Texas v. New Mexico* 484 U.S. 973 (1987) and 485 U.S. 953 (1988); For example, Meyers, "The Colorado River," 24–25.

15. Meyers, "The Colorado River," 27, 46 ff.

16. Ibid., 41–43.

17. *Texas v. New Mexico,* 484 U.S. 973 and 485 U.S. 953 (1988), unpublished opinions of the Supreme Court. In the second decision Justice Blackmun filed a vigorous written dissent on a routine application by Meyers for allowance of fees to him; Interviews with Meyers's assistant Diana Poole, June 13, 1994; June 27, 1996; Order, November 16, 1984. Meyers's order directed Texas and New Mexico to deposit "$25,000 each with the Special Master on or before December 31, 1984, for the purposes of establishing a fund for the payment of the expenses of the litigation and such interim fees of the Special Master as the United States Supreme Court may from time to time allow. The Special Master will periodically account to the parties for payments made under the fund," *TvNM-RP.*

18. "Pre-trial order," December 10, 1984, *TvNM-RP. In the Matter of the Application of Angel Fire* 96 N.M. 651, 634 P.2d 202 (1981).

19. "Texas' Status Report on Disputed Technical Issues," May 15, 1985, *TvNM-RP;* "New Mexico's Objection to Stipulation on Disputed Technical Issues," August 6, 1985, *TvNM-RP.* New Mexico objected because Texas had proposed using a statistical technique "substantially different than that developed by the USGS, Texas's method adds artificially to the data set used to develop the equation by

repeatedly introducing the mean value of the data set to force the equation through the mean value of the data."

20. Slingerland, interview, March 22, 1994.
21. E-mail, William F. Fleming to Hall, May 15, 1997. At the time Fleming was chief of the technical division in the State Engineer Office.
22. Remarks of Special Master Breitenstein, March 9, 1977, *TvNM-TR*, 267; Remarks of Breitenstein, June 23, 1977, *TvNM-TR*, 306. Breitenstein said, "I think there is ["good faith"], but I think that unless the commissioners refrain from instructing their people to take the viewpoint 'Don't look at the accuracy or the correctness or the right way to do it, look at what it is going to do to use and then yea or nay it,' we'll never get anywhere in this case."
23. Fleming, e-mail to Hall, May 15, 1997.
24. Report of Charles J. Meyers, Special Master, July, 1986, *TvNM-RP*, 2 footnote 2.
25. "Order Directing Briefs," June 17, 1985, *TvNM-RP*. The issue had arisen in late May, 1985 at a time when two new lawyers, Peter White and Renea Hicks, had taken over from long-gone predecessors. During the summer, the two lawyers exchanged a series of briefs on the issue. See "New Mexico's Memorandum on the Burden of Proof Issue," July 8, 1985; "Texas' Response to New Mexico's Memorandum on the Burden of Proof," July 16, 1985; "New Mexico's Reply on the Burden of Proof," July 22, 1985; "Texas' Response to New Mexico's Reply on the Burden of Proof," July 30, 1985, *TvNM-RP*. Remark of Special Master Breitenstein, June 28, 1977, *TvNM-TR*.
26. White and Simms had joined the legal division of the State Engineer Office at about the same time, in 1969. Once the lawyer Paul Bloom left in the middle 1970s White had taken over the Pueblo Indian litigation and Simms the interstate litigation. Only after Simms left in the early 1980s did White become seriously involved in interstate litigation. See generally, *Office of the State Engineer & Interstate Stream Commission Annual and Bi-Annual Reports, 1970–1985* (Santa Fe: State Engineer Office).
27. Peter T. White, "New Mexico's Memorandum on the Burden of Proof," July 8, 1985 and "New Mexico's reply on the Burden of Proof," July 22, 1985, *TvNM-RP*.
28. Renea Hicks, "Texas' Response to New Mexico's Memorandum on the Burden of Proof," July 16, 1985, *TvNM-RP*, 2.
29. Hicks, "Texas' Response," 3, 4–5.
30. Exchange between lawyer White and Special Master Meyers, May 20–21, 1986, *TvNM-TR*, 433–34.
31. Slingerland, interview, March 22, 1994; Report of Special Master, July 29, 1986, *TvNM-RP*, 6.
32. See footnote 81, chapter 5 and accompanying text.
33. Report of Special Master, July 29, 1986, *TvNM-RP*, 11–13.
34. "Stipulation No. 3 between Texas and New Mexico," November 18, 1985, *TvNM-RP*, 9; Remark of Special Master Meyers, November 19, 1985, *TvNM-TR*, 9.
35. Report of Special Master, July 29, 1986, *TvNM-RP*, 23.
36. Fleming, interview; Geohydrologist and former State Engineer employee Zane Spiegel, interview, July 31, 1994, Silvermine, Connecticut; Report of Special Master, July 29, 1986, *TvNM-RP*, 27.
37. William Hiss, Ph.D thesis, New Mexico Exhibit 105, *TvNM-Ex*; Spiegel, interview, July 31, 1994; Remarks of Special Master Meyers, November 19, 1985 and December 3, 1985, *TvNM-TR*, 65–67, 82–86.
38. Report of Special Master, July 29, 1986, *TvNM-RP*, 22–26 and 26–30.

39. See Slingerland to Bloom, (undated, probably spring 1976), *TvNM-Files*.
40. Meyers Draft Report, March 18, 1986, *TvNM-RP*, 9.
41. Ibid., section VIII, Remedy, 28–30.
42. Ibid., 31 (emphasis added).
43. See footnote 13, chapter 6, and accompanying text.
44. Remarks of attorney White, Oral Argument on Draft Report, April 16, 1986, *TvNM-TR*, 85–86.
45. Remarks of Special Master Meyers, Oral Argument, April 16, 1986, *TvNM-TR*, 94; Report of Special Master, July 29, 1986, *TvNM-RP*, 41 ("no finding that New Mexico acted in a reprehensible manner").
46. Slingerland, interview, March 22, 1994. Remarks of attorney White, Oral Argument on Draft Report, April 16, 1986, *TvNM-TR*, 85–86.
47. Remark of Special Master Meyers, April 15, 1986, *TvNM-TR*, 99.
48. Testimony of Texas engineer Robert Whittenton, August 30, 1978, *TvNM-TR*, 2153–2201.
49. Remarks of Special Master Breitenstein, August 30, 1978, *TvNM-TR*, 2198–2200; Remarks of Special Master Meyers, May 20, 1986, *TvNM-TR*, 284; Exchange among witness Whittenton, lawyers White and Hicks, and Special Master Meyers, May 20, 1986, *TvNM-TR*, 241–58.
50. Interstate Stream Commission hydrologist John Whipple, interview, New Mexico State Engineer Office, May 12, 1996.
51. Exchange between lawyer Hicks and witness Murthy, May 21, 1986, *TvNM-TR*, 318.
52. Exchange between Special Master Meyers and witness Murthy, May 21, 1986, *TvNM-TR*, 318–19.
53. Testimony of Texas engineer Murthy, May 21, 1986, *TvNM-TR*, 320–21.
54. Report of Special Master, July 29, 1986, *TvNM-RP*, 9.
55. Remarks of Special Master Meyers, May 20, 1986, *TvNM-TR*, 79, 104, 146: (Meyers: "I don't know whether it could have been stipulated, but you are not making a record, I don't think, on this for the Supreme Court. I don't think that they are going to look at it that closely. Is there any way that we can shorten this up?")
56. Remarks of Special Master Meyers, May 20, 1986, *TvNM-TR*, 240–41.
57. Ibid., 347.
58. Exchange between lawyer White and Special Master Meyers, May 21, 1986, *TvNM-TR*, 348–49.
59. Remarks of lawyer White, May 21, 1986, *TvNM-TR*, 433–34.
60. Remark of Special Master Meyers, May 21, 1986, *TvNM-TR*, 434.
61. Ibid., 413, 432, 440.
62. Report of the Special Master, July 29, 1986, *TvNM-RP*, 35–37, 38.
63. Ibid., 45–46.
64. Hicks and Elliot, interview, June 3, 1993; Letter, Uram to Hall, July 7, 1997.
65. Letter, Uram to Hall, July 7, 1997.
66. Testimony of Steve Reynolds, May 20, 1986, *TvNM-RP*, 14–68; Report of the Special Master, July 29, 1986, *TvNM-RP*, 33–34.
67. "New Mexico's Exceptions to the Report of the Special Master and Brief in Support of Exceptions," December 20, 1986 and "New Mexico's Answer Brief in Response to Texas' Brief in Support of Exceptions," January 20, 1987, *TvNM-RP*.
68. "Official Transcript of Oral Argument, No. 65 Original, April 29, 1987, Washington, D.C." (Washington, D.C.: Alderson Reporting), *TvNM-Files*. Letter,

Uram to Hall, July 7, 1997. By this time Justice Scalia had joined the court and he did ask questions that indicated an understandable lack of familiarity with the case to that point and a characteristic impatience with what to his mind was New Mexico's over-intellectualized view of the "man's activity" problem. See "Transcript," 23–25.

69. *Texas v. New Mexico* 482 U.S. 124, 127, footnote 5 (1987).

70. *Texas v. New Mexico* 482 U.S. 129.

71. E.g. Charlotte Crossland, "'Breach' of an Interstate Water Compact: Texas v. New Mexico," 28 *NRJ* 2 (fall, 1988): 849–62. *Texas v. New Mexico* 482 U.S. 129 (1988).

72. Diana Poole, law clerk to Meyers, interview, June 13, 1994; June 27, 1996.

73. Simms, interview, December 4, 1994.

74 Pursuant to the Supreme Court's 1987 decision, the special master was asked to determine as well the amount of damages to Texas in terms of money. The fall 1987 hearings were addressed to the question of the future administration of the compact.

75. Testimony of S. E. Reynolds, October 15, 1987, *TvNM-TR*, 39, 73,;

76. "Table 1, Departures from Table 2, Texas Exhibit 79 Adjusted for Changes Above Alamogordo Dam, McMillan Dike and Operation of Malaga Bend," New Mexico Exhibit 137 *TvNM-Ex.*, introduced October 15, 1987 at *TvNM-TR*, 50.

77. Testimony of State Engineer Reynolds, October 15, 1987, *TvNM-TR*, 36–70.

78. Remark of Special Master Meyers, October 15, 1987, *TvNM-TR*, 59, 66.

79. Testimony of S. E. Reynolds, October 15, 1987, *TvNM-TR*, 46.

80. Phil Mutz and S. E. Reynolds, "The Rio Grande Compact of 1938," 26 *NRJ* 2(summer, 1968).

81. Remark of Special Master Meyers, October 15, 1987, *TvNM-TR*, 127.

82. Poole, interview, June 13, 1994, June 27, 1996.

83. See chapter 3, endnotes 2–3 and accompanying text, and Special Master Report, November, 1987, filed December 2, 1987, *TvNM-RP*, 4. *Texas v. New Mexico*, 482 U.S. 129 (1988).

84. Poole, interview, June 13, 1994.

85. Henry Bohnhoff, "Pecos River Settlement: Why We Won," XII *Divining Rod* 4 (December, 1989), (Las Cruces, N.Mex.: New Mexico Water Rights Institute, 1989.)

86. Riesner, *Cadillac Desert;* Remarks of Special Master Meyers, May 20, 1986 and May 21, 1986, *TvNM-TR*, 198–203, 375.

87. Charles Howe, "The Benefits to New Mexico from Breaches of the Pecos River Compact, 1950–1983," and "The Economic Damages to Texas from Breaches of the Pecos River Compact, 1950–1983," May 25, 1988, and Donald L. Snyder, revised draft, "The Impact of Water Transfer, New Mexico and Texas," May, 1986 in *TvNM-Ex.*

88. Simms, interview, December 12, 1994; Poole, interview, June 27, 1996.

89. "Order Appointing Special Master," *Texas v. New Mexico* 488 U.S. 917 (1988); Hicks, interview, June 3, 1993.

90. Bohnhoff, "Pecos River Settlement: Why We Won," 1.

91. Ibid., 1–2.

92. "Entry of Stipulated Judgment and Exhibit B," *Texas v. New Mexico* 494 U.S. 111 (1990).

93. *Albuquerque Journal*, August 14, 1988, A-1.

94. Amended Decree, March 28, 1988, *Texas v. New Mexico* 495 U.S. 388 (1988).

1. Typescript, Reynolds address to Roswell Rotary Club, October 19, 1989, *SER-ISC*, 1.
2. N.Mex. Stat. Ann. 73-1-1 to 73-1-27 (1978). Jack Russell, "Memorandum on New Mexico Efforts to Meet Compact Obligations," July, 1989 in *Texas v. New Mexico, TvNM-Files.*
3. By the late 1980s the PVACD had stopped its program of buying and retiring rights in the basin. Russell couldn't explain the new, desultory attitude. Former legal chief Peter Thomas White, interview, Santa Fe, New Mexico, March 4, 1998. *Texas v. New Mexico*, 462 U.S. 557 (1983).
4. Reynolds, Rotary Club, October 19, 1989, 5, 9. State Engineer Staff, "Presentation to the Pecos River Basin Public Meetings, House Memorial 47, September 17–20, 1990, *Texas v. New Mexico* by the State Engineer Office," *ISC.*
5. Reynolds, "Memorandum on Pecos River Administration." Testimony of S. E. Reynolds, 20 May 1986, *TvNM-TR*, 57–58.
6. See, generally, chapter 5.
7. Reynolds and Mutz, "Water Deliveries under the Rio Grande Compact," 200. Gary Daves, Water Resources Department, City of Albuquerque, 12 March 1999, presentation to New Mexico Society of Professional Engineers. "Comparison of Cumulative Change in Three Reaches of the Rio Grande, San Felipe to Bernardo," in *Waterline* (summer, 1999): 6.
8. Chapter 5. Reynolds's chief lawyer late in the litigation believed that New Mexico's efforts at least would establish the state's good faith in trying to comply with an uncertain decree. Peter White, interview, March 4, 1998.
9. Reynolds, "Memorandum on Pecos River Administration."
10. S. E. Reynolds, "Statement before the Committee on Energy, Natural Resources and Extractive Industries, Interim Committee of the New Mexico Legislature on *Texas v. New Mexico*," November 20, 1989, *SER-ISC*. Reynolds did tell the legislators that if the state wells had to be pumped to meet a compact deficit, junior Roswell private wells would have to be curtailed the following spring to offset the effects. He hadn't mentioned this aspect of his program in his Roswell presentation.
11. Reynolds, "Statement before the Committee," November 20, 1989; Doug McClellan, "N.M. to Pay Texas Water Debt in Cash," *Albuquerque Journal*, 10 August 1989, 1. House Memorial 47, 39th Legislature, second session. "A Memorial Requesting the State Engineer to Consider Options to Satisfy Pecos River Compact Obligations," *ISC.*
12. S. E. Reynolds, State Engineer to State Senator Pauline Eisenstadt, February 5, 1990, with attached three-page memorandum on House Memorial 47, *SER-ISC.*
13. House and Senate Journals, 39th Legislature, 2nd Session (Santa Fe), show passage of House Memorial 37 in February, 1990.
14. ISC Engineer Jay Groseclose, interview, January 21, 2000. Ironically, this understanding guaranteed that some of Reynolds's last hospital visitors included his putative enemies, those opponents of his policies who had great respect for him nonetheless but who hadn't heard of the visitation policy of those more intimate with him. One member of the Water Quality Commission, with which Reynolds had battled for years, even brought him in the ICU unit a copy of David Muench's lavish and beautiful photographs of the New Mexico landscape. Dignified as ever, the suffering Reynolds, always a devotee of anything New Mexican, accepted the gift gracefully. UNM Law Professor Ruth Kovnat, interview, October 14, 1999.

15. See Editorial, *Albuquerque Journal,* April 26, 1990. Editorial, *Santa Fe, New Mexican,* April 27, 1990.

16. "New Mexico State Engineers," *State Engineer Office, Annual Report, 1995–1996* (Santa Fe), 6. Carl Slingerland, interview, March 22, 1994.

17. "Presentation to the Pecos River Basin Public Meetings, House Memorial 47, September 17–20, 1990, Texas v. New Mexico by the New Mexico State Engineer Office," (Santa Fe: ISC). "Options" p. 1.

18. "Summary of Public Meetings Held by State Engineers (*sic*) Office; Facilitated and Documented by Western Network; Ft. Sumner, Roswell, Carlsbad, September 17–19, 1990," *ISC,* 2, 7–8.

19. "Summary of Public Meetings," "CID Support for No Alternative Option" p. 8.

20. White, interview, March 1999.

21. Personnel, Legal Division, State Engineer Office Biennial Reports, 1974, 1990, *SEO.*

22. Former SEO attorneys Susan Kery and Laura Harper, interview, August 14, 1994, Santa Fe.

23. Interstate Stream Engineer John Whipple, "Study of Options Available in Response to Amended Decree in *Texas v. New Mexico,*" (1990) *ISC,* 1–2, 4, 5–6.

24. Interview, Special Assistant Attorney General D. L. Sanders, legislative liaison to southeastern New Mexico representatives, March 17, 1991. *Rep. Murray Ryan and Rep. Ben Lujan vs. Secretary of State Stephanie Gonzales* 114 N.M. 346, 838 P.2d 963 (1992).

25. *New Mexico State Engineer Office, Annual Report, 79th Fiscal Year (1990–1991),* 74. The arcane differences reflected the complexity of state government finance, the bailiwick of the few legislators and bureaucrats who really understood it. The cognoscenti understood that $1.0 million of the $6.8 million would be available for short-term emergency solutions, such as leasing water that presumably could quickly be delivered to the state line. The rest, $5.8 million, would be available for the purchase of existing rights whose retirement presumably would permanently add water at the state line. House Bill 582, "An Act for the Purchase of Pecos River Water Rights," 40th New Mexico Legislature, 1st Session, 1991.

26. Bruce King, *Cowboy in the Roundhouse: A Political Life* (Santa Fe, N.Mex.: Sunstone Press, 1998), 288–89. *Annual Report, State Engineer of New Mexico, 78th Fiscal Year (1989–1990),* 7. Special assistant general D. L. Sanders, interview, January 17, 2000.

27. "Reporting Assignments for Management of the Pecos River," organizational flow chart, July 1992, *ISC.*

28. Resume of John Whitlock Hernandez, Jr., February 2000, Department of Civil Engineering, New Mexico State University, Las Cruces, New Mexico. See Ralph Blumental, "Environment Unit Greets New Chief," section A, page 18, *New York Times,* March 11, 1983. Stuart Taylor, "Answers Still Lacking, the Questions Go On," section A, page 14, *New York Times,* July 19, 1983. Raymond Bonner, "Five More Officials Resigns from EPA; Inquiries to Go On," section 1, page 1, *New York Times,* March 26, 1983. Hester, "The Water Boss," 4. See *In Re Applications of the City of El Paso, Texas, Public Services Board Nos. HU-12 through HU-71 and LRG 92 through LRG 357,* New Mexico State Engineer Findings and Order 6–8 WRD-SEO (1987). Reynolds to New Mexico Attorney General Paul Bardacke, May 5, 1987, *WRD-SEO.*

29. Norman K. Whittlesey "Economic Effects of Irrigated Land Retirement in the Pecos River Basin," preliminary and confidential report, 10 February 1992, *ISC;* "Preliminary Analysis, Retirement of Irrigated Lands in the Pecos River Basin,"

1 page, undated, *WRD-SEO*. Turned on their head, the dates and corresponding acres showed not how the basin would have to shrink but how it had grown: steadily and enormously. The New Mexicans always had told the Texans that they couldn't produce numbers like these, but when they wanted to they certainly could, down to the nearest acre.

30. Neil S. Grigg, River Master of the Pecos River, "Pecos River Compact, Report of the River Master, Water Year 1991, Accounting Year, 1992," *ISC*.

31. Special assistant attorney general D. L. Sanders, interview, January 17, 2000. In *Ryan and Lujan v. Gonzales op. cit.* original mandamus, August 28,1992 the state Supreme Court raised the hurdle for Chavez and Eddy County legislators a couple of notches higher. In response to the petition of a northern New Mexican politician out to sink the southern New Mexicans' attempt to raid state funds, the court ruled that the Pecos River general obligation bonds had to be separately listed on the ballot and not "log rolled" with a bunch of other, more attractive, state-wide bond projects.

32. Confidential Memorandum, "Plan of Action to Increase State-line Flows," Pecos River Project Management Team to Eluid Martinez, State Engineer, September 10, 1991, *ISC;* "Action Plan to Increase Pecos River Flows at the New Mexico-Texas State Line," State Engineer Office/Interstate Stream Commission, September 15, 1992, *ISC*.

33. "Action Plan II:B Priority Enforcement by Court Injunction," *ISC*, 3; Former special assistant Attorney General Laura Harper, interview, PERA, Santa Fe, March, 1994. See "Decision Chart for the Initiation of the Injunctive Process," describing the steps that would lead to long-term and short-term priority enforcement. The chart provided for certain "triggers" that would lead to the injunctive process. In a couple of post-1992 years, events pulled at least a couple of triggers and the state did nothing. Steve Farris, interview.

34. Minutes of the Interstate Stream Commission, Minutes of the Interstate Stream Commission March 5, 1993, 8, motion of commissioner Phelps White, passed unanimously, *ISC*.

35. Fifth Judicial District Judge Jay Forbes, interview, Carlsbad, New Mexico, February 19, 1993.

36. House Bill 582, "An Act for the Purchase of Pecos River Water Rights," 40th New Mexico Legislature, 1st Session, 1991.

37. See "Annual Diversions by River Pumpers," New Mexico Exhibit 79, *TvNM-Ex*. The table shows a high annual diversion of 26,500 acre-feet in 1956 and a low of 6,900 acre-feet in 1986, with a wide range of diversions in between.

38. Over the 1950–1988 period pumper depletions had varied widely from year to year, dropping in the period by almost 13,000 acre-feet. Yet that voluntary reduction had not reduced the manual's determination of the amount of water New Mexico owed Texas at the state line. The problem may have lain with the manual but if the 1950–1988 historic period was any indication, reducing Pumper diversions after 1988 wasn't guaranteed to help at all with New Mexico's obligation to Texas as it hadn't before 1988. Geophysicist Francis West, interview, Santa Fe, New Mexico, February 1999. "Water Rights Acquisition Program—Summary of Expenditures, 1992–1996," *ISC*, shows that the state spent around $500,000 a year leasing water rights from individual farmers within the CID and, in addition, paid the CID itself $25,000 a year to administer the leases.

39. Water Rights Acquisition Program, Summary of Expenditures 1991–1997, *ISC*. Armand Smith, Appraisal of Buffalo Valley Water Rights, 1991, *ISC*. ISC Minutes, 5 March 1993, *ISC*. The ISC set the amount to be paid at $1750 an acre-foot for

surface water "estimated accrual rate at the state line." The details of the Buffalo Valley Farm purchase show how the program operated. The farm was located south of Morgan Nelson's basic spread in East Grand Plains and *east* of the Pecos River. Buffalo Valley had had a spotty history of irrigation and a long list of owners, more speculators than farmers. Indeed, the last two owners of the Buffalo Valley, the Langeneckers and Robert O. Anderson, were two of Roswell's most prominent and richest banking and investment leaders. Cautious not to pay too much for the farm water rights, the ISC hired a Clovis, New Mexico appraiser to set the fair market value of the water rights and paid him $20,000 to do it. In his late 1991 report the appraiser said that he lacked comparable data. Nevertheless, he estimated that the farm's 3,460 acre-feet of water rights were worth $375 an acre-foot or $1,297,500. In the end the ISC agreed to pay more than $3 million for the water rights, more than twice their appraised value. Buffalo Valley Farm, *ISC*.

40. Chapter 2. Ray Sharbutt, UNM Law student and husband of ranch owner Katie Madeira, interview, March 16, 1994, Albuquerque, N.Mex. M&M Ranch file, *ISC*.

41. Annual Report, New Mexico State Engineer Office, Fiscal Year 1995, 6–7.

42. Interviews, Special Assistant Attorney General D. L. Sanders, January 7, 2000; former Special Assistant Attorney Steve Farris, January 8, 2000; former ISC general counsel Peter T. White; retired State Engineer geohydrologist Francis West, December 18, 1999 and retired water resources engineer David Stone.

43. "Report, Office of the State Auditor, Santa Fe, New Mexico," 21 March 1996, copy in *ISC*. The audit was supposed to determine whether the water rights acquired under WRAP were purchased or leased in accordance with "State Engineer/ Interstate Stream Commission policies and procedures, state statutes and accounting standards." The report reviewed the Darr Angel, David Harris, Vernon Underwood, Kathy Glover, Rhodes Estate, and Robert Utterback transactions. It did not consider either the Hondo Company or the M&M Cattle purchases detailed here.

44. Karen Aubrey, Attorney at Law and Francis West, Professional Engineer, "A Review of the Water Rights Acquisition Project: Pecos River," May 1, 1998, *ISC*. Texas had developed that manual in the course of the Supreme Court litigation. By using statistical procedures Texas claimed that the complex Pecos River system consisting of main stem flows and tributary inflows, springs, aquifers, and precipitation, all these complex factors whose interrelationship was as poorly understood as some of the factors themselves, could be reduced to one number: "1947 condition state line flow." The process, argued the 1998 Report, amounted to scientific reductionism, which is explaining partly random, large-scaled and irreducibly complex phenomena by the behavior of the smallest parts. Then the manual treated this abstract explanation as if it were real. None of New Mexico's responses to the Supreme Court decree, concluded the report, were really likely to reduce the risk that New Mexico would face a large shortfall under the compact and a very short time to make it up. Only chance had prevented that from happening.

45. "Lease Purchase Program Appropriations from Irrigation Works Construction Fund," Summary, June 2000. ISC Engineer Bhasker Rau, "Water Rights Purchases: Pecos River, Revised 8/13/97," *ISC. Field v. Interstate Stream Comm'n*, No. CV 98–193 (N.M. Dist. Ct. 5th Judicial Dist., Lea County), dismissed November 19, 1998, appeal withdrawn.

46. Interview, geohydrologist David Jordan, Daniel Stephens, and Associates, July 3, 2000.

47. 1997–1998 Annual Report, Office of the State Engineer, Interstate Stream Commission *ISC*; House Bill 363, 43rd Legislature, Second Session, 1998,

introduced by Rep. Richard Knowles, Roswell. Telephone interview with
Interstate Stream Engineer Norman Gaume, July 17, 2000.

48. Morgan Nelson, "Senate/House Joint Resolution, Repeal of the Pecos River
Compact," August 21, 1993; Morgan Nelson to Pecos River Commissioner Bob
Bickley, November 5, 1996, proposing among other things that the Red Bluff
Irrigation District sell its irrigated land to New Mexico, *MNPP*.

49. Rene Kimball, "Groups Target Salt Cedar to Help Habitat, Save Water,"
Albuquerque Journal, April 4, 1993, D-1; "Killing a common thief may let N.M.
pay water debt to Texas," *U.S. Water News* (June 1993): 17. G. E. Welder,
"Hydrologic Effects of Phreatophyte Control, Acme-Artesia Reach of the Pecos
River, New Mexico, 1967–1982," USGS WRIP 87–4148 (1988). Welder to
Albuquerque Journal, April 24, 1993, A-13.

50. *State ex rel. State Engineer and PVACD v. Lewis (Corn sub-file)* 118 N.M. 446, 882
P2 37 (1994); PVACD attorney Fred Hennighausen, interview, August 22, 1996.

51. Morgan Nelson, letter to author, February 16, 2000; Shomaker, "Studies related
to administration of the Pecos Compact for the Pecos Valley Artesian
Conservancy District," (1995) *MNPP*.

52. See Rod Adair, "The Water Pirates of New Mexico (and the Planned Death of
the Pecos Valley): The Story of Senate Bill 860," *Legislative Update 10* (April 6,
2001). Adair is a state representative from Chaves County.

53. Chapter 2 for the early involvement of the Tracys and the CID with the federal
government.

54. Regional Director, Bureau of Reclamation to Acting Regional Director, Fish
and Wildlife Service, August 5, 1991, "Endangered Species Act, Section 7
Consultation, Biological Opinion for Pecos River Water Operations, New
Mexico," (Albuquerque: Bureau of Reclamation); Ian Hoffman, "Ft. Sumner
Dam Opens for Minnow," *Albuquerque Journal*, November 19, 1998, D3.
Denise D. Fort, "Instream Flows in New Mexico" 7:2 *Rivers* (summer, 2000):
155–63. 1995–1996 Annual Report, State Engineer Office, 44.

55. Contract No. 00-WC-40-R6490, 28 January 2000 lease of water agreement
between the Bureau of Reclamation and the Interstate Stream Commission
governing federal releases from Sumner (Alamogordo Dam), *ISC*.

56. Interview with Texas assistant attorneys general Renea Hicks and Paul Elliot,
Austin, Texas, June 3, 1993.

57. Slingerland to Bloom, undated chart (probably spring, 1976), *TvNM-Files*. See
chapter 1.

58. Charles Wilkinson, *The Eagle Bird: Mapping a New West* (New York: Pantheon
Books, 1992).

59. Neil S. Grigg, *Water Resources Management: Principles, Regulations and Cases*
(New York: McGraw-Hill, 1996).

60. For example, the river master had had to decide whether tributary inflows, a critical
and confusing factor in annual computations, should be estimated or measured.
Separating base flow and flood flows in the Acme to Artesia reach of the river was
critical to the annual computation of New Mexico's obligation. The higher the flood
inflow, the greater New Mexico's relative state line obligation. Determining what
part of the flow of the river was base inflow and what flood inflow involves dividing
the measured flow of the river between the two categories. Surface water hydrologists refer to the process as "scalping the hydrograph."

61. Letter, Grigg to Hall, December 10, 1998.

62. Letter, Tom Bohl, Assistant Attorney General, Natural Resources Division, Office

of the Attorney General, State of Texas to Dr. Neil S. Grigg, River Master of the Pecos, December 29, 1998, cc to author.

63. "Pecos River Compact, Accumulated Shortfall or Overage, 1987–1999," *ISC.*

CHAPTER 9

1. F. Lee Brown, *The Value of Water: A Report to the City of Albuquerque in Response to RFP95-101-SV,* (Albuquerque: City of Albuquerque, 1995), and "Water Markets and Traditional Values: Merging Commodity and Community Perspectives," 22 *Water International* 1 (1997): 4. See Riesner, *Cadillac Desert,* 1: "One late November night in 1980 I was flying over the state of Utah on my way back to California . . ."

2. New Mexico's water law of prior appropriation is based on a fairly primitive rule of capture. The rule is based on an even older law of the acquisition of private rights to wild animals.

3. Stanley Crawford, *A Garlic Testament: Seasons on a Small New Mexico Farm* (New York: Harper Collins Publishers, 1992); Stanley Crawford, *Mayordomo: Chronicle of an Acequia in Northern New Mexico* (Albuquerque: University of New Mexico Press, 1988); and Stanley Crawford, "Dancing for Water," in 32:3 *Journal of the Southwest* (autumn, 1990): 265–67.

4. Upper Rio Grande Hydrographic Survey, Santa Cruz River, Sheet 16, Acequia del Molino, Tracts 11 and 12 (Hydrographic Survey Division, Office of the State Engineer, Santa Fe).

5. C. T. Dumars and S. C. Nunn, eds., *Middle Rio Grande Conservancy District, Water Policies Plan,* (MRGCD, 1993).

6. Lisa D. Brown, "The Middle Rio Grande Conservancy District's Protected Water Rights: Legal, Beneficial, or Against the Public Interest in New Mexico," 40 *NRJ* 1 (winter, 2000): 1.

7. Brown, "The Middle Rio Grande Conservancy District's Protected Water Rights."

8. "Precision Air Density Separators," *Seed Tech +, Agri-Research and Consulting,* Salem, Oregon.

9. Eliot Coleman, *The New Organic Gardener, A Master's Manual of Tools and Techniques for the Home and Market Gardener* (White River Junction, Vt.: Chelsea Green, 1995), 321.

10. Alice Waters, *Fanny at Chez Panisse, A Child's Restaurant Adventure* (New York: Harper-Collins, 1992); Thomas Keller, *The French Laundry Cookbook* (New York: Artisan, 1999).

11. For example, Peter van Dresser, *A Landscape for Humans: A Case Study of the Potentials for Ecologically Guided Development in an Uplands Region* (Albuquerque: Biotechnic Press, 1972)

12. Don Haakenson, *The Small Commercial Garden: How to Make $10,000 a Year in Your Backyard* (Bismarck, N.Dak.: PC-Services, 1995).

13. Prof. Paul Brest, Richard E. Lang Professor of Law and Dean, Stanford Law School, "Tribute to Charles Meyers," 23 September 1988, Palo Alto California. (Copy in author's files.)

14. See *Alexander v. Anderson,* 126 N.M. 632, 937 P.2d 884 (NMCA, 1999).

15. Worster, *Rivers of Empire,* 4–5; Donald Worster, *An Unsettled Country: Changing Landscapes of the American West* (Albuquerque: University of New Mexico Press, 1994).

Index

measuring water flow, 171–72
Mechem, Edwin, 1, 114, 116
Meyers, Charles: as dean, 166, 167;
    death of, 195; Draft Report, 178–80;
    illness of, 189, 193–95; photograph
    of, *165;* Steve Reynolds and, 166;
    Texas v. New Mexico and, 22, 52–54,
    164–96
Middle Rio Grande Conservancy District
    (MRGCD), 233
Milagro Beanfield War, The, 1
Montoya, Joseph, 114
Moutrey family, 125
Murthy, V. R. Krishna, 137–38, 165,
    182–84
Mutz, Phil, 202, 203

Nambe Creek, 246
Nambe, New Mexico, 230, 246
National Geographic, 31
National Planning Board's Pecos River
    Joint Investigation, 54
National Water Commission, 168
natural reservoir, 14–15
Neel, George, 43
Nelson, Ann, 81, *84,* 243, 244
Nelson, Clarence, 88–90, 93
Nelson, Ernest, 89–90, 93
Nelson family: farmland of, 80, 81,
    104–6; history of, 79, 85–86
Nelson, Fred M., 79, 89–90, 93, 95, 101,
    102
Nelson, Harry, 93
Nelson, Morgan, 79–107; defense of
    wells, 100–101; farming interests,
    104–6, 203, 216, 238, 243; as a
    legislator, 103, 215; photographs of,
    80, 84, 102, 244; Texas trip, 94–96;
    Texas v. New Mexico and, 107; as a
    writer, 85–86
Nelson, Swann, 79, 86–88
"New Mexico Exhibit 137," 190, 192
New Mexico Farm Bureau Association,
    124–25
New Mexico Society of Professional
    Engineers, 221
New Mexico State Legislature, 103–4,
    200–201
New Mexico State University, 215–16
*New Mexico's 4(b) Statement: Pecos
    River Commission Administrative
    History,* 133, 143, 144, 159
Nichols, John, 1
North American Free Trade Agreement
    (NAFTA), 237

North Spring Valley, 91
North Valley Farmers' Market, 239
North Valley, New Mexico, 230, 232–40
Nye, S. Spencer, 99, 106

Oasis Ranch, 96–97
Oasis, the, 14–15
Oasis Well, *98*
O'Connor, Sandra Day, 157
outflows: analysis of, 68; groundwater
    pumping and, 181; Plate 2, 74;
    under-deliveries and, 58, 66, 70, 128

Pascoe, D. Monte, 195
Pearson, Clarence, 90
Pearson, Oliver, 84, 88, 95, 100
Pecos Irrigation Company, 28, 34, 36
Pecos, New Mexico, 7, *8,* 40
Pecos River: aerial photographs, *8, 10, 13,
    16, 18, 19, 21;* beginning of, 1; chart
    for, 219; depletion of, 60–61, 64–65,
    67, 71, 121, 136, 146–49; depletion
    versus use, 144–45, 154, 162; flood
    waters, 28–32, 34–35, 37, 46, 47;
    groundwater development, 127; man-
    agement of, 243; map of, 2; measuring
    water flow, 171–72; perturbations in,
    183; photograph of, *91;* research on,
    56–58, 60; storage rights, 40; stress
    on, 197; surface flow, 55–57, 128;
    tour of, 1, 6–15, 22–23; water avail-
    ability, 58, 61; water volume, 49–50
Pecos River Basin: irrigated land,
    124–25; map of, 2; tour of, 1, 6–15,
    22–23
Pecos River Commission: impact on
    Texas v. New Mexico, 132; Interstate
    Stream Commission and, 111; R. B.
    Magowan and, 127; Royce Tipton
    and, 54, 62–63, 68–69; Steve
    Reynolds and, 122, 123; Texas repre-
    sentatives, 123, 127; tiebreakers, 155,
    156, 157–58, 159
*Pecos River Commission: A Decade of
    Progress, The,* 123
Pecos River Compact, 5; administration
    of, 193; apportionment provision,
    66–67; approval of, 68; calculations,
    222; Charles Meyers and, 191; com-
    plaints about, 203–4; complying with,
    197; demise of, 40; effects of, 224,
    245; limitations of, 29, 31, 39–40;
    new formation of, 46–49, 54, 59–60,
    66; Royce Tipton and, 54, 59–60,
    66–68; Senate Document 109, 73–74,

290